DAVID MAMET'S
GLENGARRY GLEN ROSS

STUDIES IN MODERN DRAMA
VOLUME 8
GARLAND REFERENCE LIBRARY OF THE HUMANITIES
VOLUME 1817

STUDIES IN MODERN DRAMA

KIMBALL KING, *Series Editor*

DAVID MAMET'S
GLENGARRY GLEN ROSS
TEXT AND PERFORMANCE

EDITED BY
LESLIE KANE

GARLAND PUBLISHING, INC.
NEW YORK AND LONDON
1996

Copyright © 1996 by Leslie Kane
All rights reserved

Library of Congress Cataloging-in-Publication Data

David Mamet's Glengarry Glen Ross : text and performance / edited by
    Leslie Kane.
            p.   cm. — (Studies in modern drama ; v. 8)   (Garland reference
    library of the humanities ; vol. 1817)
        Includes bibliographical references.
        ISBN 0-8153-1877-4 (acid-free paper)
        1. Mamet, David.   Glengarry Glen Ross.   I. Kane, Leslie, 1945–
    II. Series.   III. Series: Garland reference library of the humanities ;
    vol. 1817.
    PS3563.A4345G56   1996
    812'.54—dc20   96-17233
                                                                        CIP

Cover photograph: J.T. Walsh (left) and Robert Prosky in David Mamet's
Glengarry Glen Ross. Photograph © Brigitte Lacombe. Reprinted with permission.

Printed on acid-free, 250-year-life paper
Manufactured in the United States of America

FOR PAMELA AND DAVID

Contents

GENERAL EDITOR'S PREFACE

The success of Leslie Kane's *David Mamet: A Casebook* published in 1992 by Garland Publishing, Inc., confirmed a widespread interest in Mamet scholarship among professors, students, and general theater audiences. Since then Kane, as president of the David Mamet Society, has witnessed the continued popularity and growing stature of one of America's most important playwrights. Here in *David Mamet's* Glengarry Glen Ross: *Text and Performance*, Kane has assembled the first collection of scholarly essays dedicated entirely to Mamet's Pulitzer Prize–winning play. Like Kane's previous volume of essays, this one combines meticulous research with exciting new insights into the dramatist's achievement. With many conference papers, essays, and books on authors such as Mamet and Pinter, Leslie Kane, Professor of English at Westfield State College, continues her commitment to enlivening contemporary dramatic studies.

Kimball King

PREFACE

David Mamet's Glengarry Glen Ross: *Text and Performance* is the first collection of scholarly essays dedicated to a critical assessment of David Mamet's Pulitzer Prize–winning masterpiece. The twelve original essays and two published within the last year, reprised and adapted for this volume, present the most timely and provocative thinking on Mamet's play and screenplay, commence a dialectic on performance and structure, and substantially advance our knowledge of this seminal playwright. Addressing such subjects as feminism, pernicious nostalgia, ethnicity, the mythological land motif, the discourse of anxiety, gendered language, and Mamet's vision of America, *David Mamet's* Glengarry Glen Ross: *Text and Performance* also includes an interview with Sam Mendes, the director of the highly acclaimed 1994 revival of *Glengarry Glen Ross* in London, conducted specifically for this collection by the editor. A chronology of major productions and the most current and comprehensive bibliography of secondary references from 1983 to 1995 complete the volume.

Reflecting the breadth, theatricality, imagination, and complexity of Mamet's award-winning play, the essays that compose this collection provide a range of critical approaches that offer retrospectives and perspectives on Mamet's drama. Although dominant focus is accorded to *Glengarry Glen Ross,* several comparative essays foreground this play against the background of such Mamet works as *Edmond, Reunion,* and *American Buffalo,* whereas others find fascinating parallels in the work of Ralph Waldo Emerson, Jean Baudrillard, Joseph Conrad, and Caryl Churchill. Whether contradicting or complementing one another, these scholarly essays, written by international critics of broad theatrical expertise and interest, initiate a compelling dialogue on *Glengarry Glen Ross* in performance.

I thank all of the contributors for sending their manuscripts in a timely fashion, responding to my remarks graciously, receptively and immediately, assignment for many. And for his suggestion of British scholars who were interested in Mamet's work, I especially thank Lionel Kelly, director of American Studies at the University of Reading, England.

For her advice and patience, I thank Phyllis Korper, my editor at Garland Publishing. I also acknowledge my debt to David and Janice Sauer for their meticulous preparation of the bibliography and for their assistance at every stage of production, and to archivists Nicola Scadding, Royal National Theatre, and Lauren Bufferd, Special Collections Division of the Chicago Public Library, where the St. Nicholas Theatre and Goodman Theatre papers are retained, for their responsiveness to innumerable inquiries. Special mention should also be made of Lynne Kirwin, Lynne Kirwin Associates, who facilitated my interview with Sam Mendes. Pamela Kane provided expert assistance and moral support.

Brigitte Lacombe, the Goodman Theatre, and actors J.T. Walsh, Joe Mantegna, William Petersen, and Mike Nussbaum have generously granted their permission to reprint photographs from the American premiere production of *Glengarry Glen Ross*. Likewise, acknowledgment is extended to the Donmar Warehouse for permission to reprint a production photograph of John Benfield by Mark Douet from the 1994 London revival production and to Bungakuza (Literary Theater) director Emori Toru, and Robert Rolf for providing production photographs from the Japanese production of Mamet's play.

I am indebted to David Mamet for the inspiration of his work, for his accessibility, candor, and warmth. I also acknowledge my appreciation to Sam Mendes, director of the Donmar Warehouse production of *Glengarry Glen Ross,* for graciously sharing his time, expertise, and perceptions of the play in performance, and to Gregory Mosher, whose recollections of the American production have enhanced my understanding of both text and performance. Finally, I especially thank my husband, Stu, formerly a Vice President of Sales and Marketing, for his insight, support, and general good humor while the demands and dialectic of *Glengarry Glen Ross* dominated our home and lives.

Acknowledgments

The editor and the publisher would like to thank the following publishers for permission to reprint from published works: Professors Dorothy Parker, Alan Thomas, and David Blostein, eds. *Modern Drama*, for permission to reprint "How to Do Things with Salesmen: David Mamet's Speech-Act Play" by David Worster, *Modern Drama* 37, no. 3 (Fall 1994): 375–90. Ms. LeAnn Fields, executive editor, University of Michigan Press, for permission to reprint an abstracted version of "The American Male Ethos, Male Mythologies, and Absent Women," from *Act Like a Man* by Robert Vorlicky (1995).

"The men I was working with could sell . . . Ice to the Eskimos"
—David Mamet

"Marshal the leads . . . marshal the leads? What the fuck, what bus did you get off of, we're here to fucking sell. *Fuck* marshaling the leads. *What the fuck talk is that? What the fuck talk is that? Where did you learn that? In school . . . ? (Pause.) That's "talk," my friend, that's "talk." Our job is to sell."*
—David Mamet, *Glengarry Glen Ross*

Introduction

Winner of three Obies, a New York Drama Critics Award for *American Buffalo*, the Outer Critics Award for Distinguished Playwriting, and the Pulitzer Prize for *Glengarry Glen Ross*, David Mamet is a seminal American playwright whose sensitivity to language, precision of social observation, communal and moral vision, theatrical imagination, and continuing productivity account for his broad and deserved critical respect. The prolific author of more than twenty-five plays, numerous sketches, three children's plays, four collections of essays and reminiscences, a book on film direction, a collection of poetry, a novel, a novella, and more than a dozen screenplays, Mamet has also adapted Chekhov's *Three Sisters*, *Uncle Vanya*, and *The Cherry Orchard*, translated and adapted Pierre Laville's play, *Le Fleuve rouge*, directed his own work on the screen and stage, perfected a method for teaching acting, and founded numerous acting companies, most recently the Atlantic Theatre Company.

In 1969, however, having completed the first drafts of *Sexual Perversity in Chicago*, *Duck Variations*, and *Reunion*, and having studied under Sanford Meisner at the Neighborhood Playhouse in New York, Mamet, a recent graduate of Goddard College, returned to Chicago, the setting of many of his plays and the future home of the St. Nicholas Theatre Company (founded in 1973), to pursue a career in acting. He supported himself between acting jobs by working in a real estate office where salesman peddled tracts of scorched earth in Arizona and swampland in Florida to gullible Chicagoans. What was intended to be only a temporary job evolved into a year-long position that provided the young playwright, who by his own estimate was "a terrible actor," with the moral issues, human relationships, and scathing wit that he would ultimately develop in *Glengarry Glen Ross*. "Written in five days or five seconds," director Gregory Mosher recently recalled, *Glengarry Glen Ross* fulfills the playwright's fifteen-year intention to write about that experience.[1]

One of the finest post-war American plays, it has been characterized as a "sardonic, scabrous and really rather brilliant study of a human piranha pool where the grimly Darwinian law is swallow or be swallowed";[2] "a savage microcosm . . . [of] the urban jungle";[3] "death in the capitalist food chain";[4] "one of the most exciting verbal concoctions of the modern theatre";[5] and a dramatization of "the Tocquevillian connection between the public self—the hurlyburly of those caught within a business-as-sacrament world—and the private self—the anguished characters' inner reality."[6] Its four real estate salesmen have been labeled everything from "jacketed jackals,"[7] to "peddlers of false dreams,"[8] "predators preying on susceptible prospects,"[9] "pitchmen caught in the entrepreneurial act,"[10] and "fast-talking bottom-feeders"[11] whose brand of "gutter English [is] caustic enough to rust pig iron."[12]

If Mamet has struck a raw nerve and sparked controversy with *Glengarry Glen Ross*, exposing mendacity and moral bankruptcy in the marketplace, he has also generated sympathy in his unsentimental parabolic tale tempered by his admiration for the virtuosity, imagination, and temerity of working men who, in Ricky Roma's words "live on their *wits*."[13] As the playwright told director Gregory Mosher during previews for the Chicago production, "Look, this play is not a play about love. *American Buffalo* is a play about love; *A Life in the Theatre* is a play about love. This is a play about power. This is a play about guys, who when one guy is down . . . the guy who's up then kicks the other guy in the balls to make sure he stays down."[14] Much of the success of this award-winning play issues from its distinctively robust and electrifyingly vital language, at once rhythmic and ribald, elliptical and illusory, comic and corrosive. Indeed, as John Gross has correctly noted, *Glengarry Glen Ross* "lives above all through its language," in which inspired elisions and explosive invectives are peppered with "perfectly timed verbal feints and body blows."[15]

But Mamet, whose plays have not always been well-plotted, has also garnered praise for *Glengarry*'s impeccably constructed two-act structure. Comprised of three tightly framed duologues in act 1 and the inspired genius of the freewheeling Roma-Levene-Lingk skit that is set against the devastation of act 2, *Glengarry Glen Ross* stages the exploitation of the injudicious, exposes the bending of morality on all social levels, arouses suspicion and solves the mystery of criminal actions perpetrated on and by the desperate. Juggling nearly as many off-stage characters as appear on stage, the playwright employs a late point of attack—literally a sales contest for a Cadillac or a set of steak knives whose metaphoric resonance is immense—in which only two of four salesmen will survive the murderous, cutthroat competition that is enacted in the urban jungle, better known to us all as life in the working world.

In 1982, after *Edmond*, a searing drama that is possibly the most brutal of Mamet's plays, was poorly received in New York City, winning an Obie but running a scant seventy-seven performances despite a stunning production at the Goodman Theatre under the direction of Gregory Mosher, Mamet, a classicist uneasy about the asymmetric structure of *Glengarry Glen Ross*, sent the play to his friend Harold Pinter. The rest, as they say, is theatre history. Harold Pinter, to whom the play is dedicated, communicated to Mamet that all the play required was a production; he brought the play to the attention of Bill Bryden, who had previously directed the European premiere of *American Buffalo* in London. He was also instrumental in arranging for the Royal National Theatre, of which he was an associate director, to stage a production. *Glengarry Glen Ross* was first presented at the Cottesloe Theatre, London, 21 September 1983, under the direction of Bryden, where it won the 1983 Society of West End Theatres Award for the Best Play.

The Goodman Theatre in Chicago, the venue for numerous premiere productions of David Mamet's plays, staged the American premiere of the play on 6 February 1984, under the direction of Gregory Mosher. Mosher's invitations to IBM salesmen and Fuller Brush ladies to teach the salesmen to "sell the sizzle not the steak" are now legendary. With its cast intact, with the exception of William L. Petersen in the role of the hapless sucker, James Lingk, replaced by Lane Smith, *Glengarry Glen Ross*, its costumes by Nan Cibula and sets by Michael Merritt (longtime Mamet collaborators), transferred to the John Golden Theater on Broadway on 25 March 1984, where it won the 1984 Pulitzer Prize for Drama, a Joseph Dintenfass Award, four Tony nominations, including Best Play and Best Director. Joe Mantegna won a Tony for his performance of Ricky Roma.

Notable productions of *Glengarry Glen Ross* have been staged worldwide—both in English in various venues in Canada, South Africa, and Australia and in translation in Holland, West Germany, Italy, Switzerland, Denmark, France, Finland, Turkey, Israel, and Japan—despite the fact that its translation has "posed an insane problem," due to its profanity, distinctive rhetoric rhythms, and "shad[ings] of sound."[16] In 1992 James Foley's film, based on a screenplay by the playwright that added the character of Blake, a swaggering, sadistic emissary from Mitch and Murray, the Glengarry salesmen and office manager's successful bosses, garnered enormous praise for Mamet's white-hot profanity and memorable characters portrayed by a first-rate ensemble troupe, including Al Pacino in the role of Ricky Roma, Jack

Lemmon as Shelly Levene, and Ed Harris as Dave Moss. Filmed with "breathtaking wizardry" that retained the claustrophobic nature of the stage production's murkily lit interior space, it pointedly captured the mood and milieu, the sharklike competition, and scatological dialogue of men whose fear is camouflaged "under a wealth of blue-streaked street-talk."[17] *Glengarry Glen Ross* is a triumph about which Vincent Canby has averred, "There's not another such adaptation I can think of at this minute that comes anywhere near it."[18]

Biting, harrowing, and "stripped of idealistic pretenses," *Glengarry Glen Ross* is a Mamet masterpiece, so precise in its realism that as Robert Brustein noted in his review of the New York production, it takes on "reverberant ethical meanings."[19] Drawing upon the myth of the American Dream as its ideological backdrop, Mamet's play suggests obvious comparisons with Arthur Miller's *Death of a Salesman*. As Brustein has astutely observed, "Mamet follows Miller in making salesmen the metaphorical victims of a ruthless, venal, and corrupt system, but . . . divided by a gulf of thirty-five years [they] reflect significant differences in politics and practice, telling us more about the changing nature of American drama (society) than a dozen theatre histories."[20] But, in seizing upon the salesman as the focus of his play, Mamet masterfully merges personal history with that of the salesman as representative American figure to whom, Timothy B. Spears observes, "special status in American cultural history" has accrued.[21] "[A] quixotic knight . . . a liminal trickster" and performer whose ability to joke with the customer was matched by his "expansiveness [and] adaptability to the customer's perceived character and needs," the salesman and the urban drummer who preceded him, argues Spears, virtually "brought vaudeville to Main Street."[22] Indeed, for more than one hundred years peddlers, city drummers, and traveling salesmen have "played a significant role in helping to create the visual and physical spectacle that began to characterize consumer culture."[23] David Mamet has long been interested in role-playing. And, thus it is of little surprise that his salesmen are hawkers of false dreams and consummate storytellers, but the fecundity, creativity, and assertiveness of these performers—what Guido Almansi terms the "positive attributes" of the salesmen—informs the play's universality beyond a critique of capitalism, and speaks to their vulnerability and courage in the face of crushing daily challenges.

Mamet's strength lies in his ability to raise social questions on the nature of community and communication: to critique business as sacrament; to examine personal and professional betrayals; to heighten awareness of alienation and anxieties of the individual; to stimulate discourse on the relationship between public issues and private desires; to criticize our proclivity to barter morality as commodity; to portray the gaps between word and deed, act and action. Although many of these themes characterize Mamet's unique contribution to American theatre, evident in myriad works, such as *Oleanna,* which has stimulated recent controversy and prodigious commentary—both in America and throughout the world, *Glengarry* is the richer work, whose complexity is apparent in structure, trope, character development, language, and examination of power.

David Mamet's Glengarry Glen Ross: *Text and Performance* is the first collection of essays devoted solely to *Glengarry Glen Ross,* a work of blazing theatricality and brilliant originality. The rationale for such a collection is provided by David Mamet himself. Reflecting the richness, thematics, humor, and artistry of the play, I have attempted to provide a range of critical approaches that would offer retrospectives and perspectives, inviting thematic, rhetoric, gendered, and comparative readings of *Glengarry Glen Ross*— both play and screenplay—in the context of Mamet's canon and in relation to the work of other writers such as Arthur Miller, Eugene O'Neill, Joseph Conrad, Caryl Churchill, and Jean Baudrillard. Each makes a sound argument independent of other essays. Together these essays provide a cohesive overview and commence a dialectic on performance and structure. While I do not concur with some of the interpretations in this volume, the arguments have been carefully delineated and articulated, affording a stunning grasp of the playwright's dramaturgical, social, comedic, and, in the view of some scholars, tragic vision of America. That critics hold opposing viewpoints is a reflection of both the critics' philosophy and the richness of the writing.

Additionally, this volume contains a substantive interview with Sam Mendes, artistic director of the Donmar Warehouse, London, and director of the recently acclaimed revival of *Glengarry* in London, that I hope will contribute a unique and most welcome perspective on the play as text and the play in performance. This interview was conducted specifically for this collection. The essays in *Glengarry Glen Ross: Text and Performance* have been arranged tropologically, but this has often proved impossible when several critics have addressed issues of interest to many. A chronology of major productions and a comprehensive secondary bibliography appear at the conclusion to assist scholar and student.

Speaking several years ago with Mel Gussow about *Glengarry Glen Ross,* Mamet defined his perception of the playwright's role. "My job," he said, "is to create a closed moral universe," and leave the evaluation to the audience.[24] Finding the ball in our court and seizing the opportunity to act, react, and respond to *Glengarry Glen Ross,* the critics represented in this collection have, like Gogo in *Waiting for Godot*, sought to keep the game going: to present a plethora of critical views to advance the dialectic, to inspire further inquiry, and to enhance and encourage by our scholarship the pleasurable rereading and reviewing of Mamet's resonant and richly imagined work.

When not dismissed as peripheral, the detective story motif in *Glengarry Glen Ross*, observes Steven Price, is generally recognized to have a dual function: "the crime represents metonymically both 'legitimate' and 'illegitimate' business, while providing the linear plot structure that Mamet was beginning to favor." This dual function, he contends, suggests a connection between theme and form, a correlation more pervasive and more problematic than at first appears. However, the detective story in *Glengarry Glen Ross*, marginalized by the playwright, is typically trivialized by critics who have accorded it little significance. Drawing attention to elements of "the hard-boiled crime story" and "whodunit," introduced primarily in the second act, Price convincingly argues that the "bastard" nature of the detective story in *Glengarry Glen Ross* exposes "a formal and ideological tension between the classical [English] form and its "hard-boiled" [American] descendant, that provides a context in which to explore "tensions between freedom and constraint and between present and formative experience." Maintaining that what is marginalized is neither diminished nor merely metaphoric, Price contends that the play's complex construction is a key lead that furthers understanding of the play as "the act of theft from the parent company [enacted] in endless repetition," which necessarily raises the pervasive and persistent issue of the relationship between crime and freedom.

An astute reader of Mamet's works, whose earlier essay "Comedy and Humor in the Plays of David Mamet," advances our understanding of the role and function of humor in *American Buffalo*, *Glengarry Glen Ross*, and *Speed-the-Plow*, Christopher C. Hudgins turns his estimable critical talent to Mamet's screenplay adaptation of *Glengarry Glen Ross*, drawing upon broad knowledge of Mamet's work and his expertise in film studies. Echoing Price's position that audiences fail to grasp the import of that which is intentionally marginalized by the playwright, Hudgins provocatively suggests that "general audiences, reviewers and critics often misunderstand David Mamet's plays and films. Seeing only scruffy surfaces," they pay insufficient attention to "indicators pointing toward gentleness, a kind of love and a need for love, beneath often violent scenarios."

Taking as a point of departure Mamet's summary of Eisenstein's theory of montage—"a succession of images juxtaposed so that the contrast between images moves the story forward in the mind of the audience"[25]—Hudgins persuasively argues that Mamet forces the audience to do "much of the work of discovery and interpretation, a point with equal validity for Mamet's films and plays." Indeed, much of the pleasure of discovery, he continues, derives from Mamet's withholding information. It is the nature of what is withheld and the methods employed by Mamet in the successful adaptation that "[take] full advantage of its new medium's possibilities" that Hudgins addresses in his essay which matches metaphoric cuts and the film's music to the screenplay's image, dialogue, and narrative structure.

Illustrative of his contention that "*Glengarry Glen Ross*'s indirect thematic statements are both dramatically sound and effective," Hudgins supports the view that Ricky Roma's speeches—which loom large in his analysis (as they do in many critical studies in this collection) "contain the thematic core of the play, " with substantive detail and refreshing humor. While Hudgins's essay may leave some readers unsettled—as Mamet's plays happily do—it's certain to (re)focus the spectator's and reader's vision and encourage further dialogue on an area of discussion atypical of Mamet scholarship.

Several scholars, such as British critic Anne Dean, perceptively maintain that the principal action in Mamet's plays is the "speech-act." Well respected for her keen analyses of Mamet's plays, Dean, in her essay "The Discourse of Anxiety," provides a fresh reading of the differing ways in which Mamet employs language in *Glengarry Glen Ross* "to convey a verbal maelstrom of tension and fear." Although "unflinchingly portrayed by Mamet as a grasping, venal and corrupt group," the salesmen of *Glengarry Glen Ross*, she contends, "both invite and deserve our sympathy," for in her view, every day in the life of these salesmen is a "Damoclean day" in which they face fear with "febrile trepidation." Her valuable contribution consists of an exegesis of the three-card trick that comprises act 1, namely Mamet's three masterfully crafted and meticulously controlled duologues, what Dean terms "arias of anxiety and panic." Viewing the play from the perspective of early "1980s post-Reaganism, Bushism and Thatcherism," Dean reads the "relentlessly macho, materialistic" world of *Glengarry Glen Ross,* where selling is "an addiction in itself," as one in which "loyalty and trust are rare commodities."

Studying the three primary relationships—Williamson/Levene, Moss/Aaronow, and Roma/Lingk—laid before us in meticulous detail in act 1, Dean scrutinizes "the various methodology by which Mamet dramatizes [escalating] anxiety," that in her view ranges from "verbal stammering" to "all-out aggression." Advancing her central premise that the salesmen's notion of themselves as "existential heroes living on the edge" in a world in which every fight is a "war of wits," and "everyone . . . a potential target," Dean, in her persuasive, hard-hitting essay, continually rivets our attention to Mamet's peerless devaluation of three "odd couples," delineating not only their "particular neuroses" but also the intensity of a hostile environment that fosters what amounts to death-defying acts in the process of "meltdown."

Like Anne Dean, David Worster maintains that the principal action in Mamet's award-wining play is linguistic. Taking the position that if, as Stanley Fish has posited, *Coriolanus* is Shakespeare's "speech-act play," then *Glengarry Glen Ross* is surely Mamet's "for many similar reasons." Worster argues that "in the ideological world of Mamet's play, characters perform as salesmen where identity is determined solely by one's ability to employ language," that is "the ability to sell or inability to 'sell.'" In his view the discourse of capitalism that dominates the play is self-referential, "pervasively sexual," and essentially aggressive. It not only gives rise to fierce competition and voice to failure and frustration, it also "reveals . . . and ritualizes language," rendering definitions of what it means to be a success. Tracing the speech-acts in the play, Worster wisely illumines Mamet's focus on the key component of the sales speech act: as *speaker* or *listener*. Noting that close scrutiny of the salesmen's talk—aggressive, commanding, urgent, manipulative—says much about the significance that each scene attaches to distinctive set types of talk, as in Mamet's now classic distinction between "speaking" and "talking," he approaches linguistic exchanges as exchanges of power: "a transference of power predicated upon the salesman's "vision of reality." The closer the scrutiny of *Glengarry*'s language, he concludes, "the more evident it becomes that the primary purpose of language is not to communicate, but to claim power or withhold it. . . ." And, while many critics, among them Ruby Cohn, have noted that speech "powers" Mamet's world,[26] Worster presents a convincing argument that the correlation of competition and capitalism and the observed dissolution of culture and community in Mamet's play communicates that power is possessed by two unlikely silent or sniveling men in Mamet's macho world: James Lingk and George Aaronow. In other words, *Glengarry Glen Ross*, in his view, clearly articulates that the speech-act is ironic as well as integral.

Foregrounding the issue of gender in this male-cast play, Robert Vorlicky, in "Men Among the Ruins," not unlike Hersh Zeifman, Carla McDonough, and David Radavich, notes that "the explicit role of gender (as distinguished from sexuality) in male-gendered casts, not only in

Glengarry Glen Ross but in Mamet's work prior to *Oleanna*," speaks to the central "condition rather than a dramatic action" with which Mamet is concerned. And, from a critical perspective gleaned from impressive scholarship on published male-cast plays, Vorlicky finds *Glengarry* distinctive in its cryptic communication between men devoid of emotional and psychological interaction, that largely resists exposure, honesty, and vulnerability. Powered by the narrowly defined subject of work, he establishes a strong case for viewing *Glengarry* as "the quintessential male-cast play."

Paralleling Dean and Worster, Vorlicky predominantly (re)reads *Glengarry Glen Ross* as a speech-act play, but the dyadic conversations that comprise and propel the play forward and project the men's relationships to one another, rather than the sales that "kick out," are what he believes are "closed-end." Vorlicky's principal contribution to the collection is especially notable in his sensitive attention to gendered speech and culturally coded roles and to hierarchical professional exchanges that he avers typify all-male "institutional plays in which hierarchical professional authority influences/informs speech relationships." Indeed, he observes, even when the deconstruction of the real estate office interrupts the salesmen's ability to continue to function as workers in the workaday world, the work-based dialogue, what he terms "gender-based and gender-biased," exposes self-definition—and denigration—within a cultural context defined by "a system of set codes." Examining set-pieces—"in act 1 decipherable to those within the (business) community and in act 2 designed to obscure the truth"—Vorlicky deconstructs the discourse that dominates characters' dialogue, advancing yet another meaningful way to interpret the often violent, manipulative language that characterizes *Glengarry Glen Ross*.

Twice in *Glengarry Glen Ross*, Shelly Levene appeals to Williamson with the same words: "John: my *daughter . . .*" [27] "Not only is the language" of these carefully positioned elliptical phrases "the same," observes Dorothy H. Jacobs, "but the context, too, is similar." Pursuing these allusive leads in her provocative study, "Levene's Daughter: Positioning the Female in *Glengarry Glen Ross*," Jacobs considers the significance of Levene's allusive reference. Given "the rhetorical ploys of the sales force," about which several critics remark, Jacobs weighs the possibility that these anachronistic references to family in the world of business are "of a piece with his [Levene's] schemes, legitimate or otherwise, to get the leads and avoid prosecution." But that Levene's daughter is never seen, observes Jacobs, signals that she is an elusive, rather than an illusory, figure. So pervasive is the concentration of focus upon unwelcome, intrusive female characters in *Glengarry Glen Ross* that she cogently convinces by substantive analysis that "something revelatory is gained" from scrutinizing the positioning of women as well as gendered speech.

"Reinforcing the phallocentricity of this world is the language of contempt," she contends, the seemingly interminable suspicions of women voiced in such overtly dismissive, demeaning phrases that the allusive reference to Levene's daughter sounds "curiously out of place," rendered "an anomaly in the dialogue" whose distance from the materiality of the marketplace makes the powerfully assertive "female voice" of Mrs. Lingk—similarly unheard—(and Harriet Nyborg's signature) all the more remarkable. But, it is in Mamet's others works, *Dark Pony, Reunion, The Water Engine, House of Games, The Shawl,* and *Oleanna,* that Jacobs finds "corroborative evidence" that *Glengarry* may profitably be (re)read as a drama within a cycle of Mamet plays in which "on-stage women"—daughters, wives, and other female figures—"must be discarded" as powerless, nonthreatening figures. "Something has been lost, some vital," C. W. E. Bisgby has concluded about Mamet's male-cast plays,[28] and "that something," Jacobs persuasively argues, "is the female." Indeed, in her clarion call that attention must be paid to this positioning of women "outside" the world of *Glengarry Glen Ross,* Jacobs firmly focuses the spectator's vision on "the females of *Glengarry Glen Ross* [who] reveal the ideology propping up the corrupt methods and necessitating a debased language."

Deborah Geis begins her fine study of Mukherjee's story, "A Wife's Story," and *Glengarry Glen Ross* by observing, "I'm not sure whether Mukherjee's story marks the first time that a David Mamet play has served as the starting point for a work of fiction by another author, but the effect of reading this piece was for me a startling one," she admits, given that at the time Geis saw the New York production of *Glengarry* she recalls living in the East Village of New York City, an area known as Little India. To set one work against another, Geis persuasively argues, induces a second look at the "othering" of ethnic groups in America and the issues of ethnicity, gender, and sexuality that play powerful roles in *Glengarry Glen Ross.* Geis is an astute critic of Mamet's work, and her provocative examination of Mukherjee's "A Wife's Story" and *Glengarry* in each other's light, as it were, is intriguing and incisive, compelling us to view Mamet's salesmen as men who "project their anxiety of failure onto the 'others'"—"the ever-desirable and ever-frustrating 'leads'"—upon whom they rely for their success, especially but not exclusively "the inscrutable Asian." Moss, for example, she continues, communicates both his knowledge and "helplessness" in the face of the Asian's "apparent impenetrability," his tirade on Patel the centerpiece of the second scene of act 1. Taking up the issue of gendered and cultural positioning, Geis finds common to the story and the play "the ironies of self-contradiction." But in writing "to David Mamet" and appropriating *Glengarry Glen Ross* as intertext, she maintains that Murkherjee, from the position of critical spectatorship "claim[s] a space, a territory . . . that has not fallen prey to white male prerogative," playing out its own complex "gendered and cultured positioning" through echoing references to *Glengarry*.

In his perceptive contribution, "The Marxist Child's Play of Mamet's Tough Guys and Churchill's *Top Girls*," David Sauer distinguishes a series of surprising similarities between the two works, the former whose realism is integral, the latter highly theatrical. Both, he notes, have large single-gendered casts, open in restaurants, dramatize extended scenes in a work-place where dialogue is composed of sales talk and closings, demonstrate "concern for a daughter" but feature work as central to life, present highly competitive driven characters whose goal it "is to top everyone (inclusive of friends and family)" and dramatize "uncompromising views" of the "de-structiveness of their situations." However, it is beyond the surface similari-ties that Sauer's inquiry fascinates, engaging us in a close scrutiny of "a deep level of contamination" of capitalism. Informed by a Marxist analytic per-spective, inspired by the views of Adorno, Sauer sets the action of the plays "against a background of a large social issue." If one reads the matriarchal world of *Top Girls* against the patriarchal world of the salesmen of *Glengarry Glen Ross*, one immediately discerns, he suggests, a similar "invocation of the past" that is subsequently exposed as "mythic."

Focusing upon Roma's conversational technique, a microcosm of all the salesmen given that two-person exchanges comprise more than half of Mamet's play, Sauer observes that in contrast to the direct approach of Churchill's women, "the strategy of Mamet's boys' play" is indirect, resem-bling the competitive character, context, and discourse of arguing children, which serves as "the underlying referent of Mamet's depiction of men." Counterpointing the chronology, construction, "morally decentered worlds," competitive dialogue, and the comparable illusion of Marlene in *Top Girls* and Levene in *Glengarry Glen Ross*, Sauer's enlightening study leads us to new suspicions, presumptions, and "devastating" discoveries at which the characters, entrapped "in a closed loop" never arrive.

Like David Sauer, Jon Tuttle frames *Glengarry* in contrast to another engaging modern play and similarly holds the view that "capitalist excess and American-style narcissism (as in many of Mamet's plays)" are indicted, prompting an examination of "the moral mechanism whereby people jus-tify profiteerism and spiritual prostitution." However, in 'Be What You *Are*':

Identity and Morality in *Edmond* and *Glengarry Glen Ross*," Tuttle brilliantly argues that written at approximately the same time these plays may be profitably read as "companion pieces" whose "dark journey and metaphorical exploration into the lower depths of man's depravity," recalling Marlowe's journey in Conrad's *Heart of Darkness*, not only also unites but also informs the works. A talented playwright, his perceptive insights on *Edmond* reveal a stunning grasp of Mamet's elusive and disturbing work and are, in themselves, deserving of our attention, but when glossed against *Glengarry Glen Ross*, Tuttle's superb analysis of *Edmond* illumines the later work, stripping the masks of performance art in Mamet's world to expose baser instincts, desires, actions, and anarchy. Tracing the moral continuum in *Glengarry*, "one that mirrors the contest board," from the position of "the pole—the ethic"—represented by the figures of Roma and Aaronow—and foreshadowing role-playing in his discussion, as Mamet does in both plays, he leads us to comprehend more clearly the complex series of masks that Levene adopts and the pole to which Levene gravitates. In fact, Tuttle wisely observes, we glimpse the subtly shifting power dynamic through the character's choices, "conditioned at least in part by economic pressure," and to "our horror" see that "business is savage because people are."

In her provocative essay Elizabeth Klaver posits that David Mamet and Jean Baudrillard, who "at first glance may appear to have radically different viewpoints," have both "gone in search of America." Arguing from the position that Mamet's plays, like those of Baudrillard, "constitute a remarkably similar "'lighting out'—a voyage that mirrors Baudrillard's astral vision," Klaver cogently contends that their visions compose a comparable America as "search and spectacle," what she terms "opportunity-as-event." Reading *Glengarry Glen Ross* against Baudrillard's *America*, she concerns herself—and engages us—in the theatrical journey "across a vision of America" that is set in a hologram ("in which the whole is contained in each of its elements") of America, better known to most readers and audiences of Mamet's play as the real estate office of Glengarry, through which Mamet's America becomes visible.

The key to understanding Mamet's American vision, Klaver maintains, is the ability to reread signs, the most notable is of which is "the playwright's representation of the end of the twentieth century as a consumer [read 'astral'] society in which the circulation of images replaces the sense of the real." Indeed, not only does she illuminate these images by her astute reading of signs in Baudrillard's and Mamet's America, she also perceptibly advances our inquiry into the issue of criminality in the play raised by several scholars. "Rather than delineating a system that can beat down good men," Klaver maintains that Mamet, unlike Miller, "lets the edge of criminality lurk beneath every aspect of the real estate venture from initial bribery to final robbery." In concluding her original reading of Baudrillard's and Mamet's visions, Klaver asserts that they reach their "purest point of intersection" in the "post-commodity culture," a dystopia that enacts America's "fatal attraction for the conman," a figure that even novice sign readers will recognize as Mametic and read as "the archetypal postmodernist figure."

Tony Stafford shares the commonly held view that Mamet is a "socially conscious playwright," but rather than viewing *Glengarry Glen Ross* from the perspective of "greed and gain," Stafford sets his sights on its more "cohering and devastating" central trope of illusion. From this vista, he argues, its salesmen inhabit "an illusory world, create a phony reality, and use false appearances" to peddle nonexistent land. In an imaginative study of the geographical, national, and international place names whose repetitions evolve into "a litany" of farms, highlands, and mountain views, and cluster images, Stafford focuses attention on the correlation of places, names, and invocations of land and place-as-concept not unrelated to illusory leads and people. Turning his sharp eye to shady land deals that typically exchange "promised land" for frequently worthless checks, he is equally adroit at pursuing historical paradigms and biblical—both Old and New Testament—allusions that he contends are aligned to the idea of "promised land," or rather the perversion of this sign. In concluding his whirlwind tour of places, real estate terms, and land-based phrases, he brings us round to the stunningly simple perception that in spite of the discourse, "no one goes anywhere, no land is actually seen, and the audience is left with vague illusions and even vaguer promises which remain unfulfilled."

Paralleling Stafford's search for the illusory in *Glengarry Glen Ross*, Linda Dorff's fine essay, "Things (Ex)change: The Value of Money in David Mamet's *Glengarry Glen Ross*," addresses the invisibility of money in Mamet's play. "Money is the medium of exchange," Dorff argues, for all of "the play's transactions, including sales, robbery, talking, bribery." As Levene tells it, money was clearly "visible" when they were selling Glen Ross Farms, but these allusions to money, she contends, perform in the "utopic past which Levene repeatedly invokes." In fact, in her fresh approach to one of the most contentious and seductive subjects in Mamet's work, Dorff posits that Mamet "parallels the recent past (1960s) with American frontier mythology" because money was and remains a powerful and empowering "mirage." But, notably, Dorff reminds us that when "cash is offered as bribe at the beginning and end of the play the iconic sign of money changes things."

Tracing the semiotic transformation that money signs have undergone from the gold standard to checks, Dorff perceptively argues that "money symbols problematize exchanges—altering both the value of money and life." Briefly examining money—or the lack of it—in numerous Mamet works, she focuses on *Glengarry Glen Ross*'s "critique of capitalism" as an inquiry into exchanges, noting that money defines the historical past and present. Her incisive study zeroes in on money for land in which check or chit is equally nonexistent. Moreover, mirroring the Glengarry salesmen in search of valuable signifiers or symbolic representations of money, Dorff, in pursuit of the money, concerns herself and us with its accessibility, whether covert or overt. Addressing "the relative value" of money in a world in which the having of it or the lack of it is anything but relative, she compels us to reread money as yet another encoded sign in Mamet's America, but in illuminating "its visibility and invisibility onstage" she contributes to our understanding of its complex role in *Glengarry* by underscoring "its performative aspect" as well.

"As American culture persists in defining life economically," observes Richard Brucher, "dramatic responses to social problems (and earlier plays) become increasingly caustic, ironic, and parodic." In his essay, "Pernicious Nostalgia in *Glengarry Glen Ross*," Brucher posits the premise that "Mamet subverts a line of self-conscious nostalgia that runs from Eugene O'Neill through Arthur Miller." The clarity of his argument and the abundant use of supporting evidence substantively advance our knowledge of Mamet's place and distinction in the continuum of American drama, specifically with respect to the role of nostalgia and the salesman. Balancing fine scholarship with his own sharp wit, Brucher not only showcases Mamet's distinctive sense of humor and broad use of comedy, but also sets the stage for an engrossing study of nostalgia that he maintains Mamet "internalizes, understates and ritualizes" and shifts from the characters to the audience. Similarly, taking his cue from Robert Brustein's review of *Glengarry* that counterpoints Mamet's play about salesmen with Miller's *Death of a Salesman*, he examines Mamet's use of cultural history and clarifies his place in a long line of social critics. Ultimately, argues Brucher, in (re)viewing *Glengarry Glen Ross* we observe that "Mamet refuses to tell us whom and what to trust. Arguably," he concludes, "that is where we should be."

In a most welcome contribution to the collection, Robert Rolf provides a unique perspective on the performance and reception of *Glengarry Glen Ross* in Japan. His essay is composed of two parts: the first, a study of Japanese theater, the second, a critical analysis of the play within this cultural context. Rolf sets the scene in his discussion of the play's productions (1988 and 1990) and translation. Under the direction of Emori Tōru, an accomplished actor who also translated *Glengarry Glen Ross*, Emori and the Bungakuza, the oldest and perhaps most prestigious theater group in Japan, staged two *different* productions, each of which traveled to numerous venues within Japan. Emori, in particular, was inspired by the credibility of diction and dramatic situation, greatly animated—as were the actors—by *Glengarry*'s "masculinity," and especially welcomed the challenge of re-creating "its powerful psychological reality." But the challenge of "psychological reality" proved far easier to address than a translation. Not only is the translation from English to other languages especially difficult given the rhythms of Mamet's speech—as Pierre Laville, Mamet's friend and French translator has noted—but, as Rolf explains, Mamet's reliance on scatological language created some "nearly impossible situations," given that the Japanese rarely employ obscenities.

Drawing upon a wealth of knowledge, access to the director and translated script, production photographs, and a tape of the performance, Rolf frames his discerning study of the play's second production and its reception with an overview of the historical and cultural context that informs it. His essay is equally fascinating in his examination of the appeal of *Glengarry Glen Ross* in Japan. If the "universality of *Glengarry Glen Ross* is relevant in Japan," he observes, "it is about what the Japanese performance implies about Japanese or all business." And, it is here that his extensive knowledge of Japanese literature, language, culture, and politics casts light upon an area quite removed from most readers and audiences of Mamet's play, aware that Mamet "plays" worldwide, but rarely privy to how it "plays" or possibly why. For example, we note Rolf's observation that a Japanese Moss "is slick, sleazy, self-important, in short, a distasteful character." Moreover, we learn that several characters, Lingk and Levene included, evidenced "the conventions of *shingeki* realism," a whining sound not indicated in stage instructions—which Mamet rarely employs—but rather credible and realistic behavior for a Japanese character in a similar situation. Additionally, Rolf's direct access to Emori, who contributes his perceptive responses to the work, which he "understands [as] modern life's corrosive effect on community" rather than capitalism as the play's central trope—together with production photos that he has graciously made available to us—further enrich his study and, I hope, readers of this collection.

NOTES

1. Gregory Mosher spoke with the editor about *Glengarry Glen Ross* in a lengthy telephone interview, 2 August 1995.

2. Benedict Nightingale, "The Sharks Still Have Bite," *Times* (London) 24 June 1994, 35.

3. Clive Barnes, "Mamet's *Glengarry*: A Play to See and Cherish," *New York Post*, 26 March 1984, 15.

4. Jay Carr, "Potent Adaptation of *Glengarry Glen Ross*," *Boston Globe*, 16 September 1992, 72.

5. Michael Coveney, "*Glengarry Glen Ross*," *Observer*, 26 June 1994. Rpt. *Theatre Record*, 18 June–1 July 1994, 793.

6. Matthew C. Roudané, "Public Issues, Private Tensions: David Mamet's *Glengarry Glen Ross*," *South Carolina Review* 19, no. 1 (1986): 39.

7. Jack Kroll, "Mamet's Jackals in Jackets," *Newsweek*, 9 April 1984. Rpt. *New York Theatre Critics' Reviews*, 5–11 March 1984, 337.

8. Barnes, 15.

9. John Beaufort, "A Searing Look at the Sordid World of Salesmen," *Christian Science Monitor*, 10 April 1984, 25. Rpt. *New York Theatre Critics' Reviews*, 5–11 March 1984, 339.

10. Richard Corliss, "Pitchmen Caught in the Act," *Time*, 9 April 1984, 105. Rpt. *New York Theatre Critics' Reviews*, 5–11 March 1984, 338.

11. Rita Kemply, "Mamet's Moral Swamp," *Washington Post*, 2 October 1992, C1.

12. Brendan Gill, "The Theater: The Lower Depths," *New Yorker*, 2 April 1984, 114.

13. David Mamet, *Glengarry Glen Ross* (New York: Grove, 1984), 96.

14. Gregory Mosher, interviewed by the editor, "Interview with Gregory Mosher," in *David Mamet: A Casebook*, ed. Leslie Kane (New York: Garland, 1992), 239.

15. John Gross, "Tragedies of Good and Bad Manners," *Sunday Telegraph*, 26 June 1994. Rpt. *Theatre Record*, 18 June–1 July 1994, 788.

16. Pierre Laville, *Pays de Vaud*, 4 December 1986. Quoted in *File on Mamet*, comp. Nesta Jones and Steven Dykes (London: Methuen Drama 1991), 60.

17. Billington, Michael. "Glengarry Glen Ross." *Daily Telegraph*, 22 September 1983, 15. Rpt. *London Theatre Record*, 10–23 September 1983, 822.

18. Vincent Canby, "Mamet's Real Estate Sharks and Their Prey," *New York Times*, 30 September 1992: C15.

19. Robert Brustein, "Show and Tell," *New Republic* 7 May 1984. Rpt. *Who Needs Theatre: Dramatic Opinions* (New York: Atlantic Monthly Press, 1987), 71.

20. Brustein, 67–68.

21. Timothy B. Spears, *One Hundred Years on the Road* (New Haven: Yale University Press, 1995), x.

22. Spears, 17, 106, 12.

23. Spears, xiii.

24. Mel Gussow, "Real Estate World a Model for Mamet," *New York Times*, 28 March 1984, C19.

25. David Mamet, *On Directing Film* (New York: Viking, 1991), 2.

26. Ruby Cohn, "Phrasal energies: Harold Pinter and David Mamet," in *Anglo-American Interplay in Recent Drama* (Cambridge: Cambridge University Press, 1995), 63.

27. David Mamet, *Glengarry Glen Ross* (New York: Grove, 1984), 26, 104.

28. C.W.E. Bigsby, *David Mamet* Contemporary Writers Series (London: Methuen, 1985), 136.

A NOTE ON THE TEXT

Contributors to *Glengarry Glen Ross: Text and Performance* have used both the Grove and Methuen editions of *Glengarry Glen Ross*. Please consult the Notes or Bibliography following each essay to ascertain the specific edition to which the author refers.

DAVID MAMET'S
GLENGARRY GLEN ROSS

NEGATIVE CREATION

THE DETECTIVE STORY IN *GLENGARRY GLEN ROSS*

Steven Price

Murder is negative creation, and every murderer is therefore the rebel who claims the right to be omnipotent.

—W. H. Auden[1]

The detective story in *Glengarry Glen Ross* is literally marginalized: the office break-in occurs in the interval between the play's two acts, and the investigation in act 2 is conducted in a room off-stage by a detective who barely appears. Criticism of the play has tended to enforce this marginalization. When noted at all, the robbery itself tends to be seen either as peripheral, or metonymically, as "*merely* an objectification of the crimes daily perpetrated in the name of business,"[2] and therefore as having little significance in itself. It has also been noticed that the crime story provides Mamet with the kind of linear plot structure he was beginning to favor, but this too has generally been little valued: "It is difficult to understand his anxiety to work within conventional forms,"[3] writes one critic, while another states that in *Glengarry Glen Ross* "conventional 'plot' . . . is a red herring for a more significant underlying structure of interrelationship between characters."[4]

A frequent consequence of this devaluation of "conventional" plot is that the play's tensions are collapsed into commonplaces and its suggestiveness seen to reside in something as vague as the "metaphysical source for the crisis in decent human relations."[5] By contrast, the dramatist himself tends both to speak of this play in quite concrete terms (although his insistence that he was simply trying to "write about my experiences in a real-estate office"[6] has been described as "calculatedly disingenuous"[7]), and to insist upon its heterogeneity. He has described it as "a bastard play. It's formally a gang comedy in the tradition of *The Front Page* or *Man in White*. And the first act is episodic, although like a detective story, almost gothic. The second act is a very traditional formal last act of a comedy drama." For the playwright himself, then, the detective element is at least as prominent in the first act as in the second, although he is careful to note that "*Glengarry* really isn't a 'whodunnit,' it is a gang comedy."[8]

In describing elements of the play in terms of the detective story, while rejecting the term "whodunnit," Mamet was perhaps consciously drawing a distinction between, on the one hand, the American "hard-boiled" crime story, in which he already had an interest through having worked on a screenplay based on James M. Cain's *The Postman Always Rings Twice,* and on the other hand, that form of detective novel, predominantly associated with English writers such as Agatha Christie, in which the unmasking of the murderer is of paramount importance. Despite Mamet's distinction, however, certain features of the whodunnit are deliberately introduced into the play's second act, for example the emphasis on exposing the culprit and the linear progression of events, both of which are of greater importance in the "English" than in the "American" subgenre. The foregrounding of this particular kind of plot can be dismissed as merely "conventional" because it appeals to a perception of order that is increasingly difficult to maintain yet continues to exert a powerful ideological appeal. The combination of detection and linear sequence, then, carries with it further ideological associations traceable to the whodunnit: the fixing of guilt onto named individuals (and the consequent affirmation of the innocence of the rest of us), and the appeal to a nostalgic, pastoral, and comic order.[9] In its residual pastoralism, in particular, the play is related intertextually to both English and American literary traditions and conventions. The names of the properties sold in Mamet's real estate office—"Glengarry Highland," "Glen Ross Farms," "Homestead" (3–7)—conflate the appeal of romantic Scottish detachment and a specifically American, Jeffersonian vision of the farm as idealized family retreat; but of course it is precisely this ideology of innocent rural detachment that makes the imaginary properties commercially valuable, and thereby reinstates them into the structure from which they ostensibly offer an escape.

This reappropriation shows that it is precisely because the innocent worldview of the whodunnit is not only untenable, but actually exemplifies the world of vicious financial extortion to which it appears to offer an alternative, that the play has to reject it. Unlike the whodunnit, the detective element in this play does not finally impose a form upon otherwise seemingly inchoate experience. Instead, like the burglary committed between the play's two acts, it represents a disruption of normal business, foregrounding the structure of repression by which the office operates while refusing either the characters or the audience the Aristotelian consolation of catharsis.[10] Despite the naming of the burglar, the play finally resists closure, so that submerged tensions become apparent without being exorcised: tensions between employers, employees, and clients (realistically), between parents and children (metaphorically), and between different literary and dramatic forms (generically). The play suggests that capitalism is fraud and that the true relation of employer to employee is that of parent to child, but because neither the bosses nor the salesmen can afford to acknowledge this openly these thoughts are driven underground, only to reemerge, like the Freudian unconscious, in the language and structure of everyday life.

The "bastard" nature of the detective story in *Glengarry Glen Ross,* then, exposes a formal and ideological tension between that form's subgenres: between on the one hand the "classical" variety (linear, comic, pastoral, communal, and English), and on the other hand its "hard-boiled" descendant (circular or unresolved, tragic, urban, individualistic, and American). This particular struggle enacts at the level of genre various other tensions expressed in the play, all of which may be, and frequently are, characterized by the metaphor of something or someone struggling to break free of the authority of the parent. Consequently, although at a realistic level the salesmen are thieves, at a deeper psychic and metaphorical level the crime they really want to commit is murder. Crime in this play represents a necessarily futile attempt by the child to establish itself by killing the parent.

The air of criminality is pervasive. According to Mamet, in the sales parlance of the real estate office in which he worked an appointment between salesman and client "was called a *lead*—in the same way that a clue in a criminal case is called a *lead*—i.e. it may lead to the suspect, the suspect in this case being a *prospect.*"[11] Early in the first scene the connection is established as Williamson describes his job, in which he is "*hired* to watch the leads" (6), in terms befitting Dashiell Hammett's Sam Spade; and as in the "hard-boiled" school of crime fiction that Hammett helped to initiate, the language and role-playing of the office tend to erode simple distinctions between detective, criminal and victim.

The related blurring of the line between business and crime is repeated in Mamet's later screenplays for *The Untouchables* and *Things Change,* which seem on occasion to express a measured admiration for the Mafia hierarchy precisely because it embodies the values of American capitalism, without the hypocrisy of official business exposed in the response of an audience of businessmen to *American Buffalo,* who "were angry because the play was about them."[12] The connection is an open secret. In *Glengarry Glen Ross* crime is simultaneously what Mitch and Murray strive to keep hidden (it disrupts their world) and what most precisely expresses their ethos (business as crime). The detritus-strewn set of the second act encapsulates this contradiction, as Roma tries to conduct business as usual while the police conduct a criminal investigation in the next room. When the truth can no longer be hidden the embarrassment emerges in Williamson's wonderfully understated explanation that "[w]e had a slight burglary last night" (55). Because crime is simultaneously omnipresent and forbidden it is never fully demystified, and the salesmen's fantasies of escape can only be fantasies of further criminal action. They are thereby caught in a network of relationships that has already defined the range of possibilities open to them.

In this way the play begins to explore tensions between freedom and constraint, and between present experience and formative myth, which are particularly focused on this question of crime: whether crime offers the possibility of freedom and represents the eruption of social energy, or whether on the contrary the world is so systematically criminal that it has prefigured and provided for every attempt to escape from it. Like a latter-day Hamlet, for example, Moss knows that the "hard part" of "[g]oing to business for yourself" is "[j]ust the *act*" (15). Moreover, he shares with Hamlet an ill-concealed death wish directed against the father, in his case the bosses. This revelation, and its immediate containment, emerges as he describes to Aaronow his plan for the downfall of Mitch and Murray:

> Moss: Someone should stand up and strike *back*.
> Aaronow: What do you mean?
> Moss: *Somebody* . . .
> Aaronow: Yes . . . ?
> Moss: Should do something to *them*.
> Aaronow: What?
> Moss: Something. To pay them back. *(Pause.)*
> Someone, someone should hurt them. Murray and Mitch.
> Aaronow: Someone should hurt them.
> Moss: Yes.
> Aaronow: *(Pause.)* How?
> Moss: How? Do something to hurt them. Where they live.
> Aaronow: What? *(Pause.)*
> Moss: Someone should rob the office. (17)

The first part of this exchange unmistakably intimates a threat of physical violence, especially in the context of criminal resentment already established in the previous scene between Levene and Williamson, and Aaronow's characteristic uncertainty as to what is happening around him intensifies this air of menace. The less drastic proposition Moss finally puts, however, is in keeping with a pattern repeated throughout the play, whereby significant action is promised only to be retracted; other examples include the threats to defect to Jerry Graff, Levene's sale of land to the Nyborgs, and Roma's offer of friendship to Levene at the end of the play. In each case the promise signals an attempt to escape from the constraints imposed by the office, and in each case it fails.

Robbery, the alternative means of escape Moss finally proposes, is in fact no escape at all, since it merely repeats the same course of action pursued by others and which at a different level the salesmen are already pursuing themselves. In remarking how difficult it is to "act," Moss ironically indicates that they are like actors constantly repeating a role scripted for them in advance. This accounts in part for the atavistic quality of their language and actions: they reenact crimes so ancient, so formative, so paradigmatic, that they have already passed into myth. They are a "dying breed" in a "fucked-up world" with "no adventure," a world of "clock watchers, bureaucrats, office holders" (62), in contrast to whom the salesmen think of themselves as buddy pioneers at the frontier: "a man who's your 'partner' *depends* on you . . . you have to go *with* him and *for* him . . . or you're shit, you're *shit*, you can't exist alone . . ." (58).

Given this self-image it is peculiarly appropriate that the salesmen should be recast within a detective story, for like them the lone private eye of the "hard-boiled" crime stories of Dashiell Hammett and Raymond Chandler is heir to the tradition of the pioneering frontiersman. In *The Pursuit of Crime*, Dennis Porter has argued that the private eyes of the American detective story—Hammett's Sam Spade and Continental Op, or Chandler's Philip Marlowe, for instance—represent neither the police nor the criminals, but are instead populist heroes, acting as "urban frontiersmen who because of sociopolitical circumstances have some of the characteristics of social bandits," while also resembling "the Indian scouts and gun-slinging cowboys of frontier myth."[13] These populist heroes share with Mamet's salesmen such characteristics as a potential for bigotry, misogyny, and xenophobia, anti-intellectualism, and a distrust of institutional power (whether governmental, financial, or criminal). In discussing the elements of crime and detection in the play it is important to stress their relation to these specifically American literary antecedents, because in drawing on them the characters reveal not only a desire for significant individual action but also their actual enslavement to a caricature constructed for them in advance and expressed as myth.

Mamet's view of American myth is decidedly lacking in nostalgic illusion. The problem confronted by his salesmen is different from that confronted by the cowboys of Arthur Miller's *The Misfits,* whose worldview has been superseded. The problem for Mamet is that the myth was always corrupt and that the distinction Roma draws between the salesmen and the "office holders" like Williamson is ultimately false. As Mamet says, "[f]amiliar American pieties are always linked to criminality. That's why they are familiar American pieties."[14] The burglary in the office is symptomatic of a general condition and an originary moment. The salesman's self-perception as cowboy or frontier pioneer looks to this originary moment for both security and an enabling myth of freedom; but those American myths are always constructions, always suspect and guilty, invented as an alibi by the guy who got there first. The dream is to repeat, like Jerry Graff, an original act of appropriation in order to define oneself both as the creator of the system and as someone who can stand outside it. Consequently in the mythology of the salesmen the heroes are doing exactly the same thing as the villains. The attempt to establish individuality, difference, and freedom is conducted in terms that bind the salesmen to the same rules from which they are attempting to escape: the desire can be effected only through more crime, through an act of theft from the parent company. This recognition of the obligation to persist in an endlessly repeated and futile endeavor is the truly Beckettian side to Mamet, and what Andrew K. Kennedy said of Beckett's language is equally true of American myth in Mamet's work: "The idea of the failure of language has served Beckett as a myth *for* creation. It is a 'negative' myth which, as a source of creative energy, is comparable to the familiar power of certain negative emotions as motives to action, and to 'the negative way' as a source of spiritual life."[15]

In some respects, then, *Glengarry Glen Ross* continues the assault on American business practice begun in *American Buffalo.* In each case, however, once business has been exposed as theft this is in turn revealed as merely symptomatic of a deeper motive linked to killing. In the earlier play the faded likeness of a native American on the buffalo nickel draws a connection between the plot-line—the attempted theft of the coin—and the historical genocide of the native population. While the plot of *American Buffalo* figures American capitalism as one gigantic heist story, *Glengarry Glen Ross* is closer to the conventions of detective fiction, a connection deepened by connoting robbery, or "business," not with genocide but with homicide. (The common expression "to make a killing" is very revealing.) There is something macabre, for instance, in the runner-up's prize of a set of steak knives, while the aura of death surrounding the "leads" becomes more intense as the play proceeds. As Mamet's own explanation of the initially incomprehensible term indicates, the audience will probably first associate it with the conventions of the murder mystery; and even when its meaning within the world of business has been established, the play retains and even elaborates upon its previous connotations. Startlingly, the leads are persistently figured as corpses. Poor leads are "old," "ancient," and finally "dead" (32), while at one point Roma complains that one of them has even been extracted "from the *morgue*" (35). But the most striking example of a direct connection between selling things and killing people is Levene's account of how he "closed" two of his leads. As Levene tells it, this incident recalls nothing so much as a murder followed by a funeral and a wake: when the Nyborgs finally gave in and signed the contract, "they both kind of *imperceptibly slumped,*" after which the atmosphere became "fucking solemn"; there was a formal shaking of hands, followed by "a drink. Little shot glasses. A pattern in 'em. And we toast. In silence" (43).

That the language of the assassin finds its way into Levene's description of a property deal is no accident, for murder presents itself to the salesman's mind as the only logical way out of a vicious circle that Moss's solution, robbery, cannot escape. In a play whose language is suffused with ironic, familial imagery, the salesman-child can succeed only by killing the boss-parent, as we saw in Moss's conversation with Aaronow; but because in this play the bosses are literally untouchable, the desired homicide is either projected onto others or translated into substitute forms of revenge. The most pervasive form is a kind of anal-sadistic attack on Mitch and Murray, finally effected in the robbery, which represents the culmination in action of the recurrent strands of imagery—of killing, of family, of defecation—which together unconsciously reveal the murderous impotence of the salesmen.

Mamet's presentation of family relations is both more pervasive and even darker than is often recognized. It is true that he rarely writes explicitly about the family: prior to *The Cryptogram* (1993), only *Reunion* (1976) explores family relationships in any depth, and even in these cases the nuclear family has broken down, the broken home being "[t]he most important institution in America."[16] This absence in Mamet's writing is unusual for an American dramatist, since the security and tensions created by the family have formed the basis of what has often been regarded as the dominant—for some, almost the only—American dramatic tradition.[17]

Nonetheless the family remains a potent structure in Mamet's work, and he is apt to use it metaphorically in describing all manner of institutional power relationships. For example, he uses the metaphor of the unhappy fam-

9

ily to describe the structure of the American theatre, in which "[t]he actor is manipulated and controlled by the director, who is similarly in thrall to the producer," creating relationships that resemble "that of the parent to the child"; and this superstructure reflects the commercial base, those at the bottom being "subject to the unreasoned, unloving and frightened whims of those in (financial) power over them." Mamet concludes, ominously, that in this situation, as in any "unhappy tryanny [sic], the oppressed must free the oppressor."[18]

It has often been noted that the all-male casts of such plays as *Lakeboat, American Buffalo* and *Glengarry Glen Ross* organize themselves into surrogate families. One of the reasons why this happens in *Glengarry* is that actual families cannot be mentioned because they threaten the stability of the company: whenever Levene speaks of his daughter he is silenced by Williamson, and Lingk's wife destroys Roma's chances of completing a sale. Instead, in the mock-family of the office the Cadillac, the steak knives, and the sack function as a system of rewards for good and bad behavior as defined by the parents, whose inaccessibility means that the salesmen remain in a state of permanent childhood. Even when flushed with success Roma is worried about looking small, about having "to go out like a fucking schmuck hat in my hand and reclose" (32). Later, Roma's diatribe against Williamson fuses family, sexuality and company: "I don't care *whose* nephew you are, who you know, whose dick you're sucking on. . . . You *fairy*. You company man. . . . You fuckin' *child*" (56–57). Once again a salesman articulates his abhorrence of the company man in a context that demonstrates that he himself can be nothing else, and this time the relation to the family metaphor is clear. The ultimate insult in this office is "child" (Levene repeats it to Williamson shortly afterwards), by contrast to the "men" the salesmen insist they are. As their ritual humiliations at the hands of the company repeatedly demonstrate, the force of the word child derives from their recognition that it accurately describes their own position in relation to Mitch and Murray, who "*enslave* them, treat them like *children*" (16). Williamson is the object onto which they project their own anxieties, and his name encodes this function.

At the same time, the obsession with children has still further layers of irony in a play in which the word fucking is repeated to the saturation point while procreation is taboo. This prohibition surfaces repeatedly in connection with Levene. As noted, Williamson is quick to silence him on each of the two occasions on which he mentions his daughter. In scene 1 Williamson merely insists that "I can't do it, Shelly" (10), but the parallel exchange at the end of the play is much harsher:

Levene: Don't.
Williamson: I'm sorry.
Levene: *Why?*
Williamson: Because I don't like you.
Levene: John: John: . . . my *daughter* . . .
Williamson: Fuck you. (62)

This vicious rejoinder recalls the refrain of "Fuck the Machine" that was built up around Levene earlier in the act (38–40), a refrain that introduces connotations of sterility: taken literally, metaphorically, or as a variation on the salesmen's favorite phrase, "fuck you," it is an example of the insistence upon sex as nonprocreative. Levene represents a scandal because a "Machine" should not be producing offspring, a prohibition that once again traps the salesmen permanently in the role of children.

The scatological nature of much of the dialogue works subliminally in a similar way. Although this kind of language is in everyday use, the contexts in which it appears in *Glengarry Glen Ross* often recall the Freudian anal stage, in which the child's control over its bowels gives it the illusion of control over the world. In scene 3, for example, Roma introduces an apparently bizarre question into his opening speech to ensnare the notably childlike Lingk. "You ever take a dump made you feel like you'd just slept for twelve hours . . . ?" (24), he asks, reverting to a primal notion of personal power that Lingk might comprehend more readily than the confused philosophy of personal moral integrity that Roma has previously articulated. That Roma has now hit on the right note is evident both from Lingk's acceptance of the deal and from his explanation in the second act that he is pulling out of the deal because he doesn't "have the power" in his marriage (54).

In the first scene there is an exchange between Levene and Williamson that perhaps carries similar unconscious associations. Levene is becoming frustrated about Williamson's refusal to give him the leads on easy terms:

Levene: Ah, *shit,* John . . .
    Pause.
Williamson: I wish I could.
Levene: You fucking asshole . . . (9)

Williamson is saying that he can't give Levene the help he wants, but the syntax allows for a secondary meaning, in which "shit" is taken as an imperative verb. In either case the two men are discussing the possibility of self-assertion in the face of a repressive authority, and their status as children is confirmed in the second act when the salesmen discuss the likely response of Mitch and Murray to the robbery in terms that suggest the child's fear of the parent's wrath on discovering the mess the child has made. Mitch and Murray are "going to be upset" (33).

Given these power relations it is particularly significant that the specific nature of the robbery, which had been planned by Moss as a show of defiance against Mitch and Murray, actually reinforces their authority. The theft of the leads is banal; the theft of the *telephones,* however, is extraordinary and logically inexplicable, and Roma and Aaronow, whom Mamet has described as the play's *raisonneur,*[19] foreground it as a mystery:

> Roma: . . . Where's the phones?
> Aaronow: They stole . . .
> Roma: They stole the . . .
> Aaronow: What. What kind of outfit are we running where . . .
>   where anyone . . .
> Roma: *(To himself)* They stole the phones.
> Aaronow: Where criminals can come in here . . . they take the . . .
>   They stole the phones. (32)

The incident is motiveless, but makes perfect sense in terms of its effects, for the disappearance of the phones removes a democratizing medium from the workplace and so reinstates the power of Mitch and Murray in the act of challenging it. As Marshall McLuhan argued, "It is not possible to exercise delegated authority by telephone. The pyramidal structure of job-division and description and delegated powers cannot withstand the speed of the phone to by-pass all hierarchical arrangements, and to involve people in depth."[20] The removal of the phones reinstates the pyramidal structure of authority, since orders are now necessarily handed down by word of mouth from Mitch and Murray to Williamson, and thence to the salesmen, in terms that repeat a word used earlier in order once again to evoke the child-like fear of parental anger: "I talked to Mitch and Murray an hour ago," says Williamson. "They're coming in, you understand they're a bit *upset* . . ." (43). It is this constant imposition of parental authority that creates the connected tropes of family and killing that recur throughout the play in the language of the salesmen.

As Mamet's very apt description of *Glengarry* as a "bastard play" would suggest, the family metaphor is helpful not only in examining the composition and motives of the "gang," but also in exploring the formal complexities of the play itself. The competition in Mamet's plays between a linear, realistic form on the one hand, and a circular or fragmentary form associated with the absurd on the other, has been extensively discussed elsewhere (for example in the comments by Bigsby and Carroll noted at the beginning of this essay), as have the influences of American writers, such as Arthur Miller and British and European dramatists, such as Beckett and Pinter, although it is worth noting that the dedication of *Glengarry Glen Ross* to Pinter raises these questions even more starkly than usual. In the present context, what is more important is that the "bastard" nature of the play extends to the various elements of detection within it. The milieu is predominantly that of the urban American "hard-boiled" crime story or *film noir*, although it necessarily retains vestiges of the English, "classical" variety. Within this American form the structure of the "gang comedy," which as Mamet says presents "many, somewhat dissimilar renditions of the same attitude,"[21] creates a blurring of roles, so that the role of detective passes in different forms and at different levels between a variety of characters.

The world of *Glengarry Glen Ross,* and indeed that of Mamet's plays in general, is under constant surveillance by powers that never appear bodily on stage. In *American Buffalo* Teach is concerned about the police cars circling ominously outside; in *Speed-the-Plow* Gould's career depends on conformity to the standards of commercial success demanded by Hollywood, metonymically represented by the always-unavailable Richard Ross; and in *Oleanna* the college professor, John, is dependent on the approval of the Tenure Committee. As Mamet's career has progressed these invisible powers have become increasingly associated with the force of law. The theme of *Oleanna,* for instance, is not simply "political correctness"; it is the way in which conventions become hardened into truth, and thence into legal constraint. Carol insists that because the Tenure Committee has accepted her version of events the charges against John are no longer accusations or interpretations but facts, and he may be punished accordingly.

The real estate office in *Glengarry* is comprehensively regulated by two analogous yet competing systems. First, there is an impersonal system of regulation enforced by figures who are named but never seen: Mitch and Murray and the mysterious "Lemkin" (56). As Moss puts it, "[Y]ou find yourself in *thrall* to someone else. And we *enslave* ourselves. . . . [A]nd the guy who got there first . . . made *up* those rules" (16). A second and parallel structure of surveillance is enforced by the public legal institutions. The marginalized detective Baylen is the occasionally visible representative of these institutions, but is treated with notable contempt by the salesmen ("Cop couldn't find his dick two hands and a map," says Moss [37]). Nonetheless, that these official institutions have real authority is demonstrated not only by the threat of Lingk's wife to contact the state's attorney general, but also by the salesmen's tendency to project themselves into the shoes of those in power over them. Levene acts the part of "*the* senior vice-president American Express" (47), and Roma pretends to have been a member of the board that drafted the statute that protects Lingk and acts as a constraint on himself. These spontaneous deceptions have often been held to demonstrate the creative energy and imagination of the salesmen, as indeed they do; but the overwhelming irony is that their fictions also reveal the extent to which they have internalized the regulatory systems to which they are subjected. At a less spectacular level the same is true of Moss, not only in his fantasies about Jerry Graff but also more insidiously in his reinterpretation of what Aaronow had considered to be "only talking" as a legal exchange that makes Aaronow "an accessory. Before the fact" (22).

This internalization marks the workings of a modern Foucauldian power that has substituted for visible and spectacular punishment a system of constant external and internal surveillance.[22] In *Glengarry Glen Ross* the official detective can be ignored because the salesmen are already subject to multiple systems of regulation they have already internalized. Consequently, toward the end of the play the language of detection shifts from character to character: Baylen attempts to interview Roma, a suspect who reinvents himself as Baylen's sidekick in telling Williamson that "I can tell our friend here something might help him to catch you" (57), only for the new suspect Williamson to turn investigator himself in order to expose Levene as the culprit.

Glengarry, then, bears a strong resemblance to the urban, American, "hard-boiled" novels of Hammett and Chandler. This is evident not only in the cognate roles and real or imagined landscapes, but also in the manner in which the air of criminality spreads outward and eventually encompasses the whole world of the work. In all of these ways, for example, *Glengarry Glen Ross* has much in common with Hammett's *Red Harvest* (1929), often regarded as the first novel of the new American crime school and a book whose title, like that of Mamet's play, looks back with ironic disillusion at a pastoral or agrarian ideal. This is the ironic point of the "conventional" detective story in act 2. On the one hand, Mamet's play reworks this theme of corrupted pastoral innocence which can be traced from Thoreau through Hawthorne to Nathaniel West and beyond.[23] There is a suggestion in the play that the land has run out: that there are no more wildernesses to conquer, that even these undeveloped tracts of land are now "property." On the other hand, in the same way as the salesmen exploit an American nostalgia for the pastoral world of Crèvecoeur and Jefferson, Mamet's introduction of a linear structure in his second act appeals, as we saw, to the innocent, ordered world of the English, "classical" detective story of Christie, Dorothy L. Sayers, and others, which is repudiated by Hammett and Chandler and undermined by the "bastard" structure of the play as a whole.

At several levels, formal, generic, and thematic, there is a kind of Baudrillardian trap in *Glengarry Glen Ross* whereby the dominant structure perpetuates itself through a constant process of simulation and appropriation. As Mamet has said of the totalizing ambitions of American business, "[A]ny impulse of creation or whimsy or iconoclasm which achieves general notice is immediately co-opted by risk capital, and its popularity—which arose from its generosity and freedom of thought—is made to serve the turn of financial extortion."[24] Perhaps one of the reasons why Levene's star is fading is that he insists on presenting the properties as a business opportunity indistinguishable from the kinds of deals enacted every day in downtown Chicago. He seems to have forgotten that what the land represents to his customers is a different kind of myth.

Just as the American pastoral provides the conditions for its own commercialization, so the English detective story self-deconstructs because it can only maintain its illusion of innocent freedom by placing the subject under inescapable systems of measurement and surveillance.[25] The novels of Christie, John Dickson Carr, and Freeman Wills Crofts, for example, are replete with diagrams, timetables and detailed accounts of the logistics of the "locked-room" mystery, while the detective, increasingly assisted by forensic science, is charged with bringing to light the secrets of the world. The sales chart and the "board" are visible signs of this kind of monitoring in *Glengarry*. Innocence can be established only by regarding everyone as suspect, and in this sense the English story anticipated the American versions that followed. For all of Chandler's insistence in "The Simple Art of Murder"[26] on the radical discontinuities between the two forms, then, his novels, like Hammett's, were prefigured in the tradition from which they attempted to escape.

Mamet's interest in crime fiction can therefore hardly represent a mere regression to a conventional form; rather it indicates a Beckettian negative creativity translated into American terms. Beckett's fascination with repetition, impotence, and death becomes, in Mamet's work, a fascination with conformity, power, and murder; and where Beckett's voices suffer the compulsion to speak a language of which they can never be the origin, Mamet's characters rage against a totalizing system that has anticipated its own use for their every maneuver. As Arthur Miller said of the American Dream, "We think that if we could only touch it, and live by it, there's a natural order in favor of us," but this illusion creates "an aspiration to an innocence that when defeated or frustrated can turn quite murderous."[27] The frustrated innocents of Mamet's plays have already reached the point at which murder is the only creative option left.

NOTES

1. W. H. Auden, "The Guilty Vicarage," in *The Dyer's Hand* (London: Faber, 1948), 152.

2. C. W. E. Bigsby, *David Mamet* (London: Methuen, 1985), 114; italics added.

3. Bigsby, *David Mamet*, 125.

4. Dennis Carroll, *David Mamet* (Basingstoke: Macmillan, 1987), 28.

5. Carroll, *David Mamet*, 49.

6. National Theatre's Education Department, *Background notes for teachers and pupils for* Glengarry Glen Ross (London: National Theatre, 1983), 7.

7. Bigsby, *David Mamet*, 122.

8. Quoted in Henry I. Schvey, "David Mamet: Celebrating the Capacity for Self-Knowledge," *New Theatre Quarterly* 13, no. 4 (1988): 92.

9. Martin Priestman, in *Detective Fiction and Literature: The Figure on the Carpet* (Basingstoke: Macmillan, 1990), entitles his chapter on the traditional English detective story "A Version of Pastoral."

10. For a remarkable discussion of five canonical American plays that takes an anti-Aristotelian reading much further, see Walter A. Davis, *Get the Guests: Psychoanalysis, Modern American Drama, and the Audience* (Madison: University of Wisconsin Press, 1994).

11. David Mamet, *Glengarry Glen Ross* (London: Methuen, 1984), n.p. Subsequent references are to this edition.

12. Quoted in Richard Gottlieb, "The Engine that Drives Playwright David Mamet," *New York Times*, 15 January 1978, sec. 2, 1.

13. Dennis Porter, *The Pursuit of Crime: Art and Ideology in Detective Fiction* (New Haven: Yale University Press, 1981), 171, 182.

14. Quoted in Bigsby, *David Mamet*, 111.

15. Andrew K. Kennedy, *Six Dramatists in Search of a Language: Studies in Dramatic Language* (Cambridge: Cambridge University Press, 1975), 135.

16. David Mamet, *Reunion, Dark Pony and The Sanctity of Marriage* (New York: Samuel French, 1982), 24.

17. For representative examples of this view, see Tom Scanlan, *Family, Drama and American Dreams* (Westport, Conn.: Greenwood, 1978); Gerald Berkowitz, *American Drama of the Twentieth Century* (London: Longman, 1992).

18. David Mamet, *A Whore's Profession: Notes and Essays* (London: Faber, 1994), 130–31. The family metaphor is used also to describe the Oscars ceremony (167), political corruption (284), and even card-playing (336).

19. Quoted in Matthew C. Roudané, "An Interview with David Mamet," *Studies in American Drama, 1945–Present* 1, no. 1 (1986): 75.

20. Marshall McLuhan, *Understanding Media: The Extensions of Man* (London: Routledge, 1964), 271.

21. Quoted in Schvey, "David Mamet," 93.

22. Michel Foucault, *Discipline and Punish*, trans. Alan Sheridan (New York: Vintage, 1977).

23. For a wide-ranging discussion of Mamet's relation to "the American view of Nature," see Matthew C. Roudané, "Mamet's Mimetics," in *David Mamet: A Casebook*, ed. Leslie Kane, (New York: Garland, 1992) 3–32.

24. Mamet, *A Whore's Profession*, 198.

25. See, for example, Stephen Knight, *Form and Ideology in Crime Fiction* (Basingstoke: Macmillan, 1980), esp. 120.

26. Raymond Chandler, "The Simple Art of Murder." In *The Art of the Mystery Story*, ed. Howard Haycraft (New York: Carroll and Graf, 1974), 222–37.

27. Matthew C. Roudané, "An Interview with Arthur Miller." In *Conversations with Arthur Miller*, ed. Matthew C. Roudané (Jackson: University Press of Mississippi, 1987) 361–62; quoted in Roudané, "Mamet's Mimetics," 15.

2 "BY INDIRECTIONS FIND DIRECTIONS OUT"

UNINFLECTED CUTS, NARRATIVE STRUCTURE, AND THEMATIC STATEMENT IN THE FILM VERSION OF *GLENGARRY GLEN ROSS*

Christopher C. Hudgins

Each day we take another step to hell,
Descending through the stench, unhorrified

—Baudelaire, "To the Reader" (tr. Stanley Kunitz)

I get used to the muck as I go along.

—Samuel Beckett, *Waiting for Godot*

The general audience, reviewers, and critics often misunderstand David Mamet's plays and films, seeing only scruffy surfaces, not paying enough attention to indicators pointing to a gentleness, a kind of love and a need for love, beneath his often violent scenarios. Michael Sragow's *New Yorker* review of the film version of *Glengarry Glen Ross* is typical in its myopia. Criticizing Mamet's attempt to "imbue one of his stylized hard guys with some humanity by giving him an ailing daughter" as full of "sham pathos" he comments: "Mamet doesn't have the touch for everyday emotions; they have no place in the oversized macho fantasies of his theatrical universe" (164).

That's just not the case, though Mamet evokes the gentler emotions more subtly here than in some other instances. In Mamet's film version of his Pulitzer-winning play, fully appreciating those gentle emotions is dependent on what he calls the "uninflected cut." Placing *Glengarry Glen Ross* "in tension" with Mamet's screenplay for *The Untouchables,* where the gentler emotions of family are more obviously central, is revealing. A summary of Mamet's vision of the possibilities of family life beyond the world of work, scenes showing Eliot Ness at home are achingly beautiful and suggest the primary motivation that transforms Ness from a treasury agent unwilling to go beyond the letter of the law to a man willing to do anything to "hurt

Capone." The "trigger" for Ness's brutal behavior is his love for his family—and that motivation is similar to Shelly Levene's reasons for aggressive salesmanship and for his burglary of the real estate office in *Glengarry Glen Ross*. Uninflected cuts, that is, cuts without obvious narrative comment or emphasis, as we shift from one scene to the next, suggest such connections for audiences of both works.

In *The Untouchables*, just after we watch a little girl blown up in a corner saloon that has refused to buy Capone's product, we cut to Ness's wife, Catherine, smiling in her kitchen as she stuffs a note in a lunch bag, gentle music in the background. Later, as Ness reads it on a stakeout, we see that Catherine has written "I'm proud of you"; he comments to his companion, "It's good to be married," a line repeated several times as the film progresses.[1] For the moment, we watch Catherine sympathize with Ness as he reads the headline about the little girl's death, and she sends him off with warm encouragement to a truly awful first day on the job.

The first we see of Eliot Ness, then, is in the context of a loving marital relationship displaying an emotional sympathy for children. The cut from the bombing scene to his kitchen implies the source of his ability to empathize so intensely with the death of the little girl. Later, a cut from Capone's sybaritic breakfast to Ness's office continues to emphasize their basic moral differences. In contrast to the hoodlums' negligee-clad ladies, we see the little girl's plainly dressed mother thanking Ness for his involvement: "You see, it's because I know that you have children, too. And that this is real for you." Markedly different from Capone's smirking response to his newspaper, Ness is moved, near tears as she leaves. The next "uninflected" cut to Ness looking for Malone's apartment implies that it has been this meeting with the mother of that little girl that prompts him to go to Malone's home to ask for his help. The one scene provokes the other.

After Ness refuses an alderman's bribe, we cut to Capone's vicious hit man, Nitty, the same nattily dressed thug who has bombed the saloon, waiting in a car for Ness to come home. Clearly threatening, Nitty tells Ness: "Nice to have a family. . . . A man should take care. See that nothing happens to them." As he speeds away, Ness dashes up to his daughter's room, gun drawn. The camera focuses on an empty bed and our stomachs drop with his. Then the camera pans to the little girl on the other side of the room, at play. Ness efficiently and lovingly arranges for his wife and daughter to leave town, butterfly kisses and all. As their car roars off we cut to another vehicle squealing around the corner; Ness draws a bead on it with his shotgun, now ready to kill. But it's Malone, not Capone's men, and our tension eases as Ness tells his mentor, "I want to hurt the man, Malone, you hear me. We're taking the battle to him. I want to hurt Capone." The uninflected cut between the family leaving and the second car arriving implies relationship: the threat of losing that family, like Levene's fear for his daughter's health, leads Ness to abandon legal niceties.[2]

Perhaps most centrally for our argument, the scene at the train station as Ness and his men attempt to capture Capone's bookkeeper structurally echoes his vow to help that first mother and to protect his own family and emphasizes the moral source of his determination through the parallels. Helping a young mother struggling to get a baby carriage up a long set of broad stairs, Ness has to release his hold when all hell breaks loose, the gun battle interspersed with shots of that carriage bouncing down the steps, a bullet piercing its cloth covering, closeups of the baby. Paying homage to the famous Odessa steps sequence in Eisenstein's *Battleship Potemkin,* with shots of men in sailor uniforms as innocent victims, the scene associates Capone's men with the Cossacks, Eisenstein's forces of evil. Here, though, Ness begins to defeat those forces with a brutality learned in service of family. At the conclusion of the film, the job finished, echoing an earlier line to Malone on the bridge, Ness answers a reporter's question about what he's going to do next with "I'm going home."

The point of this analysis is twofold. In the first place, it demonstrates that Mamet is capable of depicting a loving, healthy family life, that he believes it a possibility even in the context of a violent world. And in the second, it emphasizes that such love and belonging as he has said we all want motivate the efforts and decisions of many "working men," even within all-male workplaces where the family is not physically present. There are significant parallels in the film *Glengarry Glen Ross,* a much gentler work in its thematic implications than the original play.

In conjunction with additions to or changes from the play, three closely connected elements of the film point toward such a response: its cuts or editing techniques; more broadly, the film's narrative structure; and its use of "indirect thematic statement." In *On Directing Film,* Mamet writes that the best way to make a movie is to create "a succession of images juxtaposed so that the contrast between images moves the story forward in the mind of the audience" (2), his summary of Eisenstein's theory of montage. He adds that the director should tell the story in cuts, "through a juxtaposition of images that are basically uninflected," without a narrative or thematic component present in the image itself. The contrast or relationship between these "objective" shots should tell the story, pull the audience toward understanding or meaning. In a later section of the book, he writes: "[The medium] operates best through that juxtaposition [of uninflected images] because that's the nature of human perception: to perceive two events, determine a progression, and want to know what happens next" (60).

Mamet's uninflected cuts serve narrative structure and point toward theme, making the audience do much of the work of discovery or interpretation. In the structuralist and post-structuralist atmosphere of much of our recent criticism, the traditional term "structure" has fallen out of fashion. In Mamet's instance that is unfortunate, for he is a very traditional playwright in his concern for form. Like many contemporary writers, he has little sympathy with critics' fashionable theoretical concerns. As he tells Matthew Roudané, "I'm sure trying to do the well-made play" (77). In context, that "old" term suggests that Mamet struggles to write plays whose elements fit together in an overall, aesthetically pleasing design, creating a unity, a "quiditas," dependent on the interrelatedness of all of the elements of the drama. The unifying structure in Mamet's "well-made" plays and films relies on parallels, repetitions, and foreshadowing, subtle exposition; one element or scene comments on another, informing it, pointing toward meaning through the ordering of content. The intended subjective inference he hopes audiences glean is part of both the "instruction" and the "delight," the aesthetic pleasure, we take in watching a Mamet play or film.[3]

Much of that pleasure results from the subtlety of Mamet's exposition, his withholding information, refusing to give the audience too much. In *On Directing Film* he observes: "Twenty minutes in[to most movies], we say, '*why*, they should have started the movie *here*. . . .' Get into the scene late, get out of the scene early, tell the story in the cut" (28). He concludes that "The less you narrate, the more the audience is going to say, 'Wow. What the *heck* is happening here? What the *heck* is going to happen next? . . .'" "The real artistry of the film director is to learn to do without the exposition, and so involve the audience" (71, 86). Or, in another context, keep the audience's attention "by withholding all information except that information the absence of which would make the progress of the story incomprehensible" (20). Mamet describes a kind of "uninflected exposition" here: "Part of the art of a play is to introduce information in such a way, and at such a time, that the people in the audience don't realize that they have been given information. They accept it as a matter of course, but they aren't really aware of it so that later on, the information pays off. It has been consciously planted by the author . . . [but] delivered almost as an aside" (*Playboy* interview, 56).

Such comments on the expository element of narrative structure emphasize that Mamet's aesthetic relies on the audience to ferret out "conscious" structural connections and the meaning they point to. In a recent interview, Mamet responds to the charge that his plays are unclear: "It occurs to me that what they mean is 'provocative.' That rather than sending the audience out whistling over the tidy moral of the play, it leaves them unsettled" (*Playboy* interview, 52). Still, as early as "First Principles," Mamet suggests that "the theater affords an opportunity uniquely suited for . . . inspiring ethical behavior" and argues that human beings "always strive to do good—to the limit of their ability and according to their best lights. . . . The theater must be a place where mutual recognition of this desire can take place" (26, 29). In "Decadence" he suggests that the real, fit subjects for drama deal with "the human capacity for choice" (58), and in "Decay" that the central idea of the true theatre is "to bring to your fellows . . . the possibility of communion with what is essential to us all: that we are born to die, that we strive and fail, that we live in ignorance of why we were placed here, and, that in the midst of this we need to love and be loved, but we are afraid" (116). He adds that the battle is between will and fear, that the highest purpose of theatre is to "to address the question 'How can I live in a world in which I am doomed to die?'" (117).

These are not "tidy morals," but Mamet's works do provide indirect thematic comment about ethical behavior in such a world as he envisions. Speaking about *Glengarry Glen Ross,* Mamet says, "I always want everyone to be sympathetic to all the characters" (Schvey 92), a kind of identification clearly impossible for large segments of his audience. That does not prohibit recognition of the negative elements of those figures, of course. Caring behaviors and viciousness exist simultaneously. The two central, flawed figures in *Glengarry Glen Ross,* Roma and Levene, at least occasionally try to do good in a bad world. As Mamet writes in "In the Company of Men": "[T]hese communal activities, even when viciously competitive, are a form of love" (87–89). He adds that "the true nature of the world, as between men, is, I think, a community of effort directed toward the outside world, directed to subdue, to understand, or to wonder, or to withstand together, the truth of the world" (90).

In sum, both Mamet's films and plays typically include a coincidental condemnation and praise or admiration for his characters, even the most vicious. And often these same apparently unsympathetic characters make statements that carry thematic weight, as suggested by those uninflected cuts, by subtle narrative structure and expository direction of the audience's attention that seems "almost an aside."

The film begins with stylized flashes of light to the rhythms of bluesy saxophone, piano, and drums illuminating the opening credits. We cut to flashes of light from train windows as the sound of the commuter train, the "El," comes up and then cut to a coin going into the slot of a pay phone.

The camera pulls back to reveal Shelly Levene calling his daughter. The film's first uninflected cuts, acting as metaphoric "vehicle," carry several suggestions, or "tenors." Repeated throughout, the throbbing intensity of those train wheels, rushing on, inexorably carrying people to their work, or home from it, emphasizes that Levene is a working man; and Dave Moss's entrance, bitching that it's "a bunch of bullshit; waste a good man's time," both labels some of their mutual working conditions and serves as an expositional aside, in retrospect a comment on the horrifying sales meeting that's coming.

Levene's call to his daughter includes similar expositional detail. We hear the gentle caring in his voice as he asks what her doctor said during his latest visit, promising to come see her after the meeting. The lines indeed make us wonder "what the heck is going on here" on two fronts, one about the meeting, one about the state of the daughter's health. As with Ness's generous reply to his daughter's request for butterfly kisses, one of our first impressions of Levene is his deep concern for family, a motivating force for all his economic actions following that meeting. The cut to Moss on the phone trying to set an appointment shows us the nature of this business, and the cut back to Levene making a second call, this time to his daughter's doctor, is in emphatic contrast to Moss's insincerity on the phone as he claims to be the president of the firm in town for just one day. Crosscutting between Levene's frustration at not being able to speak to the doctor and Moss's disgust as he says with a similar desperation in his eyes, "I'll call you back in ten minutes," suggests that the two activities are very different, the one sincere, caring, centrally important in the most humane ways, and the other manipulative, hostile, inhumane, duplicitous. At the same time the parallel lines, as both Moss and Levene say they'll call back, point toward their similar and admirable tenacity in the face of difficulty.

At the end of Blake's outrageously inhumane sales talk, we cut from Moss, again bitterly complaining, to Levene once more calling his daughter's hospital. This cut emphasizes that Levene's first response to the now heightened desperation of his situation is to call to explain to his daughter that he cannot visit until later because of the new threat to his job. He discovers from a nurse that the doctor has been in and that his daughter is asleep. As the camera unobtrusively but clearly shows us many times, Shelly has placed a framed photograph of that much loved daughter on his desk, where he and we can see it readily while he's on the phone. These shots suggest her constant presence in Shelly's thoughts during much of his business day, and make his actions more sympathetic. We cut to a shot over his shoulder of John Williamson, the office manager, at the file cabinets; a second shot shows him locking the new leads in the drawer. The unobtrusive detail about the whereabouts of those leads provides subtle exposition about Levene's reason for his theft, coincidental with that third hospital call, and emphasizes his "opportunity"—as the crime boys would say, "motive, means and opportunity."

The following series of uninflected, subtly metaphoric cuts suggests the desperation that drives Levene over the edge. Just after the sales meeting, he first appeals to Williamson for better leads because of "personal problems," which he mentions twice. The ever-present rain in these nighttime shots, pounding on the office windows, the restaurant canopy, car windshields, umbrellas, and poor Levene's drooping hat gradually accrues metaphoric weight partly due to such cuts. Failing in his personal appeal and in his attempt to bribe Williamson to give him good leads, Levene emerges from Williamson's old Pontiac into that soaking rain once more; we cut to Moss and George Aaronow coming off a sheltering porch into the same rain after a failed "sit," heading for Moss's midsize car and then a doughnut shop. With the rain echoing off the street and the shop windows, Moss bemoans their situation, Aaronow echoing, saying what do you do "if you do not have the goddam leads?" We cut to a shot of Levene, in the rain, at the door of the Spanos home. The cut suggests that this is what you do, essentially cold calling off of terrible leads and failing. The second scene concretely illustrates the abstractions of the first. Both the cut and the situation suggest the desperation Shelly tries to camouflage as he makes his pitch.

Another example of uninflected exposition, the new scene in the Spanos's living room provides details that underline how tenacious Levene is and point to the family values behind that tenacity, which, at the same time, he is willing to violate in his effort to sell another family man a questionable investment. We see a teddy bear and dolls on an orange couch and an elaborate doll house that dominates several shots. The juice of living close together is clear and warm in this "working man's" living room, not shuffled away in a family room, and provides context for Shelly's loyalty to family and for Williamson's deciding not to take those contracts to the bank on the night of the burglary but to stay at home to play with his kid. After Levene's incredibly persistent efforts, Spanos complains about unsolicited calls resulting from his wife's filling in an inquiry card "without my knowledge." Levene replies, "I don't want to tell you how to handle your wife," which puts him out in the rain again. The line foreshadows and comments on exactly what Roma does more skillfully with Jim Lingk, who wants to be told just that, contrasting Roma's and Levene's skills. It also contrasts Lingk's and Spanos's willingness to "talk with salesmen" about relatively intimate matters.

We cut from Levene's leaving the Spanos home to Moss and Aaronow in Moss's car and then to Roma launching into the second movement of his conversation with Lingk. In general, crosscutting between these three experiences of the evening suggests the contrasting ways the salesmen cope with their similarly desperate lives. More specifically, the cuts point toward thematic statement and establish narrative relationships or patterns.

For example, now in the sheltering bar, after Moss's suggestion of the theft, though resisting, Aaronow is clearly interested in Moss's offer of a job with Jerry Graff. We cut to Levene, shot through his rain-sheeted car window, ominous, blue music coming up slowly; we see his face more clearly, defeated, miserable, and hear a siren in the background. We should remember the film's first mention of Jerry Graff, echoed in both of the previous Moss/Aaronow exchanges: Levene has said in reply to Moss's threat in the restroom to go across the street to Jerry Graff, "I've got half a mind to go with you if he'd take me." Here, Levene gets out of the car, enters the restaurant through the rain, with that rumbling train in the background, and makes his fourth call of the evening to the hospital from the restaurant phone booth. After a brief conversation, he says: "Where's the duty nurse? They cancelled her. . . . I'll have the money there tomorrow." He hangs up.

This series of cuts and transitions works wonders. It gives us a further hint of motive, an element of the narrative we cannot do without, as Mamet would have it. Given the conversation between Moss and Aaronow about robbing the office just before this phone call, the news Levene gets about yet another desperate situation, in addition to the threat to his job, is connected by the first cut to the idea of the theft. After the call we cut to Moss saying to Aaronow, "This is a big decision George," adding "Times a guy's gotta make one. And it's a big reward. Twenty-five hundred . . . for one night's work." The uninflected cuts and the accompanying structural dialogue prepare us for the revelation late in the film that Shelly has made that "big decision" to rob the office. Mamet has given us just enough detail without being obtrusive. The threat of the loss of Levene's job through the sales contest, Levene's knowledge of where those leads are locked up, the failure of both his personal appeal and bribery offer to Williamson for better leads, his failures that evening to make a sale, his newly desperate situation springing from his inability to pay his daughter's medical bill, all point, in retrospect, to the inevitability of the conclusion. In turn that depends on Levene's off-camera conversation with Moss, which, given Mamet's careful structuring, we don't need to hear to understand; the omission adds to suspense and audience involvement.

The film's music also guides our understanding of image and dialogue, providing narrative structure and additional direction on how we should respond to those uninflected cuts. For instance, as Roma finally brings out the real estate brochure to show Lingk, we cut to a train rushing by, fading to a momentarily black screen. The next cut is jarring, bright sunlight, bass and drum very up tempo, as we see Roma getting out of his late-model Riviera near the yellow police lines. Echoing the pace of those train wheels, this music is worlds apart from the low, bluesy backdrop for Roma's conversation. This "morning music" is the instrumental introduction to Al Jarreau's version of "Blue Skies," the piece over the closing credits. Commenting on Roma's early morning optimism, the way he begins his day, victorious sounding, it prepares us for the revelation that he has sold Lingk when he tears down the poster for that Cadillac first prize. In retrospect, that this instrumental is the prelude for Jarreau's lyrics at the film's conclusion is wonderfully ironic, labeling both Roma's attitude and that of his colleagues in almost Brechtian fashion: "Blue skies, smiling at me/Nothing but blue skies/Do I see. In the morning there's blue birds/Singing a song/Nothing but blue birds/From now on. I never saw the sun shining so bright/Never saw things going so right/Never saw the days hurrying by. . . ."

That the sale will collapse, that the days are indeed hurrying by, is ironic, something that will occur in spite of Roma's energy, his tenacity, his concentration on those things going right. The title "Blue Skies," too, ironically connects the piece to the "blues," the fitting genre of most of the film's music. Like Mamet's plays, the blues is about suffering and tenacity, and often includes a sympathetic laughter at the human condition.

That more typical music contributes to narrative structure throughout the film. For example, at the end of Levene's first attempted bribery in Williamson's old Pontiac, a blues piece comes up as he gets out into the rain once more. The same music continues as we cut to the next scene with Moss and Aaronow coming off the porch of their "sit." The continuity comments on the similarity of their desperation and on the connectedness of Levene's plight to Moss's, an important foreshadowing of their eventual involvement in that theft. When Shelly calls the Nyborgs from the phone booth in the rain, a very sad sax and a mellow electric keyboard comment on Levene's emotional state; beneath the surface of Shelly's efforts, he's "ready to do the Dutch," as he tells Roma the next day. And as we cut to Roma's train compartment speech to Lingk, very quietly a new piece comes up, Duke Ellington and Gordon Mill's popular "Prelude to a Kiss." If we know the title, it labels the sales pitch that's coming; even if we don't, that the same piece continues under the next scene, Moss's trying to convince Aaronow to rob the office, underlines the similarity of these situations, one man's trying to seduce another to his own benefit. The music reinforces a narrative connectedness beyond the literal dialogue, serving as subtext.

At times the absence of music on the soundtrack provides a structural index of response, too. That almost always occurs at moments of high tension—during Levene's confession to Williamson, during the scene in which Moss blows up at Roma over Roma's slighting of Moss's sales record, during the conversation between Roma and Aaronow just after Levene has gone in to the detective. The sales meeting scene in the office with Blake emphatically establishes this structural pattern.

Though Mamet's narrative structure avoids obvious exposition, the film version of *Glengarry Glen Ross* does "give" his audience considerably more than does the play. In part, that's because responses to the visual film medium are more subjective than responses to the more language-centered medium of theatre. Instead of relying on an audience to infer the importance of Levene's family life from his brief references to his daughter in the play, Mamet provides additional expository information in those four phone calls and elsewhere. The same is true with regard to the basically abstract comments in the stage version about Mitch and Murray, the bosses downtown. The film provides a more concrete image of the system and its evils in Blake, the sales motivation person who comes in to run the meeting. This new scene evokes our sympathy for the abused salesmen, provides the additional motivation of intense resentment for Levene and Moss, and structurally serves as the central image for the economic system entrapping and belittling these men. It makes blatantly clear the reality of the salesmen's subservient position—they are dispensable slaves, pawns. The most chilling in the film, the scene also suggests the brutality of "downsizing," one of the prevalent economic realities of the 1990s, a shift in chronology from the play's 1980s milieu.

The camera lingers on a red BMW as Shelly crosses the street in the rain and goes into the office. With Aaronow complaining about the quality of the leads, Moss enters with "The rich get richer, that's the law of the land," providing a more explicit label. Comically, he asks, "Who belongs to the BEE M," which humorously associates Blake and his materialism with excrement, underlines Moss's resentment of success, structurally important later in the film in his attitude toward Roma, and gets him off on the wrong foot with Blake. The line also punningly suggests that materialism is controlling this man, that he does belong to his things, his BMW, his gold watch, his thousand-dollar suits—that his attitude toward life is impoverished.

As Blake describes the front office's plan to provide "incentive" to the sales staff through competitive downsizing, that all three of the sales-men just "take" his insults makes clear that they feel that they have no choice, no alternative, but to accept these new rules and play by them as best they can. As we cut from the elegant Blake to Levene, in his short sleeved shirt and suspenders pouring a cup of coffee from the office pot, Blake in stento-rian tones orders him to put that coffee down. Levene looks bewildered, pathetic, defeated; we cut back to the "salesleader": "Coffee's for closers only." As Blake continues to abuse Levene, Moss gets up, saying, "I don't have to listen to this shit." But that choice of open revolt doesn't last, as Blake tells Moss, "You certainly don't pal, 'cause the good news is you're fired." We cut back to Levene, who puts the coffee pot down, a gestic em-blem. Blake adds, "The bad news is that you've got just one week to regain your jobs starting with tonight's sit." As he continues to rub it in, we cut to a shot of Levene at his desk, seated, to Aaronow seated, and then to Moss, who sits down, choosing to swallow the abuse with the rest of them.

Mamet also emphasizes that choice is involved in the men's actions through Blake's structural, echoing dialogue. He says he knows the sales staff is interested now, "Because it's fuck or walk. You close or you hit the bricks. Decision. Have you made your decision for Christ?" The line echoes Williamson's earlier comment to Levene in the restroom, preparing the au-dience without their knowledge: "Well, Shelly, you ready to do or die to-night?" Because the men do make the decision the system dictates for them the scene is horribly discomforting—we almost want to look away. At this point choosing to play by the rules, all three men try to close those sales in the first part of the evening, not getting up and out. They see no alternative for themselves other than the abuse of the straight commission system. Blake's comment that if they don't close they'll become bums at a bar is ironi-cally just what they see as their only other option. Structurally, the scene encourages our wish for something better for these men, allows us to sym-pathize with Levene in his decision to rob the office, and makes us under-stand the resentment underlying these men's actions much more emphati-cally than Mamet's infamous gutter language that is its reflection.[4]

The sales meeting scene also structurally emphasizes that responsi-bility to the family is a central reason that working people feel so trapped. To Moss, who's asked his name, Blake says, "Fuck you, that's my name. . . . I drove an $80,000 BMW [to get here tonight]. That's my name." Just a bit later, he takes off his watch, apparently a gold Rolex, and says, twice, "You see this watch? . . . That watch costs more than your car."[5] As Moss con-tinues his admirable attempts to put down Blake, he asks: "You're such a hero, you're so rich. Why're you coming down here to waste your time with a bunch of bums?" He is again browbeaten into craven silence as Blake says, "I made $970,000 last year. How much you make? You see pal, that's who I am and you're nothing. Nice guy, I don't give a shit. Good father, fuck you, go home and play with your kid. You wanna work here, close." Coming from the most unsympathetic character in the film, these extremely negative sentiments about family life point us in the opposite direction, as Roma might say. Blake's comments are structural in that they relate to both Levene's contrasting attitude to his daughter and to Williamson's attitude toward his family.

The play implies that Williamson is just as concerned about his job as "his" salesmen but leaves his family life a blank. The film subtly makes that family life crucial to its narrative structure. In the first scene of the play, when Levene can't come up with the cash for the bribe, Williamson says simply, "I have to go" (9). In the film, Williamson replies that he has to get home "so that I can spend one hour with my kid, come back here to see if any of you closed a contract." The tone is clearly critical of the job situation itself—that is, Williamson is not pleased that the nature of his work allows him such little time with his family, an admirable emotion. In his final scene with Levene, the older man rebukes Williamson for not feeling bad that he destroyed Roma's sale, unable to resist, prideful: "A *child* would know it, [Roma's] . . . right. *(Pause.)* You're going to make something up, be sure it will *help* or keep your mouth closed" *(Pause.)* (98). In both versions, Williamson realizes that Levene could only know that he'd made up the story of taking the contract to the bank if Levene has seen the contract on the desk during the burglary. In the play, he says in explanation to Levene: "Shel, usually I take the contracts to the bank. Last night I didn't. How did you know that?" (99). In the film, he says: "Usually I take the contracts to the bank. Last night I didn't. Last night I stayed home with my kids. How did you know that?"

Whether or not Williamson's decision not to come back has been motivated by his own disgust with the Blake meeting, his wish to be with that "off-screen" family is pivotal to his ability to extract a confession from Levene. His wish to succeed as best he can at this rotten job flows from the same concern for his family, at least in part. He turns Levene in rather than take the second bribe because he understands that more will accrue to him, and his family. As he's said before the onslaught begins, face shot half in darkness, half in light, "This is my job! This is my job on the line!" His last line to Levene, as he says "my daughter," a slight shake of his old wrinkled throat, is a belted out "Fuck You."

Such structural finesse cumulatively points toward theme. There are four thematic subjects in the film version of *Glengarry Glen Ross,* all implied in the play, some more emphatically stated in the film. The first is the relatively obvious criticism of the "system," of what materialism or capitalism does to the gentler human tendencies that Mamet repeatedly finds in his characters. Anne Dean captures this theme well: "Mamet is a moralist who bemoans, through his drama, the fecund venality he believes exists at all levels of American society, whether in the form of media propaganda, spurious business negotiations at either end of the social spectrum, devalued emotional and sexual relationships, or simply an arrogant capacity for selfishness and greed" (223).

A second "negative" thematic area, also frequently analyzed, glaringly presents the harsher elements of human nature, of our tendency to be competitive, aggressive, jealous, and fearful. In Mamet's world, much of this failure to live virtuous lives grows out of a profound sense of insecurity. As Dennis Carroll suggests, the play reveals "something perverse in human nature" beyond its emphasis on the deleterious impact of capitalism; the problem, he argues, is a combination of "a faulty social system and a masochism of the personal psyche" (*David Mamet,* 49). C. W. E. Bigsby emphasizes, too, that beyond the corrosive spirit of business, "Beyond the fast paced patter of the salesmen is a desperation which is not simply the product of a competitive society" (122).

In this film, desperation ultimately springs from a spiritual poverty in the face of death, aging, and a vision of personal failure and isolation—most eloquently captured in the images of the aging Levene, apparently dealing with his daughter's illness on his own, without a supportive wife/mother, and in Roma's more explicit conversations with Lingk, which are about how we are to live in a world where we know we are going to die. The third and fourth thematic areas, then, in the context of this death consciousness, make more positive statements about friendship, on the one hand, and advocate conscious choice and positive action as a way to live on the other. Mamet summarizes this theme in "First Principles": the theater should reveal that "it is possible and pleasant to substitute action for inaction, courage for cowardice, humanity for selfishness" (27).

Glengarry Glen Ross often depends on its audience inferring positive themes through negative examples; but Mamet also provides explicit though indirectly presented thematic statements for our consideration. Many critics miss or underemphasize these implied positive responses for two reasons. In the first place, such thematic ideas often are spoken by characters who are apparently unsympathetic, inept, or ridiculed in various ways. As Guido Almansi suggests, "The new playwrights . . . do not seem to care if the innocence (the purity) of their judgements is corrupted by the prejudices and emotional outbursts of their creatures. This gives a special ambiguity to the authorial voice, be it Pinter's, Stoppard's or Mamet's" (194). In the second place, many refuse to take such positive statements seriously because Mamet loves to couch them in the language of the exigent, the lowest common denominator. Don's advice to Bobby in *American Buffalo* springs to mind: "Action talks and bullshit walks," a concise restatement of Mamet's paean to actions being more pleasant and valuable than inaction.

Glengarry Glen Ross's indirect thematic statements are both dramatically sound and effective—that is, they're not so obvious as to violate the aesthetic that Mamet sets for himself. Still, some are relatively clear. For example, as Moss and Aaronow complain about the new rules of the game, Moss sums up: "All this garbage, you sell ten thousand you win a Cadillac . . . fire your ass. . . . It's *medieval* . . . it's wrong." Aaronow agrees with a simple "Yes." He responds to Moss's line that the fault lies with Mitch and Murray, "'Cause it don't have to be this way," with a simple "No." Both responses underline the correctness of Moss's vision, despite his self-serving goal, here, as he's just about to introduce the idea of the theft.

Repetition emphasizes the validity of Moss's thematic lines as they approach the restaurant in the rain: "I'll tell you what the hard part is; it's to stop thinking like a goddam slave." Very shortly thereafter he reiterates: "George, we're men, here, and I'll tell you what the hard part is, starting up, starting up, breaking free of this bullshit, this enslavement to some guy because he's got the upper hand." He concludes: "this is the difference, listen to me now, George, when Jerry Graff went into business for himself, he said 'I'm going on my own now.' And he was free, you understand me?" The emphasis on choice, on freedom, on courageously revolting from slavery is thematic; these men should not put up with such abuse. But ironically the only alternatives they see to unemployment are either creating another immoral business endeavor—Graff, after all, targets a list of nurses he regards as both well paid and naive—or, as Moss suggests in his next pitch, replicating the thievery of capitalism by robbing the office. The first part of Moss's statement suggests a legitimate ethical judgment; the second emphasizes just how difficult that is to act on, given the system.

Shelly Levene also makes several indirect thematic comments. His tale of his sale to the Nyborgs echoes the idea behind Moss's lines about the "opportunity" of the theft he proposes to Aaronow—Talk about a chance. "It's when a chance presents itself" that a man must make a decision, Moss tells Aaronow, lines not in the play. Shelly describes his saying to the Nyborgs, "What we have to do is *admit* to ourself that we see that opportunity . . . and take it *(Pause)."* Again, the idea reflects Mamet's vision of the importance of the moment and of action; the context demonstrates how easily ethical ideas can be used to justify unethical behavior, making the thematic statement indirect and ironic. Levene's paean to friendship as he chastises Williamson is another example: ". . . Your partner *depends* on you. Your partner . . . the man who is your 'partner' *depends* on you. . . . You have to go *with* him and *for* him . . . or you're shit, eh?, you are *shit,* you can't exist alone." Though Mamet intends us to take this ideal seriously, the thematic statement is indirect because Levene makes it to aggrandize his own power, to kick Williamson while he's down, to claim a moral superiority he doesn't deserve, given his own indirect betrayal of his "partners" through his theft of "their" leads.

Roma's two major scenes with Lingk include the most moving and emphatic statement of the central theme of choice. Despite repeated emphases in Mamet's essays, and despite parallel statements throughout the canon, many critics refuse to take Roma's lines seriously because of their vision of Roma's character, his patois, and his purpose in speaking the lines. For example, Matthew C. Roudané understands Roma's lines to Lingk about doing things that seem correct to him today to be "a well-known rationalization" (12). Henry I. Schvey finds the "apparently friendly conversation . . . full of banal 'insights' about how to live" (105). Anne Dean understands the speech as "an amalgam of simplified existentialism, intrusive sentimentality, and preacherlike exhortation for the necessity to stand up and be counted." She goes on to comment: "Rather perplexingly, Mamet has described this speech as 'inspirational . . . classic Stoic philosophy' but most critics have taken it to be little more than cleverly worded nonsense. . . . It is difficult to disagree with them" (203–4).

Actually, as Mamet's appeal to his beloved Stoics suggests, Roma's speeches contain the thematic core of the play. In a number of instances, too, Roma practices what he preaches. In the film, as Williamson leaves the restaurant after his bullying suggestion that the men be at that sales meeting, Roma is coming in, comically denouncing the rainy weather. Williamson does not issue him any instruction about the meeting, for Roma is too strong for the office manager to stand up to. As Levene and Roma approach the bar together, Roma comments that it was so hot downtown today "that grown men on the street corner were going up to cops, begging the cops to shoot them." The line is both funny and subtextually labels the desperation these men deal with, day and night, a comic echo of Levene's line about suicide. Roma continues that "they say you should not drink alcohol when it's so hot" for "they" say it dehydrates you; "they say you should drink water."

33

And then this: "But I subscribe to the law of contrary public opinion. If everyone thinks one thing, then I say bet the other way."

"Giving the audience more" in the way of exposition and implied themes, this addition to the play shows us that Lingk, drinking by himself, around the corner of the bar, makes the initial contact, hungry for conversation, lonely, willing to accept the validity of a stranger's opinions to get it. That makes Roma a slightly more sympathetic figure. Unlike Eliot Ness, Lingk hasn't gone home after work, structurally establishing the "beat" for our wish to learn more about Mrs. Lingk as the film continues. As Levene, chugging his drink, leaves for the meeting, Roma's staying behind, sipping, makes us wonder why he's doing so. He is, indeed, going against common behavior, revolting from the dictates of the system. His line about the majority being wrong is thematic in its implied praise for the strong individual who chooses his own path freely, echoed by Moss's lines about Graff's freedom. As in *Hoffa*, this indirect statement of theme reverberates. Told that he should call off a demonstration, Jimmy replies: "Fuck me. . . . Tobin and the President and the newspapers and every fucking body else in the world says I'm wrong, then I gotta be right." In both Hoffa's case and Roma's, there's a pronounced echo of Ibsen, though the language is much different.

The second movement of the first Lingk scene follows Blake's sales meeting and the scenes depicting Levene's, Aaronow's and Moss's fruitless evenings. We cut to Roma in close up as he opines: "all train compartments smell vaguely of shit. It gets so you don't mind it. That's the worst thing that I can confess." Echoed as Roma later tells Aaronow that thieves are the only ones who don't mind talking to cops because, as the play has it, "They're inured to it," rhythmic and evocative, this opening line is a vernacular statement of an old idea, one reflected in modern literature from Brecht to Beckett, from Baudelaire to Pinter: Habit is the great deadener. Looking at our world through habitual glasses, thinking that what we are used to is the only way to do things, blinds us to the world, forces us to accept the Blakes. That train compartments smell like shit, given those train shots of the "El" taking people to their work, labels these lives. That the worst thing Roma can tell about himself is that "you get used to it" reveals a self-consciousness, a contemplative side, even if he has partially yielded. Within the context of the job, he is the best, the most adventuresome, the man most clearly making some of his own choices. Unlike Baudelaire's persona in "To the Reader," he is at least horrified at the stench of hell, and resists.

The rest of this movement of the speech is a vernacular, not banal, version of existentialism. Roma, of course, doesn't sound like Sartre, but he is clearly intelligent and reasonably well read.[6] He first suggests that the fact of death makes what we have of life, that brief moment, all the more important: "When you *die* you're going to regret the things you don't do." From that follows the suggestion that only individual choice is "legitimate": recounting a litany of "sins"—being queer, being a thief, cheating on your wife, fucking little girls—he says "So *what?* You get befuddled by a middle-class morality . . .? Get *shut* of it. Shut it out. . . . There's an absolute morality? . . . Bad people go to hell? I don't *think* so. If you think that, act that way. A hell exists on earth? Yes, I won't live in it."

Roma's version of existentialism emphasizes that even the choice of a different moral system can be legitimate, but underlines that his own choice is to do everything he can to make the "hell on earth," that metaphoric existential commonplace, as bearable as possible. His advice on morality is much like the mentor psychiatrist's in *House of Games:* "When you've done something unforgivable, you forgive yourself" and go on. Given such a decision, Roma suggests that the moment is what is important. Believably in character, his examples are off-putting for many critics—the experience of great "dumps" that are better than the great meals we can't keep, wonderful gestures of kindness after making love that are better than the orgasm itself. A similar food motif is prominent in both Pinter and Beckett: We eat, we digest, we defecate, and then we start all over, the Thinker eating while seated on a toilet. Roma implies that we should enjoy even the "decay," the elimination of the remnants, as immediately satisfying, visceral, of the moment. His imaging of his memory of sex is even more evocative. The giving of a cigarette, the making of café au lait, loving eyes, this is what moves him, human kindnesses, not mere physicality. He sums up this segment of the speech: "What I'm saying, what is our life? *(Pause.)* It's looking forward or it's looking back. And that's our life. That's *it.* Where is the *moment? (Pause.)*" (48).

We cut back to Roma after Lingk has gone to the restroom. As Lingk slips in beside Roma, now in a booth, their intimacy advanced, Roma opens with a familiar barroom joke, "They say you don't buy it, you rent it." "The thing," Roma continues, "You really, uh, what do you keep? I mean, you don't keep anything, really." The joke, even in the lowest of lowlife bars, carries a metaphoric load beyond the difficulty of retaining beer or whiskey consumed in quantity. The tenor is something like "Whatever you strive for, and think you have, and spend your hard-earned money on, vanishes," or, up a notch in intensity, "Life is only loaned to us, and we can lose it at any moment." In this context, the lines echo the film's earlier food-to-excrement subtext, and serve as transition back into the conversation.

Roma's scotch-fractured syntax roughly translates: "The central issue is, what do you keep in this life?" His answer, "You don't keep any-thing," leads to his vernacular summary of the ground of existential thought: "Things, things. You know, it's just you strive to stave off insecurity. You can't do it." Lingk agrees with a simple "No." Before the cut to Moss and Aaronow, Roma has commented to Lingk that our insecurity springs from our fear of loss, the bank's failure, our own illness, the wife's death, the stock market crash, asserting that amassing wealth will not counteract this inse-curity. In the play, Roma concludes: "I say *this* is how we must act. I do those things which seem correct to me *today*. I trust myself. . . . The *true* reserve that I have is the strength that I have of *acting each day* without fear. *(Pause.)* According to the dictates of my mind" (49).

The film's omission of these lines and a few others works well, elimi-nating elements that would result in far too "stagy" a speech for film, even given the crosscutting that breaks up the original scene. The film's line, "You strive to stave off insecurity," points us in the same direction, and it retains the summary lines from the play: "Stocks, bonds, objects of art, real estate. What are they? An opportunity. To what? To make money? Perhaps. To lose money? Perhaps. To indulge and to learn about ourselves? Perhaps. So fucking what. They're an opportunity, that's all they are. They're an event. . . . Things happen to you." And then Roma says, "Glad I met you. I'm glad I met you James," and pulls out the brochure for Glengarry High-lands.

The logic here is that though we know that acquisition cannot stave off insecurity, we still try, tenaciously, even in our knowledge of futility, to make choices, to pursue opportunity, to deal with the things that happen to us. Recognition of certain defeat and then going on, as Camus would have it, is a startling revelation of man's nobility. Roma knows that most people make investment decisions not so much on financial grounds but "to indulge and to learn about ourselves." Lingk desperately wants to learn about him-self, to participate in the activity, to join Roma in a partnership, to not re-gret what he has not done. Like so many of Mamet's characters desperately seeking friendship, for Lingk playing in this game makes him a part of the community, makes him belong. He wants to make a decision, a choice, about what to do about opportunity, about events that happen to him, apparently by chance. He wants to follow Roma's advice about how to live.

David Worster sums this up nicely from the perspective of the more explicit speech in the play: "Roma manipulates Lingk's need for security in an unstable world, offering the strength to act each day without fear" (380). But he misses the element of sincerity, caring, that is a part of the reason for Roma's success, in contrast to the sales abilities of his colleagues. Joe

Mantegna, who played Roma in the play's 1984 American premiere in Chicago, in a valuable interview with Leslie Kane provides a fuller perspective: Roma's positive attributes "were confidence, they were power, they were respect, they were compassion, caring. . . . whereas I don't doubt that [Roma's] main drive and his pursuit of success is for himself, what also helps make him successful is that he's doing what he actually thinks is beneficial for another person. . . . There's a genuine compassion there" (256).

In retrospect, we discover that Lingk's seeking out the company of men, not going home, springs from his dissatisfaction with his subordinate role in his marriage. We have left the scene early, before the sale, making us wonder what's coming next. From Roma's first call on the cellular in the burgled office, we know that after their drinks the pair went to Lingk's home; we know, too, from the conversation between Roma, Lingk, and Levene that Lingk's wife, Jinny, fixed a good home-cooked meal—another part of the food subtext—and that she acquiesced to her husband's wish to buy the land. We discover, though, that she has forced her husband into the embarrassing situation of informing Roma of her reneging on the deal he regards as both his "legitimate" choice, a participation in a manly game, and an emblem of friendship. The second major scene with Lingk in the office echoes and expands on Roma's indirect thematic statements in his first conversation and reveals additional good elements within his complex character.

As Levene plays American Express executive "D. Ray Morton" with gusto, Roma intuitively tries to reassure Lingk that he's made the right choice, the right investment decision. He's acting courageously, extemporaneously responding to threatening events. Praising Jinny's meal, Roma improvises a story about home cooking, supposedly a plan to be institutionalized by American Express for business men on the road. The fiction subtly implies how much we all need some sense of community, of home, on our various roads. The major thematic statement in this scene, though, is once more about how to live one's life.

When Lingk manages to stumble out that his wife has called a consumer protection agency, Roma recognizes that his first ploy, delaying beyond the three-day limit, won't work. He momentarily flounders, but comes up with what he thinks to be the lie that Lingk's check hasn't been cashed yet. Reassured that time is no longer a problem, Lingk believes in Roma again and offers an implied apology as a mark of friendship: "It's not me. It's my wife." Both Roma and Lingk continue to be shot in half light, half shadow throughout the scene, the film noir device suggesting the mixed motives of each. Roma takes Lingk's hint, asking him to talk about himself, repeatedly offering help. As Lingk reveals that he's upset with his wife's dictating his behavior to him—"she wants *her* money back" (my emphasis), "she told me right now." "She won't listen." "She said if I don't get my money back I have to call the State's Attorney"—Roma both sees his angle and sympathizes with this very human predicament. He tells Lingk that "that's something she said. We don't have to do that." The plural subject again claims camaraderie, an offer of help, but Lingk twice says, "No, I have to," and starts out the door when the detective's calling for Roma gives him the opportunity to escape.

Once Roma manages to get Lingk to come back, his voice becomes markedly more gentle, more sympathetic. In the first place, he thinks that the lie about the check has bought him some time. But he is also genuinely concerned for Lingk; he wants to listen, to council, which has overtones of power, of superiority, but which can still be a generous activity. Roma tells Lingk: "Jim, anything you want, you want it, you got it. . . . Something upset you. You tell me what it is. Am I going to help you fix it? You're goddam right I am." Though embarrassed to have to reveal what he regards as his own weakness, Lingk finds sympathy in Roma, who once more offers the guidance Lingk wants: "Tell you something. Sometimes we need someone from outside. . . . Sit down, talk to me, come on." As if discussing a marriage on the brink of disaster with an intimate friend, Lingk shamefacedly admits that "I don't have the power. Ha. I said it," almost a triumph in the admission, in the feeling of genuine communication. But Lingk still does not have enough courage to act; he retreats several times, despite Roma's blandishments, his reassuring Lingk that he's no longer interested in the deal. Finally, when Roma attempts to change to a more intimate venue, to go to the bar, Lingk says he can't: "She told me not to talk to you," and Roma suggests first that she won't find out, and then, "Please, let's talk about you."

The picture of Lingk that emerges here is of a man desperate in a life situation that bewilders him, that leaves him powerless and ashamed, but which he sees no way to escape. Structurally and thematically, that's a parallel to the work situation of the salesmen. This tale of belittlement, even though Jinny is no doubt right in her dictate, evokes in the audience the same kind of nervous sympathy for Lingk as has the scene depicting Blake's belittlement of the sales force and their inability to do anything about it. Roma, the music soft, on one level, is genuinely sympathetic as he utters the scene's central indirect thematic statement: "I'm going to tell you something. Your life is your own. You have a contract with your wife. There are certain things you do jointly. You have a bond there. And there are other things and those things are yours, and you needn't feel ashamed and you needn't feel untrue, or that she would abandon you if she knew. This is your life." As Lingk shakes his head, Roma gently says "Yes? Now I want to talk with you because you're obviously upset and that concerns me. Now let's go, come on right now, let's go." And, echoing Beckett's tramps, they are on the way out the door.

Despite mixed motives, Roma sensitively offers good advice. In his own vernacular, to be sure, he emphasizes that marriage, or any relationship, should not destroy one person's independence, that one person in a relationship should not so completely dominate another as to subsume a life. The repetition of the idea emphasizes its centrality: at the beginning of the speech, "Your life is your own"; at the conclusion, "This is your life." Keying on Lingk's clear shame and guilt at his feelings, Roma emphasizes that he should not feel untrue or ashamed if he occasionally acts on his wishes that differ from his wife's. Thus, Lingk's making the choice to go with Roma is a kind of revolt, a small gesture of strength, and he welcomes the opportunity. At the same time, of course, Roma still hopes to save his sale, to talk Lingk into a more substantial revolt from his wife's good advice, which is detrimental to Roma's financial well-being. More complexly, Roma, "outside," evidently single, is almost wistful when he comments on the bond of marriage, the things you do jointly.

Joe Mantegna again provides insight on Roma in this scene. When Kane asks him if Roma is trying to help Lingk with his wife, Mantegna replies: "I do feel that I'm doing a good thing. . . . Of course, I want to be handsomely rewarded for that by selling the land, but . . . that moment exists in the play where . . . I stop talking about real estate. I'm basically talking to the guy about his life. . . . The beauty of it is that [Roma's] genuinely getting at a real problem here and maybe this guy will learn something from it. Everybody wins. . . . I get the money; maybe this guy is able to deal with his life a little better" (258).

Lingk's final leave-taking suggests just how desperately he's needed such help, and relied upon it. As the detective attempts to delay Roma's heading across the street, Williamson blurts out the lie that the check has been cashed, thinking that he's reassuring a nervous client. Lingk turns to Roma, "You cashed the check?" The horror in his voice is primarily at the betrayal of what he has come to value as a fruitful friendship. Ironically, Lingk's final lines are guilt-ridden, apologizing for his own betrayal: "Oh Christ. Hey, don't follow me. Just don't follow me. . . . I let you down. I know I let you down. I'm sorry, forgive me. I don't know. I don't know anymore. I'm . . . Oh . . . Forgive me."

Lingk feels guilty both for not having the strength to stand up against his wife and for violating what he regards as the trust of friendship, for going back on a deal important to his friend. Since he's also distraught at

Roma's chicanery, that the advice he was depending on is tainted, he just doesn't know how to live, what to believe anymore. He's not been able to live up to the "contract" of this relationship with Roma, and he's going back home to a marriage in which he'll continue to be dominated, unhappy, and lonely, because he sees no alternative.

Roma's response first echoes our feeling sorry for Lingk, despite the fact that he's escaped a bad investment; we feel sorry for his loss of what he'd believed was a genuine camaraderie and for his lack of courage. The camera focuses on Roma in closeup; initially, his eyes look downward, saddened, unfocused, reflecting continuation of his sympathy for Lingk. Then, he looks toward Williamson, new life in his eyes, as he lashes out. Two central lines emerge from the vituperation: "Anyone in this office lives on their *wits*"; and, as the speech concludes, "You want to learn the first rule you'd know if you ever spent a day in your life. . . . You never open your mouth till you know what the shot is."

In the first instance, Roma's generous attribution of talent to his colleagues underlines their tenacity and courage in an untenable situation. In the second, his labeling Williamson a child suggests that he, like Lingk, has not lived his life very fully, that his secondhand knowledge is not the equivalent of the "wits" earned on the street of hard knocks. "You'd know if you ever spent a day in your life . . ." on one level is an incomplete sentence that might be completed to something like: "You'd understand if you'd ever spent a day in your life actually trying to make a sale." On another level, typical of so many Mamet elliptical speeches, the line is existential in tenor. Williamson hasn't spent a single day fully living, because he, too, is afraid, and doesn't have the courage to act beyond the kind of cowardly cunning we've seen him display throughout the play.

Thematic response in *Glengarry Glen Ross* certainly emerges not only from indirect thematic statements but also from the play's situations, its characters' actions, which are often not labeled or commented upon. Levene's love for his daughter is clearly genuine and fine, an example of ethical behavior that is as it should be. The friendship and loyalty of these men should provoke a thematic inference from action, as well, despite their concurrent willingness to betray one another when the stakes are high enough. The film concludes with Ricky's genuinely affectionate and genuinely self-serving proposal to Levene to become sales partners. Structurally prepared for by Levene's own paean to partnership as he's condemned Williamson, the line echoes, and is not undercut in the film version. In the play, Roma tells Williamson that the agreement is a scam: "My stuff is *mine*, whatever he gets for himself, I'm talking half" (107).[7]

In the film version, once Roma comes into the office from his interrogation, he comments to Levene that they have to stick together because they're members of "a dying breed," two of the few who can remember when there was "some adventure in it." He praises Levene's reputation as a sales "Machine," and he praises "that shit you were slinging on my guy today," as "like the old days," concluding, "There's things I could learn from you. You eat today?" In context, Roma does not know that Levene has just confessed to Williamson. But in the film, Levene still turns his chair to Roma, putting his work aside and smiling at Roma's line about working with him, another big smile on "that was so good."

This concluding thematic vision of friendship, with all its irony, is structurally prepared for by three earlier scenes. The brief scene in the bar, not in the play, shows us Roma having a drink with Levene with warm banter establishing their friendship. The scene showing Roma praising Levene's sale to the Nyborgs emphasizes that he performs the function of a friend by providing Levene an audience for a tale he thinks central to his life and by defending him against Moss's belittling attack. Roma puts Moss in his place as self-centered and inhumane with revealing language: "Your pal closes, all that comes out of your mouth is *bile*, how fucked *up* you are." And Levene is simply ecstatic over Roma's line that this sale has been like the old days, "Like you taught me. . . ." The scene in which they brilliantly improvise for Lingk comments on their friendship, too; Shelly pays Roma back for his friendship, on one level; on another, the two unite against that outside world, further cementing their relationship.

In the final moments of the film, that emphasis on friendship continues. Roma repeatedly invites Levene across the street, defends his dignity against the onslaught of the detective, and is kind to Aaronow. In the film, Roma cannot talk with Levene before he goes in with the detective for that second visit because Roma is busy setting an appointment with Mrs. Schwartz, a vignette not in the play. Aaronow utters his last line from the play, "O God, I hate this job," sitting at his desk in half light, and Roma exits to the restaurant, patting Aaronow on the shoulder on the way by in rough sympathy, "I'll be at the restaurant," fully expecting to meet Levene later to discuss their partnership. Unlike the play, in the film Aaronow gets back on the phone and calls Mrs. Delgarry. We cut to that train in daylight, taking working people to their jobs, and the ironic "Blue Skies" comes up over the soundtrack.

The film's ending, then, though dark, is considerably softer than the play's, emphasizing admiration for these men rather than criticism of the system. With the idea of partnership echoing in our ears, we're even more sorry for Levene, who has been crushed by one of those circumstances we all fear, a central concern of Roma's first talk with Lingk. We're sorry for the pressure his daughter's illness has brought upon him; we're sorry that the only alternative that he's seen has been the theft, with its leitmotif of vengeance, and we're sorry that his belief that the sale to the Nyborgs has rejuvenated him has been crushed, and that he'll not work his magic with Roma as partners. The alternative to Levene's behavior is to choose one's actions more as Roma advocates, with strength and will and courage. The near-tragic irony is that Levene has tried to do that. His attempt has not worked because, despite good motives, his choice has been wrong and has been discovered through missteps caused by his own anger and pride.

Eric Bentley pointed out years ago that tragedy and comedy are both "negative arts in that they characteristically reach positive statement by inference from negative situations." He adds, "What tragedy achieves in this line by its incredibly direct renderings of sympathies and antipathies, comedy achieves by indirection, duality, irony" (308–9). Mamet's refusal of direct thematic statement, of an easily discernable authorial voice, is what confuses many members of his audience. On reflection, we should be able to identify with these characters, as Mamet suggests, and to recognize and take to heart their often ironic and indirect statement of theme, of ethos.

Mamet's plays almost always celebrate "work," even if the work is corrupt. Echoing several of Ibsen's and Chekhov's characters as well as the Thackeray lines he uses as an epigram for *Speed-the-Plow,* he emphasizes just how central our vision of our work is to our visions of ourselves. But his plays repeatedly suggest that neither failure nor success in work is a valid ground for judgment of character or moral well-being, and that success, no matter how great or small, may vanish at any instant. That is a central emphasis of Roma's first sales pitch to Lingk, and in content it is not unlike the Chorus's lines at the end of *Oedipus Rex,* though certainly very different in form. It's within this ephemeral world, within this uncertainty, that Mamet's characters must choose, must try to be good men or women. That the serious and unexpected illness of Shelly's daughter is the dominant motivation for the central action of the play is terribly ironic. Motives of both love and friendship dictate many actions even within this venal world, but not always to good ends.

The film still suggests that it is stoically noble to strive to deal with such uncertainties, that it is better to try to nurture friendship and belonging and love even if such actions are never selfless, and that one should choose to live one's life with as much dignity as possible. *Glengarry Glen*

Ross's evocation of a hostile reality should not detract from our recognition of the kindness and the ethical interchange going on because of (or in spite of) the very nature of the world Mamet mirrors.

The broadest thematic suggestions springing from Mamet's portrayals of the similar worlds of his Chicago junkmen, drunken attorneys, hypocritical physicians, Hollywood moguls, convicts, policemen, government agents, hoodlums, and salesmen are the most important and the most often given short shrift. As Frank says to his client, the sister of the comatose young woman, in *The Verdict,* "Finally we're none of us protected. We just have to go on." Echoing Frank's "cliché" at more length in *We're No Angels,* once again putting words of wisdom in the mouth of a near illiterate, Mamet has the escaped convict posing as Father Brown describe the risk of destruction in a dangerous world. He concludes: "It's all in your head. They could take the money from you. They could take the position from you. I don't know. They can whip you. People turn their backs on you. Everything happens to everybody. And you ain't going to find nothing in your pocket to stave it off. Nothing can stave it off. . . . All I know is, something might give comfort. If it comforts you to believe in God you do it. That's your business."

"Father Brown's" lines echo Ricky Roma's description of the world to James Lingk. The ersatz priest suggests that in a world where there is no defense against disaster there are still things in one's life that one must choose for oneself; "that's your business," parallels Roma's advice to Lingk on how to negotiate his marriage and still keep the part of his life that belongs to him. In broader terms, Mamet's *Glengarry Glen Ross* suggests that we should struggle not to get used to those train compartments smelling vaguely of shit; we should struggle against the Blakes of the world and their world view, and strive to behave morally toward one another, even if, like Mamet's Stoics, we fear the bad omens. Friendship, family, belonging are limited defenses, but they are the ultimate value in Mamet's world; endurance, tenacity, passionate pursuit of work, talent and wit follow in close succession. We see them all in *Glengarry Glen Ross.*

I heartily agree with Vincent Canby's assessment: "There's not another adaptation I can think of at this minute that comes anywhere near it" (C18). I'd add that the adaptation succeeds because it takes advantage of its new medium's possibilities so well, evoking very traditional themes indirectly with wonderful and evocative subtlety. As Levene tells Williamson in his diatribe of attack, "What I'm saying to you is that things change." Echoing Mamet's film *Things Change,* as well as one of Frank's lines in *The Verdict,* this is vernacular for what *Oedipus* is about, for what *The Cherry Orchard* is about, for what *The Homecoming* is about. As audience, we must struggle to learn how to deal with such literal and ontological insecurity in our own lives. By indirection, *Glengarry Glen Ross* points us toward several possibilities and at the same time celebrates a variety of attempts to deal with our work-a-day lives that are very human in their richness, entailing strength and weakness, flaws, recognition, and noble behavior.

NOTES

1. All dialogue from the films is based on transcription. Differences between scripts and films are beyond my scope. I've cited the films under Mamet, despite standard practice, since he argues that having written the scripts, they are "his."

2. Dennis Carroll perceptively comments that Ness's family life provides a satisfying center for his work and serves as a "strengthening force," observing that "De Palma underlines [the point] by often including Ness's wedding-ring hand in facial closeups, when Ness is depressed or exhausted" ("Films," 178–9).

3. My understanding of audience response largely springs from Hans Robert Jauss, but space prohibits detailing that aesthetic. Interested readers might consult my essay "Intended Audience Response, *The Homecoming*, and the "Ironic Mode of Identification" in *Harold Pinter: Critical Approaches,* ed. Steven H. Gale (Rutherford, N.J.: Fairleigh Dickinson University Press, 1986).

4. Space also does not allow full discussion of Mamet's use of cursing. My thoughts on this much-discussed topic may be found in "Comedy and Humor in the Plays of David Mamet" in *David Mamet: A Casebook,* ed. Leslie Kane (New York: Garland, 1992), 191–226.

5. To those who think this scene comes dangerously close to caricature, I would observe that anyone who has sat through a sales meeting will recognize even this one. Mamet's use of the Rolex and the BMW reflects the iconography of popular culture's mockery of this period. An extraordinary political consultant in sensitive touch with such matters, Suzanne Bruner tells a joke that captures that *zeitgeist:* Jockeying for a parking spot, an attorney in a BMW cut off an old truck. As the lawyer triumphantly opened his door, the angry loser rammed into the car, ripping off both the door and the attorney's arm. Discovering the lawyer muttering "My BEEMER, my BEEMER!" a passer-by says, "My god, your arm is torn off." The attorney, in shock, looks down: "My Rolex, my Rolex!"

6. As his line about "Patel" suggests: "Fuckin' *Shiva* handed him a million dollars . . . he wouldn't sign. And *Vishnu* too."

7. Dennis Carroll comments that the scene was added in American rehearsal, retained in the published version because Mamet liked it as pointing to the evanescence of all relationships (*Mamet* 46).

BIBLIOGRAPHY

Almansi, Guido. "David Mamet, A Virtuoso of Invective." In *Critical Angles in European Views of Contemporary American Literature,* ed. Marc Chénetier, 191–207. Carbondale: Southern Illinois, 1986.

Bentley, Eric. *The Life of the Drama.* New York: Atheneum, 1964.

Bigsby, C. W. E. *David Mamet.* London: Methuen, 1985.

Canby, Vincent. "Mamet's Real Estate Sharks and Their Prey." *New York Times,* 30 September 1992, C15ff.

Carroll, Dennis. *David Mamet.* New York: St. Martin's, 1987.

———. "The Recent Mamet Films." In *David Mamet: A Casebook,* ed. Leslie Kane, 175–90. New York: Garland, 1992.

Dean, Anne. *David Mamet: Language As Dramatic Action.* Rutherford, N.J.: Fairleigh

Dickinson University Press, 1990.

Kane, Leslie, ed. *David Mamet: A Casebook*. New York: Garland. 1992.

Mamet, David. *American Buffalo*. New York: Grove, 1977.

——. "Decadence." In *Writing in Restaurants*, 57–59.

——. "Decay: Some Thoughts for Actors, Theodore Spencer Memorial Lecture, Harvard, 10 February, 1986." In *Writing in Restaurants*, 110–17.

——. "First Principles." In *Writing in Restaurants*, 24–27.

——. *Glengarry Glen Ross*. New York: Grove, 1982.

——. "In the Company of Men." In *Some Freaks*, 85–91.

——. *On Directing Film*. New York: Viking, 1991.

——. *Some Freaks*. New York: Viking, 1989.

——. *Writing in Restaurants*. New York: Viking, 1986.

Roudané, Matthew C. "Mamet's Mimetics." In *David Mamet: A Casebook*, ed. Leslie Kane, 31–32. New York: Garland, 1992.

Schvey, Henry I. "Power Plays: David Mamet's Theater of Manipulation." In *David Mamet: A Casebook*, ed. Leslie Kane, 87–108. New York: Garland, 1992.

Sragow, Michael. "Stick Shifts." *New Yorker*. 5 October 1992, 164.

Worster, David. "How to Do Things with Salesmen: David Mamet's Speech-Act Play." *Modern Drama* 37 (1994): 375–90.

INTERVIEWS

Mamet, David. With Geoffrey Norman and John Rezek. *Playboy* (April 1995), 51–60, 148–50.

——. With Matthew C. Roudané. *Studies in American Drama 1945–Present* 1, no. 1 (1986): 73–81.

——. With Henry I. Schvey. *New Theatre Quarterly* 13 (1988): 77–89.

Mantegna, Joe. With Leslie Kane. In *David Mamet: A Casebook* 248–69. New York: Garland, 1992.

FILMS

Mamet, David, screenplay. *Glengarry Glen Ross*. Dir. James Foley. With Al Pacino, Jack Lemmon, Alec Baldwin, Ed Harris, Alan Arkin, Kevin Spacey, and Jonathan Pryce. Music by James Newton Howard. "Blue Skies" by Irving Berlin. New Line, 1992.

——. *Hoffa*. Dir. Danny DeVito. With Jack Nicholson and Danny DeVito. Twentieth Century-Fox, 1992.

——. *House of Games*. Dir. David Mamet. With Joe Mantegna and Lindsay Crouse. Based on a story by David Mamet and Jonathan Katz. Orion, 1987.

——. *The Untouchables*. Dir. Brian De Palma. With Kevin Costner, Sean Connery, and Robert De Niro. Paramount, 1985.

——. *We're No Angels*. Dir. Neil Jordon. With Robert De Niro and Sean Penn. Paramount, 1989.

——, and Sidney Lumet. *The Verdict*. Dir. Sidney Lumet. With Paul Newman, Jack Warden, and James Mason. Based on the novel by Barry Reed. Columbia, 1982.

——, and Shel Silverstein. *Things Change*. Dir. David Mamet. With Joe Mantegna and Don Ameche. Columbia, 1988.

THE DISCOURSE OF ANXIETY

Anne Dean

Glengarry Glen Ross is a very violent play: highly charged, vividly concentrated and bloody with verbal slaughter. This is *Reservoir Dogs* with filofaxes, *The Wild Bunch* with staplers. It is also the most perfect example of Mamet's black comedies, satirizing the iniquitous back-biting mores of the times. Its violence resonates in every line, straining the boundaries of the printed page, spilling out in meticulously controlled arias of anxiety and panic.

To the salesmen in this play, fear is the motivating factor. Willy Loman's hold on his career may have been precarious, but his anxieties were at least only fully realized at an advanced stage. In Mamet's Darwinian nightmare, fear is omnipresent: it is a permanent pollutant that can never really be eradicated. For these men, there is no rest, only exhaustion. They live on their nerves, anxiety fueling adrenaline already in overdrive. Here, the term *cutthroat* takes on new significance; it is no coincidence that the second prize in the salesroom competition is a set of knives. Betrayal is always a possibility, and a metaphorical knife in the back a likely outcome of a botched deal or error.

Although the play was written in the early 1980s, the viciousness of its sensibility is perhaps even more fitting in the 1990s, post-Reaganism, Bushism—and Thatcherism. In its relentlessly macho, materialistic, and existential world, loyalty and trust are rare commodities, indeed, and "friends" can turn into enemies with alarming speed. Success is measured purely in terms of work, and turns on the ability to exploit a client, to deceive a colleague, or to hone a fabric of lies so dense that the execution of the deed can be boasted of like a particularly thrilling sexual conquest. To keep on "the board" is the all-important motivator; to be top of the list is, to these men, better than sex, better even than the money it will bring. Although greed is ostensibly a prime ingredient, and certainly it is high on the agenda, money is in fact a secondary component. For them, selling has become an addiction in itself, a "high" more exhilarating than cocaine that can take them soaring above their colleagues, proof of a ruthless ability to close the deal, to "sell" the client, to be a man, to take on a hostile world—and win—against extraordinary odds.

But such successes are rare; luck and worthwhile leads are in short supply. More usually, the salesmen must endure the almost unbearable pressure of merely getting through each day, scrabbling without dignity for anything they can get, even the dreaded leads from the "B" list. Without a sale, they are essentially impotent; their *raison d'être* is lost, they feel emasculated, and unworthy of the (spurious) friendship their colleagues may offer. Fear of failure forces them to new heights of ruthlessness: they must live each moment as though it were their last; use language as a cudgel to berate or entrap, or adapt it in moments of crisis to approximate a sincerity that would not seem out of place from a priest; perform amazing feats of creative thinking, and act out a part for a faltering client with a conviction that the most accomplished actors would envy.

If ever an environment was a breeding ground for nervous excess, this is it. In this sweating office, a poor lead can be almost lethal—the text positively flutters with the rhythms of a faulty pacemaker. One wrong move and the salesmen's lifeblood is stemmed, his career over and, by association, life itself. As one says, "A man's his job"—there is nothing else. Every working moment teems with threat, outrage, and panic, coupled with a skin-deep braggadocio that aspires toward a camaraderie of sorts.

To study in more detail Mamet's various methods of dramatizing anxiety, it is instructive to look at his delineation of the three main relationships: Levene and Williamson, Moss and Aaronow, and Roma and Lingk. There is here more than one variety of fear: the repeated interruptions and lightning changes of mood and approach conveyed by Levene in his opening plea to Williamson; Moss's horrifying, though hilarious, stalking of Aaronow and his implication of him in the robbery "[b]efore the fact"; Aaronow's nervous flounderings as he strains to be accepted by his more bullish colleague, prior to his disbelief as Moss plays his final ace, and, finally, a combination of Roma's brilliant verbal dexterity as he works on Lingk's stammering uncertainty, and his manic interrogation of Williamson when he finds that the office has been burgled and some of his "leads" stolen.

LEVENE AND WILLIAMSON

Shelly Levene is down on his luck; he has been unable to make enough sales to get on the all-important "board," and he must therefore grovel to his cold-hearted office manager, a man for whom he feels only derision, an office boy who has never experienced the slings and arrows of cold calling and broken deals. Levene's opening speech repays study in some detail, since it accurately demonstrates crucial aspects of his febrile speech patterns and anxious personality. It can be read simultaneously as the opening gambit of a sales pitch, a heartfelt plea or, probably most accurately, a sly combination of the two. It is structured to reflect the salesman's rapid shifts of mood and changing tone, as he strives to convince his boss of his innate worthiness. Of all the speeches in the play, it is perhaps this one that most perfectly demonstrates the discourse of anxiety. That it does so with such stylistic economy and deft character delineation confirms Mamet's position as a master of linguistic versatility.

Mamet builds into this speech Williamson's frequent attempts at interruption. Levene's verbosity and insistence do not permit him to get more than a few words out at a time, and are indicative of the salesman's burgeoning fear and fretfulness. Should Williamson manage to disagree with, object to, or dismiss any of Levene's assertions, the frantic salesman may flounder, succumb to confusion, panic, and thereby lose in what almost amounts to a one-way battle of words. The fact that the more powerful adversary is almost silent is an ironic paradox in a play filled with the sounds of linguistic warfare.

> Levene: John . . . John . . . John. Okay. John. John. Look: *(Pause.)* The Glengarry Highland's leads, you're sending Roma out. Fine. He's a good man. We know that he is. He's fine. All I'm saying, you look at the *board,* he's throwing . . . wait, wait, wait, he's throwing them *away,* he's throwing the leads away. All that I'm saying, that you're wasting leads. I don't want to tell you your *job.* All that I'm saying, things get *set,* I know they do, you get a certain *mindset* . . . A guy gets a reputation. We know how this . . . all I'm saying, put a *closer* on the job. There's more than one man for the . . . Put a . . . wait a second, put a *proven man out* . . . and you watch, now *wait* a second—and you watch your *dollar* volumes. . . . You start closing them for *fifty* 'stead of *twenty-five* . . . you put a *closer* on the . . .

One can almost see Levene's expression as he carefully plans his attack. An eminently reasonable, if slightly patronizing, manner is evident; he seeks to establish himself as the professional, the man with years of experience on which to draw, the salesman with the most to offer and the ability to use such expertise to succeed and excel. That it quickly becomes apparent that none of these attributes have been evident in recent times both adds to the darkly persistent humor of the scene, and also to its underlying pathos. Levene is, after all, a sad and desperate man, who will try anything to get back on the all-important sales board, a position from which he has so dramatically fallen with little hope of recovery.

He repeats the manager's name no fewer than five times in the first line, pausing for effect, and, finally, launching into the diatribe he hopes will persuade his boss to give him another chance. In his strategy, it is first of all essential to personalize the exchange, and to hint at the existence of a "bond" between the two men. Levene adopts a confiding air as he weighs up the situation, citing Roma's undoubted talent so that Williamson will view him as a fair and honorable colleague: "Fine. He's a good man. We know that he is. He's fine." There is a subtle rhythm in these few lines: Levene begins and ends with the word *fine,* and takes care to use words with positive connotations, bringing Williamson into this small paean of praise by his use of "We," striving to establish and underline a camaraderie that simply isn't there. He structures his verbal onslaught so that the only possible inference (he thinks) that can be made is that he is doing Williamson a favor. By pointing out his concern regarding Roma's performance, he seeks approbation. Direct criticism is not an option—his real motives would become transparent—and so Levene plays it down: "All that I'm saying . . ." Above all, he strives to appear eminently fair, and to acknowledge Roma's worth—but at the same time he feels he "must" do the right thing by the manager, too. Although the whole point of his speech is to persuade Williamson to give him another chance, Levene's words hint at an altruism that is plainly out of character and spurious in the extreme; for such a man, self-interest and advancement are the only motivating factors.

Having failed to elicit the desired response by praising his colleague's efforts, he raises his attack by a notch; it becomes necessary to engage in some direct criticism. Roma is then accused of "throwing the leads away" and, by implication, Williamson shares some responsibility in allowing this to happen. In an unguarded moment, Levene comes straight to the point (a rarity here) and blurts out that Williamson is wasting leads. Realizing with a sinking, if palpitating, heart that he has just indicted Williamson as an incompetent, he quickly counters this with a strident, "I don't want to tell you your *job,"* and moves into a jocular "we're all human" phase wherein he acknowledges the ease with which expectations about a colleague's performance can become slightly skewed, and "a certain *mindset"* is developed. Even the best of us can sometimes err, he implies. Sensing Williamson's imminent dismissal of this, he is forced to become a little more strident, but still takes care to repeat his mediating phrase, "[a]ll I'm saying," so that he does not appear to be too aggressive.

His use of sales jargon, exhorting Williamson to "put a *closer* on the job" is clearly intended to impress, and to remind his boss that he is the consummate salesman, vendor without rival. But Williamson's impatience threatens to intervene and Levene panics: "There's more than one man for the . . . Put a . . . wait a second, put a *proven man out* . . ." He dare not finish his sentences lest Williamson should manage to speak. That he exhorts him to use a man who has already proven his worth (that is, himself) indicates a rapid switch of loyalty away from his recently lauded colleague. So much for camaraderie. Williamson's irritation becomes yet more threatening, and Levene tries a different, more aggressive, approach: "Wait a second," and begins to cite the financial rewards that could ensue if the manager had the foresight and vision to give the best leads to him. Thus he tries a direct approach to Williamson's wallet, a tactic he must know has at least some chance of success.

Eventually, Williamson manages to speak a word or two, and harshly criticizes Levene's recent performance. To the frenzied salesman, this is an almost fatal blow. The scene continues with Levene realizing that he must again change tone and mood; now he tries obsequiousness and adopts an air of concern. The "bad luck" he has recently experienced is just that:

Levene: Bad *luck*. That's all it is. I pray in your *life* you will never find it runs in streaks. That's what it does, that's all it's doing. Streaks. I pray it misses you. That's all I want to say. (4)

Clearly, Levene wants to—and will—say a great deal more! His hypocrisy and self-righteousness are wonderful to behold, as are his supposed prayers for the man who can make or break his career. Williamson is still dismissive, explaining that it is his job to "marshal those leads" (5), and Levene's anxiety reaches new heights. He becomes sarcastic, angry, and reckless:

Levene: Marshal the leads . . . marshal the leads? What the fuck, what bus did *you* get off of, we're here to fucking *sell*. *Fuck* marshaling the leads. What the fuck talk is that? What the fuck talk is that? Where did you learn that? In school . . .? *(Pause.)* That's 'talk,' my friend, that's 'talk.' Our job is to *sell*. I'm the *man* to sell. I'm getting garbage. *(Pause.)* You're giving it to me, and what I'm saying is it's *fucked*.

All of Levene's pent-up contempt for the despised office manager flows out and builds to an explosion of bile. The repeated use of the word "fuck" underscores his fury; for Levene at this moment, no other word can express his derision. So incensed is he that he repeats the same sentence twice for effect: "What the fuck talk is that?" He implies Williamson is nothing more than a child, who has learned such terminology in school and, with great unconscious irony, relegates the manager's words to "talk." Levene compounds this by stating that the salesman's job is to sell and, by implication, not to waste words merely talking. That he and his colleagues have spent their lives perfecting the ability to talk and elevating it to an art form is lost on him at this time. He then emphasizes that he is a "man" (unlike Williamson, who has already been relegated to the schoolyard) who is being unjustly treated, "getting garbage." He pauses for effect and then goes for the final assault: "You're giving it to me, and what I'm saying is it's *fucked.*" That he ends his tirade with an expletive is no accident; Levene's best laid plans have fallen apart and he has degenerated into screaming obscenities and insults at the only man who can help him. Desperate moments indeed.

Not surprisingly, Williamson is deeply unimpressed with Levene's behavior, and the argument continues with the manager gaining ground and setting the pace, refusing to allow the salesman any further leeway. Levene continues his hopeless quest to browbeat Williamson, violently berating him one moment and pleading with him for help the next, veering wildly between attempts to reestablish some form of empathy and denouncing the manager's job as pathetic. Williamson's constancy of mood and his cold, dismissive tone take hold and seriously frighten the older man, and Levene must change tactics once again in a frantic attempt to save the situation—and his job. He begins to beg for understanding in his hour of need, and to throw himself upon Williamson's mercy: "I NEED A SHOT," he cries, "I got to get on the fucking board" (7). To men like Levene, being a salesman is an addiction, not merely a job. Like a junkie, he craves a "fix," the chance of a new "high," a "shot." Knowing he is beaten, he debases himself, offering Williamson a share of his earnings, which the manager then forces him to increase, and, when even this desperate measure looks sure to fail, he tries once again to personalize the matter: "As a favor to me? *(Pause.)* John. *(Long pause.)* John: my *daughter.*" The verbal stammerings of defeat can be detected in these crushed words.

Levene capitulates to Williamson's outrageous financial demands, and is even forced to accept inferior leads: ". . . I'd like something off the other list. Which, very least, that I'm entitled to. If I'm still *working* here which for the moment I guess that I am . . . *(Pause.)* What? I'm sorry I spoke harshly to you" (11). Although Levene is beaten down as far as he can go, Mamet builds even more dejection into his words. Nevertheless, a feeble attempt to retain some dignity and hint at his own worth momentarily intrudes: "Which, very least, that I'm entitled to." However, Levene immediately realizes that this may further antagonize Williamson, and counters it with what he hopes will be taken as a spirited show of joviality under duress: "If I'm still *working* here . . ." What follows is interesting: either Levene is in such a state of despair and distraction that he thinks Williamson has spoken when he has not ["What?"], or this single word is Levene's way of buying a moment of calm so he can prepare himself to apologize to his hated and victorious colleague. As Williamson gets up to leave, Levene's final stumbling words underline his shame and mortification: "Good. Mmm. I, you know, I left my wallet back at the hotel" (11). Clearly, nothing is fine for Levene; his humiliation at the hands of the younger man is complete.

AARONOW AND MOSS

Two different kinds of anxiety can be detected here: Aaronow's alarm as he gradually realizes he is being irrevocably drawn into criminal conspiracy, and Moss's outraged indignation as he rails at the injustice of a system he himself has served to perpetuate. Aaronow appears to be of a nervous disposition in any case, and he spends a great deal of time agreeing with and backing up Moss's arguments. His tentative struggles to say the correct thing reveal an insecure and frightened man for whom the approbation of a stronger colleague would mean so much. Faced with the all-out aggression of Moss's prolixity, poor Aaronow can only try to fill in the gaps:

> Moss: They killed the goose.
> Aaronow: They did.
> Moss: And now . . .
> Aaronow: We're stuck with *this* . . .
> Moss: We're stuck with *this* fucking shit . . .
> Aaronow: . . . *this* shit . . .
> Moss: It's too . . .
> Aaronow: It is.
> Moss: Eh?
> Aaronow: It's too . . .
> Moss: You get a bad month, all of a . . .

Aaronow: You're on this . . .

Moss: All, of, they got you on this "board . . ."

Aaronow: I, I . . . I . . .

Moss: Some *contest* board . . .

Aaronow: I . . .

Moss: It's not right.

Aaronow: It's not.

Moss: No. (*Pause.*) (13)

This reads like a double act between two comedians, the wise-guy and his stooge. Aaronow tentatively offers criticism of the firm, but dare not *quite* finish what he wants to say, just in case Moss should disagree—which would be very unlikely in the circumstances! It is clear in any case that Aaronow is not the most articulate of men; on the evidence of this exchange, it is of little wonder that his recent exploits as a salesmen have been doomed to failure. He waits for Moss's approval and then quickly responds, often using the same vocal inflections, a linguistic habit in which both men like to engage during this scene. The two build up a kind of debased harmony with the repetition of the stressed (in every sense of the word) *"this."* Aaronow fields what he feels might be the desired response, "It is," without knowing what is in Moss's mind, prompting his colleague's query, "Eh?" Aaronow has of course absolutely no idea, and counters again with a repetition to buy a little time in the hope that Moss will bridge the gap—and he predictably obliges. They feed off one another's assertions, and Moss succeeds without really trying very hard in gaining Aaronow's agreement about the inequity of their lot.

Even at this stage, there is an underlying frisson that suggests Moss's deadly skills in the manipulation of the weaker man, although we do not yet know the extent of his ruthlessness or his motives. Aaronow is browbeaten by the sheer force of Moss's outrage; even if he did disagree, he would keep quiet. He wants to be accepted, to be one of the boys. Like Levene, he too has experienced lean times in the recent past and is feeling vulnerable and possibly isolated. The domineering Moss is completely aware of Aaronow's situation, which is why he has chosen him as his "co-conspirator" in the proposed heist. He knows full well that Aaronow is ripe for manipulation. As he says after delivering a fantastic (and inspired) confection of verbal bamboozlement and double-cross: "I took you in on this, you have to go" (21), even though Aaronow has at no point agreed to be involved, believing his colleague when he said they were "just talking" (18) about a hypothetical situation. "Why would I *do* it?" cries the hapless salesman, to which

Moss responds: "You wouldn't, George, that's why I'm talking to you" (22).
Knowing he has success within his sights, Moss blackmails Aaronow:

> Moss: . . . I have to get those leads tonight. That's something I have
> to do. If I'm not at the *movies* . . . if I'm not eating over at
> the inn . . . If you don't do this, then *I* have to come in
> here . . .
> Aaronow: . . . you don't have to come in.
> Moss: . . . and *rob* the place . . .
> Aaronow: . . . I thought that we were only talking . . .
> Moss: . . . they *take* me, then. They're going to ask me who were
> my accomplices.
> Aaronow: Me?
> Moss: Absolutely.
> Aaronow: That's ridiculous.
> Moss: Well, to the law, you're an accessory. Before the fact.
> Aaronow: Why? *Why,* because you only *told* me about it?
> Moss: That's right. (22)

Aaronow's panicky "you don't have to come in" is very telling. He
is like a child who believes that by saying the words aloud his fears will
not come true, and his echo of Moss's last sentence compounds this fantasy. Moss senses his desperation and starts spicing up his sentences with
inflammatory and "loaded" words, such as an emphasized *"rob,"* and
stressing that Aaronow's lack of cooperation will result in the police having to *"take"* him. To compound this, and to go for the verbal jugular, he
says he will have to cite Aaronow as his accomplice in the crime, as "an
accessory. Before the fact." By his use of legal-sounding terminology, Moss
hopes to play his trump card and force Aaronow into complicity. The period between "you're an accessory" and "Before the fact" allows just
enough of the horror of his situation to dawn on Aaronow, and his feeble
rejoinder is dismissed.

In the web of connivance woven by Moss, Aaronow is now a fel-
low-criminal, simply because he listened to Moss's theoretical notions
about "getting even." A conversation that had appeared to Aaronow as
an opportunity to bolster his confidence, gain an ally, and consolidate a
valuable friendship with a "real" salesman has disastrously backfired. His
gullible naiveté has been exploited by the corrupt and ruthless Moss for
his own gain.

Moss's own patterns of anxiety are best demonstrated in the sheer speed of his conversation, his unending supply of expletives, and his tendency to leave sentences hanging in mid air, unfinished:

> Moss: The whole fuckin' thing . . . The pressure's just too great. You're ab . . . you're absolu . . . they're too important. All of them. You go in the door. I . . . "I got to *close* this fucker, or I don't eat lunch." "Or I don't win the *Cadillac*. . . ." We fuckin' work too hard. You work too hard. We all, I remember when we were at Platt . . . huh? (12)

These are the words of a man suffering from extreme stress. His anger is palpable, arising out of the unfair working conditions he has been forced to endure. He interjects new issues without concluding the previous sentence and his words race ahead, almost incoherently, toward a reminiscence of better times. To further compound the fact that a salesman's life consists of thousands of little plays, meticulously acted out for the benefit of his clients, Moss performs for Aaronow's benefit succinct one-line dramas, with himself as the hard-pressed and abused protagonist. The liberal use of commas suggests a mind full of trepidation and uncertainty; he seldom ends a sentence with a full stop when a comma will permit a further assertion, another expletive. For Moss, to rail against the world, and to vocalize his outrage is essential; so tightly coiled is the combination of anguish, deceit, and ruthlessness he has honed for himself, that one fears his health would be dangerously compromised without this safety-valve of exploding anger. He might well succumb to hypertension and suffer a coronary. A man like Moss resembles a shark—to stop is to die. He—and by implication, his language—must always keep moving, toward a distant and possibly unattainable goal of genuine success.

ROMA AND LINGK

Roma is a man who lives on his nerves; quick-tempered and impulsive, he seldom fails to take the opportunity to display his arrogant frustration with the world in general, and with his colleagues in the sales office in particular. A deep-seated anxiety becomes blazingly apparent during his many outbursts of aggression: at such times he is frightening and intimidating, and his liberal use of obscenities compounds the general effect of someone whose patience is on a very short fuse. A good example of this, which also highlights his fundamental insecurity and fear, occurs at the beginning of act 2 when he storms into the ransacked office and repeatedly interrogates Williamson as to whether his own contracts are among those that have been stolen. His repetitions underscore a terror of failure, even that occasioned by theft. When he finds that the all-important (and expensive) Lingk contract has already been filed and that he is, therefore, out of "danger," his language empties out in an exhalation of profanities:

> Roma: Then I'm over the fucking top and you owe me a Cadillac.
> Williamson: I . . .
> Roma: And I don't want any fucking shit and I don't give a shit,
> Lingk puts me over the top, you filed it, that's fine, any
> other shit kicks out *you* go back. You . . . *you* reclose it,
> cause I *closed* it and you . . . you owe me a car. (31)

His pent-up anxiety does not permit him to succumb to immediate relief on hearing the good news; his words rush ahead, punctuated only by commas, never pausing long enough to justify a full-stop. Although fully aware that Williamson is no salesman, Roma irrationally puts the onus onto the manager to reclose any other contracts should they fall through. The repeated use of "you" emphasizes Roma's need to distance himself from any kind of failure or negative situation; by implication, he stresses that *he* has done his job well; *he* is the consummate professional who cannot be expected to "reclose." His time is precious, and it would be unworthy of him, he implies, to have to duplicate his efforts. Thus, a violently explosive mix of panic and tentative relief renders Roma, for once, almost incoherent. Such uncharacteristically disordered speech does not last for very long. In a final flourish, he reiterates the fact that Williamson owes him the car, and reestablishes his claim to be the salesman *par excellence*—the kind of man who when queried on his identity by the detective can respond with a puffed-up, arrogant "My name is Richard Roma" (31) confidently reasserting his position as a superbly professional one-man sales dynamo, without rival.

Roma's adrenaline-driven sales technique comes to the fore most vividly during his brilliant double-act with Levene, which he performs for the benefit of the quaking and apologetic Lingk when the latter comes to the office to renege on their deal. The text that Mamet creates to demonstrate the terrible plight of both men is at once replete with black comedy and an overwhelming sensation of fear. Although Lingk is all but monosyllabic in the face of the verbal bravura he receives, his stammerings acutely convey his suffering and feelings of guilt. As for Roma, the sight of Lingk coming through the door works like behavioral psychology; it triggers an immediate, Pavlovian reaction. His sixth sense tells him that the only possible reason for Lingk's presence in the sales office is that he has come to cancel their agreement, thereby losing Roma not only his place on the famous board (and, resultantly, his reputation) but also the Cadillac. This must not be allowed to happen, and his mind lurches into furious overdrive, and his imagination—like his pulse rate—races violently. Clearly, such events must have occurred in the past, because the unrehearsed spiel in which he and Levene engage has a polish and élan that could come only with years of practice and subterfuge.

Roma's first strategy is to pretend that his "executive" lifestyle puts him under inordinate pressure, leaving him virtually no time to see anyone without an appointment. Playing this to the hilt, he tries to confuse Lingk with the following:

> Roma: I've got to get Ray to O'Hare . . . (To Levene:) Come on,
> let's hustle . . . (Over his shoulder.) John! Call American
> Express in *Pittsburgh* for Mr. Morton, will you, tell them
> he's on the one o'clock. (To Lingk:) I'll see you. . . . Christ,
> I'm sorry you came all the way in . . . I'm running Ray over
> to O'Hare. You wait here, I'll . . . no. (To Levene:) I'm meet-
> ing your man at the bank . . . (To Lingk:) I wish you'd
> phoned. . . . I'll tell you, wait: are you and Jinny going to be
> home tonight? . . . (Rubs forehead.)
> Lingk: I . . .
> Levene: Rick.
> Roma: What?
> Levene: *Kenilworth . . . ?*
> Roma: I'm sorry . . . ?
> Levene: *Kenilworth.*
> Roma: Oh, God . . . Oh, God . . . (Roma *takes* Lingk *aside, sotto:*)
> Jim, excuse me . . . Ray, I told you, who he is is *the* senior
> vice-president American Express. His family owns 32 per . . .
> Over the past years I've sold him . . . I can't tell you the dollar
> amount, but *quite* a lot of land. I promised five *weeks* ago
> that I'd go to the wife's birthday party in Kenilworth tonight.
> *(Sighs.)* I *have* to go. You understand. They treat me like a
> member of the family, so I have to go. . . . We'll go out to his
> home sometime. Let's see. *(He checks his datebook.)* Tomor-
> row. No. Tomorrow I'm in L.A. . . . *Monday* . . . I'll take you
> to lunch, where would you like to go? (47–48)

Roma tries everything possible to inject a frantic hustle and bustle into his voice. To compound the impression of the pressurized industriousness he seeks to create, he carries out a three-way conversation, ordering

Williamson to contact American Express as though he were a secretary used to carrying out his demands, sincerely apologizing to Lingk for his wasted journey, and underlining the importance of "D. Ray Morton's" standing in the world of international business by mentioning his "man at the bank." Sensing Lingk's intransigence in the face of all this, Roma begins to panic. Earlier, he had told Levene that, should he rub his head at any point, Levene should say the word *Kenilworth* as a prompt for further action. Levene is ready for the cue; he knows exactly what is required, and the two men slip into a wonderfully inventive improvisation.

Roma decides to inflate his ersatz client's importance even further, to assure Lingk of his own standing as a salesman and to underline the importance of the kind of men with whom he does business. He changes Mr. Morton's job title from "director of all European sales and services for American Ex[press] . . ." (46) to "*the* [his emphasis] senior vice-president American Express," whose incredibly wealthy family owns huge amounts of land. Roma then drops heavy hints implying that he and this extremely important man are great friends, as well as business associates; he implies that their friendship is just like the "relationship" he has established with Lingk and his wife and, by so doing, compares the Lingks with his "old" friends.

To further emphasize the atmosphere of trust and familiarity that prevails, he even invites Lingk (without Mr. Morton's permission) to the Morton home. Roma's trepidation is almost tangible; no matter how hard he tries, he sees that Lingk's own deep-seated fear (of his wife!) prevails and renders it impossible for Roma's fantasy lifestyle to make any impact. Even Roma's assertion that his high status with the Morton family means that he *must* attend the birthday party, and that his jet-setting job will take him to L.A. the following day fails to sidetrack Lingk from his awful intention. In a last desperate effort to escape, Roma starts for the door to follow Levene. Lingk sees things catapulting out of control as the only man who can help him disappears into the street, and sheer terror forces him to say the words that Roma (and Lingk himself, for that matter) has dreaded to hear: "My wife said I have to cancel the deal" (48).

Once Lingk has committed himself, there is no going back; it has cost him dear to get even this far, and he simply dare not back down, even under the severest pressure and intimidation—and Roma certainly uses every trick he knows to coerce him. Realizing Lingk's predicament, Roma again utilizes his strategy of not allowing his pathetic victim to speak, his machine-gun sentences ricocheting off the walls. After a long wrangle in which he strives to confuse Lingk about the number of days he is allowed to cancel the agreement, Roma mercilessly continues:

Roma: No, I'm saying you don't include Saturday . . . in your three
    days. It's not a *business* day.
Lingk: But I'm not *counting* it. *(Pause.)* Wednesday. Thursday.
    Friday.
    So it would have elapsed.
Roma: What would have elapsed?
Lingk: If we wait till Mon . . .
Roma: When did you write the check?
Lingk: Yest . . .
Roma: What was yesterday?
Lingk: Tuesday.
Roma: And when was that check cashed?
Lingk: I don't know. (50)

Lingk's fear turns to exasperation as Roma's maneuverings show no
sign of abating, and he even dares to indulge in a little irate emphasis: "But
I'm not *counting* it." However, the fact that this is immediately followed by
a pause indicates that he realizes he may have offended Roma, something
he wishes to avoid at all costs. To antagonize the man who has the power
to help him face his wife once again is unthinkable. He becomes more deliberate, carefully stating the relevant days of the week, each separated with
a full stop for gentle emphasis. Roma senses his hesitancy and fear, smells
blood and immediately steps up his attack with yet another display of verbal double-dealing and intimidation, not even letting Lingk complete his
words: "Mon . . ." and "Yest . . ."

Later, Lingk's panic forces him to openly admit to Roma that his wife's
dominance means that he does not have "the power to negotiate," thereby
verbally emasculating himself: "I can't talk to you, *you* met my wife, I . . ."
and then, "She told me not to talk to you" (54). Lingk's humiliation is complete; he believes that his retraction of the deal under such ignominious circumstances renders him pathetic, less than a man, and certainly not one who
has the right to speak to such a "stand up" guy as Roma. Lingk's subjuga-
tion is so complete that even when he realizes that he has been duped, he
apologizes: "Oh, Christ . . . *(Starts out the door.)* Don't follow me. . . . Oh,
Christ. *(Pause. To Roma:)* I know I've let you down. I'm sorry. For . . . Forgive . . . for . . . I don't know anymore. *(Pause.)* Forgive me" (56).

In conclusion, it is patently evident that *Glengarry Glen Ross* is replete with conversation fueled by nervous energy and anxiety. Indeed, it is
one of the primary motivating forces of the play. The salesmen's notions of
themselves as existential heroes living on the edge and fighting a war of wits

depends on such dynamism, but they pay a high price for it—and so do their ill-starred clients. Whatever loyalty and camaraderie exist among them disappear as quickly as they emerge if it suits their purposes. Treachery is everywhere, and everyone is a potential target. They must live in the moment, the now, dismissing sentiment and encouraging duplicity. For these men, competitiveness is everything; when there is nothing left to sell, they sell themselves—and each other.

BIBLIOGRAPHY

Mamet, David. *Glengarry Glen Ross*. London: Methuen, 1984.

4 HOW TO DO THINGS WITH SALESMEN

DAVID MAMET'S SPEECH-ACT PLAY

David Worster

Stanley Fish once called *Coriolanus* Shakespeare's speech-act play, because it is "about speech acts [and] the rules of their performance. . . . It is also about what the theory is about, language and its power."[1] If *Coriolanus* is Shakespeare's speech-act play, then *Glengarry Glen Ross* is David Mamet's, for many of the same reasons. The ideological world of Mamet's play is not the legal institution of Roman law, but rather the economic institution of American capitalism (mythologized as the American Dream), within which Mamet's characters are constituted as salesmen, pivotal figures in the economic world of business. The institution has already predetermined how the salesmen will define themselves, their relationships to each other and to their conditions of existence, and how they will employ language to compose those definitions.[2]

Writing of the central action/talk paradox in *American Buffalo*, Thomas L. King suggests that talk is "an active agent in shaping the world and the terms of human relationships."[3] What is true of Mamet's earlier work is even truer of *Glengarry Glen Ross,* in which a particular way of using language (the ability or inability to "sell") is central to the characters' identities and relationships to each other. This play is about salesmen and selling, and, since selling is almost entirely utterance, the play is thus about talk and sales talk. According to speech-act theory, discourse acquires meaning in the context within which it is uttered, so any play about language must also be about speech context—the ideological, social, and cultural conventions and rituals which constitute and are in turn constituted by language.[4] *Glengarry Glen Ross* reveals to its audience how the discourse of capitalism posits within its subjects what it means to be a success, to be a man, to be a *sales*man, as well as what it means to be anything else (like a failure, a woman, a customer—these terms are all vaguely synonymous pejoratives to the salesmen). The play also identifies the manipulation of language within the ritual of selling—the ability or inability to articulate effective (or "felicitous") speech acts—as a primary constituent of identity. Close attention to language and how the salesmen use it reveals the distance between how the characters define themselves through their discourse and their genuine positions in the American business system. The language of the salesmen is emphatically self-referential, saturated with characteristics typical of "sales talk," pervasively sexual, and indicative of real and imagined power relationships.

In no other Mamet play is talk so insistently about talk. Aside from the ubiquitous "fuck" (a verb that itself becomes a metaphor for aggressive talk), verbs that denote utterance occur more frequently than any other significant words in the play. *Say, said, tell, told, talk, talking,* and *speaking* appear a combined total of over two hundred times. These verbs frequently are used as seemingly unnecessary reminders that the speaker is speaking and the hearer is listening: "What I am saying is. . . ." In this play, talking is so critical to the composition of identity and power that just to speak is not enough, the speaker must call attention to his speech. The constant reminder of the speaker/hearer relationship may be seen most clearly in the subject/tells/object construction: "Let me tell you," or "What I am telling you is. . . ." The proclamation of utterance is particularly aggressive because it firmly positions the hearer as the listening object, the nonspeaker. This pointed construction also appears more frequently than any other self-referential utterance, at least twenty-eight times by my own count; the three most aggressive salesmen in the play (Levene, Moss, and Roma) employ it the most frequently (twenty-five out of twenty-eight times).

In the first scene of the play, the aging salesman Levene has failed to convince the sales office manager, Williamson, to give him better sales leads:

> Well, I want to tell you something, fella, wasn't long I could pick up the phone, call *Murray* and I'd have your job. [5]

Levene's superfluous reference to his own utterance, "I want to tell you something, fella," could be deleted without changing the meaning of the sentence significantly; it serves as a vain device for asserting a verbal authority which, in this speech context, Levene does not have.

In addition to asserting verbal authority, this semantic construction often acts as a verbal "filler" in *Glengarry Glen Ross,* a way for the speaker to keep talking and to prevent the hearer from taking his turn in the conversation. The second scene of the play is a dialogue between Moss and Aaronow, two older salesmen who are not doing well in the office sales competition. At one point, Moss performs the equivalent of a musical "vamp" as he tries delicately to approach the subject of robbing the office to steal the sales leads:

> Moss: . . . I want to tell you something.
> Aaronow: What?
> Moss: I want to tell you what somebody should do.
> Aaronow: What? (37)

Aaronow does not have "permission" to speak; he can only respond with a verbal prompt as he waits for Moss to continue. As is the case with Levene's line above, Moss prefaces his utterance by saying that he wants to say something. In addition to italicizing his own speech act and preventing Aaronow from speaking, this construction ("I want to tell you") expresses a need on the part of the speaker to speak—a need that is about to be self-fulfilled. A key component of salesmanship is the creation or identification of the customer's needs, which the salesman can then offer to meet (a point to which I shall return). As the speeches of Moss and Levene reveal, the very act of speaking is a consummation of a desire to tell—a desire almost sexual in its implications (a point to which I shall also return).

All speech communities categorize important information through use of language. In fact, a close examination of the way a language orders and composes reality reveals much about the users of that language.[6] The salesmen talk about talking in a way that indicates the significance they attach to distinctions between different kinds of talk—another indication of how important utterance is to them. The most amusing and obvious example of this categorization of talk occurs during the second scene of the play. After Moss finally suggests the possibility of breaking into the office, he and Aaronow discuss it:

> Aaronow: Yes. I mean are you actually *talking* about this, or are we just . . .
> Moss: No, we're just . . .
> Aaronow: We're just *"talking"* about it.
> Moss: We're just *speaking* about it. *(Pause.)* As an *idea.*
> Aaronow: As an idea.
> Moss: Yes.
> Aaronow: We're not actually *talking* about it.
> Moss: No.
> Aaronow: Talking about it as a . . .
> Moss: *No.*
> Aaronow: As a *robbery.* (39)

As these lines show, just "speaking" about a subject keeps it in the comfortable realm of abstract "idea"; actually "talking" about a subject crystallizes it as an action—a robbery, or a business deal or a sale (in this play, these actions are roughly equivalent).

Although the difference between "just speaking" and "actually talking" is not maintained throughout the play in those specific terms, the distinction between ineffective talk and effective talk is. In the first scene of the play, Levene makes a distinction between two different kinds of talk: "Marshal the leads? . . . What the fuck talk is that? . . . That's 'talk,' my friend, that's 'talk.' Our job is to *sell*" (19). The impression that real talk is talk with the intent to transact business (and every other talk is just "talk") is reinforced moments later when Levene suspects that Williamson might make a kickback deal in return for some sales leads: "Good. Now we're talking" (25).

The distinction between just talking and actually talking is similar to the distinction between felicitous and infelicitous speech acts. In *Glengarry Glen Ross,* talk cannot perform as actual talk unless it contains some element of authority: The parties have the power and the desire to negotiate a deal, strike an agreement, or close a sale. As long as Aaronow and Moss are only talking about breaking into the office as an intangible "idea," their conversation is "just speaking." After Moss reveals that he really wants to do it and he wants Aaronow to join him, suddenly they are "actually talking" about an act:

> Moss: You *went* for it.
> Aaronow: In the abstract . . .
> Moss: So I'm making it concrete. (46)

Just as Levene earlier had tried to maintain a verbal authority over Williamson which did not exist, here Moss attempts a different kind of verbal transformation: making the abstract concrete simply by saying so. As John Austin wrote in *How to Do Things with Words,* this type of utterance is the most blatantly "performative" kind, a statement that enacts as it is uttered. "I'm making it concrete" is the equivalent of "I now pronounce you man and wife" in that reality changes as the words are spoken, if the hearers recognize the intended illocutionary force of the utterance. Such recognition depends upon the authority of the speaker to make such statements felicitous, or valid. A priest can felicitously say "I now pronounce you man and wife," a college professor cannot. Whether Moss has the authority to do what he says he is doing depends upon whether Aaronow recognizes his authority to do so. As the audience eventually will discover, he does not. The salesmen, who make their living through the use of language, are not only acutely aware of utterance (their own and others'), they also have a vague but powerful sense of the difference between infelicitous speech acts ("just talk") and felicitous ones ("actual talk"). *Glengarry Glen Ross* is not only about speech, it is also about speech acts.

The primary illocutional function of utterance in *Glengarry Glen Ross* is to persuade, to sell, and the practical business maxim, "Always Be Closing," hovers over the play like a perverted golden rule. Not only are the salesmen always selling, they talk about selling almost as much as they talk about talking; the words *sell* and *close* occur at least 45 times in the play. According to J.R. Searle, the following appropriateness conditions must obtain if a request (under which category persuasion and selling fall) is to be performed felicitously:

1. There exists the proposition of a future act (A) of the hearer.
2. The speaker wants the hearer to perform A.
3. The hearer is able to perform A, and the speaker believes the hearer is able to perform A.
4. It is not obvious to both the speaker and the hearer that hearer will do A in the normal course of events of his own accord.
5. The illocution "counts as" an attempt to get the hearer to do A.[7]

In the making of a request, the hearer has power over the speaker— the speaker makes the request, and the hearer has the ability to agree or to refuse. This relative power relationship is the reverse of an order or a command, in which (if the speech-act is to be felicitous) the speaker has authority over the hearer. This distinction is important because, although the salesmen are obviously in the position to make requests, they always speak as though they are in the position to give orders. An utterance will carry the intended illocutionary force of a command only if the hearer recognizes the authority of the speaker to do so, an authority which the salesmen simply do not have (thus the relationship between customer and salesman is analogous to the one between Moss and Aaronow in their scene together). This irony raises the interesting possibility that, if a customer does recognize and obey the salesman's nonexistent authority, that recognition indicates a need on the part of the customer not so much for whatever the speaker is selling, but for an authority—someone to tell him what to do and how to act.

During the second act of the play, Levene, while describing to Richard Roma the successful close of a sale to Bruce and Harriett Nyborg, reproduces part of his sales talk:

"... I don't want to go *round* this, and *pussyfoot* around the thing.... Why take an interim position? *The only arrangement I'll accept* is full investment. Period. The whole eight units. I know that you're saying 'be safe'.... But this won't do, and ... that's not the subject of our *evening* together." Now I handed them the pen. I held it in my hand. I turned the contract, eight units eighty-two grand. "Now I want you to sign ..." (73)

Because he believes that "business transactions hinge on personal domination over another,"[8] Levene attempts to establish himself as in control; he clearly articulates to his prospective customers what will and will not "do," and which arrangements he will and will not accept. The customers should recognize Levene's sales talk as having the illocutionary force of a request and should have the authority to say yes or no; however, Levene's verbal acrobatics transform the request into a demand, and the issue subsequently becomes whether or not the customers will obey that demand. If the customers do recognize the salesman's authority, the speech act becomes felicitous and carries the illocutionary force of an order. If the customers do not recognize it, the utterance is infelicitous—it becomes "just talk" not culminating in a sale.

Levene also tries to establish a sense of urgency about the deal that is typical of sales talk ("act *now* to take advantage of this incredible offer"). Earlier, Levene had told the Nyborgs, "This is now. This is that *thing* that you've been dreaming of ..." (72). "Now" and "today" are the habitual words the salesmen employ to create an artificial imperative to buy; these terms are often used in conjunction with dynamic action verbs like "act" or "do." For instance, Richard Roma offers the following as part of his sales routine to James Lingk:

"I do *today* with what draws my concern today." I say *this* is how we must act. I do those things which seem correct to me *today*. I trust myself. And if security concerns me, I *do* that which *today* I think will make me secure. And every day I *do* that, when that day *arrives* that I need a reserve, (a) odds are that I have it, and (b) the *true* reserve that I have is the strength that I have of *acting each day* without fear. (49)

Within this short stretch of monologue, the profusion of the verbs *to act* and *to do,* in combination with the frequent repetition of the words *today* or *each day,* has the cumulative effect of a command: "Act today." Roma also attempts to assert verbal authority over his customer—he does not hesitate to inform Lingk how we must act. Roma has, in fact, usurped his customer's power, and subsequently offers to sell it back to him. Lingk, apparently eager to acquire the ability to act with authority and certainty, ironically surrenders his real power to say "no" to Roma as he obeys the salesman's demand to listen and to buy. Roma's line to Lingk that closes act 1 is a request in the form of an imperative command: "Listen to what I'm going to tell you now:" (51).

Roma's sales talk to Lingk reveals not only two qualities typical of such utterance—requests in the form of commands and a sense of urgency to act—but also indicates a third hallmark of sales talk, which has already been mentioned in passing: the attempt to create a need or manipulate one already present in the customer. As Thomas L. King has written of *American Buffalo,* "Words relate not to things but to human motives and desires."[9] Roma manipulates Lingk's need for security in an unstable world, offering the strength to act each day without fear. Levene exploits the Nyborgs' "something-for-nothing" capitalist desire for wealth, telling them, "This is that *thing* that you've been dreaming of, you're going to find that suitcase on the train, . . . the bag that's full of money" (72). Later in the play, Levene describes his sales success in the old days:

> Walk up to the door. I don't even know their *name.* I'm selling something they don't even *want.* You talk about soft sell . . . before we called it anything, we did it. (77)

The salesmen may be selling something consumers don't even want, but the ideology of capitalism posits that happiness is purchasable and whatever needs the customers do have can be met within the system: just buy the right material possessions as quickly as possible, and you will be happy. The salesmen exploit that belief to meet their own far more desperate needs; they are involved in a cutthroat sales competition and have an urgent need to act— to talk in order to sell—NOW (those who lose the sales competition will be fired at the end of the month). As Anne Dean has written, the specific and immediate predicament of the salesmen in *Glengarry Glen Ross* presents a "paradigm of capitalism."[10]

Sales talk expresses the salesmen's vision of reality, transferring the most obvious and urgent needs from the salesman to the customer, and the power from the customer to the salesman. The existence of this transformative attempt in the context of a salesman/customer discourse is interesting enough, but the salesmen talk in all contexts as if they were selling something to the hearer; they always explicitly seek to address the desires of the listener, although linguistic constructions like "I want to tell you" indicate whose needs are really at stake. In scene 2, David Moss, realizing that George Aaronow is not doing well in the sales competition, tries to persuade him to steal the sales leads from the office:

> Moss: And it's a big reward. *(Pause.)* It's a big reward. For one night's work. *(Pause.)* But it's got to be tonight.
>
> .   .   .   .
>
> Aaronow: You're, you're saying so you have to go in there tonight and . . .
>
> .   .   .   .
>
> Moss: *You* have to go in. *(Pause.) You* have to get the leads. *(Pause.)* (42)

Although Aaronow has the right to refuse Moss's proposal, Moss couches his conversation in urgent, imperative demands: Aaronow has to do it, and it has to be tonight. Like Levene with the Nyborgs, Moss tries to emphasize the material opportunity he is presenting, the "big reward." Moss keeps the conversation focused on what *Aaronow* needs, although Moss himself urgently needs the money and someone to do his dirty work:

> Aaronow: You need the money? Is that the . . .
> Moss: Hey, hey, let's keep it simple, what I need is not the . . . what do *you* need . . . ? (46)

By the end of the scene, Moss seems to have persuaded Aaronow that he is already implicated in the crime because he "listened" (46). Yet in act 2 the audience will discover that Levene actually has broken into the office and is working with Moss, not Aaronow. Moss lacks the authority to make his request a demand, to make the abstract concrete; Aaronow ultimately recognizes this lack, rendering Moss's speech act infelicitous.

The urgency with which the needs are expressed, the demands that are actually pleas, and the desirability of the object (material gain, security, happiness, money) transform the sales talk into seduction—another form of persuasion. In the world of *Glengarry Glen Ross*, the measure of a real man is how successfully seductive a salesman he is. As Levene says early in the play, a "proven man" is a "closer" (15). Since they live by their golden rule, "Always be Closing," the most successful salesmen are always selling, always trying to persuade a listener to close with them—actions often described in sexual terms.

In the first scene of the play, Levene attempts to convince the office manager, Williamson, to give him some of the premium sales leads. "Put a *closer* on the job," Levene demands, "put a *proven man out* ..." (15). Moments later he asserts, "Our job is to *sell*. I'm the *man* to sell" (19). The conflation of a man and his job is solidified later in the play, again by Levene: "A man's his job" (75). Accomplishment as an aggressive salesman translates into enhancement of one's stature as a real man. As Roma says to Moss in act 2, "[If] *you* make a close the whole *place* stinks with your *farts* for a week ... what a big *man* you are" (71). Near the play's conclusion, Roma sadly confides to Levene that they are the last of a dying breed: "[I]t's not a world of men" (105).[11]

This professional definition of a real man as a persistent closer becomes easily and consistently fused with the sexual definition of a real man as an accomplished sexual aggressor. David Mamet has defined the capitalist American Dream as "basically raping and pillage,"[12] so it follows that a successful capitalist, a good salesman, a "proven man," would play a brutally aggressive sexual role. The continuous use of variations on the verb "to fuck"—far from a mere gratuitous and liberal proliferation of obscenity—is an important component of the defining metaphor of the play: salesmen as violent sexual males. The law of the jungle has become sexually mutated: Rape or be raped. A successful salesman is a sexual predator who achieves many closings because he has "the balls."[13]

If a good salesman is always a sexual aggressor, then customers are denigrated into sexually passive roles; they become rape victims. Customers, "by definition, are there to be screwed."[14] More than once, Levene crows, "I *closed* the cocksucker," creating an image of the customer as a sexual object, kneeling and humiliated before the dominant salesman. Levene's description of his sale to Bruce and Harriett Nyborg provides an excellent example of sexual metaphor applied to the closing of a deal. As Levene describes it, he is in total control—he does all the talking, while the Nyborgs are silent, listening:

> Now I handed them the pen. I held it in my hand. .... I sat there. Five minutes. Then, I sat there, Ricky, *twenty-two minutes* by the kitchen *clock*. (73)
>
> .   .   .   .
>
> They signed, Ricky. It was *great*. It was fucking great. It was like they wilted all at once. No *gesture* ... nothing. Like together. They, I swear to God, they both kind of *imperceptibly slumped*. And he reaches and takes the pen and signs. (74)

As Guido Almansi has written, "What a great erotic scene": Levene holding the erect pen out to the Nyborgs, the tension building for twenty-two minutes, then the physical release as they finally take it from him and sign.[15] Later in the same scene, Levene explains to Williamson the effect this sale has had upon him:

> I turned this thing around. . . . *I'm* the one's going to close 'em. . . . And now I'm back, and I got my *balls* back. (101–102)

The successful sale has given Levene his confidence back, and his description indicates that the successful *seduction* has restored his sexual potency.

If the most successful salesmen—the real men—are always sexual aggressors and seducers, then less successful salesmen, like George Aaronow, are "fucked" in the sales competition and "can't close 'em" because of a lack of seductive ability. This metaphor of those who fuck and those who are fucked applies not only to the salesman/customer relationship, but also to the salesmen in their relationships to each other. All their talk is sales talk, and their sales talk is sexual. The favorite insults are "[I'm going to] Fuck you" and "You're fucked," comments that verbally reduce the listener to a seminal receptacle and claim for the speaker the dominant sexual role of a "real man." The claim to dominant sexual positions is a verbal trick similar to putting a request in the form of a demand—it is a way of transferring power from the hearer to the speaker. The violent sexual metaphor does give a clear indication of where the real need lies, however. Rapists, even metaphorical ones, rarely act out of consideration of the needs of their victims.

During another interesting moment (and one that gives valuable insight into the true position of the salesmen within the system), Moss is complaining about the company-sponsored sales competition:

> [Y]ou find yourself in *thrall* to someone else. And we *enslave* ourselves. To *please*. (35)
>
> .   .   .   .
>
> [men] *build* your business, then you can't fucking turn around, *enslave* them, treat them like *children,* fuck them up the ass. (36)

While the subject of the conversation is clearly Moss's sense of economic bondage in a system he earlier described as "medieval," the language he uses creates a metaphor of sexual slavery as well. He says his role is to *please* someone else; he is being treated like a child, who has no sexual identity, or like a humiliated object for some other man's sexual pleasure. Economic power (or lack of it) is described in terms of sexual power (or lack of it). The allusions to slavery, children, and sexuality convoluted here also plant a vague and unsavory idea of these men as catamites for their supervisors in the firm; like all abused children, the salesmen, in turn, become abusers themselves.

The more closely the use of language in *Glengarry Glen Ross* is examined, the more evident it becomes that the primary purpose of utterance is not to communicate, but to claim power or to withhold it from others. As C.W.E. Bigsby has written, "Dominance and subservience are established independently of the lexical content of the exchanges."[16] If he who speaks is asserting dominance (and he who listens is passive), then the assertion that "I am talking" and "You are listening" is the primary function of utterance—the construction of a power relationship that has nothing inherently to do with locution.

Further evidence for this point might be seen in the constant misunderstandings between the characters, for language requires the object to *listen,* but not, necessarily, to *hear.* "What?" is by far the most frequently asked question in the play, and "What does that mean?" or "What do you mean by that?" occur at least a dozen times. Similar questions, like "What are you saying?" or "What are you telling me?" also abound. In the following exchange, Moss and Aaronow discuss the possibility of starting up their own office:

> Moss: . . . you know what the hard part is?
> Aaronow: What?
> Moss: Starting up.
> Aaronow: What hard part?
> Moss: Of doing the thing. . . . The hard part is . . . you know what
> it is?
> Aaronow: What?
> Moss: Just the *act.*
> Aaronow: What act?
> Moss: To say "I'm going on my own." (35)

Aaronow, in spite of giving every indication of intense listening, doesn't seem to hear or understand what Moss is saying. Also of interest in this exchange is the equating of speech to action. The act of going out on one's own is equated by Moss with the speech act of saying "I'm going on my own." As is typical of the way Moss (and other salesmen) think, to say it is to do it.

An insistence upon speaking (and calling attention to one's own speech) is a claim to verbal, sexual, and economic power in this play; an insistence (subtle or blatant) that others shut up and listen is a strategy to deprive one's listeners of that same power. But in the world of *Glengarry Glen Ross*, perhaps the most brutal speech act is forcing another person to speak when he wishes to remain silent. If utterance is power, then controlling the utterance of another strips all power away from him. During two of the most humiliating moments in the play, characters force other characters to speak against their will. After Williamson has discovered that Levene is the one who broke into the office and stole the leads, he insists that Levene tell him with whom he was working:

> Williamson: If you tell me where the leads are, I won't turn you
> in. . . . I'm walking in that door—you have five seconds to
> tell me: or you are going to jail.
>
> .   .   .   .
>
> Williamson: How much did you get for them?
> Levene: Five thousand. I kept half.
> Williamson: Who kept the other half? *(Pause.)*
> Levene: Do I have to tell you? *(Pause.* Williamson *starts to open the*
> *door.)* Moss. (100–101)

A moment similar to this one represents perhaps the lowest point in the play, as Roma forces Lingk to confess that he has no power to make a deal. In the world of *Glengarry Glen Ross,* where speaking is by ideological definition a claim to power, to force a person to speak a renunciation of power—to say that he cannot really "talk"—is the ultimate humiliation:

> Roma: What does that mean?
> Lingk: That . . .
> Roma: . . . what, what, *say* it. Say it to me . . .
> Lingk: I . . .
> Roma: What . . . ?
> Lingk: I . . .
> Roma: What . . . ? Say the words.
> Lingk: I don't have the *power. (Pause.)* I said it.
> Roma: What power?
> Lingk: The power to negotiate. (92)

The power to negotiate—to utter "actual talk" for the purpose of making a deal—is the only power that counts to the aggressive salesmen in *Glengarry Glen Ross*. That power lies with Mrs. Lingk and her ability to say no to the salesmen. Roma reassures Lingk that "we'll speak [talk] to her," but Lingk demurs: "She won't listen" (90). A customer who will not listen cannot be sold.

A very different kind of power—unrecognized by the characters in the play but there nonetheless—is the power to remain silent under great pressure to speak. James Lingk and Levene do not possess it, but one character does: the least respected and most laconic of the salesmen, George Aaronow. Not only does he ultimately retain his authority to say "no" to Dave Moss's command to rob the office, he also does not reveal that conversation to the police detective, Baylen, in spite of what Aaronow describes as a brutal interrogation ("*gestapo* tactics"). It is a credit to Mamet's artistry that Aaronow's strength in silence is easily missed. At that point in the play, the members of the audience are far more likely to be distracted by the entertaining efforts of Roma and Levene to keep James Lingk from canceling a sales contract. If they do think of Aaronow, it is likely to be in the interest of discovering whether or not he was persuaded by Moss to break into the office, and they are likely to overlook the fact that Aaronow knows of Moss's probable guilt but does not reveal it. Aaronow's silence presents him as a character in contrast not only to Lingk and Levene, but also to Williamson, who does not hesitate to betray Levene and Moss once he knows of their guilt. The quietest (but perhaps most significant) irony of this play is that, in spite of the pervasive insistence on speech as action and power, the refusal to speak is also action and power.

The power of a speech-act analysis of *Glengarry Glen Ross* lies in its revelation of the depth of irony in the way the salesmen use language. These characters claim their power with almost every word they utter: verbal power through imperative demands and the ubiquitous insistence that they are talking and others must listen, and sexual power through metaphor that equates talking with aggressive sexual seduction, listening with passive sexual submissiveness, and the closing of the deal with sexual intercourse of the most mechanical and degrading kind. However, for all this verbal thrusting, the salesmen fail to enact. During the course of the play, we see no deals successfully concluded. Lingk cancels his deal with Roma, and Levene's deal with the Nyborgs "kicks out" when it turns out their check is no good. Their efforts to sell each other also fail: Levene does not convince Williamson to give him better sales leads, Moss does not convince Aaronow to participate in the robbery, Roma and Levene fail to form a partnership.

The only successfully concluded agreement is the one between Moss and Levene made offstage for the purpose of ripping off the office; Levene betrays that deal at the play's conclusion. The claims to enact felicitous speech-acts abound in *Glengarry Glen Ross,* but the actual felicitous speech-acts we see may be counted on one hand. Levene and Roma insist that they closed deals with the Nyborgs and the Lingks, respectively, so it might be argued that those customers recognized the illocutionary force of Levene's and Roma's commands to buy.[17] But Mrs. Lingk withdraws her recognition when she changes her mind, and the Nyborgs apparently recognize everybody's authority to order them around. Williamson reveals at the play's conclusion that the Nyborgs have no money: "The people are insane. They just like talking to salesmen" (104) (they would have to be insane to like talking to salesmen). By Williamson's definition, neither of these deals closed.

In fact, of all the characters in the play, only Williamson has the position and power to make what he says reality. He has the authority to set the conditions of a hypothetical deal with Levene, and when Levene asks, "Why?" Williamson is accurate in his response, "Because I *say* so" (26, emphasis added). Mrs. Lingk, who does not appear in the play, also possesses the power to negotiate—the authority to utter "actual talk." As a woman, she reconfigures the gender-power hierarchy in sharp contrast to the salesmen's claims about the need for balls to enact powerful speech-acts.[18] It is surely no coincidence that two characters who possess verbal authority (Williamson and Mrs. Lingk) are not salesmen, and a third character who retains a measure of strength and dignity by refusing to speak (Aaronow) is perceived by the other characters as an unsuccessful salesman.

The salesmen verbally have constructed artificial identities (very real to them) as "proven men" and successful salesmen at odds with their actual positions of powerlessness within the ideology of capitalism. Their function as salesmen is vital to business, but they merely serve as the necessary interface between those parties really in control: the Williamsons of the system whose "because I say so" carries authority and the Mrs. Lingks of the world who have the power to negotiate. If, as is the case according to speech-act theory, what their words do or fail to do affect what characters are or fail to be, then Mamet's salesmen are failures acting (or failing to act) under the delusion of success.[19] Most of their locutions fail in their illocutionary intent; ultimately all of their talk is "just talk" masquerading as "actual talk." They are always closing, but they never close.

NOTES

1. Stanley Fish, "How to Do Things with Austin and Searle: Speech-Act Theory and Literary Criticism," in *Is There a Text in This Class?* (Cambridge, Mass: Harvard

University Press, 1980), 244. By calling *Glengarry Glen Ross* Mamet's speech-act play, I do not wish to imply that I agree with Fish when he claims that speech-act theory is applicable only to works of fiction about what the theory is about. I align myself rather with the tradition of Mary-Louise Pratt (*Towards a Speech Act Theory of Literary Discourse,* 1977), Sandy Petrey (*Speech Acts and Literary Theory,* 1990), Shoshana Felman (*The Literary Speech Act,* 1983), and others who maintain that speech-act theory is applicable to a wide range of texts because of its power to illuminate the way characters productively or unproductively use language in speech contexts. *Glengarry Glen Ross* is a "speech-act play" because it is *about* language in a particular context, as well as being composed *of* language in a particular context.

2. Mamet has expressed his own opinions in ideological terms, noting that the "code of an institution ratifies us in acting amorally." Mamet goes on to observe that even actions that might, in other contexts, be considered immoral are "somehow magically transformed and become praiseworthy" when performed "in the name of some larger group, a *state,* a *company*" (as quoted by C. W. E. Bigsby, *David Mamet* [London: Methuen, 1985], 123).

3. Thomas L. King, "Talk and Dramatic Action in *American Buffalo,*" *Modern Drama* 34 (December 1991): 539.

4. Speech-act theory was first developed and articulated by John Austin in his book *How to Do Things with Words* (Cambridge, Mass: Harvard University Press, 1962), and further developed most notably by John R. Searle in *Speech Acts: An Essay in the Philosophy of Language* (Cambridge, Mass.: Cambridge University Press, 1969). According to speech-act theory, in speaking we perform at least three different kinds of speech acts: (1) we utter a sentence (Austin called this "locution"); (2) we perform an illocutionary act; and (3) sometimes we also perform a perlocutionary act.

The illocutionary act is what the locution "counts as" in the speech context within which it was uttered. The same sentence may, in different speech contexts, count as a command, a question, a request, a promise, or any one of a number of different illocutions. The prime criterion for an illocutionary act is not its truth or falsehood, but whether or not the act has been performed successfully or unsuccessfully (Austin's terms are "felicitously" and "infelicitously"). The felicitous performance of any illocutionary act depends upon "appropriateness conditions" that obtain for that act, which are the understood linguistic, social, or institutional conventions shared by competent speakers and hearers of a language.

For instance, to issue a command felicitously, a speaker must have the authority over the hearer to make such a command, the hearer must be capable of performing what is commanded, and so forth. If all of the appropriateness conditions are not met, the hearer will not recognize the illocution (Austin's term for this recognition is "uptake"), and it will be infelicitous (for a more detailed description of speech-act theory, see M.H. Abrams, *A Glossary of Literary Terms,* 6th ed. [Fort Worth, Texas: Harcourt Brace College Publishers, 1993], 277–280).

5. David Mamet, *Glengarry Glen Ross* (New York: Grove, 1984), 26. All subsequent references to the play are from this edition and are cited parenthetically in my text. All emphasis is Mamet's own unless otherwise indicated.

6. For instance, Peter Farb notes that Americans think of chairs and couches as related to each other because they both belong to the category in English of "household furniture." But some African speech communities might lack a category of "household furniture" altogether, or think of "chairs" as related to "spears" since both are emblems of a ruler's authority. This difference in categorization reveals different ways of thinking about domesticity and civil authority (*Word Play: What Happens When People Talk* [New York: Knopf, 1974], 189).

7. J.R. Searle, *Speech Acts* (Cambridge, Mass.: Cambridge University Press, 1969), 66.

8. Edward Lundin, "Mamet and Mystery," *Publication of the Mississippi Philological Association* (1988): 107.

9. King, 547.

10. Anne Dean, *David Mamet: Language as Dramatic Action* (London: Associated University Press, 1990), 192.

11. Hersh Zeifman has recently written a valuable essay on machismo in the work of David Mamet. Zeifman argues that "the values of machismo—toughness, strength, cunning—which have become appropriated and apotheosized by American business" (125) are the sole criterion of worth in *Glengarry Glen Ross* and *American Buffalo*. See "Phallus in Wonderland: Machismo and Business in David Mamet's *American Buffalo* and *Glengarry Glen Ross*," in *David Mamet: A Casebook*, ed. Leslie Kane (New York: Garland, 1992).

I would qualify this statement as it applies to *Glengarry Glen Ross* by noting that the values of machismo are the sole criteria of worth according to the *salesmen*. During the second act, Williamson, the office manager, upsets an elaborate ruse constructed by Roma and Levene to keep Jim Lingk from canceling the deal he has made with Roma. The very worst pejoratives the aggressive salesmen can articulate impugn Williamson's role as a mature heterosexual male; to them, he is a "stupid fucking *cunt*," a "fucking *child*," and a "*fairy*." Women, homosexual men, and children are sexually powerless objects, worthy only of scorn and ridicule, to be used and discarded by "real men." Yet characters scorned by the salesmen ultimately possess greater power and authority than they do in the play; Williamson gets the last word on both Roma and Levene. The values of machismo are false values.

12. Quoted by David Savran, *In Their Own Words: Contemporary American Playwrights* (New York: Theatre Communications Group, 1988), 133.

13. Recently, columnist Debra J. Saunders has written about the neologism "O.P.P." The terms stands for "other people's pudendum" and is "rap" slang for sexual affairs, particularly those which "betray a pledge of fidelity." "There's something highly competitive in the motives of O.P.P. practitioners," Saunders writes. "People aren't people; they're other people's possessions. Hence, a sexual fling is a way of cleverly absconding with someone who belongs to someone else. It makes every cheater into a Donald Trump and turns adultery into a sharp deal" ("Calling Others 'O.P.P.' on MTV Must Be Commercially Correct," *News & Observer* [Raleigh, NC], 3 December 1991, A11). This comparison of a sharp business deal to a sexual act is a fascinating contemporary manifestation of Mamet's sexual metaphor in an age of Trump, Michael Milken, and Ivan Boesky.

14. Zeifman, 130. Another clue as to how the salesmen view the customers may be seen in an odd transformation in which the indirect object (object of the preposition "to") of the sentence: "I sell the land to the customer" becomes the direct object, and the original direct object ("the land") is deleted, producing the sentence "I sell the customer." Moss advises Aaronow, "Don't ever try to sell an Indian" (29), when what he clearly means is something like "Don't ever try to sell (something) *to* an Indian." (In this speech context, Aaronow knows exactly what Moss means; he assures Moss that he'd "never try to sell an Indian.") The actual commodity has vanished and the customer himself has become the object in the transaction. Williamson describes Roma's deal with Jim Lingk: "You closed him yesterday" (54). Late in the play, Levene rhapsodizes over how the salesmen closed deals back in the good ole days:

The *old* ways. The *old* ways . . . convert the motherfucker . . . *sell* him . . . *sell* him . . . *make him sign the check* (72).

15. Guido Almansi, "David Mamet, A Virtuoso of Invective," *Critical Angles: European Views of Contemporary American Literature*, ed. Marc Chénetier (Carbondale, Ill.: Southern Illinois University Press, 1986), 206.

16. Bigsby, 115.

17. Further incidental evidence for the primacy of utterance in the imaginations of the salesmen is the distance between their definition of "closing" and Williamson's. Early in the play, Levene and Williamson disagree over whether or not Levene closed two previous real estate sales:

Levene: One kicked *out,* one I closed . . .

Williamson: . . . you didn't close . . .

Levene: . . . I, if you'd *listen* to me. Please. I *closed* the cocksucker. (16)

Later, Williamson insists that both deals "kicked out," to which Levene responds that "they *all* kick out" (22) and continues to maintain that he closed them, anyway. As far as the salesmen are concerned, once they have successfully concluded the verbal negotiation and secured the promise to buy, the deal is closed regardless of the customer's actual economic power to meet that commitment.

18. Guido Almansi has written of Mamet that "his best plays are immune from any female contamination; the existence of women only filters on the stage through the preconceived ideas of the opposite sex" (191). Yet Mrs. Lingk succeeds in screwing up this deal for Roma (a comment by Levene earlier in the play foreshadows this possibility as he describes a sale that was canceled because of the customer's ex-wife). Hersh Zeifman admits that Mrs. Lingk "implicitly challenges" the salesmen's macho code of behavior (132), but she accomplishes more than that; she has the power to negotiate the deal (or refuse to negotiate the deal) and, as such, defies the code of machismo and the derogatory preconceptions of women articulated by the salesmen.

19. This delusion is a very necessary one, already written into the discourse of capitalism. If the salesmen are to continue to perform their role within the system, they must continue to perceive their own success or at least the future potential for success. As Sandy Petrey has written, "One of the things we do with words is make a life we can get through" (103).

5   MEN AMONG THE RUINS

Robert H. Vorlicky

Near the conclusion of David Mamet's male-cast *Glengarry Glen Ross,* Richard Roma, a sleazy, cutthroat salesman, stands amid his employer's burgled real estate office. The surrounding destruction heightens Roma's lament that "it's not a world of men . . . it's not a world of men" (1984, 105). Just a day earlier, Roma had mesmerized a lead, a potential buyer named James Lingk, with the fantasy that in his desired world of men, a (white) man embodies his own absolute morality: he not only trusts himself, which enables him to overcome any fear of loss, but he also knows that he can "act each day without fear" (49). This, for Roma, is the way of the world, the way the world is intended to be. But Roma's fantasy of man's moral rightness—man's fearlessness—is nearly dashed when he considers his own position within the destroyed office: it is a scene of chaotic disruption that suggests, paradoxically, an imminent dismantling of the myth-driven world that "naturally" empowers (all) men within American patriarchy. It is a scene whose real and symbolic meanings even Roma cannot ignore.

In a bold stroke of self-confidence, however, Roma reasserts his own "difference" from other men as the key to his personal survival (50). He distinguishes his subject position from all others (who, to him, are women, unmasculine men, and men of color). Like the phoenix, Roma is determined to rise from the rubble that signals the demise of other less shrewd businessmen. He, after all, never loses faith in his ability—in his power—to exploit anyone at any time. This is his right, he assumes, within the capitalist system his actions help to perpetuate. This is his right, Roma demonstrates, as a male in American culture. Roma's lust for material success is matched by his belief in the rewards extended to a male for having done well at his job—a success that is determined by the American masculine ethos and perpetuated through familiar male mythologies. Such a belief feeds Roma's ambitious behavior, which is at once touching in its apparent concern for his fellow man's losses while deceptive in its underlying selfish greed.

I have intentionally stressed Roma's maleness to foreground the issue of gender in *Glengarry Glen Ross*. In general, critics ignore the central, explicit role of gender (as distinguished from sexuality) not only in this play, but in Mamet's work before *Oleanna* (1992).[1] For this reason, it can be misleading to universalize the characters' experiences in *Glengarry*. Frank Rich (1984) and Christopher Bigsby (1985), for instance, collapse the characters' gender-coded identities into representations of a non-gender-specific human condition, for the sake of more sociophilosophical, non-gender-related readings. Mamet himself acknowledges the importance of distinguishing the basis upon which his characters' position arises in male-centered plays like *Glengarry* (or *American Buffalo* and *Edmond*): their anguish is a result of the failure of the American dream, Mamet concludes, for "the people it has sustained—the white males—are going nuts" (qtd. in Leahey). And it is the male protagonists' "condition rather than a dramatic action," Mamet adds, that serves as *Glengarry*'s distinguishing dramaturgical feature (qtd. in Savran, 1988, 135).

Mamet consciously favors the world of men via the male-cast play when he writes for the theater. When his men are in women's company, they nonetheless remain acutely aware of their dominance over the Other, a positionality that recalls the binarism of Simone de Beauvoir's gender system of Self/Other (xvi–xvii). At all times, Mamet's male characters see the world through men's eyes, with a vision that assures them that they exist in a culture that promotes the values of the masculine ethos as well as privileges them over women by virtue of their masculine gender. It is a vision that finds its expression in social dialogue, a quality of talk throughout the male-cast canon that favors as its topics employment, consumerism, families, women, and men's active identification with the cultural ideal of male virility. These subject matters surface in the initial dialogue in the vast majority of the nearly one thousand published American male-cast plays.

Mamet's language is also the language of men who activate, in H.P. Grice's term, the "Cooperative Principle"; that is, when one makes a "conversational contribution such as is required, at the stage at which it occurs, by the accepted purpose or direction of the talk exchange in which [one is] engaged" (45). Yet, while the men communicate cooperatively by engaging in talk exchanges, they do so without self-disclosure, without overstepping the cultural codings that dictate acceptable male interaction. These cultural codings, in turn, inform the semiotic of the play's "discourse coherence," which, as defined by Keir Elam, is the "strategic order" or the sequence of topic selections that occurs in stage dialogue (182–84). The dialogue, then, reflects both the linguistic-literary codes and the cultural codes operating within the dramatic system, including whiteness and the American masculine ethos. Most realist male-cast plays rely upon this cooperative level of social dialogue for their initial dramatic structure, but very few preserve it for the duration of their characters' interaction. Upholding the latter quality, *Glengarry* is a quintessential male-cast play of this type.

Mamet's characters consciously choose to remain on the level of social dialogue. "Their language, gestures, desires, and values are social products," Jeanette Malkin suggests, "not expressions of individual will" (160). They prefer foremost to sustain cooperative communication without becoming emotionally or psychologically vulnerable to the other men. Unlike the dialogue in other office plays, where the hierarchy of authority often promotes characters' self-disclosures, Mamet's dialogue resists any such private access to the individual. What results in *Glengarry* is a cryptic, inarticulate coding system that deliberately fluctuates between clarity of meaning and ambiguity while it propels the men's conversation forward. This social dialogue is narrowly confined to the topic of the men's employment. As Julius Novick remarks, Mamet's play depends solely upon the "imperatives of business." It "derives a special purity, a special power, from the fact that it is about nothing but the necessity to sell—which means, in this play, to bend other people to your will and take what you want, or need, from them." In general, the characters forgo an involved discussion on the remaining topics that usually surface during social dialogue, choosing instead to promote a coded language of business, of capitalism, that is defined semiotically—as a system related to other systems, including extratheatrical, cultural systems.

The structure of *Glengarry* is shaped according to two dominant features: a coded language of business, with a hierarchical relationship firmly established between speaker and listener; and a dominant, though diversely realized, thematic of business. This latter feature refers to the various meanings of *business*: from the business of one's public employment to one's personal business (that is, the details of one's private life). The coded language of business and the thematic of business are technically linked to one another via the characters' dialogue, an association realized in the practical sales maxim that serves as the play's opening epigram: "Always be closing" (13).[2]

As crafted by Mamet, the social dialogue in *Glengarry* is dramatic talk that is "always closing," as it were, not only because of its limited selection of topics (its nearly exclusive, closed focus on one's job) but in its conversational dynamic between participants as well. Mamet restricts the social dialogue in order to illustrate the linguistic constraints that influence how a men's closed conversational relationship is constructed, and how that relationship easily becomes the power struggle between speaker and listener as each attempts to secure the position of authority. Because of their topic selections, Mamet's male characters are locked into culturally coded roles as speaker and listener—that is, the men activate a socially sanctioned, predetermined relationship to one another simply because they are discussing, in a nonpersonal manner, a topic determined in accord with the masculine ethos. The balance of power resides with the participant who most adamantly adheres to the principles of the ethos.

In each of the three scenes of conversational dyads that comprise the first act, the answer to the question "Who really holds the power?"—the speaker or the listener—is determined by the individual who adheres unwaveringly to the restrictions advocated by the masculine ethos. Those who wield the conversational power in act 1 are Williamson, who is predominantly the listener in the first scene (much of his interaction with Levene is metalinguistic, as the two talk about talk in their efforts to understand one another), and the verbose, goal-oriented Moss and Roma. Each man is staunchly committed to dialogue that reinforces the masculine ethos and its attendant mythologies. Consequently, they bulldoze their conversational partners into submission, whether through calculated silences or evasive remarks, as in Williamson's case, or energetic talk, as in Moss's and Roma's cases, completely denying the value of a topic other than that which is employment related. While the men adhere to a kind of dramatic cooperative principle in their talk, Williamson, Moss, and Roma discourage their respective conversational partners from engaging in self-disclosing, personal dialogue. Whether as listener or speaker, each maintains a closed conversational relationship with the other man as he backs up the authority of his own restricted position with the culture's coded authority of appropriate masculine behavior and verbal interaction. As William Demastes remarks, "These men are trapped in their worlds, and their words are trapped in their culture" (91).

In numerous interviews, Mamet harshly criticizes American capitalism—the "world," the "culture" of men's lives: "The American Dream has gone bad. . . . This capitalistic dream of wealth turns people against each other. . . . The dream has nowhere to go so it has to start turning in on itself" (qtd. in Leahey). White men, according to Mamet, are coming to realize that the cultural mythologies that traditionally have sustained them are, in fact, in jeopardy. Why? Because "the white race . . . [has] no tragedy." For Mamet, the white man's condition is that he has no "spirit"—no identity outside his culturally coded power of domination. Certainly one sign of man's "spiritlessness" is his impoverished, crippled relationship to language—and to feeling. Herein lies the desperate state of Mamet's males in *Glengarry*, despite the author's recent insistence that the play is a "gang comedy" (1988, 92).

Prominently located on Mamet's matrix, white (straight) men usually reject any options (and their attending responsibilities) that might conflict with the masculine ethos. Nonetheless, they inhabit a realist dramatic world shaped not by fate, but by free choice. For this reason, "the only redemption for the individual is not to change with the institution," Mamet states, for him "not to become part of the institution" (qtd. in Freedman). Whether on- or offstage, however, Mamet rarely comments on social movements, including feminism, as having the power to affect men's lives in a constructive way, creating a more balanced cultural power between the sexes. Despite his awareness of its severe limitations in terms of the quality of human interaction, Mamet is still obsessed with the power, the camaraderie, the potential strength in the exclusivity of male bonding (1989a, 85–91). Prior to *Oleanna* and subsequently *The Cryptogram* (1994), women's issues were not a central social reality in any of Mamet's plays; his characters and their worlds exist independent from any larger cultural context in which gender roles are challenged and changed. Yet, as Novick points out in respect to *Glengarry*, "Has any professed feminist ever given us so unsparing a picture of the masculine ethos at its most barren, destructive, anguished, futile?" *Glengarry Glen Ross*, asserts Demastes, "very clearly focuses on the business ethic, but it is a much broader topic that Mamet is addressing—the decaying of America as a result of this ethic, not just in business, but throughout" (87).

The ethics of Mamet's business world, and its intended metaphoric and actual associations to American patriarchy, are directly linked to the culture's masculine ethos. As dramatized by Mamet, this gendered ethos appears unethical: it promotes corruption, exploitation, prejudice, and violence. One could say that Mamet's men communicate through a coded language whose end is also unethical, not only in its subordination of the Other, but in its calculated resistance to personal, frank communication among men. Mamet's men "no longer have access to words," surmises Bigsby, "that will articulate their feelings" (123). In the mouths of Mamet's characters, this unethical (use of) language is committed to the business of deliberate obscuring of the truth; it encourages illusion, not the actual, as it fosters frustrated isolation rather than meaningful connections among those who speak it. In *Glengarry*, therefore, "It is less the plot development than Mamet's language," as Demastes concludes, "that succeeds in capturing the essence of his themes" (91). It is the pervasive, unrelenting power of the American masculine ethos and male mythologies manifest in Mamet's language that reveal the play's cultural and dramaturgical dynamism.

The plot of Mamet's play is relatively inconsequential compared with the dynamics of the characters' verbal interaction, most strikingly captured in their social dialogue. The men's involvement with one another reveals what each man thinks of himself, as he talks about or relates to business. In Mamet's male world, one's identity is determined by the way he engages in business (as in Lingk's circumstance), or by his success or failure at his job (as in the case of the real estate personnel and the detective). Significantly, as Carla McDonough proposes, "If a job is what defines a man, then failure in business is what defines the non-man, the woman" (202). A man measures his self-worth (and has it measured by others) against the gendered cultural standards associated with economic power. In such a system, it is not uncommon for a man to experience the roles of both victim and victimizer.

This cultural context for self-definition is actually a system of set codes, one spelled out in the opening speech of *Glengarry,* when Levene tells Williamson, "I don't want to tell you your *job.* All that I'm saying, things get *set,* I know they do, you get a certain *mind-set*" (15). Levene's language (and eventually every other character's language) reveals paradigmatic codes that characterize the men's social dialogue: "job," "set," and "mind-set" anticipate other codes to follow—"board," "policy," and "lead." Such codes are "known to both transmitter and destination—which assigns a certain content (or meaning) to a certain signal. In linguistic communication the code allows speaker and addressee to form and recognize syntactically correct sequences of phonemes and to assign a semantic content to them" (Elam, 35). What is crucial to note in Mamet's dialogue is that the characters rely upon these codes, which are both dramatic and cultural (Elam, 52), as each resonates with meanings that are gender based and gender biased. Mamet's characters are represented as having freely chosen to maintain this level of interaction (distinguishing these men from those in *American Buffalo,* for instance, where Don and Teach consciously transcend the conversational limits imposed by social dialogue). In the closed patriarchal microcosm of *Glengarry,* therefore, the coherence in the men's dialogue is firmly entrenched, reflective of a mind-set that adheres solely to the principles of the masculine ethos and its attendant mythologies. Although the men communicate cooperatively, they remain inflexible in their efforts to restrict the discourse coherence, and consequently the thematics, of their talk.

Introducing initial codes in the first two scenes that will characterize the men's dialogue for two acts, Levene and Williamson, followed by Moss and Aaronow, establish another critical feature of Mamet's social dialogue: metalinguistics. Each pair talks a great deal about talk. Explicitly, they indicate the discourse coherence of their conversation through their topic selection; implicitly, they struggle to establish the power relationship between speaker and listener, identifying who occupies the position of authority. The men's moment-to-moment metalinguistic dialogue reinforces the play's construction as a closed language system, one in which specific meanings are obscured in favor of ambiguous, nonspecific references. No one is ever certain that he is heard or understood. Their talk about talk—and its concomitant relationship to the process of receiving and comprehending information—does not, however, diffuse the power of codes in the men's dialogue. In fact, the linguistic-cultural codes in the men's social dialogue, those that are informed by the masculine ethos, provide the only irrefutable foundation for communication between the men. The codes essentially ground the men in their interaction with one another. For example, when Williamson asserts that he's "given a *policy. My* job is to *do that.* What I'm *told*" (19), Levene knows with certainty that the policy about which his boss speaks is the same one that structures both their professional and personal relationships to one another. For this reason, they favor familiar and predictable socially engendered roles that feed off cultural clichés and stereotypes of maleness. From this more comprehensive perspective, therefore, one can identify the social construct of the Beauvoirian Self/Other, the "policy" of gender, that polices the men's dramatic language (of subject/object) and behavior in Mamet's America.

Moss and Aaronow, like Levene and Williamson, generate much dialogue between them in scene 2 that challenges the meaning of what is being spoken. Following Levene's failure to persuade Williamson to sell him the leads, or prime real estate customers, Moss presents an idea to Aaronow on how the two might steal those same leads and sell them to Jerry Graff, a competitor (who, in turn, may reward the men with jobs). The two men do not directly discuss a specific plan; rather, they allude to the idea of a robbery, then question through metalinguistic exchanges their potential relationship to its possible execution. For example, after being asked by Aaronow if he has discussed this possible robbery with Graff, Moss replies:

> Moss: No. What do you mean? Have I talked to him about *this*?
> (*Pause.*)
> Aaronow: Yes. I mean are you actually *talking* about this, or are we
> just . . .
> Moss: No, we're just . . .

87

Aaronow: We're just *"talking"* about it.

Moss: We're just *speaking* about it. *(Pause.)* As an *idea.* . . .

Aaronow: So all this, um, you didn't, actually, you didn't actually
      go talk to Graff.

Moss: Not actually, no. *(Pause.)* (39–40)

The talk between Moss and Aaronow is dotted throughout with these
metalinguistic interactions. They are unable (or unwilling) to use language
to convey specific meanings. Rather, they choose to maintain a social dialogue that is vague and ambiguous, or as Moss might estimate, a language
that is pleasingly "simple" (35). To "keep it simple" (46) is also for Moss
and Aaronow to keep their sights on a basic cultural power—economic potency—that they can (re)gain, if only for a while, if a robbery is successful.
Their fantasy to possess this power—and thereby to experience the anticipated ancillary patriarchal powers that come from a psychological boost of
having achieved a cultural goal—is strong enough to push aside any individual realities that might challenge its realization.

The language and thematic of business continue to dominate the characters' dialogue and determine its discourse coherence throughout act 1,
scene 2. Most strikingly, however, the men relish the thought of being dis-
loyal to their current employers in hopes of securing jobs with their competitor. Moss even goes so far as to suggest that someone should "hurt" their
bosses (37). This evocation of the power of violence to effect change—and
its attraction as an actual undertaking—is a typical position men assume
among themselves after they discuss their perceived lack of power. From
Martin Flavin's *Amaco* to Edward Albee's *The Zoo Story,* Charles Fuller's
A Soldier's Story, and OyamO's *Let Me Live,* male characters repeatedly
resort to violence as a final solution to their immediate professional or private conflicts. Moss's plan that Aaronow and he should rob their employer's
office, therefore, lines up behind a long-standing tradition in American male-
cast drama in its appeal to men to engage the power of violence in order to
get the job done. And, of course, that violence does occur in the dramatic
time that separates acts 1 and 2 in Mamet's play; it also occurs outside the
spectator's vision, outside his or her immediate experience of the drama. By
presenting the effects of the violence rather than staging the violence itself,
however, *Glengarry* further distinguishes itself from most male-cast plays in
which violence is a prominent, enacted feature.

Throughout Moss's rigorous defense of the plan to rob the real estate office, Aaronow remains an ambivalent, inconsistent listener. From
moment to moment the idea either appeals to him or seems the illegal act

that it is. Tempted by avarice, this decentered man becomes a postmodern everyman in Mamet's contemporary morality play; he appears to be the central, pivotal character around whom the play's construction and (cultural) ideology develop. As the everyman figure, Aaronow initially wields a great deal of power—especially in the spectator's identification with him—in terms of the significance of the choices he makes. He is free in Mamet's democratic dramatic world to choose whatever he wants: he can either agree or disagree with Moss, the vocal defender of a kind of male power that is essentially based on economic reward through violence. Accordingly, in Moss and Aaronow's interaction, Mamet returns to the critical consideration that surfaces in nearly all male-cast plays—that is, who really holds the power. And what is sacrificed, if anything, when one participant dominates the other(s) through restricted, ambiguous talk? This becomes Aaronow's dilemma as Moss increasingly dominates their conversation.

Aaronow's predicament links two complementary strands that are characteristic of the male-cast canon. The first strand identifies several terms by which a given male in a talk exchange becomes the more dominant participant, privileging that which he says (or, as the case may be, that which he refuses to say). The second strand focuses on the dramaturgical significance of male characters who willfully create and sustain fictions when speaking among men as a means of (personal) survival.

When a speaker and listener (or respondent) focus on the thematic of the masculine ethos during their mutually agreed upon social dialogue, the speaker establishes a closed dynamic with his listener that effectively secures the listener's compliance with that thematic. In this regard, a listener chooses during social dialogue to agree (or appear to agree) with the principles advanced within the thematic of the masculine ethos. In act 1, scene 2, Aaronow eventually chooses to entertain Moss's conversational position; Moss does not force him to do so. Their dynamic illustrates the extent to which social dialogue initially creates, in their words, "abstract" images between speaker and listener that are then realized, or made "concrete," simply through the articulation of their properties, or codings (46).

On the level of plot development, for example, Moss cites Aaronow as an accomplice to the robbery simply because Aaronow hears the plan; the abstract scheme is, according to Moss, concrete once it is articulated. Even though he challenges Moss's logic, Aaronow is unable to convincingly deny or refute it. One could say that between speaker and listener a kind of "truth" is voiced when the abstract is materialized in the language of social dialogue. And the listener is either "in or out" (46) of agreement with that truth. In this instance, Aaronow listens "in" agreement with the position Moss advocates.

Mamet utilizes this same solipsistic logic in establishing a dramatic logic that operates on the construction of his social dialogue. The power of language, as used by Mamet's men, creates the thematic of the masculine ethos that is so crucial to the characters' collective male identity, but it also has the capacity to make one's self-image "concrete" (46) in its compliance with that ethos. Yet, each man is "free," so to speak, to choose his relationship to the construction of that identity, which, as rendered in Mamet's dialogue, is most readily determined by the character's choice of dialogue: social or personal.

The second strand that surfaces in Aaronow's situation is the relationship between the play's closed speech dynamic and the conversational participants' tendency to create fictions as a method of survival. What links this strand with the previous one is its relationship to the creation of "truth." Certainly, Moss weaves a seductive fiction when he suggests that both Aaronow and he will somehow benefit if their attempted robbery is successful. What Moss overlooks and Aaronow fails to challenge, however, is the penalty that each will pay if caught for committing this crime. Both men construct a fiction that they will acquire lasting economic power, a wish that will be immediately gratified when they are hired for more lucrative positions by their current competitors. Yet, Moss and Aaronow manufacture the illusion of truth out of lies. Their social dialogue fosters this indulgence as their language moves in and out of the unlimited possibilities that surface in a closed speech that accommodates illusion over truth, fiction over reality. Simply because he listened to Moss's fiction—and finally succumbed to its allure as truth through its representation in language—Aaronow fails to self-identify.[3] Rather, like Roma in scene 3, he embraces the fantasy of male cultural power as his means of survival. But unlike his assertive co-worker, Aaronow is incapable of creating fictions on his own. He is a decentered, postmodern everyman who responds only to that which is thrust in front of him; he, himself, exerts no convincing effort to initiate alternative action or ideas. Aaronow's survival, therefore, is solely dependent upon piecing together others' lies. He relies upon coded cultural fictions not only for their indication of the choices he is to consider, but also for the establishment of his own sense of meaning as well—his own sense of himself. That self is finally, tragically false; Aaronow appears painfully conscious of the absence of personal depth in his life.

In act 1, scene 3, Roma demonstrates the skill, the "act" as Moss calls it (35), of the successful, persevering salesman—the one who, unlike Aaronow, is determined to survive according to the terms of the masculine ethos. Whereas Aaronow is everyman, Roma could be considered the representative, classical (white) everyman who appears in most American male-cast plays. He epitomizes the male characters (regardless of their race) who remain staunchly committed to the values advanced by the masculine ethos. Like the Coach in Jason Miller's *That Championship Season,* Alan in Mart Crowley's *The Boys in the Band,* Ora in Amiri Baraka's *The Toilet,* and Waters in Charles Fuller's *A Soldier's Play,* Roma unhesitatingly upholds the virtues of masculinist ideology, most readily recognizable in his buddy-buddy, cutthroat approach to business. As speaker, he also depends upon the power of language to create fictions that in turn create the illusion of empowering the listener. These efforts establish the fantasy of interpersonal connections between men that are vital to the continuance of patriarchal authority, to the culturally coded gender system of Self/Other.

Expressing what at first appears as a stream-of-consciousness monologue, Roma seduces the unsuspecting, but emotionally and psychologically vulnerable, Lingk with what in fact is a strategically calculated speech and performance, much like Jerry's mode of communication with Peter in Edward Albee's *The Zoo Story.* In effect, Roma delivers a highly manipulative sales talk, which, according to Deborah Geis, is the essence of "monologue" (6); his solo talk is initially masked in pseudophilosophical musings intended to allure Lingk into the web of what could be called "Roma Reasoning." One comes to understand Roma's reasoning on the meaning of life through a series of rapid questions and answers (48), each designed to refocus the emphasis from the anonymous human condition to the more crucial status of the little guy, Lingk, who exists amid an overwhelming, faceless condition. Roma's speech is intended to empower Lingk; it is about conventional patriarchal dynamics of action, control, and power. He argues the position that any man can feel powerful simply by acting without fear. And this power of direct action is extended to Lingk by virtue of his gender privilege, a privilege about which Roma intends to remind his attentive customer. Furthermore, Roma implicitly reminds Lingk that a commitment to action is a demonstration of support for masculine ideals.

The logic in Roma's monologue moves from the universal to the specific, always with the clear objective to convince Lingk to buy land from him. Roma offers this reasoning as the key to Lingk's empowerment: man is afraid of "loss" and has traditionally turned to "greed" as a false sense of security; unwilling to believe himself to be "powerless," man must "trust" his own power to "do those things which seem correct to [him] *today*"; as a result of his independent thinking, therefore, man can experience himself as secure, "*acting each day* without fear" (48–49). Once Roma suggests the importance of action as an expression of one's personal power, he then focuses his attention on motivating Lingk to take personal action on an "opportunity": "stocks, bonds, objects of art, real estate" (49)—each of which, according to Roma, can mean "what [Lingk] *want*[s] it to mean" (50).

Real estate, in particular, Roma suggests, might "mean *nothing*" to Lingk, or "it might not" (50). Roma skillfully maneuvers the power to define the meaning of things into the rhetorical control of his nearly silent listener. How Lingk names things, Roma implies, is direct evidence of Lingk's relationship (or lack thereof) not only to the culture's expectations of gendered power, but to his sense of himself as a Man. "[T]o talk is to *act*, talk is power," writes Malkin, and "*men* know how to talk" (156). Although men are "all different" from one another, according to Roma (50), each, as a man, has access to the power to define. Man, not God, has the power in Mamet's world to name things, to give definition. He indeed has free choice. Yet free choice is an illusion for many Mamet characters based on a certain notion of identity quite specific to American patriarchy. What passes as free choice is ideologically shaped. The dictates of the impersonal masculine ethos and its social conventions are repeatedly embraced by Mamet's men. Despite voicing his freedom from social constraint, therefore, a Mamet character often contradicts that freedom by reengaging stereotypical action: while he may say one (potentially liberating) remark, he will usually do what he has always done. In this way, Roma represents himself as one who is authorized to name things anew. However, he does nothing of the kind.

Certainly the gender privilege of naming is not lost on Mamet's salesman. Each man, Roma implies, has power over the Other to name the value of life's experiences and expenditures. In fact, it is a man's duty, Roma intimates, to take it upon himself to exercise that power. At no point does the salesman underestimate the importance of inflating his lead's ego with the rhetoric of masculine privilege. He speaks soulfully and hyperbolically to his listener. Bigsby's pointed assessment about Roma's verbal seduction of Lingk is, in fact, an accurate description of all Mamet's salesmen—as well as most American male characters—who sustain social dialogue: "What masquerades as intimacy is in fact the betrayal of intimacy, confidence, trust, the shared experience implied by language" (119). To this end, the final irony of their interaction occurs when the two men reconnect in act 2, as Roma realizes that he must rescue his fellow man from the real influence of the Other: he must do battle with Lingk's wife, one of *Glengarry*'s absent women, in order to win back his weakening, vacillating customer.

Act 2 is set in Williamson's ransacked real estate office. Despite its burgled setting, this act nonetheless manifests a common characteristic of many all-male institutional plays: a hierarchy of professional authority exists at any one time in the dramatic space. As in other office plays, bosses interact with employees, seasoned employees counsel younger employees, and employees court clients. Added to the setting, however, is Baylen, a police detective, whose appearance overrides the authority of both boss and workers. Baylen thrusts patriarchal law into the office space as his invested legal authority informs both the boundaries (that is, the constraints) and the freedoms that operate on the characters' immediate interaction. His physical presence or absence from a conversation profoundly influences what other men do and do not say to one another.

Amid this hierarchy of male authority, Mamet's men nonetheless exercise a range of verbal gymnastics within the dynamic of social dialogue. Act 2 is characterized by sustained reliance upon social dialogue, with two unique features of that dialogue— metatheatrical and metalinguistic—occurring midact. The characters' persistent engagement of social dialogue is an unusual quality in an office play, since most men in such settings eventually embrace personal dialogue as a response to the hierarchy of authority. What distinguishes *Glengarry* from most office plays, however, is the fact that the authority figures of Williamson and Baylen are mainly in an unseen room that adjoins the dramatic space in which the play's action develops.

When Moss leaves Baylen's interrogation room to join his colleagues in the main office space, the men's communication is anxious and resistant to personal interaction. Not one wants to speak truthfully. Each valiantly strives to protect himself from exposure, as each has something to hide from at least one of the remaining fellows: Levene knows he robbed the office; Moss knows he masterminded the robbery and secured Levene's help; Roma knows he wants a percentage of Levene's commissions; and Williamson knows that he left Lingk's contract on his desk. Confident in his private knowledge when among his co-workers, each man feels extremely powerful—particularly as he anticipates his ability to survive the immediate crisis in a personally satisfying manner. Both Levene and Moss believe that their robbery is a success; Roma trusts that he can bribe his boss when need be; and Williamson recognizes that by lying, he can generally get what information he needs from the others to guarantee his own authority. Each man presumes that he can exercise a power play over the other, that he can secure his domination over all others—if his secrets remain private. Very simply, each strives to keep the dialogue social and not personal.

Just as someone stole the leads from the office in order to become more powerful, so every character tries to "steal," to acquire, information from the other men. Characters aim to rob otherwise guarded knowledge from their co-workers, not only to secure more power over their colleagues, but to reorder the chaos represented by the ransacked office. Language is the men's weapon of choice; social dialogue, their ammunition. Yet Mamet's men fail to recognize fully the pervasive impact of the most influential component of their social dialogue: the power of a masculine ethos that insists on the presence of hierarchical authority. All men cannot be all-powerful in a male-male context. In the absence of women, therefore, some men among men necessarily become "other," while some do not. Men who experience the loss of power automatically become objects. Here, within the realm of social dialogue, a man's identification as "other," as one who is differently masculine, occurs because he appears vulnerable, insubstantial, and ineffectual: in effect, he is relatively powerless in a world where male power is all.

One way in which "the Machine" Levene distinguishes himself from "other" men (and thereby hopes to secure power over them) is through metatheatrics. In a mock performative voice, Levene plays out before some of his office mates the conversation of his property sale to the Nyborgs. Through his performance he illustrates the good "*old* ways" of selling real estate (72). He demonstrates the language skills and techniques that his protégé, Roma, undoubtedly called upon during his hard sell to Lingk in act 1. Levene's business talk, his social dialogue, materializes through language, and not just action, the philosophy of "always be closing." Through aggressive association between the values of the masculine ethos and the Nyborg's presumed desire for ownership, Levene uses language to manipulate his leads. "Believe in your*self*" (67), Levene tells Bruce and Harriett, as he encourages them to grab his real estate offer as a real opportunity for personal empowerment. According to Levene, there is no reason for any Nyborg who lives in a prosperous land driven by traditional male values to believe that "this one has so-and-so, and I have nothing" (68). "What we have to do is *admit* to ourself that we see that opportunity," Levene coaxes, "and *take* it" (72).

Levene's enactment of the couple's purchase, which is based essentially in social dialogue, occurs simultaneously with Moss's hard-nosed social dialogue about the realities of business—the loss of jobs for those who fail to top Levene's apparent success. Mamet creates dramatic tension between the two speakers' distinct uses of this level of interaction: Levene's self-centered metatheatricality (which calls for role-playing) and Moss's attempts at a regular conversation that reject Levene's "fucking war stories" (67). On the narrative level, tension surfaces between Levene's mock-heroic story of successful selling and Moss's woes of failure at selling. On the level of conversational dynamics, Levene relies upon a variation of a stream-of-conscious monologue and playacting, while Moss encourages realized, interactive conversation (albeit prompted by his display of anger and anxiety).

It is ironic, however, that just as Levene assumes a character in his imaginary scenario with the Nyborgs, so Moss is possibly also role-playing in the "real" interaction with his colleagues. One cannot trust that Moss's angry words are justified; he is revealed later on, after all, to be the instigator of the robbery. Whether engaged in metatheatrical or actual social dialogue, therefore, Mamet's men play at talking. The only persistent connection among the men is their perpetual language usage—the fact that they continue to activate social dialogue with one another while in the same space. They move from coded languages decipherable to those within the (business) community (act 1) to self-absorbed diatribes constructed to obscure the truth (act 2).

Levene's inflated ego is deflated by Williamson's observation that a sale to the Nyborgs, who turn out to be perennial customers, may not materialize. Williamson's remark challenges Levene's skill and judgment as a salesman, as well as questions his capabilities, his credibility as a Man. But the Machine will not be derailed, as he equates his rejuvenated success with his male prowess: "A man's his job," he tells his younger boss, "and you're *fucked* at yours. . . . You don't have the *balls*" (75–76). Levene relies upon his track record as a salesman as the primary indicator of his manhood. He reminds Williamson that one's history changes one's fortunes of the future. To Levene, his identity, which was shaped by the "old ways" (72), the tried-and-true principles of the masculine ethos, has never really lost its potency, its ability to resurrect. "[T]hings can *change*," he tells his boss. "This is where you fuck *up* because this is something you don't *know*. You can't look down the *road*. And see what's *coming*. . . . It might be someone *new*. . . . And you can't look *back*. 'Cause you don't know *history*" (76). Levene's notion of change focuses only on the shift that can impact on a man's success at business—a shift that reveals the amount of power a man wields. It has nothing to do with a transformation in an individual's attitude or behavior toward self-improvement. Furthermore, while social privilege may certainly give immediate gratification to men as it marginalizes women and "other" males, it is, in fact, a cultural system that thrives on the bankruptcy of men's self-identification.

What Levene does not know is that Williamson represents a new generation of men not so unlike his own. While they may refuse to link success and survival with any historical, "factual" personal achievements, they rely upon the power of stable gender codings, the culture's historically grounded positioning of their social privileges as males. Williamson, like many men before him, believes that he has the right to activate any powers to which he has access. He considers this act his privilege as a man within American society. Such efforts of his do not require the achievement of any desired end; rather, the end and the means are one and the same: his goal is the sheer execution of male power.

The key scene in act 2 occurs after Williamson leaves the conversation with his employees to return to the interrogation room. Alone in the outer office, Levene and Roma are interrupted unexpectedly by Lingk. Anticipating that any conversation with Lingk may spell trouble for the closure of their real estate deal, Roma instantly creates another metatheatrical scenario to divert attention. The speed and precision with which Roma directs his partner Levene into action clearly indicates that these guys are old pros at playacting their way out of personal confrontations: "You're a client. I just sold you five waterfront Glengarry Farms," Roma hastily instructs Levene. "I rub my head, throw me the cue Kenilworth'" (78). Roma and Levene know only too well how to read the signs of potential conflict within their business; Lingk, indeed, has come to talk to Roma about his backing out of the sale.

The social dialogue in this scene is complex. The three men converse on topics supported by the thematic of the masculine ethos and myths, while assuming a variety of speaking positions not necessarily representative of their own voices. Each man takes on a voice that is, in effect, outside of himself. In so doing, each assumes that he can get what he wants only by using a voice other than his own, one not inside himself. Roma and Levene speak from their metatheatrical positions as, respectively, wheeling-and-dealing salesman and wealthy, satisfied customer. Lingk, on the other hand, sporadically interrupts them through metalinguistic intrusions: "I've got to talk with you" (78, 81). Once the very nervous, self-conscious Lingk does talk, he only reports on his wife's legal efforts to back out of the deal. Much is then made between Lingk and Roma about when they will talk about her actions. Eventually, Lingk can assert his presence before the domineering Roma only by adopting his wife's voice, the authority of the absent woman. "It's not me, it's my wife," Lingk claims. "She wants her money back. . . . She told me 'right now.' . . . She told me I *have* to. . . . I can't negotiate" (89–91). The male-cast play often dramatizes the absent woman's power by presenting her transformation into, or her "becoming," the voice of a present male who struggles to assert his own personal voice. This is certainly one way in which "the gender confusion" of Mamet's men, "while not complicated by the physical presence of women," as McDonough points out, "is constantly evoked in language" (204).

The presence of Jinny's voice in Lingk's dialogue disrupts the fictional dialogue of the other men. It is the only authentic voice to be heard; the men, including Lingk (if using his own voice), wish only to obscure the truth. The absent woman's words, however, penetrate the social dialogue and, in effect, demand to be heard, redirecting the conversation away from Roma and Levene's fantastic performance. Yet while Jinny's opinions are spoken by her husband, another new, dynamic topic is added to the men's discourse coherence: the absent woman, herself. She inserts her presence into the men's dialogue, therefore, not only through a character's reiteration of her words but also through the characters' discussion of her role. In *Glengarry,* the topic of the absent woman diminishes the metatheatrical and metalinguistic dimension of the men's social dialogue. Roma knows that he must defeat the power of the absent woman if he is to win over Lingk. As Hersh Zeifman observes, Jinny is the "'missing link' whose values could destroy Roma's very existence" (132). Predictably, manly Roma instructs the now wavering Lingk: "That's just something she 'said.' We don't have to do that" (90). "Jim, anything you *want,* you *want* it, you *have* it. You understand? This is *me,*" the role-playing Roma confides, as he positions himself as someone from the *"outside"* who, through "talk" (91), can put Lingk in touch with the powers of the masculine ethos—those collective, mythic powers that can finally subordinate the power of the internalized absent woman.

Another provocative and complicated level of social dialogue also disrupts the communication when Aaronow returns to the main office after being interrogated by Baylen.[4] "No one should talk to a man that way. How are you *talking* to me" (87), the anxious, paranoid salesman pleads after his session with the police. With no knowledge of the situation he is walking into, Aaronow tries to establish actual conversation. He is desperate to create a dialogue that respects how he imagines men are supposed to talk, a dialogue in which each man, because he is a man, has access to power, to some integrity and courtesy through talk. Aaronow's efforts, however, serve only to comment on the failures of the metatheatrical dialogue between Roma and Lingk, which Williamson loosely calls *"business"* (88). Aaronow unknowingly mimics Lingk in the Roma-Levene-Lingk interaction as he inquires, "Is anybody listening to me . . . ?" (87). Aaronow, like Lingk, struggles to be heard among men as well as to be respected as a man among men. But he fails to engage the other men in either social dialogue or, what he most desires, personal dialogue. The salesman departs for the restaurant, frustrated and humiliated.

Aaronow, using his own voice, fails to capture the attention of his colleagues, and Lingk secures their concentration only when he speaks in the voice of the absent woman. In telling Roma that he cannot negotiate any deal, Lingk moves their dialogue back to a metalinguistic level. Lingk's response to the demanding Roma—"I don't have the *power*" (92)—is an astounding admission for a (white) male character to make. He means that he does not have the power to negotiate the real estate deal, but he reveals a more engrossing, powerless state that many characters experience in the male-cast canon but are afraid to articulate. Male characters are repeatedly presented as not trusting one another and therefore refusing to be vulnerable and truthful in one another's company.

Men feel powerless to create such moments of truth because in doing so they lose the power to control the listener's response to their openness. Partially for these reasons, Lingk chooses to hide behind the words of his wife rather than to speak personally to Roma. Lingk consciously resists Roma's efforts to get closer to him through conversation. Although Lingk is clearly drawn to the male bonding that Roma seductively offers him, he is driven by the more familiar demands of the absent woman. But Roma's loyalty to Lingk as a trusted listener is specious at best. "I can't talk to you, *you* met my wife," Lingk asserts (92), as he consciously pits a man's Man, Roma, against the absent woman, Jinny. Lingk essentially steps outside the battle as he lets these two powerful figures battle over the definition of his manhood—as well as over the possession of his money.

True to male characters throughout the male-cast canon who want to break down other men's conversational barriers, Roma offers several times to take Lingk out for a drink. Lingk responds, "She told me not to talk to you" (93). Getting nowhere with the customer, who is now the full-blown Jinny surrogate, Roma tries to appeal to Lingk's ego through another self-empowering monologue that recalls his original sales pitch to Lingk in act 1. "Let's talk about *you*," Roma contends, "Your life is your own. You have a contract with your wife. You have certain things you do jointly . . . and there are *other* things. . . . This is your life." Once again, Roma appeals to the powers of the masculine ethos, male privilege, and male bonding and naming as a means by which Lingk can overcome the influence of the Other. Roma believes that by appealing to Lingk's sense of manhood, appearing to bond with him in this battle against the Other, he can sell real estate. In a blatant violation of human intimacy, Roma adopts a pseudotherapeutic voice to exploit Lingk's personal life. His motives for encouraging Lingk's personal dialogue are entirely self-serving. Like Levene, Roma has no scruples when it comes to "selling something they don't even *want*" (77). A salesman, after all, must "always be closing." Roma has almost succeeded in getting Lingk to go for that crucial drink when Williamson remarks that Lingk's check has already been cashed. This admission, to Lingk, means two things: he has failed to meet his wife's demands and Roma has lied to him by saying that Lingk had time to cancel the deal and the check.

His loyalties torn between the omnipotent figures in his life, Jinny and Roma, Lingk makes a hasty exit from the real estate office. "Oh, Christ . . . Oh Christ. I know I've let you down," Lingk tells Roma. "I'm sorry. For . . . Forgive . . . for . . . I don't know anymore. *(Pause.)* Forgive me" (95). Lingk's final words recall the closing moments in Mamet's *Edmond* as well as Albee's *The Zoo Story* in their metaphysical evocations. Unlike Albee's Jerry, who finds some connection with Peter by the end of their tragic interaction, Lingk feels no lasting "link" with Roma. Lingk has no awareness of powers within himself that can give him direction, insight, and a sense of individualization. He repeatedly turns to those outside of himself to define himself, both externally and internally. In confessing to Roma that he has let him down, Lingk reveals his delusion that Roma actually cares personally for him; conversely, it reveals Roma's success at playacting. But Lingk is also admitting that he has failed to live up to the expectations of a "real" man within the male power structure. He has let down the male ethos, neither enacting nor professing his power over the Other. For all intents and purposes, Lingk is emasculated by Jinny (or so he thinks), prompting him to seek out Roma's camaraderie.

In the final scene of act 2, the men return to social dialogue as actual, realistic conversation. The code of their linguistic interaction, determined by the masculine ethos, is rendered in familiar terms and without roleplaying. In no uncertain words, Roma and Levene chide Williamson for contradicting Roma's story to Lingk. "Whoever told you you could work with *men?*" (96), Roma bitterly challenges his boss. Williamson is guilty of breaking the vital code of businessmen's ethics—that of which the "old stuff" is made: "A man who's your 'partner' *depends* on you. . . . You have to go *with* him and *for* him . . . or you're a shit, you're *shit,* you can't exist alone" (98). The credo for any man, according to the salesmen, is to accept that he is in a partnership with other (straight) men, a relationship that may require him to lie about, to be silent about, but most certainly to agree about anything that will help maintain their power position in the "business" of living in America. This strategy has nothing to do with the solidification of self-disclosing, personal relationships. It is purely a survival tactic, based upon a bonding of male ideology, which ensures men's economic power.

But it is Roma who is most cruel as he angrily releases a litany of abusive epithets that clearly align Williamson with the "other," those marginalized in American society over whom the (white) straight male wields cultural power. For breaking the male code, Williamson is a "fucking shit," "asshole," and "idiot"—all of which warrant his being named a "stupid fucking cunt," a "fairy," and a "fucking child" (96, 97). To align him with women, homosexuals, and children is, according to Roma, the worst humiliation for a (white) male. If a man is not working *for* men, then he must necessarily be working *against* them, siding with the Other.[5] Roma reminds Levene that their survival—as businessmen and implicitly as white men—is in jeopardy: "We are members of a dying breed. That's . . . that's . . . that's why we have to stick together" (105).

In the end, however, the "child" solves the mystery of the office robbery. During his tirade against Williamson, Levene reveals his knowledge of Williamson's trick on Roma—that Lingk's contract was not submitted. The boss notes that Levene could know this detail only by having been in his office the previous evening. Levene is exposed as the robber; he hangs himself with his own words. In Mamet's world of men, thieves and salesmen are one and the same. They are all perpetrators of the corrupted American frontier ethic of exploitation in the name of economic gain. And right up to the end, Levene hopes to bribe Williamson not to turn him in to the police. As with his previous efforts, Levene knows that he can succeed with Williamson only if the ante is high enough; his only recourse is to draw from his recent sale to the Nyborgs. This time, however, the boss humiliates his employee by pointing out that Levene is still a loser: the Nyborgs are "insane," their checks are worthless. Like the old system of which he used to be an integral part, Levene is broken down, corrupt, obsolete, and pathetic.

Several new faces on the old system, nonetheless, appear to be existing without diminished authority at the conclusion of *Glengarry Glen Ross*. Collectively, as the recast voice of the masculine ethos in "a world of men" (105), they represent the first of two conflicting, though surviving, ideologies in the play. This male voice is manifested differently, however, in the dialogue and presence of three characters: Roma, Williamson, and Baylen. Their voices diverge in respect to their position on patriarchal law; they converge in their attitudes toward the masculine ethos.

Embodying a classic (white) everyman, Roma presumes that the patriarchal system should bend to his immediate needs. This, he believes, is his rightful privilege as a male. While he unabashedly lives outside the law (consider his final directive to Williamson that he expects to claim half of Levene's commissions [107]), Roma still commits himself to the masculine ethos and its myths of masculine power. The boss also lives inside masculine privilege but outside legal law. He, too, likes to play with power. But unlike Roma, Williamson has the entitlement of position to protect his authority. Both men survive in Mamet's impersonal world because each is committed to and skilled at manipulating the powers of the masculine ethos. Each knows how to exploit other men in order not to become one of the "other" men.

As a police detective, Baylen represents the uncorrupted authority of patriarchal law. Unlike Roma and Williamson, Baylen lives inside the law and inside the masculine ethos. This combination assures him privilege, security, and power, his for keeping in the American system. His presence affirms that a secular order, one defined in patriarchal terms, exists to dispel chaos. Yet, only one other voice in the play completely embraces the legal law that Baylen courts—and it is not another male.

The voice of Jinny Lingk, the absent woman, is the second distinct ideology to survive in *Glengarry*. Although she has a different relationship to patriarchal law than Baylen, she relies upon that law to protect her rights: she contacts the district attorney's office for protection in her case against Roma. In this instance, Jinny lives inside the patriarchal law and it empowers her. However, Jinny obviously lives outside the male ethos. She does not have access to the same cultural privileges that men enjoy in the patriarchy. But this social imbalance of power does not weaken Jinny when confronted with the male ego. Through her husband's mouth, Jinny challenges the wisdom, the integrity, and the actual and the mythic value of the masculine ethos. She insists that her subject position be heard, or as David Worster notes, she "possesses the power to negotiate" (387). In denying Roma all that he wants, including conversation with Lingk, Jinny's voice disempowers the classic everyman. She effectively resists the power play of the masculine ethos by turning its own premises and authority against itself. By simply saying no to Roma through Lingk, she gives voice—and power—to all "others" whom Roma and fellow advocates of the masculine ethos have dominated and silenced.

As these two surviving, clashing voices move toward the center of Mamet's text, the spectator's last sight is Aaronow, sitting at his desk, alone in the destroyed real estate office. His final admission is filled with raw truth: "Oh, God, I hate this job" (108). His words signal the death of the salesman, capturing the defeated man's pathetic awareness that things in life should be better than they are. As Jack Barbera notes about Mamet's plays, "Notions of the American way—democracy and free enterprise—become corrupted when they enter the look-out-for-number-one rationalizations of crooks and unethical businessmen" (275). Aaronow struggles to understand the all-pervasive corruption in *Glengarry Glen Ross,* a "moral play," according to Benedict Nightingale, "not a moralizing one" (1984, 5). The play "seeks to 'tell the truth' about the usually invisible violence men inflict on themselves and each other as they grab for gold."

In Mamet's dramatic worlds, characters are challenged to take moral responsibility for men's corruption. Aaronow seems to know that someone needs to create order out of the chaos. Matthew Roudané suggests the importance of Aaronow's "semblance of moral seriousness" (44). Mamet himself comments,

> Aaronow has some degree of conscience, some awareness; he's troubled. Corruption troubles him. The question he's troubled by is whether his inability to succeed in the society in which he's placed is a defect—that is, is he manly or sharp enough?—or if it's, in effect, a positive attribute, which is to say that his conscience prohibits him. So Aaronow is left between these two things and he's incapable of choosing. This dilemma is, I think, what many of us are facing in this country right now. (1986, 75)

Aaronow knows that in a "world of men" it simply is not enough for law enforcement to police the public's actions. Such authority, according to Aaronow, does not always know the proper way "to talk . . . to a working man" (88). But Aaronow has no idea how to use his gender privilege to his advantage; he has no sense as to how, when, or where to use this culturally coded power to help to understand it any better. On the other hand, he has no idea of the power that he can unleash through his freedom of choice: he can choose to live—to speak—as a differently masculine man outside the definitions of the masculine ethos.[6] Like Jinny Lingk, Aaronow is aware that life should be better for those who choose not to break the law. But unlike the absent woman, Aaronow cannot envision a new kind of power, which is flourishing within his grasp, if he only explores his profound discontent with the values of the masculine ethos. Such a vision would necessarily signal the dismantlement of the gender-coded system, and Aaronow fails to envision the potential powers of the "other." His lack of imagination appears to "always be closing" his mind and heart. He also has no voice of an absent woman to listen to; he has no idea of the powers of individualization that reside in her voice. As McDonough astutely argues, Mamet's men resist the "discovery of new identities that would release them from a stance which is antagonist to the female without as well as to the feminine within them" (205). Mamet's own experience complements McDonough's vision: "Men *generally* expect more of women than we do of ourselves. We feel, based on constant evidence, that women are better, stronger, more truthful, than men. You can call this sexism, or reverse sexism, or whatever you wish, but it is my experience" (1989b, 24).

Despite his inability to become a different kind of subject, Aaronow resists immersion in the institution, in the corrupted manifestations of the masculine ethos. The hapless salesman signals some hope for personal change simply in his passionate urge to understand what is going on around him and thereby to understand his deeper rage. In *Glengarry,* Mamet dramatizes the institutional oppression generated by social constructions of gender. He masterfully displays through Aaronow an American man's often contradictory struggle to realize and to claim his individuality among men. This struggle exists for all men who, consciously or unconsciously, yearn for the authenticity of self-identity. All male characters confront the overwhelming context of the American masculine ethos and its male mythologies on their journey to individualization and self-identity. Yes, *Glengarry* is an indictment of the horrors of capitalism and corrupt business. But men among themselves sustain these structures. The degree to which men are victims and victimizers, as dramatized by Mamet, is debatable. Less debatable is the poignancy of his morality play about the lives of the many men in whom human feeling is absent.

NOTES

1. For recent exceptions to this critical trend see the analyses of *Glengarry* by Carla McDonough; David Worster; Hersh Zeifman. While providing an otherwise very useful analysis of *Glengarry* and *American Buffalo,* Jeanette Malkin, by shadowing the trend, neglects to make explicit the connection among the gender features of her own observations: The social ethos she cites operating in the plays is a masculine ethos; the debased verbal existence is men's verbal interaction; the world of business manipulation is a "male" world; and the distortion of friendship occurs in male friendship. Like many critics, Malkin chooses not to draw attention to the feature of gender that, perhaps, most significantly determines the plays' action and the characters' dialogue: *Glengarry* and *American Buffalo* focus only on men among themselves.

2. See Zeifman for a gendered reading of "Always be closing" (132). Although Zeifman rightly cites the significance of Jinny Lingk to the action in *Glengarry,* he underestimates the profound, practical influence that absent women in both *Glengarry* and *American Buffalo* have upon onstage dialogue and actions, as well as the presence of the feminine in some men's words and deeds. The absent woman, therefore, has more than "metaphorical import" (133) in Mamet's all-male setting. Analysis of discourse coherence is one method that reveals the absent woman's considerable impact on the plays' form and content.

3. Moss's response to Aaronow is, according to Anne Dean, "the ultimate betrayal of the trust implied in ordinary conversation; Aaronow is designated as a criminal simply because he 'listened'" (201).

4. This is comparable to the moment in act 2, previously discussed, when Moss, who desires actual conversation, interrupts Levene's performance.

5. This sexist, homophobic, ageist attitude is not unlike the racist, sexist, and homophobic stance of the bigoted Coach in Jason Miller's *That Championship Season.* Coach, the quintessential white extremist, warns his former team of white basketball players to beware of "niggers," "kikes," "Jews," "queers," "commies," and "bitches." "We are the country, boys, never forget that, never. . . . But no dissension.

We stick together" (18). See also Worster's recent, insightful comments on Roma's "pejoratives" (389); the critic's remarks were published after *Act Like a Man,* from which this essay is a revised reprint, had already gone to press.

6. For this reason, Worster's identification of Aaronow's silence as a "kind of power" (385–86) is arguable if the action (and the play) is positioned within the rigidly coded semiotic system of male-cast plays. At the very least, Worster's observation is paradoxical, finally, since the voiceless salesman (that is, one without authority) neither disrupts the gender-coded actions of his colleagues nor ruptures the semiotic of maleness that controls the construction of Mamet's dialogue. Aaronow's silence neither redirects nor imagines differently the communication dynamics between men. Rather, it is a coded feature of character behavior in male-cast plays based upon established speaker-listener dynamics, reflected here in Aaronow's previous "roles" in talk exchanges. His silence (which, in effect, is Mamet's silence), is a confirmation of Aaronow's relative powerlessness when he is among men. If his silence, as Worster suggests, is "action and power" (and to/for whom?), it goes unnoticed for good reasons: Aaronow exists in a heavily coded semiotic world of maleness where "other" male voices are, out of necessity, inactive (that is, silent) and powerless.

BIBLIOGRAPHY

Barbera, Jack V. "Ethical Perversity in America: Some Observations on David Mamet's *American Buffalo.*" *Modern Drama* 24, no. 3 (1981):270–75.

Beauvoir, Simone de. *The Second Sex.* Trans. and ed. H.M. Parshley, Gallimard, 1949. Rpt. New York: Knopf, 1953.

Bigsby, Christopher W. E. *David Mamet.* New York: Methuen, 1985.

Dean, Anne. *David Mamet: Language as Dramatic Action.* Rutherford, N.J.: Fairleigh Dickinson University Press, 1990.

Demastes, William. *Beyond Naturalism: A New Realism in American Theatre.* Westport, Conn.: Greenwood Press, 1988.

Elam, Keir. *The Semiotics of Theatre and Drama.* New York: Methuen, 1980.

Freedman, Samuel. "The Gritty Eloquence of David Mamet." *New York Times Magazine,* 21 April 1985, 32.

Geis, Deborah. "David Mamet and the Metadramatic Tradition: Seeing 'The Trick from the Back.'" In *David Mamet: A Casebook,* ed. Leslie Kane, 49–68. New York: Garland, 1992.

Grice, H. P. "Logic and Conversation." In *Speech Acts,* ed. Peter Cole and Jerry L. Morgan, 41–58. Vol. 3 of *Syntax and Semantics,* ed. John P. Kimball. New York: Academic, 1975.

Leahey, Mimi. "The American Dream Gone Bad." *Otherstages,* 4 November 1982, 3.

McDonough, Carla. "Every Fear Hides a Wish: Unstable Masculinity in Mamet's Drama." *Theatre Journal* 44, no. 2 (1992): 195–205.

Malkin, Jeanette R. *Verbal Violence in Contemporary Drama: From Handke to Shepard.* New York: Cambridge University Press, 1992.

Mamet, David. *Glengarry Glen Ross.* New York: Grove Press, 1984.

———. Interview by Matthew C. Roudané. *Studies in American Drama, 1945–Present* 1 (1986): 73–81.

———. Interview by Henry I. Schvey. "Celebrating the Capacity for Self-Knowledge." *New Theatre Quarterly* 4, no. 13 (1988):89–96.

———. "In the Company of Men." In *Some Freaks,* 85–91. New York: Viking Press, 1989a.

———. "Women." In *Some Freaks,* 21–26 (1989b).

Miller, Jason. *That Championship Season.* New York: Dramatists Play Service, 1972.

Nightingale, Benedict. "Is Mamet the Bard of Modern Immorality?" *New York Times,* 1 April 1984, sec. H, 5.

Novick, Julius. "Mamet." *Village Voice,* 3 April 1984, 89.

Rich, Frank. Review of *Glengarry Glen Ross* by David Mamet. *New York Times*, 26 March 1984, sec. C, 3.

Roudané, Matthew C. 1986. "Public Issues, Private Tensions: David Mamet's *Glengarry Glen Ross*." *South Carolina Review* 19, no. 1 (1986):35–47.

Savran, David. *In Their Own Words: Contemporary American Playwrights*. New York: Theatre Communications Group, 1988.

Vorlicky, Robert. *Act Like a Man: Challenging Masculinities in American Drama*. Ann Arbor: University of Michigan Press, 1995.

Worster, David. "How to Do Things with Salesmen: David Mamet's Speech-Act Play." *Modern Drama* 37, no. 3 (1994):375–90.

Zeifman, Hersh. "Phallus in Wonderland: Machismo and Business in David Mamet's *American Buffalo* and *Glengarry Glen Ross*." In *David Mamet: A Casebook*, ed. Leslie Kane, 123–35. New York: Garland, 1992.

6 LEVENE'S DAUGHTER

POSITIONING THE FEMALE IN GLENGARRY GLEN ROSS

Dorothy H. Jacobs

Glengarry Glen Ross opens with Shelly Levene trying to talk the sales manager, Williamson, into giving him the good leads to real estate customers. Near the conclusion of the play Levene is again trying to convince Williamson to do what Levene needs, to be spared from arrest for stealing the very leads he coveted in act 1. Within these parallel scenes of persuasion, Levene exercises his abilities at harangue, self-aggrandizement, insult, and bribery confidently but ineffectively. A curious refrain in his performance is a reference to a female relative outside the scene set in the Chinese restaurant and, later, in the trashed office. Both times he begins but says nothing further than "John: my *daughter* . . ."[1] Placed near the end of Levene's dialogues with Williamson and surprising in its personal reference, the mention has unusual weight. Yet the dialogue gives no further indication of its significance. Indeed, Williamson's immediate responses—first, "I can't do it, Shelly," and second, characteristically, "Fuck you,"—cut off any possibility of elaboration.

With its sentimental expansion upon the play and its Lomanizing of Levene, the 1992 movie places the daughter in a hospital, her photograph on his desk, and the pathos thick in the celluloid. "Shtick Shifts," Michael Sragow's insightful review of that movie, likewise categorizes Hollywood's reach for "some humanity" in the Glengarry world of "stylized hard guys" as unconvincing, inappropriate, and false.[2] The cinematic failure to maintain the integrity of the play damages not only the consistency of the original version but also the innovative and suggestive quality of Levene's remark. Therefore I shall concentrate my argument upon the 1983 precursor, the staged *Glengarry Glen Ross*.

Without the movie's sentimental padding, Levene's evocation of an off-stage female is consistent with the masculine ideology propounded in this as well as in Mamet's other works. Reinforcing the phallocentricity of this world is the language of contempt, hatred, and dehumanization that is insistently allied to matching attitudes toward women. So pervasive are the insults based upon obscene renderings of essentially female body parts that reference to a daughter sounds and is curiously out of place. It hints of another world, a familial relationship beyond the place of business, an existence whose voice is as silent as the ellipsis that follows mention of her. So far as the dialogue goes, there is every reason to question Levene's bringing her into the arguments with Williamson. If he is seeking sympathy, why so? Should she be a consideration in the deliberations with the office manager? The man in charge of the leads thinks not. Given the fabled skill of "Shelly, the Machine, Levene" isn't it likely that he is simply using another sales approach, one more method from his word hoard? Isn't it he, not the daughter, who is in desperate need? Levene may be running out of linguistic resources. Furthermore, Levene, like a professional actor, slides easily into any role, any stance. Why, then, should we entrust any statement of his with veracity? At an extreme of skepticism, an attitude certainly fostered by the play, we might even question the existence of a daughter at all, since she so fleetingly exists merely in the faltering negotiations. As an anomaly in the dialogue, this suggestion of a daughter haunts the play, for it calls up the possibility of a feminine world distant from and at odds with the hustle for leads and the frank materiality of the Cadillac.

Glengarry Glen Ross includes references to other females. Although they all remain off-stage, each has a defining function within the ideology of the all-male cast. Least important referentially are the nurses on the prime list, but even they represent for the salesmen the most promising marks. Moss's estimate of Jerry Graff's success depends upon Graff's list of "four, five thousand nurses, and he's going wild . . ."(14–15). Because the leads are so indicative of success, overhead, Moss claims, shrinks to insignificance: "A telephone, some broad to say 'Good morning,' nothing . . . nothing . . ."(15). To Aaronow, Moss's estimate of office expenses is too simple, but there is no argument about the salability of nurses nor any rift in the contempt for a female's job as receptionist. "Some broad" is a nameless functionary, part of the "nothing" that is insignificant to the men who sell real estate.

Women receive more intimate but just as dismissive references in those existential monologues of Roma's that initiate his engagement with James Lingk. "You cheated on your wife . . . ? You did it, live with it. (Pause.) You fuck little girls, so be it." Then, as though in reverie, Roma summons up the servicing female: "Some broads, forearms on your neck, something her eyes did. . . . the next day she brought me café au lait. She gives me a cigarette, my balls feel like concrete"(24). Roma's reminiscence of "some broads" insinuates Lingk into a shared ideology of *Penthouse* sex, but the terminology for women is exactly the same when Moss refers to despised Indians: "Their broads all look like they just got fucked with a dead *cat* . . ."(12). Casual as these comments are, they yet indicate a common language of degradation of women. Categories for them are fixed, distancing, and undifferentiating. Roma's "she" is one of "some broads," like Indian wives and secretaries. Even "little girls" are just a segment in the sexual catalogue. None of these females have names or identities or claims to any other representation than the generalizations voiced by the salesmen of *Glengarry Glen Ross.*

Coming in for closer articulation, though, are two females who figure in the sales game. Wives and co-signers of contracts, Harriett Nyborg and Jinny Lingk achieve namehood. Supposedly both wives have been sold, along with their husbands, parcels of real estate, and both prove to be only temporarily contracted. While each situation has its individual character, both reinforce the theme introduced at the very beginning of the play: the wife as spoiler of the deal. During the initial dialogue between Williamson and Levene the problem of a "close" that stays closed immediately surfaces. Williamson accuses Levene of not closing, but Levene defends himself by insisting "I *closed* the cocksucker. His *'ex,'* John, his *'ex,'* I didn't know he was married . . . he, the *judge* invalidated the . . ."(3). Thus the play immediately establishes the cause or blame for a failed sale: the unknown female, the "ex," the wife at one remove but still the spoiler. Shelly Levene implies that the deal would have remained closed were it not for the unseen "ex." Such, too, is the predicament in Roma's sale to James and Jinny Lingk, for James disavows Jinny's determination to cancel the sale. An understanding between men is undermined by wives past or present. Like an earlier mythic woman, the "ex" and Mrs. Lingk deprive their partners of eight units of Mountain View or their equivalent. More significantly, the salesmen are cheated out of the paradise of being on the Cadillac board. Each wife has a spokesman; Mrs. Lingk has her hesitant and apologetic husband, but Mrs. Nyborg has that inspired storyteller, Shelly Levene.

Mood, tone, and innuendo are essential elements in Levene's recounting of his "eighty-two fucking grand" (36) sale. Starting with the usual expletive has particular pertinence here, for what Levene relates to Roma is a tale of seduction. Anne Dean, in her study of Mamet's language, refers a few times to Levene's "almost orgasmic evocation of a great sale," his "almost sexual excitement as he details the moment when his clients signed," and the "climax that seems almost orgasmic."[3] Dean echoes the "almost" in the actor Jack Shepherd's recollection of Mamet talking about the "almost sexual quality to the quest for selling."[4] Following a quotation of Levene's climactic description, Guido Almansi is more definite than Dean: "What a great erotic scene. . . . This is the intensity of coition: Levene has buggered his customers."[5] From the same scene Hersh Zeifman has found a suggestion in the language of "both an epic battle and, in its compulsively orgasmic rhythm, a sexual conquest."[6] Corroborating the linkage of warfare and sexuality is Moss's put-down to Levene's accomplishment: "I don't want to hear your fucking war stories . . ."(38). This combination of belligerence and sexuality has, in Moss's voice, a particularly vicious tonality, but it shares the ideology that informs the entire drama. The female should be securely placed at home, preferably in the kitchen, precisely where Levene positions Harriett Nyborg.

In his excitement as he enters the sales office, Levene gives out specific information on the contract, including the names of Bruce and Harriett Nyborg. As her name authenticates the contract, so does it grant her the distinction of a name, although it is one that Aaronow recollects disparagingly. His cautionary remark, "Fuck. I had them on River Glen" (36), goes unacknowledged as Levene concentrates on the shambles around him. That Levene ignores the warning is evidence of the insistence upon winning that both drives and deludes the salesmen. Later Levene will learn from Williamson that, far from being "had," the Nyborgs regularly have salesmen for their own purposes. But the sexual innuendo of "had" is too ordinary in their parlance for Levene to interrupt the staging of his return to glory amid the ruins. Actually, his questions about the break-in are, in themselves, an act. Thus his story of the Nyborg sale is an act-within-an-act. For this metadramatic feat "the Machine" has the necessary histrionic skills for voicing over some of Moss's running insults so that he can concentrate upon his setting of selling Harriett and "blah blah Nyborg." Roma's linguistic substitution for Bruce's name is a complicit erasure of the husband, the male degraded by being sold the units of Mountain View. In his setting of the scene, however, Levene has to wait for Roma's attention to shift from Moss to Harriett's crumb cake. Then, prompted and encouraged, Levene resumes the narration. Immediately the information that the cake came from the store prompts the usual insult: "Fuck *her* . . ." says Roma. And Levene continues, ". . . convert the motherfucker . . . *sell* him . . . *sell* him . . . *make him sign the check. (Pause.)* The . . . Bruce, Harriett . . . the kitchen, blah" (42). The kitchen, the traditional locale of the mother and the wife, becomes the scene of Levene's assertion of dominance. Emphasizing their names, Levene continues the seduction, with Roma "reflectively" offering a refrain of

"Harriett." Levene assures Bruce, "I don't want to fuck *around* with you," and their compliant stillness while he holds the pen in his hand makes him confident that he "*did* it," that he "locked on them." Sharing the coital analogue with Roma, Levene exults in his successful double fuck: "They signed, Ricky. It was *great*. It was fucking great. It was like they wilted all at once. No *gesture* . . . nothing. Like together. They, I swear to God, they both kind of *imperceptibly slumped*. And he reaches and takes the pen and signs, he passes it to her, she signs. It was so fucking solemn. I just let it sit. I nod like this. I nod again. I grasp his hands. I shake his hands. I grasp *her* hands. I nod at her like this. 'Bruce . . . Harriett . . .' I'm beaming at them. I'm nodding like this" (42–43).

Although there are no arms around the neck or any *café au lait,* as in Roma's evocation of memorable fucks, Levene's story features a gestureless dual slump, a twenty-two minute hold of the pen before each Nyborg takes it, nods as frequent as Molly Bloom's "yes," and a ceremonial toast in little shotglasses. If cruder in its celebratory images, the recapitulation still earns Roma's compliment, "That was a great sale, Shelly" (43). Realizing parallels between sales and sex was part of the education of the English actors for the premiere of *Glengarry Glen Ross.* According to Jack Shepherd, who played Roma, learning how to sell was very difficult "until the author pointed out that the process of salesmanship has much more in common with the act of 'getting laid' than it had to do with hustle and fast-talking and so on."[7] Mamet's explanation to the actor clearly establishes authorial direction for Levene's scene; the absence of hustle and fast-talk is part of the sales process, as in "getting laid," and there is no "almost" about it. David Radavich, too, has noticed how Mamet has articulated "the intimate connection between sexual and business practices,"[8] and William F. Van Wert has seen the same seductive process employed by the con men of *House of Games.*[9]

Harriett Nyborg's position is established through Levene's rhetoric. From "deadbeat magazine subscription leads" (13) Levene has plucked a pair of actual buyers, he claims. It is his excitement upon entering the sales office, his triumph, his story of the sell that gives her identity more than does her signature on the contract. Her subservience is obvious not only in her taking of the pen, but, more important, in her silence. Neither she nor "blah blah" speak. But Roma, the top salesman, savors the syllables of her name. Probably Luce Irigaray's essay "The Power of Discourse and the Subordination of the Feminine" is the strongest theoretical link to this particular scene in *Glengarry Glen Ross.* There she defines the *"exclusively* 'masculine' parameters" of "a phallocratic order" that stages the representation of the feminine. Most pointedly Irigaray stipulates the objectification of women as a means of commerce: "In our social order, women are 'products' used and exchanged by men. Their status is that of merchandise, 'commodities.'"[10] Solely through the male-created and controlled language does Harriett Nyborg achieve identity; all we know of her is from Levene's story. While Irigaray acknowledges Lacan's theory of the exclusion of women through and because of language, Ann Rosalind Jones has synthesized much of his thinking when she writes about women's "negative position in language"; for Lacan, she says, "woman is a gap or silence, the invisible and unheard sex."[11] Just so is Harriett in her kitchen, as told by Shelly Levene.

Levene has framed Harriett's silence within the omnipresent atmosphere of male domination. "Fuck" is a constant, and the usual insults are contemptuous of any sexual position perceived as inferior. Having balls is superior, whereas someone sold or unable to sell is a "cocksucker," a "cunt," or a "secretary." As Robert Stoller so neatly put it, "The first order of business in being a man is don't be a woman."[12] Mamet echoes Dr. Stoller's psychoanalysis when he states that "it's useless to define yourself in terms of a woman. What men need is men's approval."[13] The Lacanian mirror is in place. Yet the demeaning language is but a crude indicator of the prevailing homosocial attitudes.[14] Fear begets the frequent denigration and persistent distancing of the female. *Glengarry Glen Ross* is, in this sense, a dramatization of how necessary the marginalization of women is to the maintenance of patriarchal ideologies.

Surprisingly useful in understanding the significance of the positioning of Harriett, Lingk's wife, and Levene's daughter is that tired metaphor for the world of business, the jungle. In her insightful analysis of patriarchal ideologies in Conrad's *Heart of Darkness,* Johanna Smith argues that Marlowe's need for belief in an imperialist ideology is sustained by patriarchal underpinnings. The savage woman, the laundress, and The Intended are incongruous to the world of experience which, he maintains, "should be a man's world."[15] Just as Marlowe rejects their entrance into the narration of the jungle, so do Levene and Roma attempt to keep the feminine from intruding upon their masculine territory and autonomy. From Conrad's literal jungle to Mamet's sales contest is an easy metaphorical leap. Robert Brustein, reviewing a revival of *Glengarry Glen Ross,* claims that the play shows "life stripped of all idealistic pretenses and liberal pieties—a jungle populated with beasts of prey. . . ."[16] Likewise, Elaine Showalter's review of the movie version refers to "the jungle law of the sales contest."[17] But, before the critics, one of Mamet's earlier father characters, Bernie in *Reunion,* explained to his estranged daughter, "It's a fucking jungle out there."[18] This is the easily assumed ideology that reserves the jungle for the male and helps keep the feminine distanced from it. Yet the damage extends beyond exclusionary territories to ethical wastelands, as Hersh Zeifman reminds us: ". . . the perverse denial of an entire gender and its metaphorical import brilliantly exposes the moral wilderness of a business 'ethic' ruled solely by the vile and violent values of a debased machismo."[19] Within this wilderness, this jungle, the language of feminine debasement has its luxuriant growth. The Cottesloe Theatre's program for the 1983 premiere of *Glengarry Glen Ross* provides the same sort of metaphorical link: "Mamet's extraordinary dialogue exposes the spiritual failure of the society even while it relishes the barbarous poetry of street talk."[20] The brutality of attitude so evident in the repetitious language of rape is representative of the salesmen's appropriation of the methods of the hunter in snaring the leads, of the trophy-seeker in prizing the contract and the Cadillac, and of the Marlowe-like maintainer of patriarchal ideology in positioning the female.

Keeping her isolated becomes a problem for the top salesman. Roma, with his name suggestive of a great, past empire, perhaps like Levene's "old days" of great sales, is unable to maintain the image of Jinny Lingk as the server of a commendable dinner and the gender-specific trait of prudence. He wants to position her just like Harriett Nyborg, safely in the kitchen. "[Y]ou haven't had a *meal* until you've tasted . . . I was at the Lingks' last . . ."(46), Roma intones to Levene, now acting in the assumed role of an American Express executive. Responding to Lingk's message from his wife, Roma, in his assumed superior attitude, extends and deepens the gender difference as he stalls Lingk and tries to draw him back into the all-male deal: "It's a common reaction, Jim. I'll tell you what it is, and I know that that's why you married her. One of the reasons is *prudence*. It's a sizable investment. One thinks *twice* . . . it's also something *women* have. It's just a reaction to the size of investment. *Monday,* if you'd invite me for dinner again . . . (*To* Levene:) This woman can *cook* . . ."(48). Reinforcing the male bond, Levene says, simultaneously, "I'm sure she can. . . ." But Roma's depersonalization of Jinny to "common" reactions in a series of "it's" does not work. Despite Roma's imperial stance, Lingk keeps referring to her, trying to complete the message. Two important sentences emerge:

My wife said I have to cancel the deal (48).

   .   .   .   .

She called the consumer . . .(49).

Out of the kitchen and out of the type-casting comes a voice. Complicit silence, as with Harriett, is broken, and it is coincident with the damaged office. Now not only are the leads stolen, but a contract is about to be taken away by a woman. The quiescence is over. Again and again, the man who claims, "It's not me, it's my wife," (52), reiterates the insistence in her voice:

> She wants her money back.
>
> .   .   .   .
>
> No. She told me "right now."
>
> .   .   .   .
>
> She won't listen.
>
> .   .   .   .
>
> She told me I *have* to.
>
> .   .   .   .
>
> She told me not to talk to you. (53-54)

Jinny's daring disturbance of Roma's complacency occurs through the agency of a Lingk whom Dennis Carroll categorizes as bullied by his wife; Elaine Showalter, more Mametly, as "a pussy-whipped mark;" and Carla McDonough as evidence of a relationship that "does not reflect the masculine dominance/feminine submission dichotomy."[21] Whether sexually weakened or unwillingly cooperative, James Lingk in this scene subverts the ruling masculine ideology as he becomes the agent of female power. Jinny Lingk is male fear made audible, the domestic in combat-boots, the intruder into the male domain of business deals. So powerful is she, she can command the actions of her husband, order him not to talk to Roma, superimpose her voice on the proceedings, insist upon her wants, all through a spokesman. Her voice, despite her physical absence, seeps into the wreckage of the sales office and its dreams of conquest. Roma, the top salesman, fails to make her irrelevant. Like Levene, who lost a contract because of "the ex," Roma loses six thousand dollars, one Cadillac, and the placing of Jinny Lingk outside the deal-making dialogue. Naturally, in blaming Williamson for the loss, Roma's first address, one which he repeats, is, "You stupid fucking cunt" (56). Those at fault are female.

Just as Roma claims the primacy of man's work, the brought-in voice of Jinny Lingk denies its hegemony. Indeed, this female's position parallels Jane Gallop's psychoanalytic critique of Luce Irigaray's disruption of the Freudian text: "The Man's order is disturbed by the woman with the impertinent questions and the incisive comments."[22] She is one of those women who, according to David Radavich, "more seriously" intrude upon the male enclaves in Mamet's dramas.[23] Such a serious intrusion is what Betty Caplan, in her review of *Oleanna,* posits as evidence of Mamet's rigid notion of gender when she states that "if a woman comes into his plays, she literally destroys them."[24] Jinny Lingk does not, however, destroy this play. Rather, she disconnects, as Irigaray would have it, a staging of feminine representation. She modifies the phallocratic order. She breaks the silence and asserts the power of the female voice. She reveals the swamp that the Glengarry sales-pitch on Highlands tries to obscure.

Given this significant disruption in the dominantly patriarchal text, the positioning of Levene's daughter requires further study. Whereas the audience hears, via messenger, that Jinny Lingk wants her money back, and the audience learns, through Levene's story, that Harriett Nyborg acquiesces to the sale, the audience hears nothing about Levene's child beyond the invocation of her in the unfinished phrase, "John: my daughter . . ." and the reference to the "kid" he brags about putting "through *school*" (45). Even though Levene uses the first reference to highlight his past accomplishments as a salesman and the second to attempt to persuade Williamson to help him avoid arrest, there is an obvious hesitancy in Levene's introduction of her into the dialogue. In her study of the language of silence Leslie Kane posits an imperative for the reader and audience "to question why" the writer has remained silent, thus "directly, dramatically, and implicitly" reflecting "doubt and disjunction."[25] The space left by Levene, then, is where questioning must begin.

To Dennis Carroll the daughter is Levene's "last card," one he plays for sympathy.[26] If so, the metaphor suggests reduction of her to an object, a singleton in a serious poker game (a well-known favorite pastime of Mamet's). The ploy or play, however, is ineffective. Both times Williamson responds with a decisive negative. The sales-manager's tough deflection of Levene's blandishments maintains the tone of ruthless business procedures that informs the entire drama. Virtually every critic agrees upon the amoral machinations of the salesmen. Only a few notice indicators of male friendship—Robert Brustein, for example, finding "a kind of unexpected camaraderie" among the competitors. He also praises the actor playing Levene for maintaining "a manly resolve and courage."[27] A searching for redemptive qualities in these characters reaches incredulous levels in Kenji Oba's apologetics, which credit the daughter as the clear influence upon Levene and which assume "soft, flexible, sensitive, and precise" traits behind the "roughness" of Mamet's male world.[28] That these assumptions are at variance with the play is clear in the text itself. Notions of friendship are absurd in a drama in which Williamson refuses anything but ready cash, where Moss traps Aaronow into being an accomplice by talking to him, and where Roma pretends teammanship while reserving the rights to his own "stuff" and claiming half of Levene's. Frank Rich's review of the 1984 New York production reflects the tone of the play when he notes "the only strong male-female" bond as, "curiously and sentimentally enough," between a father and a daughter. He doubts that Levene's "mere mention of the fact that he has a daughter will somehow redeem his sense of self-worth."[29]

Glengarry Glen Ross does not offer redemption, and looking for hints of morality in its salesmen is like expecting increased value from a Glengarry plot. Indeed, Levene himself dispels any such cobwebs of conventional ethics when he announces that, having sold the eight units, he is "going to Hawaii!" (36). Parental concern is not part of his itinerary. Convincing as the drama is, David Mamet's instructive letter to Gregory Mosher, director of the Chicago production, adds authorial insistence to the prevailing effect of ruthless, friendless competition: "Look," Mamet wrote, "this play is not like American Buffalo—it is not fueled by love. These are guys who kick the other person when he is down, and you must find this in the production."[30] It was found in the productions I saw in London and Providence, and it remains intact in the text.

This cutthroat, all-male business world is the context wherein Levene's mention of his daughter has its curious effect. Anomalistic, at least, disturbing, surely, it hints at another world, one separate and distinct from that staged in the Chinese restaurant and the trashed office. For a brief moment, as from a suddenly opened window, a whiff of innocence enters the harsh business atmosphere. Whatever the purpose—sympathy, self-respect, reminder—the mention fails, not just because of Williamson's rejoinders, but because she cannot be allowed to enter into this world of bogus land deals. Her absence, like that of The Intended's, keeps the ideology of the patriarchy operative. Levene's daughter does not belong in a world described by Henry Schvey as one "of competition in which human feeling is completely absent."[31]

There is a further, corroborating reason why Levene's articulation falters at the mention of his daughter. He does not, in this environment, have the words necessary to bring her beyond an introduction into the bargaining with Williamson. Everyday parlance has robbed him of the necessary vocabulary. C. W. E. Bigsby finds precisely here, where "the flow of language falters," evidence that "anxieties are exposed." The cause resides in the fact that the salesmen "have so thoroughly plundered the language of private need and self-fulfillment and deployed it for the purpose of deceit and betrayal that they no longer have access to words that will articulate their feelings."[32] Bigsby's use of the language of conquest ("plundered" and "deployed") is an apt reminder of the useful jungle metaphor. Consistently and insistently the maintenance of a phallocentric ideology through its repetitive expletives and insults results in the silencing of the feminine and any contrary notions associated with her. Amidst the schemes to win over Williamson, therefore, Levene only faintly begins to offer his daughter on the bargaining table. Language fails that man of words, Shelly "the Machine" Levene. The meanness of his vocabulary leaves him speechless about his daughter and acquiescent to his antagonist's curt dismissal of the daughter as chip, card, or ploy. So far does a ruthless language rule the characters that, as Jeanette Malkin says, "Business terminology has invaded and colonized the minds of Mamet's characters."[33] Again the metaphors of conquering the jungle reinforce the interrelation of patriarchal, imperialist, and business ideologies.

Thus, according to Bigsby and Malkin, the Glengarry salesmen have become victims of their own lingo. Certainly Levene, in both scenes of failed negotiations with Williamson, is unable to find the words to say anything beyond "my *daughter . . .*" Perhaps he knows, at least in an experiential sense, as well as Malkin does, that "In such a world the very act of speech is a betrayal. . . . Words can only buy and sell, and they sell trust and friend-ship just as easily as land."[34] Succinctly put by Matthew Roudané, the loss of authenticity in the salesmen's speech is evident and conclusive: "In brief, the business response necessarily cancels the human response."[35] Essentially, then, Levene's daughter is a reference to the feminine which cannot be sus-tained, even in conversation, in the exploitive and denigrating world of *Glengarry Glen Ross.*

Mamet tends to reserve some possibility for gendered communication and reconciliation between fathers and daughters in *Dark Pony* and *Reunion.* But even in these significantly short dramas, tentative dialogues, heavily re-liant upon the father's gift for storytelling, briefly speak to the long-term separation between the two characters. One other familial relationship, that of Charles Lang and his sister Rita in *The Water Engine,* allows for speech, via telephone, indicating mutual, sustained affection; but this mutuality is doomed to a shared death brought about by corrupt business forces. Oth-erwise, where female characters appear in Mamet's plays, they are objects of conflict and alienation. Distrust, founded and reinforced by sexist atti-tudes, severs the lovers of *Sexual Perversity in Chicago.* In the spent ener-gies of Nick and Ruth, *The Woods* studies the final scenes of marital dis-cord. For Edmond, woman—as wife, B-girl, whore, and waitress—is so detestable that he contentedly ends his existential quest imprisoned with his male rapist. The nameless Miss A of *The Shawl* is a mark for John and Charles. Karen, too, has merely temporary importance within the dramatic frame formed by the male characters in *Speed-the-Plow;* like the screenplay

she favors, she is an easy throwaway. Mamet's most assertive female character, Carol, of *Oleanna,* accrues power by learning from a feminist group
until she becomes the threat incarnate. Physically beaten, knocked to the
floor, she acknowledges and appears to accept John's contemptuous "you
little *cunt* . . ." when, head lowered, she says, two times, "Yes. That's right."[36]

Mamet's on-stage women must be discarded. When they enter into
the offices of the male spiritualist, movie-producer, or professor, they do not
lose their identities as Others. Karen's attempt at influence fails, Carol's tres-
pass is punished, and Miss A remains outside the loop of the con. The movie
House of Games replicates the plot of the conned female with the intriguing variation of a highly educated, professional female seduced and "driven"
to criminality by male sharks of the game. In all of these dramas where an
adult female character is on stage, silencing is the preferential treatment. Lead
male characters, Danny and Bobby Gould, stop listening to Deborah and
Karen; instead, they attend to their buddies' deprecatory analyses of the
women. Acceptance, as by Miss A, is an alternative to silence, as it is also
by the intimidated student, Carol.

Of the well-known plays in which no female characters appear, *Prairie
du Chien* more gently and mysteriously features an ephemeral female in a
ghost story told in counterpoint to a tense cardgame played on the other side
of the train; like Harriett Nyborg, this woman is speechless within the con-
fines of the male narrator's tale. *Lakeboat* and *American Buffalo* refer to
women in the same crude, sexual terms that *Glengarry Glen Ross* inscribes.
So routine is the debasement that Hersh Zeifman speaks for more than
American Buffalo when, in his clever phrasing, he accuses Mamet's world
of American business of being "*literally* ruthless and graceless."[37] Several
critics have noticed similar consistencies within Mamet's work. For Guido
Almansi, Mamet's "best plays are immune from any female contamination;
the existence of women only filters on the stage through the preconceived
ideas of the opposite sex."[38] Where these oppositional notions originate is
some of the concern of David Radavich, who sees in the play's marginalization and exclusion of women a concentration upon the "myriad variations
on homosocial male order."[39] Most conclusive, because most inclusive of
feminist psychoanalytic criticism, is Susan Harris Smith's study, "En-
Gendering Violence," which translates the verbal and transferred violence
staged by Mamet, Shepard, and Rabe into a demonstration of sexist and
imperialist attitudes.[40] Yet again the analogue of imperial with patriarchal
ideologies indicates the intertwined rationalities which sustain the dominating
urges so clearly revealed in the characters of Levene, Roma, Moss, and
Williamson.

In his essays Mamet has not hesitated to ally his own ruminations with some of the attitudes manifested by the characters in his plays. Extolling male companionship necessitates, for him, absolute distinctions between male and female roles: "The true nature of the world, as between men and women, is sex, and any other relationship between us is either an elaboration, or an avoidance. And the true nature of the world between men, is, I think, community of effort directed toward the outside world, directed to subdue, to understand, or to wonder or to withstand together, the truth of the world."[41] Thus granting grand and imperialist endeavors to the poker players, Mamet excludes women from community and positions them in the limited role of sex, all for the maintenance of "the truth" of the male world. It is not surprising then to see the men on stage mimic this ideology, subduing Harriett, withstanding together Jinny, and wondering at Levene's daughter.

Corroborating this insistence upon the privileges of the all-male domain are the reminiscences in *The Cabin*. These range from Mamet's infatuation with the male smells of his private retreat; through joyous memories of the male radio voice which bespoke calm, reason, and self-esteem to the youthful male audience; to a description of Wabash Avenue as a noisy, masculine, business street.[42] Savoring these male atmospheres gives a congratulatory tone to some of Mamet's stage-scenes, particularly those in *Glengarry Glen Ross*, where a man is cornering a client or stalling the forces of law and order. Anarchical license, strutting triumph, instant playacting for profit promote the male identities of the salesmen. Any entering female is a disruption, as "the ex" and Jinny Lingk prove. Harriett Nyborg exists only in the kitchen, and Levene's daughter must be somewhere beyond the business locales. By separating, silencing, distancing the feminine, the masculine can proceed to rape the leads.

"Something has been lost, something vital," C. W. E. Bigsby has concluded about Mamet's male environments.[43] That something is the female. The language that replaces and denigrates her loses, too, for it substitutes expletives for needs and bluster for insecurity. "You really have to love that kind of talk to write it," Mamet says. "More than that, you have to need it. The people who speak that way tell the truth. They don't institutionalize thought. They speak from a sense of need."[44] Mamet's empathic explanation for the language of the salesmen accounts for the dual pleasure of loving to speak what one needs to say, but, as Michael Billington notes in his review of the London premiere of *Glengarry Glen Ross*, the production "exactly catches this feeling of a nervous closed society."[45] So must it be when that group of men is so intent upon identification in opposition to women. The strain is obvious in Levene's solemnizing of the Nyborg sales scene, in

Roma's dodging of Lingk's message from Jinny, and in Levene's repeated gaps when he starts to speak of his daughter.

Analyzing the battles for power in Mamet's *House of Games* and *Speed-the-Plow,* Ann Hall writes what holds true for *Glengarry Glen Ross* as well: "Mamet's texts mimic the patriarchy and the role of women in them. His female characters create disturbances, admittedly behind the scenes, in effect behind the 'yellow wallpaper,' but they succeed in creating subtle disruptions in these texts that tempt us to return, rethink, and reconsider."[46] Frank Rich categorizes their appearances as recent, problematic, baffling, and crazing for the males.[47] Actually, the disruptions occur throughout Mamet's works, and the effects are deeper and more revelatory than a comic interpretation allows. Positioned outside the office and the restaurant, the females of *Glengarry Glen Ross* reveal the ideology propping up the corrupt methods and necessitating a debased language. In the imaginative re-creation of a passive sit, in the hurried construction of a false identity, and in the halting invocation of a daughter, this community of men acknowledges the identity of Harriett Nyborg, recoils from the determined voice of Jinny Lingk, and momentarily goes mute at the mention of a female child. Something revelatory is gained.

NOTES

1. David Mamet, *Glengarry Glen Ross* (London: Methuen, 1984), 1, 62. All further references are to this edition and will be cited parenthetically.

2. Michael Sragow, "Shtick Shifts," *New Yorker,* 5 October 1992, 164.

3. Anne Dean, *David Mamet: Language as Dramatic Action* (Rutherford, N.J.: Fairleigh Dickinson University Press, 1990), 193, 207, 209.

4. Quoted by Dean, 196.

5. Guido Almansi, "David Mamet, a Virtuoso of Invective," in *Critical Angles: European Views of Contemporary American Literature,* ed. Marc Chénetier (Carbondale: Southern Illinois University Press, 1986), 206–207.

6. Hersh Zeifman, "Phallus in Wonderland: Machismo and Business in David Mamet's *American Buffalo* and *Glengarry Glen Ross,*" in *David Mamet: A Casebook,* ed. Leslie Kane (New York: Garland, 1992), 131.

7. "*Glengarry Glen Ross*—Performance," in National Theatre's Education Department's *Background Notes for Teachers and Pupils* (London: National Theatre, 1983), 9.

8. David Radavich, "Man among Men: David Mamet's Homosocial Order," *American Drama* 1 (Fall 1991): 59.

9. William F. Van Wert, "Psychoanalysis and Con Games: *House of Games,*" *Film Quarterly* 43, no. 4 (1990): 4.

10. Luce Irigaray, *This Sex Which Is Not One,* trans. Catherine Porter (Ithaca: Cornell University Press, 1985), 68–85.

11. Ann Rosalind Jones, "Inscribing Femininity: French Theories of the Feminine," in *Making a Difference: Feminist Literary Criticism,* ed. Gayle Greene and Coppelia Kahn (London: Methuen, 1985), 83.

12. Robert J. Stoller, *Presentations of Gender* (New Haven: Yale University Press, 1985), 183. Quoted by Susan Harris Smith, "En-Gendering Violence: Twisting

'Privates' in the Public Eye," in *Public Issues, Private Tensions,* ed. Matthew C. Roudané, (New York: AMS Press, 1993), 115.

13. Quoted by David Richards, "Mamet's Women," *New York Times,* 3 January 1993, sec. 2, 1.

14. See Radavich, 46–60, for an analysis of the implications of male exclusivity in Mamet's plays.

15. Johanna Smith, "'Too Beautiful Altogether': Patriarchal Ideology in *Heart of Darkness,*" in Joseph Conrad, *Heart of Darkness,* ed. Ross C. Murfin (New York: St. Martin's Press, 1989), 190.

16. Robert Brustein, *Who Needs Theatre: Dramatic Opinions* (New York: Atlantic Monthly Press, 1987), 71.

17. Elaine Showalter, "Acts of Violence: David Mamet and the Language of Men," *Times Literary Supplement,* 2 November 1992, 16.

18. David Mamet, *Reunion* and *Dark Pony* (New York: Grove Press, 1979), 23.

19. Zeifman, 133.

20. Program notes in Cottesloe Theatre program for *Glengarry Glen Ross* (London: National Theatre, 1983): 3.

21. Dennis Carroll, *David Mamet* (London: Macmillan, 1987), 44; Showalter: 16; Carla J. McDonough, "Every Fear Hides a Wish: Understandable Masculinity in Mamet's Drama," *Theatre Journal* 44, no. 2 (1992): 203.

22. Jane Gallop, "The Father's Seduction," in *The (M)other Tongue: Essays in Feminist Psychoanalytic Interpretation,* ed. Shirley Nelson Garner, Claire Kahane, and Madelon Sprengnether (Ithaca: Cornell University Press, 1985), 35.

23. Radavich, 48.

24. Betty Caplan, "The Gender Benders," *New Statesman,* 2 July 1993, 35.

25. Leslie Kane, *The Language of Silence: On the Unspoken and the Unspeakable in Modern Drama* (Rutherford, N.J.: Fairleigh Dickinson University Press, 1984), 15–16.

26. Carroll, 49.

27. Brustein, 70–71.

28. Program for a Japanese production, cited in *File on Mamet,* comp. Nesta Jones and Steven Dykes (London: Methuen, 1991), 60.

29. Frank Rich, "The Theatrical Gender Gap Is a Chasm," *New York Times,* 30 September 1984, sec. B1, 4.

30. Quoted from an interview with Mosher in *File on Mamet,* 59.

31. Henry I. Schvey, "The Plays of David Mamet: Games of Manipulation and Power, " *New Theatre Quarterly* 4, no. 13 (February 1988): 88.

32. C.W.E. Bigsby, *David Mamet* (London: Methuen, 1985), 123.

33. Jeanette R. Malkin, *Verbal Violence in Contemporary Drama: From Handke to Shepard* (Cambridge: Cambridge University Press, 1992), 159.

34. Malkin, 159.

35. Matthew C. Roudané, "Public Issues, Private Tensions: David Mamet's *Glengarry Glen Ross,*" *South Carolina Review* 1, no. 1 (1986): 45.

36. David Mamet, *Oleanna* (London: Methuen, 1993), 79–80.

37. Zeifman, 129.

38. Almansi, 191.

39. Radavich, 46.

40. Susan Harris Smith: 115–30.

41. David Mamet, "In the Company of Men," in *Some Freaks* (New York: Viking, 1988), 90–91.

42. David Mamet, *The Cabin* (New York: Vintage, 1992), 55, 92, 109.

43. Bigsby, 136.

44. Cottesloe program notes, 3.

45. Michael Billington, review of *Glengarry Glen Ross, The Guardian,* 22 September 1983. Quoted in *File,* 56.

46. Ann C. Hall, "Playing to Win: Sexual Politics in David Mamet's *House of Games* and *Speed-the-Plow*," in Kane, *Casebook*, 158.

47. Frank Rich, "Mamet's Tasteful Hell for a Movie Mogul," *New York Times*, 4 December 1989, sec. C, 15.

7

"You're Exploiting My Space"

Ethnicity, Spectatorship, and the (Post)colonial
Condition in Mukherjee's "A Wife's Story" and
Mamet's *Glengarry Glen Ross*

Deborah R. Geis

Patel? Fuck you. Fuckin' Shiva *handed him a million dollars, told him "sign the deal," he wouldn't sign. And Vishnu, too. Into the bargain. Fuck that, John. You know your business, I know mine.*

—Roma, in David Mamet, *Glengarry Glen Ross*

So Patels are hard to sell real estate to. You buy them a beer, whisper Glengarry Glen Ross, *and they smell swamp instead of sun and surf. They work hard, eat cheap, live ten to a room, stash their savings under futons in Queens, and before you know it they own half of Hoboken. You say, where's the sweet gullibility that made this nation great?*

—Panna, in Bharati Mukherjee, "A Wife's Story"

The narrator—and uneasy spectator—of "A Wife's Story" is Panna, a woman of upper-class Indian background who has been living in Manhattan and working on her Ph.D. in special education while her husband (through a traditional Hindu arranged marriage) is back in Ahmadabad (north of Bombay) overseeing a factory. Their relationship consists of strained long-distance phone calls as Panna becomes increasingly independent and immersed in American ways and develops friendships with other men, including Imre, a Hungarian immigrant determined to introduce her to the arts and with whom she attends *Glengarry Glen Ross*. When Panna's husband comes to New York to visit her, she experiences alternating feelings of affection (especially as she watches with bemusement her husband's newfound enthusiasm for American consumerism) and the sense that she will not be able to return to her old life in India as he expects. We also get the impression that there is an unacknowledged sorrow between the two: Panna says early on that they have no children, but makes several references to a dead son about whom the husband apparently will not speak. At the end of the story, her husband receives a cable saying he must return to India immediately because of a labor confrontation at his factory; Panna prepares herself to make love with him and admires her own body in the mirror, but implies in the process of this physical and sensual self-affirmation that she is ready to leave him and move on to the next stage of her independence.

I am not sure whether Mukherjee's story marks the first time that a David Mamet play has served as the starting point for a work of fiction by another author, but the effect of reading this piece was for me a startling one—especially to do so not too many years after sitting in the audience for the Broadway production of *Glengarry* during the same sweltering summer described in the story (and, like Panna and Imre, in near–front row seats obtained from the half-price booth). If memory serves, I was living at the time in a sublet on East 7th Street in the Village, one block away from the area of East 6th Street known as Little India, surrounded every day by women in saris and by Indian grocery stores and restaurants. Yet to read Mukherjee's story was a revelation of sorts because suddenly I was asked to imagine sitting in the audience for *Glengarry* again (the tale actually begins with Panna watching the play), but to see and hear the performance with the eyes and ears of someone confronted by the "othering" of the "Patels" who (among others) are the butt of the salesmen's jokes in the drama. To set Mukherjee's story in dialogue with Mamet's play is to open up questions both works raise—sometimes in conflicting ways—about the "othering" of ethnic groups in America, as well as about postcolonialism, structures of class and gender oppression, and capitalist culture. Mukherjee's appropriation of Mamet's play as intertext both enriches a reading of *Glengarry* and encourages a second look at Mamet's handling of issues of ethnicity and exploitation.

Ethnicity, gender, and sexuality play central roles in the power relationships in the real estate office of *Glengarry*. The older salesmen (Moss, Levene, Aaronow) are apparently Jewish, and the up-and-coming Ricky Roma is Italian-American; only Williamson, the reviled boss and outsider, has a WASP (White Anglo-Saxon Protestant) name. As is so often the case in Mamet's plays, the place of business is a place of homosocial bonding and a site of the projection of intense anxiety about the heterosexual masculine ideal (see also *Lakeboat, American Buffalo, Speed-the-Plow,* and others). When characters feel their power threatened, they express their aggression and anxiety in terms that mark the threatening or dismantling of this ideal; when Williamson blows Roma's deal with Lingk, for instance, Roma calls him a "cunt," a "fairy," and a "child."[1] As Hersh Zeifman puts it in his discussion of male bonding in *Glengarry* and *American Buffalo,* "Since machismo is the sole criterion of worth in the 'closed moral universe' these plays depict, it therefore follows that the worst term of abuse in such a universe is one that questions masculinity . . . [thus] Mamet's businessmen are both deeply misogynistic and deeply homophobic."[2] Carla McDonough underscores the connection between this machismo and the salesmen's implication within the structures of capitalist competition:

> [T]he definition of masculinity within *Glengarry Glen Ross* is too limited for the majority of the characters to maintain, leaving them perpetually unsure of their identities. As in *Edmond,* it is the limited structure of their definitions which fails these men; the system of patriarchal capitalism that promises to define them, to position them in a place of power, is precisely what disempowers them by setting up a competition which always positions the majority of players as losers and, therefore, as not-men. Any comfort they might take from each other, any support or friendship, is constantly undercut by competition.[3]

An overlapping set of anxieties (and corresponding epithets) is assigned to clients and potential clients, the ever-desirable and ever-frustrating "leads" to whom the salesmen must pitch their properties. Part of what makes a lead valuable or worthless is the name on the lead itself, as the name's ethnicity and its implied willingness or unwillingness to invest suggests gullibility or stinginess. In other words, the salesmen project their anxiety of failure onto the "others" upon whom they rely for their success. Since what they are selling hinges on a vision of the American dream as fulfilled through the acquisition of property (and specifically, through marketing property in magical-sounding Florida to middle-class inhabitants of Chicago), it is not surprising that many potential clients would come from first, second, or third-generation immigrant families. Again, given the Chicago setting, it is also not surprising that many of these leads would be of Polish descent. Here is Levene's lambasting of the unusable leads Williamson is trying to give him near the beginning of the play:

> I'll tell you why I'm out. I'm *out,* you're giving me toilet paper, John. I've *seen* those leads. I saw them when I was at Homestead, we pitched those cocksuckers Rio Rancho nineteen sixty-*nine* they wouldn't buy. They couldn't buy a fucking *toaster.* They're *broke,* John. They're cold. They're deadbeats, you can't judge on that. Even so. Even so. Alright. Fine. Fine. Even so. I go in, FOUR FUCKING LEADS they got their money in a *sock.* They're fucking *Polacks,* John. (21)

Under different circumstances, Levene's "you can't judge on that" could be taken to mean that one can't be judgmental—but the democratic ideal is subservient to the capitalist one: he is actually telling Williamson not to "judge" his ability to make a sale, given the Poles' reluctance or inability to spend money.

Moss echoes these sentiments at the beginning of the following scene when he tries to comfort Aaronow (who has apparently just lost a sale), by saying, "Polacks and deadbeats . . . How you goan'a get on the board sell'n a Polack?" (29). It is at this moment that he goes into his tirade about the similarly miserly Indians, the "Patels" that to him mark a sure no-sale. The manner in which Moss feels threatened by the Other—here, literally the face of the Other—is apparent:

> You had one you'd know it. *Patel.* They keep coming up. I don't know. They like to talk to salesmen. *(Pause.)* They're *lonely,* something. *(Pause.)* They like to feel *superior,* I don't know. Never bought a fucking thing. You're sitting down "The Rio Rancho *this,* the blah blah blah," "The Mountain View—" "Oh yes. My brother told me that. . . ." They got a grapevine. Fuckin' Indians, George. Not my cup of tea . . . I never got a cup of tea with them. You see them in the restaurants. A supercilious race. What is this *look* on their face all the time? I don't know. (29–30)

In invoking the stereotype of the inscrutable Asian, Moss conveys a simultaneous sense of "knowing" the Patels well enough to be able to "teach" Aaronow about them—and of feeling helpless about their apparent impenetrability. This reflects Homi Bhabha's characterization of the way that "colonial discourse produces the colonized as a social reality which is at once an 'other' and yet entirely knowable and visible."[4] According to Bhabha, ethnic stereotypes are constructed, paradoxically, by the process of just such ambivalence: the stereotype, "as a form of multiple and contradictory belief, gives knowledge of difference and simultaneously disavows or masks it."[5]

Christopher Hudgins, in his analysis of humor in Mamet, argues that the audience's laughter at Moss's narrative comes "partly out of our liberal superiority, laughing at the character" and that we might also retain some level of recognition that this is an expression of Moss's own feelings of frustration and inferiority.[6] While Hudgins's point is well taken, it is nevertheless worth noting that the "we" who laugh in "liberal superiority" to Moss are still implicitly not Patels ourselves (nor would "we" admit to being

Mosses). Mukherjee calls apt attention to the ways that such assumptions about spectatorship need to be re-viewed. And it is at this moment that "A Wife's Story" begins, with Panna sitting in the audience of *Glengarry* and listening with increasing horror, anger, and embarrassment as Moss continues his series of vitriolic comments. The narrative allows the reader to witness his diatribe through Panna's reactions to it as she sits self-consciously in the front row: "[I]n my red silk sari I'm conspicuous," she says, even wondering for a moment whether the actors spotted her in the audience before the play began and said, "Let's get *her* today."[7] Sitting in the front row has thus also broken the theatrical illusion; Panna says that "we see things we shouldn't be seeing" (24), and the implication is that the performance of racism has become visible.

What particularly strikes Panna is that this is simultaneously a performance of sexism, for the audience members—embodied for Panna in the fat, polyester-shirted man sitting next to her—roar with laughter as Moss continues (and I am quoting Mukherjee's paraphrase of Mamet here), "*Seen their* [that is, the Indian] *women? . . . They look like they've just been fucked by a dead cat*" (24). For Panna, the moment is exacerbated by her own physical displacement, the violation of her territory, as the fat man next to her "hoots so hard he nudges my elbow off our shared armrest" (24). It is as if the fourth wall has been broken and the man next to her is one of the salesmen, or vice-versa; moreover, the man's reaction points to the complicity of the spectators in accepting, appreciating, and appropriating the characters' sexism and racism (however ironic Mamet's intention in having his characters say these lines in the first place: the balance of judgment is a delicate one). Panna says:

> I don't hate Mamet. It's the tyranny of the American dream that scares me. First, you don't exist. Then you're invisible. Then you're funny. Then you're disgusting. Insult, my American friends will tell me, is a kind of acceptance. No instant dignity here. A play like this, back home, would cause riots. Communal, racist, and antisocial. The actors wouldn't make it off stage. This play, and all these awful feelings, would be safely locked up. (24)

At some level, Panna sees *Glengarry*'s salesmen themselves as victims of this "tyranny of the American dream." Yet she realizes how the marginalization and scapegoating of those who are also seeking this dream—immigrants to the United States from India and elsewhere—causes them to become participants in the cycles of victimization. She says, "I know how both sides feel.

That's the trouble. The Patel sniffing out scams, the sad salesmen on the stage: postcolonialism has made me their referee" (25–26).

This cultural conflict is reflected in Panna's divided feelings of wanting to express her rage and "make an awful scene" (25), and her desire for the "dignity" she mentions in the passage above. Even this "dignity," though, has become remolded and reappropriated in terms of postcolonial class privilege: she remarks that she does not make a scene because she has learned "exquisite" manners from the "[e]xpensive girls' schools in Lausanne and Bombay" she has attended (25). Instead, in a sublimation of her anger at the scenes being performed on stage in front of her, Panna turns to the man next to her whose elbow has displaced hers on the armrest, and with the "effortless meanness of well-bred displaced Third World women, though [her] rhetoric has been learned elsewhere," says to him, "Excuse me . . . you're exploiting my space" (25). The man jerks his arm away, startled, and Panna thinks to herself that she has probably "ruined the first act for him" (25), but these words also seem to contain some small sense of retribution. She has reclaimed her physical territory, yet has relied upon class privilege— on sounding "well-bred"—in order to do so.

One might even say that these sorts of multiple ironies—the ironies of cultural self-contradiction—are common to both Mamet's play and Mukherjee's story. The difference might be, though, that Panna is aware, even self-mockingly so, of their existence, while Mamet's salesmen are too deeply implicated in feeling that their subjectivity is determined through success in competition with others for them to be able to afford such acknowledgments. Panna's reclamation of her territory by confronting the man next to her in the audience is accompanied by her decision to write to Mamet that night, along with a letter telling Steven Spielberg that "Indians don't eat monkey brains" (27). She adds, "We've made it. Patels must have made it. Mamet, Spielberg: they're not condescending to us. Maybe they're a little bit afraid" (28). And in a sense, too, Mukherjee seems to be "writing to David Mamet" by publishing this story: to do so is to claim a space, a territory, that is both Indian and female and that has not fallen prey to the salesmanship of white male prerogative. The appropriation of *Glengarry* as intertext enacts a gesture that Stephen Slemon would describe as a strategy of postcolonial literature's oppositional political practice; in such writing, he argues, "a 'parodic' repetition of imperial 'textuality' sets itself specifically in opposition to the interpellative power of colonialism."[8]

Within "A Wife's Story" itself, the *Glengarry* episode continues to echo throughout the remaining events of the narrative, as Panna's husband arrives in the United States and seems at once mistrustful of everyone around him, yet "sold" on American consumerism to the extent that he is entranced by the tube sock vendors on the streets, by the hair dye and protein powder available in the supermarket, by Chicken McNuggets and the Rockettes. When Panna and her husband take a tour of New York City, Panna finds herself part of an audience again, in an ironic reminder of the opening *Glengarry* sequence. The actor-wannabe tour guide (he, like the salesmen of *Glengarry*, is pursuing his version of the American dream) singles her out during his song and dance presentation on the bus: "Look, we gotta maharani with us! Couldn't I have been a star?" This time, though, Panna "squeal[s]" in response, "Right," with the narrative aside, "I've been trained to adapt; what else can I say?" (36). The moment is charged with the kind of ambivalence that has carried over from her spectatorial position in the opening of the story: this time she is stereotyped as "royalty" and is given a voice of sorts, but has still been co-opted or cast as an image, a willing participant in a colonialist vision of her as quaint object of curiosity. Panna's responding squeal (with its sense of the "appropriately" feminine/animalistic) and her comment about being able to "adapt" show the complexity of her gendered and cultural positioning; she has taken on the "voice" that her colonizer expects of her in this moment, but she also seems to be aware that she is compromising, is playing along while rebelling underneath, the same way that she resolves to play along with her husband's wishes for their time together even though she knows that she cannot return to India and resume the role of the traditional wife.

"A Wife's Story" is framed by two acts of looking, beginning with Panna's position of imagining herself "looked at" in the audience of *Glengarry*, and ending with a parallel moment that also marks a progression of sorts—at least for Panna. In the final sequence of Mukherjee's narrative, as Panna looks at her body in the mirror while she waits for her husband to come back to bed, she is imaged as both subject and object of her own spectatorship: "I am free, afloat, watching somebody else" (41). Her sense of herself is split, fragmented, as she seems to have found a kind of release into a new life, but not without a certain degree of detachment (unmooring) or ambivalence—and indeed, this kind of splitting or doubleness, the sense of watching oneself as others might watch, reflects the status of the marginalized subject. Still, Panna seems to have come up with a response to Mamet's salesmen: yes, she (like them) has "bought into" the American dream—and she (unlike them) realizes the extent to which such a "purchase" is always mediated by her status as a woman and as an immigrant. Perhaps her critical spectatorship of Mamet's play, though, has been at least partially the catalyst for her decision to reinvent that dream in her own terms, in territory she will claim as her own.

NOTES

1. David Mamet, *Glengarry Glen Ross* (New York: Grove, 1984). Subsequent references to the play are to this edition and will be cited parenthetically in the text.

2. Hersh Zeifman, "Phallus in Wonderland: Machismo and Business in David Mamet's *American Buffalo* and *Glengarry Glen Ross*," in *David Mamet: A Casebook*, ed. Leslie Kane (New York and London: Garland, 1992), 126.

3. Carla J. McDonough, "Every Fear Hides a Wish: Unstable Masculinity in Mamet's Drama," *Theatre Journal* 44 (May 1992): 202.

4. Homi K. Bhabha, *The Location of Culture* (London and New York: Routledge, 1994), 70–71.

5. Ibid., 66, 77.

6. Christopher Hudgins, "Comedy and Humor in the Plays of David Mamet," in Kane, *David Mamet: A Casebook*, 22.

7. Bharati Mukherjee, "A Wife's Story," in *The Middleman and Other Stories* (New York: Fawcett Crest, 1988), 23–24. Subsequent references to the story are to this edition and will be cited parenthetically in the text.

8. Stephen Slemon, "Modernism's Last Post," *Ariel* 20 (1989): 3–17. *A Postmodern Reader,* ed. Joseph Natoli and Linda Hutcheon (Albany, N.Y.: SUNY Press, 1993), 430.

Mike Nussbaum (left) and Joe Mantegna in David Mamet's Pulitzer Prize–winning play, Glengarry Glen Ross. *Directed by Gregory Mosher,* Glengarry Glen Ross *received its American premiere in the Goodman Studio Theatre, 27 January through 4 March 1984. Photograph © Brigitte Lacombe.*

J.T. Walsh (left) and Robert Prosky are pictured in David Mamet's Pulitzer Prize–winning play, Glengarry Glen Ross. *Directed by Gregory Mosher,* Glengarry Glen Ross *received its American premiere in the Goodman Studio Theatre, 27 January through 4 March 1984. Photograph © Brigitte Lacombe.*

Joe Mantegna (right) and William Petersen are pictured in David Mamet's Pulitzer Prize-winning play, Glengarry Glen Ross. *Directed by Gregory Mosher,* Glengarry Glen Ross *received its American premiere in the Goodman Studio Theatre, 27 January through 4 March 1984. Photograph © Brigitte Lacombe.*

John Benfield as George Aaronow in Glengarry Glen Ross *at the Donmar Warehouse, Earlham Street, London, which opened on 16 June with a press night on 22 June 1994. Photograph courtesy of Mark Douet.*

Levene: "I go in, FOUR FUCKING LEADS they got their money in a sock. They're fucking Polacks, John. Four leads. I close two. Two. Fifty per . . ."
Levene (Kitamura Kazuo, left); Williamson (Sugō Takayuki, right). Act 1, scene 1, February 1990, Haiyūza Theatre, Tokyo. Photograph courtesy of Bungakuza.

Levene: "We have a deal or not? Eh? Two Sits. The Des Plaines."
Levene (Kitamura Kazuo, left); Williamson (Sugō Takayuki, right). Act 1, scene 1, February 1990, Haiyūza Theatre, Tokyo. Photograph courtesy of Bungakuza.

Roma: "How can we act? The right way, we would say, to deal with this: 'there is a one-in-a-million chance that so and so will happen . . . Fuck it, it won't happen to me'. . . . No."
Roma (Kobayashi Katsuya, left); Lingk (Takao Taka, right). Act 1, scene 3, February 1990,
Haiyūza Theatre, Tokyo. Photograph courtesy of Bungakuza.

Levene: "John: John: . . . my daughter . . ." Williamson: "Fuck you."
Levene (Kitamura Kazuo, left); Williamson (Sugō Takayuki, right). Act 2, February 1990,
Haiyūza Theatre, Tokyo. Photograph courtesy of Bungakuza.

8

THE MARXIST CHILD'S PLAY OF MAMET'S TOUGH GUYS AND CHURCHILL'S *TOP GIRLS*

David Kennedy Sauer

The similarities between Caryl Churchill's *Top Girls* (London, Royal Court Theatre, 28 August 1982) and David Mamet's *Glengarry Glen Ross* (London, National Theatre, 21 September 1983) are surprising. Both plays have large single-gender casts, open in restaurants; have extended scenes in the workplace, talk about "closing" sales, show concern for a daughter but feature work as the center of life. They share a common view of characters as highly competitive types whose aim, as Churchill's title indicates, is to top everyone, including family and friends. Finally, both plays end with uncompromising views of the destructiveness of their situations.

Beyond these factual comparisons, what most connects the plays is their lack of a moral center represented on stage—none of the characters offer the audience any kind of *raisonneur* or trustworthy central intelligence.[1] Mamet indicated this before the New York opening of the play: "'My job,' he said, 'is to create a closed moral universe,' and to leave the evaluation to the audience."[2] Yet critics and audiences seem to agree that the characters' lack of morality comes from the competitive environment in which they are placed—the economic system that forces one worker to compete against, and defeat, the others. Churchill makes this politically explicit by linking that system with the conservative Thatcher government. In the film of his play, Mamet invents Blake, the Alec Baldwin character, to make the stakes of the competition clear: "First prize is a Cadillac Eldorado. . . . second prize is a set of steak knives. . . . third prize is you're fired." It is this system that has corrupted the people inside of its domain.

Many of the critics therefore use a Marxist approach, explicitly or implicitly, to examine these capitalist victims of capitalism.[3] My view is that there is a deeper level of contamination in this system. It is not just that bosses and workers are dehumanized, but both plays present a system which is so centrally flawed that its destruction reaches everywhere in the society. In order to dramatize this, however, both playwrights have written plays with surface targets that seem to be about outside oppression of their characters—men oppressing women and bosses oppressing salesmen. These have distracted audiences and caused misunderstanding.

Beneath the surface, however, the playwrights put the blame not outside the characters, but inside of them, for the destruction they create for each other and those closest to them. The trick of this is that the ideology is invisible. So how is the dramatist to reveal the hidden codes of the society? In both of these plays the answer is found in a similar technique: they seem to be plays about adults in an adult world, but are really about adults reduced to the level of children. Ironically, the result is that the adults' own children become the victims of this confusion.

The theorist who illuminates this misdirection, from superficial targets to systemic corruption, is Theodor Adorno (and his contemporary successor Frederic Jameson). Adorno defines a more subtle Marxist interpretation of ideology. Superficially one might follow Terry Eagleton's generalization, "Literature, in the meaning of the word we have inherited, is an ideology. It has the most intimate relations to questions of social power."[4] But Adorno is much more cautious about using ideology to analyze literature:

> We must be especially wary of the present insufferable tendency to drag out at every slightest opportunity the concept of ideology. For ideology is untruth—false consciousness, a lie. It manifests itself in the failure of art works, in their own intrinsic falsehood, and can be uncovered by criticism. . . . The greatness of works of art lies solely in their power to let those things be heard which ideology conceals.[5]

This view that lesser works manifest "the false consciousness" of ideology is often used for analysis of popular culture where ideology is closer to the surface, but as Adorno indicates, this is less evident in a great work that reveals what ideology conceals. Mamet and Churchill illustrate the problem; both playwrights give a false ideology on the surface of their works, but a deeper reading reveals the more profound view of that ideology.

The Marxist literary technique for representing this kind of situation is to present the action of the play against a background of a larger social issue or movement. As Jameson says in his essay on Adorno in *Marxism and Form*, "In the realm of literary criticism the sociological approach necessarily juxtaposes the individual work of art with some vaster form of social reality which is seen in one way or another as its source or ontological ground . . ."[6] As a result, "consciousness is superposed against the pattern of a collective and institutional organization."[7]

Both plays use misdirection as they establish the background. Churchill's play at first seems to deal with feminism and patriarchy, but turns quickly to examine how women oppress other women, from girls' games in a cardboard box to the adult world of work and home. And Mamet seems to deal with bending people to one's will to make a sale, but later is revealed to be dealing instead with boys' games of outwitting, out-talking, and cheating. So in both cases there is a larger social background, but when reduced to the level of children, ideological issues are revealed more clearly. The apparent background is created by invoking a golden age of the past—then showing it to be mythic. Churchill's golden age is shown in the opening scene's dinner with great women of history and culture; Mamet's opening scenes have salesmen recollecting the ideal past of real estate sales in the 1960s when there was no cutthroat competition or exploitation of the client. In fact, both are mythic constructions. According to Adorno, such myths of the past golden age are invented when the present becomes intolerable.

CHURCHILL'S FEMINISM IN THE GOLDEN AGE

Churchill opens in an overtly Brechtian way with five famous women of history and culture at dinner together to celebrate Marlene's promotion to managing director of the Top Girls employment agency. Feminism thus becomes the background against which subsequent realistic modern scenes are presented. Churchill makes her misdirection clear in an interview:

> What I was intending to do was make it first look as though it was celebrating the achievements of women and then—by showing the main character, Marlene, being successful in a very competitive, destructive, capitalist way—ask, what kind of achievement is that? The idea was that it would start out looking like a feminist play and turn into a socialist one, as well.[8]

The problem with placing the action against one background and then changing it is that critics get distracted by the superficial feminism, and may thereby miss the deeper issues of material causes of oppression in the play.

Using women of history and culture as a background for Marlene's accomplishments illustrates this problem, for critics divide in describing that opening scene. Some see heroic women; others see victims. Geraldine Cusins takes the view that women are triumphant, "overwhelmingly, the first scene is a celebration of achievement by women in the face of seemingly insurmountable odds."[9] Michelene Wandor takes a similar view: "None presents herself as a victim; for each, taking responsibility for herself is the central thread."[10] Ironically, this language reveals my point that critics are distracted by the superficial: "taking responsibility for herself" is shown to be the dehumanizing result of Marlene's Thatcherite conservatism. Lisa Merrill, however, sees the accomplishments, but recognizes the irony: "By attempting to equate Marlene's promotion at work with the extreme circumstances overcome by the other five guests, Churchill renders Marlene's achievement petty and ludicrous."[11] Amelia Howe Kritzer takes a more dualistic view: "Their initially festive mood gradually turns bitter, with the growing realization of what each has lost in her struggle to survive and succeed."[12] Janet Brown sees only the bitter side: "In *Top Girls*, Marlene, whose rise to the executive suite many middle class feminists might unthinkingly admire, is, like her ghostly dinner companions, a selfish, isolated snob."[13] Brown's later view in *Taking Center Stage* comes close to my own: "The apparently autonomous lives of all the diners have been predicated on a patriarchal system that simply co-opted them, and at a high price in isolation and suffering."[14] This array of views demonstrates the trickiness of decentering the play, leading the audience to assume it is a play to be understood through women's history.

The opening scene seems to give one vision of women who triumph over obstacles (the misleading ideology), but in fact it gives the opposite—women who have become twisted and grotesque (the deeper ideology). The scene presents women who have been twisted by living in a patriarchal world in which the role of woman is so narrowly defined or circumscribed that a woman of spirit might have to rebel, but to do so forces her into an uncomfortable definition of herself as something other than a complete woman. This is most evident in Pope Joan, who is completely unaware of the most basic physical facts of womanhood, having no idea she is pregnant, and later giving birth in the street. With her, denial is almost total. She is not just twisted in denying her womanhood, but also in accepting the patriarchal Church construction of women. She first explains her longing: "I was seized again/with a desperate longing for the absolute. . . . Pope Leo died and I was chosen. All right then, I would be Pope. I would know God. I would know everything."[15] Becoming Pope results not from her ambition, but the pure desire to "know everything." The hope is futile only because of being a woman: "I had thought the Pope would know everything. I thought God would speak to me directly. But of course he knew that I was a woman" (14). This is the most disturbing of all the women's stories, since it shows such a complete acceptance of the views of the time. So Joan, despite her achievement in the face of such barriers, is still trapped inside this view of her own inferiority. And her story parallels the other women's stories.

The rest of the play becomes a commentary on this theme. Subsequently we are shown the super-successful scientist turned saleswoman, Win, who is locked into a self-destructive pattern of success, being cut off from (male) colleagues, drinking, self-loathing, crashing into multiple personalities, retreating, starting again.

> Any job I ever did I started doing it better than the rest of the crowd and they didn't like it. So I'd get unpopular and I'd have a drink to cheer myself up. . . . Then I . . . went bonkers for a bit, thought I was five different people, got over that all right, the psychiatrist said I was perfectly sane and highly intelligent. Got married in a moment of weakness and he's inside now . . . and I've not been to see him too much this last year. I like this better than sales, I'm not really that aggressive. (65)

Win's story is deliberately archetypal. The pattern of competing with men, beating them, then falling in love with a loser keeps repeating itself in her life. Entering into the competitive world of "the rest of the [male] crowd" destroys her—as it does the men in Mamet's play.

Mamet's Real Estate and the Golden Age

In *Glengarry Glen Ross* the background story is the patriarchal world of salesmen in America. Most of the American reviews made this connection by linking *Glengarry* with *Death of a Salesman* to praise Mamet's grittier view of the life of the salesman.[16] The background here is more specific in time and space: selling real estate in Florida. This has been a satiric dramatic target at least since George S. Kaufman and Morrie Ryskind wrote the 1925 play *Cocoanuts* for the Marx Brothers. This context also invokes a history of land swindles: as the customers are in Chicago buying land they've never seen in Florida, all they can do is trust the salesman. And a play built on real estate and sales can't be separated from Mamet's common theme of confidence men and deception. But in Mamet's time frame, the company seems to have been selling developments for at least eighteen years.

Since the salesmen find no meaning in their jobs and are exploited by Mitch and Murray, they fantasize about a time when selling real estate was really good—the golden age of real estate sales. In Adorno's view, invoking or inventing past history like this is the reaction to increasing dehumanization.[17] People seek to reconcile

> subject and objectivity, existence and the world, the individual consciousness and the external network of things and institutions into

which it first emerges. The naive projection of such logical possibility into the realm of historical chronology can only result in metaphysical nostalgia (the golden age before the fall, the blissful state of primitive man) or in Utopianism.[18]

In the first scenes the audience deduces the prehistory, "the golden age before the fall." Shelly Levene first tries to appeal to the office manager, John, by reminding him of the history of the company and the way it should be built on commitment to employees based on accomplishments:

> Lately kiss my ass lately. That isn't how you build an org . . . talk, talk to Murray. Talk to Mitch. When we were on Peterson, who paid for the fucking *car?* You talk to him. The *Seville* . . . ? He came in, "You bought that for me Shelly." Out of *what?* Cold *calling. Nothing.* Sixty-*five,* when we were there, with Glen *Ross* Farms?[19]

In Shelly's view something is owed to one who has for years worked so hard, been successful, and earned lots of money for the owners, Murray and Mitch. But John's position is that Shelly has not been the leader "lately." And the company's view is simple: whoever sells the most gets the best leads, and the Cadillac. The message is clear: competition generates enormous profits that are not split equally but instead all go to the one who sells the most. The others are essentially castaways.

Shelly continually tries to justify different treatment based on his history with the company: "I, *I* generated the dollar revenue sufficient to *buy* them [the premium leads]. Nineteen senny-*nine,* you know what I made? Senny-*nine?* Ninety-six thousand dollars. John? For *Murray* . . . For *Mitch* . . . Look at the sheets . . ."(20). Then he goes back eighteen years: "It's cold out there now, John. It's tight. Money is *tight.* This ain't sixty-five"(20). All of this constructs an idealized prehistory of land sales in Florida.

Like Levene, the other characters have lost out in sales to Ricky Roma. In response to the great pressure they feel, Moss and Aaronow construct an idyllic view of the golden age of selling:

> Moss: The whole fuckin' thing . . . The pressure's just too great. You're ab . . . you're absolu . . . they're too important. All of them. You go in the door. I . . . "I got to *close* this fucker, or I don't eat lunch," "or I don't win the *Cadillac.* . . ." We fuckin' work too hard. You work too hard. We all, I remem-

ber when we were at Platt . . . huh? Glen Ross Farms . . .
didn't we sell a bunch of that . . . ?

Aaronow: They came in and they, you know . . .

Moss: Well, they fucked it up.

Aaronow: They did.

Moss: And now . . .

Aaronow: We're stuck with *this* . . .

And it's not right to the *customers.*

.   .   .   .

Moss: I know it's not. I'll tell you, you got, you got, you know, you
got . . . what did I learn as a kid on Western? Don't sell a
guy one car. Sell him *five* cars over fifteen years. (30–31)

This is an extremely comic exchange on stage because the language is so
harsh, the sentiments so soft, and the discrepancy is funny. The use of humor here underlies the gap between the false idealization of sales and the
reality of exploitation.

As Adorno indicates, however, the attempt of the alienated workers is
to construct a past history in which there was a golden age, without "Some
contest board" (31), where there was cooperation rather than competition.
The humor of the presentation underlies the gap between the mythic past and
the real present.[20] The punch line to the exchange is poor Aaronow's concern
for "the customers." We know from their language describing customers,
however, that there is no such concern so we must assume that the whole prehistory of idyllic life at Glen Ross Farms is delusion. It was surely just as competitive then when the goal was to make sales not to benefit the customer.

The whole scene is funny because the interaction between Levene and
Williamson is so phony. We watch Levene try to weasel his way into selling
Williamson on his abilities. The main device is the one-on-one dialogue in
which a person tries to sell another on trusting him. The preponderance of
these two person exchanges (67 pages of the 108 pages) reveals the sales technique of a one-on-one competition.

The repetitions increase the humor; the live audience laughs at each
one. And the bizarre staging with two men sitting at adjoining tables facing each other on a banquette makes the conversation seem more comic.
The more ardent Shelly becomes, the more the audience laughs, and the
blank stare from J.T. Walsh as Williamson produces greater laughs.
Vincent Gardenia stresses a New York accent for Shelly: "Put a *closer* on
the job" (15). Gardenia draws out the long vowel of *"closer"* so much that
he gets the laugh.

The production style can make a comic statement as well. In New York the set was simply a long red bench seat with individual tables—only two of the tables and the part of the banquette facing them were lit—and this was the set for all three scenes of act 1, each a two-person, side-by-side dialogue.[21] As a result, the audience is given the sense of a fragmentary view of existence. We have to piece things together, and it is more comic.

The trick to each scene in the first act is twofold: first the golden age is an invented myth, not a reality—like the myth of the women overcoming obstacles. In *Top Girls* the women were still trapped inside an all-encompassing system that twisted them. The same is true of Mamet's salesmen. Second, the deception is revealed when a reversal comes at the end of the scene as we least expect it. Williamson can't help Levene until he's offered a bribe. Moss ends the second scene by suggesting that since the old love has gone out of the game, Aaronow should burglarize the building and steal the leads. When Aaronow balks, Moss threatens him as an accessory before the fact. The most startling reversal is Roma's reflection on death and the meaning of life, apparently the meandering thoughts of a person eating alone in a restaurant. It is more of a monologue than spoken to a stranger sitting in a nearby booth. In fact, James Lingk gets only thirteen words during the whole scene (47–51). It never occurs to us until the very end that Roma is not just talking about life but is selling real estate, and this indirect approach, through the meaning of life, is his pitch.

This reversal at the end is the essence of the Mamet con game. It is based on indirection and magician's sleight of hand. While we are looking in one direction, at the meaning of life, Roma suddenly switches hands and we are looking at buying Florida real estate as the key to security and a significant life. His appeal is to find meaning in life not in the future or the past, but in the present: "'If it [disaster] happens, AS IT MAY for that is not within our powers, I will *deal* with it, just as I do *today* with what draws my concern today.' I say *this* is how we must act. I do those things which seem correct to me *today*. I trust myself" (49). All of this is both a justification of his own egocentric life, as well as an inducement to Lingk to act spontaneously—impulse buying on a large scale. The logic, of course, is contradictory. First, the buyer is not acting in the moment but only buying land as a speculation in hopes of future profits and security. Second, he is fortifying himself against the very disaster that Roma says one cannot be fully protected against.

Roma's is a microcosm of the conversational technique of all the salesmen. They speak indirectly; they refuse to answer direct questions; they try to move the conversation to some other ground where they are in control. Once they lure their opponent to those grounds they completely control him.

This is in stark contrast to Churchill's women—who are absolutely direct in their conversations. The strategy of boys' play is really the underlying referent for Mamet's depiction of men.

BAIT AND SWITCH: MEN TO BOYS

The golden age of real estate sales that Levene, Aaronow, and Moss all invoke implies the fixed past of business, an adult world. But in fact, that golden age is itself a mythic construct that they use to protect themselves from their vulnerability as virtual children in the adult world. Throughout *Glengarry* there is talk about being "men," another mythic idea like the golden age. Successful salesmen are true men as Levene implies: "I got my *balls* back" (102). Conversely, as Hersh Zeifman argues, customers and unsuccessful salespeople are "not man enough" (96), often referred to as women, children, or as homosexuals. Williamson especially gets all of Roma's wrath after he loses the sale with Lingk: "asshole. . . . You stupid fucking *cunt*. You *idiot*. Whoever told you you could work with *men*?" (96); "You *fairy*. . . . You fucking *child*" (96–97). Interestingly, despite all these epithets, most of the talk is modeled on the world of boys, not men. Indeed, so much foul language as in the quotation is purely adolescent. So that beneath all the sales*man* misdirection about the golden age and real men, the truth is that these characters really speak and act like boys. Adorno posits this kind of self-contradiction as a means to recognizing the internal conflicts in the dominant ideology.[22]

There is no explicit allusion in *Glengarry Glen Ross* to the world of boys, but in his next work, a collection of essays entitled *Writing in Restaurants*, Mamet's first essay reconstructs a boys' dialogue that reveals the underlying basis of characters in the play. In this quintessential boys' dialogue, recalled from his 1950s childhood, Mamet argues that he shouldn't be held responsible for losing the baseball on the schoolyard roof:

Me: So he goes he ain't going home until we're paying him we lost the ball, he's gonna call my ma.

Tom: Where did you lose it?

Me: On the roof. So I go, "Look, you never called it, Gussie."

Tom: He *din* call it?

Me: *No!* That's what I'm *tellin'* you. He goes "I called it." I go, "No, you didn't, Gussie. No. You never called it, no. If you said 'chips' we woulda heard it, and you never called it. No." I ast the other guys, his own team, huh? Maurice goes, "I don't think you called it, Gus." I go, "Look here, your

own man, Gussie, huh?" He says that didn' mean a thing.
His own man.

Tom: Yeah.

Me: I tell him, "I ain't trine a hock the ball off you, Gus; you called
'chips' I'd pay for it right now. It's not the money . . . "

Tom: . . . no . . .

Me: ". . . and you know times that *I* have loss my ball, and you ass
Mike or anybody." Huh?[23]

Apparently unless *"chips"* is called, the batter need not take care not to hit
the ball too hard, beyond retrieval onto the roof: "[If] He *called* it, we would
all of played a little carefuller" (5). The argument made by Me (Mamet) is
that he is not responsible for losing the ball since Gussie did not call "chips."
But undercutting this argument, ME uses various diversionary tactics to keep
Gussie from holding him responsible (even alluding to balls he has lost in
the past, then of his headlight that was once broken).[24]

The passage substantially resembles Shelly's attempts to distract
Williamson from withholding the Glengarry leads. Like the boy, Mamet, in
the remembered dialogue, Levene does everything possible to distract
Williamson from the main point that Levene can't "close." But Williamson,
like Gussie, continues to hold Levene responsible. He will not be distracted
by side issues. Much of the humor of the scene involves our watching Levene
trying the same childish tactic of insisting that he had closed the last set of
leads he was given. Actually, only two of the four closed in any sense, and
both of those were quickly invalidated. Levene, however, like a child, insists
that this should not count against him:

Williamson *(Pause.):* What about the other two?

Levene: What two?

Williamson: Four. You had four leads. One kicked out, one the
judge, you say . . .

Levene: . . . you want to see the court records? John? Eh? You want
to go down . . .

Williamson: . . . no . . .

Levene: . . . don't you want to go down*town* . . . ?

Williamson: . . . no . . .

Levene: . . . then . . .

Williamson: . . . I only . . .

Levene: . . . then what is this "you *say*" shit, what is that? *(Pause.)*
What is that . . . ? (16–17)

Proposing the absurd idea that Williamson should go and investigate court records is done to verify Levene's claim that the loss of this one lead was not entirely his fault. But that ignores the other three completely. The strategy is childish, and rather like that of Me trying to distract Gussie from the key issue: that Mamet/Me lost the ball. At the end of the exchange, Levene even tries to move the discussion to trust, and with "you say" he tries to offer as another distraction which Williamson ignores.

Later in the scene Levene tries a variety of other approaches, mostly dealing with unverifiable past events used as another distraction. [What happened in] "Nineteen *eighty,* eighty-one . . . eighty-*two* . . . six months of eighty-two . . . who's there. . . . It's *me*" (17). "Sixty-*five,* when we were there, with Glen *Ross* Farms" (18). "I saw them when I was at Homestead, we pitched those cocksuckers Rio Rancho nineteen sixty-*nine* they wouldn't buy" (21). All of these mentions of history, most of which predate what Williamson could know, are the adult version of the child's attempt to distract as in the Me and Tom dialogue.

BAIT AND SWITCH: WOMEN TO GIRLS

Like *Glengarry Glen Ross, Top Girls* also places the competitive characters in the context of children. In this way it can strip the characters down so that we can see them more clearly—as children whose understanding of the world is woefully incomplete. Churchill's third scene is the play world of Angie and Kit. Since this scene does not seem to follow in sequence, it floats free, without context. In fact, however, it supplies a context of girlhood conversation for the scenes that both precede and follow: the job applicants themselves sound like children, and the final scene between the sisters, Marlene and Joyce, reveals a sibling rivalry that goes back to childhood. Their adult fights seem to reflect the same view of the world they must have had as children. Churchill connects girls and women in a way that makes women seem to act childishly, as if the system itself forces a kind of retardation or return to earlier models. *Top Girls* structures this perception directly by including the voices of children and implying their connection with the adult world.

The first act has three radically different venues: "Scene One: Restaurant, Saturday night. [Fantasy dinner]; Scene Two: 'Top Girls' Employment agency. Monday morning. [Marlene and Jeanine]; Scene Three: Joyce's back yard. Sunday afternoon. [Angie and Kit]." The sequence of events from fantasy to workaday reality to the children's world gives the audience three fragments of reality to put together. These fragments are much more disconnected than Mamet's, which, however disparate, at least take place in one locale. Churchill puts the three scenes in this scrambled order: scene 3, Sunday, should precede Monday, scene 2. As a result, the girls' world of scene 3 occurs out of place, and so the world of the girls permeates the other scenes, revealing the childish level to which adults have been reduced by a system that, on the surface, is very rational and adult in its forms of competition.

What ties the child and adult worlds together are escapist fantasies and dreams appropriate in childhood, but seemingly not for realistic adults. Yet all the adults lead lives of the purest fantasy. Marlene clearly does—the first scene is her fantasy. In scene 2, job applicant Jeanine has the childish dream of having it all—great job, husband, but a not too confining marriage: "I'd like a job where I was here in London and with him and everything but now and then—I expect it's silly. Are there jobs like that?" (32). She also reflects the girls' conversation on nuclear disaster when counseled by Marlene that one must plan such moves: "I might not be alive in ten years" (32).

The next job applicant, Louise, has a fantasy of escape from the trap of her life (as Angie dreams of escaping to Marlene in London in scene 3):

> I've built up a department. And there it is, it works extremely well, and I feel I'm stuck there. I've spent twenty years in middle management. I've seen young men who I trained go on, in my own company or elsewhere, to higher things. Nobody notices me. . . . They will notice me when I go, they will be sorry. . . . They will see when I've gone what I was doing for them. (52)

This childish refrain about being unnoticed, and how to make them notice, echoes over and over in her speech, but her fantasy of escape is not very realistic. Like Howard or Shelly Levene, she is too old to start over; the competitive world has little use for her. Even more unrealistic is the fantasy life of Shona, who wants to drive a Porsche up and down the M1 staying in hotels and living the good life selling fridges with big freezers. Nell quickly discovers that these lies about her life are all fantasy: "You just filled out the form with a pack of lies" (63). All the job applicants, in other words, are seeking to escape from their lives the same way the girls are in scene 3.

The final scene, however, is the most explicit, since Marlene's return to her home to visit Joyce and Angie after a six-year absence offers a number of models of adult siblings reverting to childhood. The most obvious is a fight over Angie's telling Marlene of her secret:

Joyce: So what's the secret?
Marlene: It's a secret.
Joyce: I know what it is anyway.
Marlene: I bet you don't. You always said that. (77)

This childish "I know a secret and you don't" is an explicit repetition of the same kind of exchange between Kit and Angie in scene 2:

Angie. I'm not telling you.
Kit: Why?
Angie: It's a secret.
Kit: But you tell me all your secrets.
Angie: Not the true secrets. (38)

Here, too, language is used simply to dominate by withholding knowledge. Both struggle for control the way that the sisters do in the final scene of the play.

Angie is the focal point of the struggle; apparently, both sisters want her and don't want her at the same time. This brings one of the possible endings to the scene, when both break down in their fight over her and seem to be reconciled like little girls:

Marlene: If I don't come for another six years she'll be twenty-one, will that be OK?
Joyce: That'll be fine, yes, six years would suit me fine.
Pause.
Marlene: I was afraid of this. I only came because I thought you wanted . . . I just want . . . (Marlene *cries*).
Joyce: Don't grizzle, Marlene, for God's sake. Marly? Come on, pet. Love you really. (81)

This looks to be offering a sentimental ending to the play, with Joyce calling her "Marly" and Joyce saying "Love you" leading to an ending where they live happily ever after. But when they take up politics their reconciliation is destroyed.

What is intriguing about the writing of the scene is how close they come at this moment—Joyce must touch Marlene to console her to get Marlene to say, "No, let me cry." And the attempt to console takes the form of childhood names, "Marly," not used anywhere else in the play. At this moment, however, they parallel the work of the actors playing Angie and Kit who are always touching each other.

In both plays, times of emotional stress cause the adults to regress to childish behavior. The irony of this is that in both plays the victims are not just the adults, Marlene and Levene, who cope in some way, but their own innocent daughters.

MOTHER/DAUGHTER

As Jameson makes clear in his essay on Adorno, the result of the pressure is indirect, rather than direct, and so is difficult to assess precisely because it is contained in "that moment of history which marks and deforms in one way or another all the cultural phenomena which it produces and includes, and which serves as the framework within which we understand them."[25] The "moment in history" that Mamet and Churchill share is that of the conservative victories (Reagan and Thatcher) and the renewed emphasis on competition as the key ingredient in capitalism.[26]

In this kind of a new synthesis about how the world should be run according to principles of natural selection, Adorno notes:

> What disappears in this notion of selection is the fact that what keeps the mechanism creaking along is human deprivation under conditions of insane sacrifice and the continual threat of catastrophe. The precarious and irrational self-preservation of society is falsified and turned into an achievement of its immanent justice or "rationality."[27]

Both plays focus largely on the public identity of their characters, but both also make clear the "insane" sacrifices that the characters make in order to keep the illusion of public persona which competes in the free marketplace. Marlene has sacrificed her family in every possible way in order to become "top girl." And physically Churchill makes that clear by locating her in the office most of the time, just as Mamet sets the men in *Glengarry* only in the office and the restaurant across the street.

We see Marlene's life in even greater detail in the final scene with her sister—the lovers, abortions, abandoned child, abandoned family—feeling cut off, reaching out, hating it. Like her sister, Joyce is equally self-destructive. She is a Marxist whose life is spent cleaning other people's houses or clothes, taking out her resentment by secretly vandalizing rich people's cars, blaming her sister and Angie for her dead-end life and her failed marriage.

Angie is the final step in the chain. She is a creative, intelligent, imaginative child whose self-image could be reduced to the same insignificance as all the other women—not by men, but by women who have accepted a patriarchal system. Her own mother, whom she thinks of as Aunt Marlene, says the best she can achieve is to be a grocery packer. Angie seems doomed to the same kind of life of self-loathing that her foremothers have all had.

The common view of the critics is that Angie is fated to such a meaningless life.[28] Paul Lawley concludes, "As Marlene says, Angie is 'not going to make it.'"[29] And her failure is "the ethic of acquisitive individualism which has been the foundation for Marlene's success is one that would condemn her own pathetic child to a life of deprivation and wretchedness."[30] His view is typical: blaming Marlene for her "pathetic child." This view is based on the visit in the last scene, when Marlene asks Angie what she wants to do and Joyce answers for her: "I don't think she's ever thought of it. . . . She hasn't an idea in her head what she wants to do. Lucky to get anything. . . . She's not clever like you" (71–72). Angie is left voiceless in this examination of her future.

Joyce's characterization of her shapes the way that we see her in the scene, as she seems a little retarded in her desire for all three of them to put on perfume and smell alike. Her friendship with Kit has already been questioned as abnormal, since Kit is four years younger. When Angie is discussed after she's gone to bed, Joyce's view is clear:

> Marlene: I don't mean anything personal. I don't believe in class. Anyone can do anything if they've got what it takes. . . .
> [But] If they're stupid or lazy or frightened, I'm not going to help them get a job, why should I?
> Joyce: What about Angie? . . . She's stupid, lazy, and frightened, so what about her?
> Marlene: You run her down too much. She'll be all right.
> Joyce: I don't expect so, no. I expect her children will say what a wasted life she had. If she has children. Because nothing's changed and it won't with them in. (86)

This exchange crystallizes many of the issues of the play. Both Marlene and Joyce view Angie as like their mother whom both see as leading a wasted life. Both resolved to live different lives from hers, but both are unhappy. Marlene's harsh view of natural selection ("Anyone can do anything, if they've got what it takes") she uses to justify her own life. And if Angie hasn't "got what it takes" because she's "stupid, lazy and frightened," so much the worse for her.

This view of Angie, however, is generated by Joyce, who gives Angie no love. The affection with Kit in the box is the only love Angie gets. This is evident in 1.3 when Joyce calls Angie:

> You there Angie? Kit? You there Kitty? Want a cup of tea? I've got some chocolate biscuits. Come on now I'll put the kettle on. Want a choccy biccy, Angie?
> *They all listen and wait.*
> Fucking rotten little cunt. You can stay there and die. I'll lock the back door. (37)

Given this aside, it is a wonder that the audience takes Joyce's point of view about Angie. Clearly Angie comes from an unloving home. Joyce resents Marlene for leaving her daughter, and blames Angie for her miscarriage. Her life is full of resentment for taking care of her mother and Angie, while to her view, Marlene has all the best parts of life, such as traveling to America.

In the chronologically last scene, 2.1, Marlene echoes her sister's negative judgment of Angie:

> Win: She wants to work here.
> Marlene: Packer in Tesco more like.
> Win: She's a nice kid. Isn't she?
> Marlene: She's a bit thick. She's a bit funny.
> Win: She thinks you're wonderful.
> Marlene: She's not going to make it. (66)

It is shocking that critics seem to accept this assessment. Clearly something about ideology in the play has become invisible if Joyce and Marlene's point of view is taken as normative.

In an exchange from the final scene, one of their confrontational moments, the misery of Joyce becomes clear to Marlene:

> Marlene: America, America, you're jealous. / I had to get out,
> Joyce: Jealous?
> Marlene. I knew when I was thirteen, out of their house, out of them, never let that happen to me, / never let him, make my / own way, out.
> Joyce: Jealous of what you've done, you're ashamed of me if I came to your office, your smart friends, wouldn't you, I'm ashamed of you, think nothing but yourself, you've got on, nothing's changed for most people / has it. (85)

Marlene's perception of Joyce's jealousy reduces them both to babbling in incomplete sentences. Saying "I had to get out" when she was thirteen (though she didn't actually leave until she was seventeen) underlines Marlene's desperation to escape the fate of her mother. Joyce's anger indicates her despair that "nothing's changed for most people" and that Marlene's Thatcherite view will never allow them to change. She also recognizes that Marlene moves in a "smart" world in which she'd be ashamed of Joyce.

Ironically, in 1.3 Angie voices the same desperation to escape which Marlene had: "If I don't get away from here I'm going to die" (36). And in the last scene chronologically, Angie does get away—escaping to Marlene without telling Joyce. That move indicates that Angie is not the dead loss that her mother and aunt think she is. In fact she always manages to get her way—with Kit, with Joyce and going to the movie, getting Marlene to come visit, and finally getting away to London on her own. All of this indicates that she has a potential and spirit to rebel, but has been so beaten down by her environment—abandoned by her mother, raised by her unloving aunt— that she is lucky to have emerged with any spirit intact.

Adorno's sense of love relationships in *Minima Moralia: Reflections from Damaged Life* is relevant to the Joyce/Marlene/Angie dichotomy. His rejection of enlightenment rationalism results in the view that one cannot stand outside of persons loved, like Angie, and make judgments of them objectively because it both reduces them to timeless commodities and thereby into possessions:

> Historically, the notion of time is itself formed on the basis of the order of ownership. But the desire to possess reflects time as a fear of losing, of the irrecoverable. Whatever is, is experienced in relation to its possible non-being. This alone makes it fully a possession and, thus petrified, something functional that can be exchanged for other, equivalent possessions. Once wholly a possession, the loved person is no longer really looked at.[31]

Both Joyce and Marlene stand outside of Angie this way, and make her into a "possession"—either to be disposed of as Marlene does, or to be collected as Joyce does. Both also stand outside of love, too, and from their seemingly objective view, they think that they can judge her. But their viewpoint is timeless, as Adorno suggests, seeing no future for her because of her past performance. That view denies change to her; it makes her into an object. In point of fact, Churchill planned out a whole future for Angie, but then decided not to include it in the play because it would make the point too explicit:

I quite deliberately left a hole in the play, rather than giving people a model of what they could be like. I meant the thing that is absent to have a presence in the play. I did wonder when I was writing, however, whether the action ought to go on, and this is a crude way I might have done it: Angie discovers that Marlene's values are false and realizes that the person she'd like to kill is Marlene, because she's such a shit. Next, Angie, though stupid, meets up with a lot of feminist women and becomes politicized, and gets a job as a bricklayer in a feminist collective. But then I thought, what the hell; if people can't see the values, I don't want to spell them out. I didn't want to put a feminist heroine on the stage.[32]

FATHER/DAUGHTER

This is the first point where there is a serious divergence between Churchill and Mamet. Churchill finishes the play, violating chronology, at Joyce's house—the first indoor domestic setting. Mamet stays inside the workaday world, and the allusions that Levene makes to his daughter, essentially the only family references in the play, never go so far as to allow us a glimpse of her, or of him in a role other than at his job. Interestingly, though defined by her absence, his daughter is at least treated much more positively than Angie is. She is clearly on her father's mind, but not made into an object or possession in the Adorno sense. In fact, Shelly is hardly able to discuss her or allude to her without checking himself to keep from making her into some kind of object of pity.

Shelly three times pleads that Williamson remember his daughter—who has some undisclosed problem that forces Shelly to stay in the real estate business working as hard as he can to care for her. He alludes to her once in the opening scene: "I'm asking you. As a favor to me? *(Pause.)* John. *(Long pause.)* John: my *daughter* . . ." (26). There is no explanation of the nature of her problem. It is a little more fully developed in the movie as a health problem: Jack Lemmon is shown in a phone booth calling a hospital to check on her. But with no national health insurance, Levene is desperate. Adorno's description from *Prisms* cited above fits perfectly: "Human deprivation under conditions of insane sacrifice and the continual threat of catastrophe." The sacrifice is implied in the second act when Levene recalls,

And, and, and I *did* it. And I put a kid through *school*. She . . . and . . . Cold *calling,* fella. Door to door. But you don't know. You don't know. You never heard of a *streak*. You never heard of "marshaling your sales force. . . ." What are you, you're a *secretary,* John. Fuck *you.* That's my message to you. Fuck you and kiss my ass. (77)

Whatever has happened to his daughter apparently occurred after she finished school, when normally she would be out on her own. While Levene is proud of the past accomplishments of working to get her through school, she is still his sole concern. He plays her off in his mind against Williamson, and ironically when he finally commits the robbery, his anger is directed against Williamson but can only hurt his daughter. The leads are his livelihood. Stealing and selling them leaves him with almost nothing. And his imminent arrest will make certain that he can't support her.

For Levene, Williamson is the obstacle to his daughter's survival. He indicates this when John says he is turning Shelly in to the police:

> Williamson: Because I don't like you.
> Levene: John: John: . . . my *daughter*
> Williamson: Fuck you. (104)

It is possible that Shelly is merely using his daughter for a final appeal—perhaps he could even use her to make sales. But this is not likely, since he never alludes to her in a complete sentence. He is unable to objectify her in language; it is clearly a subject too painful to develop or to discuss. Yet one senses that in his view all his work has been for her.

CONCLUSION: LOST IN HYPERSPACE

At the end of *Glengarry Glen Ross* script comes the final revelation that the office was a house of games. Levene and the others have been victims of a rigged game in which Williamson has fed the best prospects to Roma, presumably in exchange for a substantial kickback. Thinking back we recognize that Williamson was really engineering Shelly into offering the bribe in the first scene. So the salesmen have been deceived. Roma has been in charge all along, and wants to ensure that he stays in front. His worry is that Levene, with regained confidence, will begin to sell again and may overtake him. Roma doesn't realize that this won't happen because Levene is about to be arrested. To ensure that he stays on top Roma offers Levene a partnership, and then behind his back guarantees that Levene cannot be more successful than he:

> Roma: Williamson: listen to me: when the *leads* come in . . . listen
> to me: when the *leads* come in I want my top two off the
> list. For *me.* My usual two. Anything you give *Levene* . . .

Williamson: . . . I wouldn't worry about it.

Roma: Well I'm *going* to worry about it, and so are you, so shut up and *listen. (Pause.)* I GET HIS ACTION. My stuff is *mine,* whatever *he* gets for himself, I'm talking half. You put me in with him. . . . Do you understand? My stuff is mine, his stuff is ours. I'm taking half of his commissions—now *you* work it out. (107)

This conclusion to the play is fitting because repeatedly we have seen people playing on others' trust, then using them. Once again we, like Levene, have been taken in and duped. Roma's praise of Levene for great work in teaming up on Lingk is perfect because we know, ironically, that Levene can't capitalize on it—he's going to jail. And just as we sit thinking we've seen the tragic irony of the ending, Mamet reverses it all on us. It is not tragic, but something else. We discover that Roma is not sincere; he is simply duping Levene once again to win his confidence in order to keep him from winning the Cadillac. The final revelation that Roma is in control of Williamson, and treats him like an underling, is a shock. But it makes sense once we combine that recognition with the first scene and realize that Levene was a neophyte at bribery and Williamson was in control all along, just as Moss controlled Aaronow, and Roma controlled Lingk.

The doubly ironic point is that the true victim in this play is Levene. He accepts that, as Adorno indicates, "what he earns" equals "what he is worth."[33] When Levene thinks that he is worth nothing, after failing to persuade Williamson in scene 1 to give him good leads, then the only response is to objectify himself and commit suicide—throw away the useless commodity:

I turned this thing around. I closed the *old* stuff, I can do it again. *I'm* the one's going to close 'em. I am! I am! 'Cause I turned this thing a . . . I can do *that,* I can do *anyth* . . . last night. I'm going to tell you, I was ready to Do the Dutch. Moss gets me, "Do this, we'll get well. . . ." Why not? Big fuckin' deal. I'm halfway hoping to get caught. To put me out of my . . . *(Pause.)* But it *taught* me something. What it taught me is that you've got to get *out* there. Big deal. So I wasn't cut out to be a thief. I was cut out to be a salesman. (101–2)

The irony is that we quickly discover through Roma, though Levene does not, that to be a salesman *is* to be a thief. And Roma's control of the board and the leads makes it clear that he is more accomplished at bribing Williamson than the others, yet they never know it. Levene ironically stakes his whole identity on sales, but he can never be a success because Roma already has the best leads and thereby makes more sales—Levene can never do better than runner-up. Since he does not know this, he wants to commit suicide ("Do the Dutch"), and then hopes to get caught—"to put me out of my" misery. But the misery is not of his making, as he thinks it is. In the salesman's money equals worth theory, failure to sell is failure as a person. He alone is responsible. Levene never realizes that the game is rigged so he can never succeed.

There can be no alternative in a self-contained system that allows for cheaters to win; losers can only turn to suicide, or try to become thieves as Levene does. But there is no way to succeed in the way that Marlene assumes one can in *Top Girls:* "Anyone can do anything if they've got what it takes" (86). Levene seems to think the same thing, and never recognizes that it is an illusion. For Churchill it is not so much an illusion, as it is a motto for dehumanizing both the Top Girls and all those they had to leave behind to achieve success.

The structural parallel in *Top Girls* that gives the same box-within-box sense is the reversal of the last scene (which occurs the year before the scene it follows). Thus we see Angie at fifteen in the last scene, and sixteen in the earlier scene when she runs away from home. The reversal of chronology gives a similar impression of being trapped in circular time. Somehow the fights and errors of the past continue into the present and each generation passes on such baggage that there is no escape. The child becomes an adult and then acts like a child. That is why Churchill could not supply her projected ending for Angie. In the world of *Top Girls* (not *Top Women*), as in the world of *Glengarry Glen Ross,* there is no escape from the labyrinth of deceptions that people have created.

In this way both plays resemble Frederic Jameson's image of the postmodern condition in late capitalism, John Portman's Westlin Bonaventure Hotel in Los Angeles, which is similarly spatially disorienting:

> So I come finally to my principal point here, that this latest mutation in space—postmodern hyperspace—has finally succeeded in transcending the capacities of the individual human body to locate itself, to organize its immediate surroundings perceptually, and cognitively to map its position in a mappable external world. It may now be suggested that this alarming disjunction point between the body and its built environment—which is to the initial bewilderment of the older modernism as the velocities of spacecraft to those of the automobile—can itself stand as the symbol and analogon of that even sharper dilemma which is the incapacity of our minds, at least at present, to

map the great multinational and decentered communicational network in which we find ourselves caught as individual subjects.[34]

Jameson's argument is that the contemporary problem is one of spatial orientation—mapping. The individual is lost in the multinational corporate maze, which is totally decentered.

The smaller corporate worlds of Mamet and Churchill are equally decentered, at least morally. Both begin with disorienting misdirection, making us think we are dealing with feminism, or real estate scams, and conjuring the illusion of a golden age when there was no exploitation. Then they change direction with internal contradiction or humor to give a different focus—on socialism and variant forms of dishonesty. In doing so, both present their characters as losing their way, behaving like children, and worse, hurting their own children by being unable to cope with the disorientation they feel.

Marlene concocts a fantasy of her place among the Top Girls of History and Literature and Art but when we hear their stories we realize that they were trapped and distorted in their material circumstances as she is. We see her daughter follow in her footsteps, but a daughter she dismisses: "She'll never make it." Levene's pattern and fantasy is even more self-destructive. He finally mistakes the leads for reality, and in frustration steals and sells the leads for a pittance, yet they are what he needs to make a living. His anger is directed at Williamson but the damage he does is ultimately to himself, much like Marlene. Both are trapped at the end of their plays: Marlene in a history that will continuously enfold and frame the present, and all the salesmen in a corrupt and rigged contest world. Both fantasize that they can escape through hard work and effort, but there is no escape.

Adults are reduced to children. Child and adult are trapped in a closed loop in which one seems to become adult, then regresses into being a child. This is the next step beyond fanaticizing of an ideal time, the golden age of the past, but is again a refusal to face the unpleasantness of the future. Both are forms of escapism, because the characters cannot face the inescapable conclusion that both playwrights present of a world totally corrupt and a system completely dehumanizing. The technique of misdirection that both playwrights use is therefore necessary, despite the risks of leading critics and audience astray with obvious targets. To get to this conclusion, the audience must first think that there is a solution, then come to the devastating discovery that the characters themselves never reach. The reversing endings of both plays brings the audience to this discovery, one the characters are unable to face.

1. Mamet claims that Aaronow is "closest" to being a *raisonneur* in Matthew
C. Roudané's "Interview With David Mamet," *Studies in American Drama, 1945–
Present* 1 (1986): 75. "In *Glengarry Glen Ross,* it's interesting to watch Aaronow. He's
the one who comes closest to being the character of a *raisonneur,* for throughout the
whole play he's saying, 'I don't understand what's going on here.' 'I'm no good.' 'I
can't fit in here. . . .' Or his closing lines, 'Oh, God, I hate this job.' It's a kind of
monody throughout the play. Aaronow has some degree of conscience, some awareness; he's troubled. Corruption troubles him." This is not the usual perspective of a
raisonneur. Instead of being the one with the (playwright's) answers, Aaronow is the
one with questions, with doubts.

2. Mel Gussow, "Real Estate World a Model for Mamet," *New York Times,*
28 March 1984, sec. C, 19.

3. Amelia Howe Kritzer deals with *Top Girls* in the chapter "Labour and Capital" in *The Plays of Caryl Churchill* (London: Methuen, 1991). See also Lisa Merrill,
"Monsters and Heroines: Caryl Churchill's Women," in *Caryl Churchill: A Casebook,*
ed. Phyllis R. Randall (New York: Garland, 1988), 85, in which *Top Girls* "engages her
audience in questioning capitalist strivings"; Linda Fitzsimmons, "'I won't turn back for
you or anyone': Caryl Churchill's Socialist-Feminist Theatre," *Essays in Theatre* 6 (1987):
19, says *Top Girls* "treats the ideal of motherhood as a political issue, examining it as a
construct of patriarchy and capitalism." Of *Glengarry Glen Ross,* Dennis Carroll notes
in *David Mamet* (Houndmills: Macmillan, 1987), 32, that "American capitalism creates the incentives and the context that drive the salesmen"; C.W.E. Bigsby observes in
David Mamet (London: Methuen, 1985), 125, that the "circularity [of plot] clearly reflects the production-consumption cycle of capitalism"; Anne Dean in *David Mamet:
Language as Dramatic Action* (Rutherford, N.J.: Associated University Presses, 1990),
189, describes "a consumer society based on materialism and has, at its heart, an emptiness that cannot be assuaged by yet more money in the bank"; and Philip C. Kolin argues
that "Mitch and Murray do more than simply epitomize the corrupt bosses of capitalism. . . . [They] represent the pitfalls of false friendship" in "Mitch and Murray in David
Mamet's *Glengarry Glen Ross,*" *Notes on Contemporary Literature* 18 (1988): 4.

4. Terry Eagleton, *Literary Theory: An Introduction* (Minneapolis: University
of Minnesota Press, 1983), 22.

5. Cited by Martin Jay in *Adorno* (Cambridge: Harvard University Press,
1984), 155.

6. Frederic Jameson, *Marxism and Form: Twentieth Century Dialectical Theories of Literature* (Princeton: Princeton University Press, 1971, 1974), 4–5.

7. Jameson, 6.

8. Emily Mann, "[Interview with] Caryl Churchill." In *Interviews with Contemporary Women Writers,* ed. Kathleen Besko and Rachel Koenig (New York: Beech
Tree Books 1987), 82.

9. Geraldine Cusins, *Churchill: The Playwright* (London: Methuen, 1989), 95.

10. Michelene Wandor, *Carry On, Understudies: Theatre and Sexual Politics,*
(rev. ed. London: Routledge, 1986), 172.

11. Merrill, 83.

12. Kritzer, 140.

13. Janet Brown, "*Top Girls* Catches the Next Wave," in *Caryl Churchill: A
Casebook,* ed. Phyllis R. Randall (New York: Garland, 1988), 124.

14. Janet Brown, *Taking Center Stage: Feminism in Contemporary U.S. Drama*
(Metuchen, N.J. and London: Scarecrow Press, 1991), 106. Juli Thompson Burk also
takes a balanced view in "Top Girls and the Politics of Representation," in *Upstag-
ing Big Daddy: Directing Theater As If Gender and Race Really Matter,* ed. Ellen
Donkin and Susan Clement (Ann Arbor: University of Michigan Press, 1995), 73:
"What I tried to do was to position them [the women of history] as successful people

(for the most part) in Marlene's opinion. But I also wanted the audience to see how each woman's apparent success rested upon her ultimate oppression."

15. Caryl Churchill, *Top Girls* (London: Methuen, 1982, rev. ed. 1985), 12. Subsequent references are in parentheses following quotations.

16. Humm, [R. Hummler], "Glengarry Glen Ross," *Variety,* 28 March 1984, 104; Robert Brustein, "Show and Tell," *The New Republic,* 7 May 1984, 27–28; Richard Corliss, "Pitchmen Caught in the Act," *Time,* 9 April 1984, 105; C. Lee Jenner, "Glengarry Glen Ross," *Stages,* May 1984, 6–7; Stanley Kauffmann, *Saturday Review,* November/December 1984, 58–59; Jack Kroll, "Mamet's Jackals in Jackets," *Newsweek,* 9 April 1984, 109; Julius Novick, "Men's Business," *The Village Voice,* 3 April 1984, 89; Frank Rich, "Theater: A Mamet Play, 'Glengarry Glen Ross,'" *New York Times,* 26 March 1984, sec. C, 17; and Gerald Weales, "Rewarding Salesmen: New from Mamet, Old from Miller," *Commonweal,* 4 May 1984, 278. In contrast, in Britain only Milton Shulman, "Glengarry Glen Ross," *Standard,* in *London Theatre Record,* 10–23 September 1983, 824, alludes to Willy Loman.

17. Martin Jay, *Adorno,* 63–64, amplifies this rejection of the idea of a golden age by quoting Adorno's essay on "Subject-Object": "The picture of a temporal or extratemporal original state of happy identity between subject and object is romantic, however—a wishful project at times, but today no more than a lie. The undifferentiated state before the subject's formation was the dread of the blind web of nature, of myth; it was in protest against it that the great religions had their truth content. Besides, to be undifferentiated is not to be one; even in Platonic dialectics, unity requires diverse items of which it is the unity."

18. Jameson, *Marxism,* 38.

19. David Mamet, *Glengarry Glen Ross* (New York: Grove, 1984), 18. Subsequent references are in parentheses following quotations.

20. According to Gay Brewer, in *David Mamet and Film: Illusion/Disillusion* (Jefferson, N.C.: McFarland, 1993), 166–67, "The Foley-Mamet film is totally darker than its antecedent; it lacks the play's humor and sympathetic portrayals." In my view by dropping the humor the film gives, instead, the superficial critique that shows how dehumanized the salesmen are. The difference is most apparent in Levene. In the play he is not the sorry sad-sack victim that he is in Jack Lemmon's portrayal in the movie. In the videotape of the Broadway production at the Lincoln Center Library for the Performing Arts, Vincent Gardenia, who replaced Robert Prosky as Levene, portrays a fully self-confident, aggressive seller who sees himself as only in a streak of bad luck.

21. The London production was not fragmentary but purely realistic: Giles Gordon notes of the NT production: "Hayden Griffin has, for Act One, designed a red plush Chinese restaurant that looks like a Leicester Square steak house. Had the production been in the Olivier or Lyttelton, no doubt Chinese waiters would have served chop suey" (823). The New York production was much less elaborate; Clive Barnes thought "there could have been more decorative imaginations—the settings by Michael Merritt and the costumes by Nan Cibula are at best neutral assets" (15). But Frank Rich recognizes some of the symbolic purpose when he observes: "When the characters leave the dark restaurant for the brighter setting of the firm's office in Act II, Mr. Mamet's tone lightens somewhat as well" (C17). The point of the change in lighting is that comedy requires brighter light. But the first act leaves the audience guessing, and the darkness, illuminating just two tables, is much better demonstrated with the fragmentary, rather than fully realistic setting. On the whole subject of staging Mamet's plays, see Carroll's chapter on "The Plays in the Theatre," *David Mamet,* 118–39 which omits *Glengarry,* but explains clearly the need for a minimalist style of production for his plays generally.

22. In the Introduction to *Adorno: The Stars Down to Earth and Other Essays on the Irrational in Culture,* Stephen Crook explains that Adorno detected this kind of self-contradiction in his study of astrology columns, "The reason for this ir-

rational contradiction is that "fascist propaganda, and by analogy the wider culture, is obedient only to the 'logic' of the unconscious" (13).

23. David Mamet, *Writing in Restaurants* (New York: Viking, 1986), 4.

24. Toby Silverman Zinman, in "Jewish Aporia: The Rhythm of Talking in Mamet," *Theatre Journal* 44 (May 1992): 208–9, argues for a different model for Mamet's questions and answers: "These questions are not exactly examples of *erotesis*, the device usually called the 'rhetorical question,' in that they are answered, sometimes by another character, sometimes by the asker himself. The device seems, rather, to be a variation on *aporia*, the trope of doubt, the real or pretended inability to know what the subject under discussion is." But I don't find "doubt" the issue here; rather I see more evidence for a boy's technique of evading the issue and substituting one on which there is less doubt.

25. Jameson, *Marxism*, 52.

26. Mamet makes the connection with Reagan clear in the interview with Roudané: "Economic life in America is a lottery. Everyone's got an equal chance, but only one guy is going to get to the top. 'The more I have the less you have.' So one can only succeed at the cost of, the failure of another, which is what a lot of my plays— *American Buffalo* and *Glengarry Glen Ross*—are about. That's what Acting President Reagan's whole campaign is about" (73).

27. Theodor Adorno, *Prisms,* 1967; trans. Samuel and Sherry Weber (Cambridge: MIT Press, 1981), 38.

28. Joseph Marohl, in "De-realized Women: Performance and Identity in Top Girls," *Modern Drama* 17 (1987): 388, concludes "Marlene's world cannot account for or accommodate her. The world continuing to be what it is, Angie, like most women, can never be a 'top girl.'" Janet Brown similarly sees this as Marlene's fault: "If Angie, representing those children who will never be at the 'top' of any hierarchy, has only Marlene to depend upon, then she and the society have every reason to fear" (*Taking Center Stage*, 113). Fitzsimmons simply sees Angie as victim: "The story ends . . . with Marlene's dismissal of her: 'She's not going to make it' (66). This system and the attitudes which support it are what Gret and Joyce demand we fight" (23). Her essay takes a much more positive view of Joyce than I do. Merrill simply notes that "Churchill has already shown her audience the dim prospects for Angie's future" (87). Kritzer sees that "Angie's final lines reveal her as stranded between her own 'frightening' powerlessness and Marlene's power to be 'frightening'" (149).

29. Paul Lawley, "*Top Girls,*" *International Directory of Theatre: 1 Plays,* ed. Mark Hawkins-Dady (Chicago: St. James Press, 1992), 818.

30. Lawley, 818.

31. Theodor Adorno, *Minima Moralia: Reflections from Damaged Life* (1951), trans. E.F.N. Jephcott (London: NLB, 1974), 79.

32. Stone, 81.

33. In the early *Dialectic of the Enlightenment* (1944), trans. John Cumming, 1972 (New York: Continuum, 1993), written with Max Horkheimer, Adorno analyzes economic prosperity as a cause of dehumanization: "Here in America there is no difference between a man and his economic fate. A man is made by his assets, income, position, and prospects. The economic mask coincides completely with a man's inner character. Everyone is worth what he earns and earns what he is worth. He learns what he is through the vicissitudes of economic existence. He knows nothing else. . . . Contemporary men have rejected . . . idealism" (211).

34. Frederic Jameson, *Postmodernism: Or, the Cultural Logic of Late Capitalism* (Durham, N.C.: Duke University Press, 1991, 1992), 44.

9

"Be What You Are"

IDENTITY AND MORALITY IN *EDMOND*
AND *GLENGARRY GLEN ROSS*

Jon Tuttle

"Oh, but I will wring your heart yet!" he cried at the invisible wilderness.
—Joseph Conrad, *Heart of Darkness*[1]

Marlowe's journey down the Congo in Joseph Conrad's *Heart of Darkness* becomes a metaphorical exploration into the lower depths of man's depravity, his capacity for rapacious exploitation. The wilderness is an objective correlative for an encroaching and atavistic savagery; it is "invisible" to Kurtz in the epigraph above because, having fought it on its own terms, it is now within him. By the time Marlowe encounters him crawling through the bush, Kurtz has abandoned his civilized morality—a concept the novel deals with ironically—and reverted to a primal condition, indulging his most base and destructive instincts in order to survive and even profit. With his dying breath, Kurtz acknowledges "the horror" at seeing what he truly is.

Post-Darwinist literature revisits the dark continent of man's soul regularly. Many of David Mamet's plays make the same journey, particularly *Edmond* and *Glengarry Glen Ross*. Written at approximately the same time, these two plays bear so much in common thematically and structurally that they may reasonably be considered companion pieces. Despite some arguments that in each play Mamet has posited avenues for his characters' redemption, both ultimately and decisively strip Urban American Man of his moral pretensions and expose his essential barbarism.

At stake in each play is the soul of its protagonist, Edmond Burke and Shelly Levene. Both seek to discover the key not only to survival but gratification in their respective urban jungles (New York, Chicago), and along the way cast off the socialized behavioral constraints that Mamet has called "the veil of the world."[2] Revealed in the end as fundamentally feral and bound for incarceration, both attempt to re-create themselves in their former, civilized image—to travel, as it were, back up the river. Edmond admits, "I've been confused, but, but . . . I've learned my lesson and I'm ready to go home,"[3] and Levene wants to do "whatever it takes to make it right."[4] But having engaged the wilderness on its own terms, each finds that he is one with it: he embodies the horror he had feared would subsume him.

Both plays also constitute speculations on principles enunciated by Edmond's namesake, British statesman and philosopher Edmund Burke. In his letters and his *Reflections on the Revolution in France* (1790), Burke took issue with his contemporaries' belief in the "perfectibility of man" as well as the French revolutionists' insistence on the "rights of man." Because evil exists in nature and nature is immutable, man cannot, Burke argued, "perfect" himself to the extent that he exorcises his capacity for evil; rather, whatever moral order he constructs must strive for a balance between virtue and evil. Moreover, he cannot superordinate his "rights" over traditional social conventions, however artificial those may be, without inviting imbalance and therefore anarchy.[5] To the extent that Edmond and the salesmen in *Glengarry Glen Ross* indulge their appetites for sensual or material gratification, they exercise what they perceive as their rights at the risk of creating or perpetuating social evils that would themselves culminate in anarchy.

Edmond is an updated and Americanized version of George Kaiser's *From Morn to Midnight* (1916), which has by now fallen far enough into obscurity that a brief summary is in order. In it, an anonymous business functionary called simply "Cashier" steals money from his bank, abandons his family, and, in a series of disconnected episodes or *stationen* plotted similarly to those in *Edmond,* exhausts his loot and indulges his senses in a fatal quest for "pinnacles" and "passion." Stimulated first by the touch of a woman, he breaks out of the literal cage he works in at the bank and sets out to find "what's for sale."[6] Money, he finds, "works like magic" (85) in dissolving social and sexual morays, revealing a "free humanity . . . untroubled by class, unfettered by manners. Unclean, but free" (99).

Ultimately disenchanted by this revelation, however, he takes the platform at a Salvation Hall and delivers a speech that functions as the play's thesis:

> You can buy nothing worth having, even with all the money of all the banks in the world. You get less than you pay, every time. The more you spend, the less the goods are worth. The money corrupts them: the money veils the truth. Money's the meanest of the paltry swindles in this world! (150)

To symbolize his own moral rebirth, he scatters what's left of his money into the hall, but despairs as the fallen-again penitents scramble for the cash. A skeletal apparition appears, reminding him of "the final truth—emptiness" (54), and he shoots himself in the chest, gasping "Ecce Homo" with his arms outstretched. This last image, that of a man assuming a Christlike posture— if not stature—as he martyrs himself for a fallen race, underscores the statement the play makes about free humanity: behold the man—debased, salacious, and for sale.

In its rather misanthropic essence, and in certain significant particulars, *From Morn to Midnight* prefigures *Edmond.* Mamet's New York (which he says he doesn't like[7]) resembles Kaiser's unnamed "asphalt city" where "disease and crime are everywhere" (132). Edmond, like the Cashier, is an interchangeable cog in the business machine who seeks to escape the workaday grind and find the meaning of life in extremes of physical and emotional sensation. Early in each play, both abandon home lives they find dry and stultifying, and embark on nearly parallel hedonistic sprees, indulging their sexuality and inner violence, arriving finally at a mission/salvation hall, where their attempts to "testify" result in their capture and destruction.

In *Edmond,* as in *From Morn to Midnight,* interpersonal contact is usually a financial transaction. Everyone is for sale, but usually, direct access to one another is complicated by some business mechanism designed to profit someone else. The barrier between Edmond and the B-Girl, for instance, is a prohibitive fee (twenty dollars) and a bartender who gets a fifty-percent commission. When Edmond attempts to negotiate the price and eliminate the middleman, saying, "I came here to be *straight* with you" (13), he is summarily escorted out. At the whorehouse, he fails to subvert a system whereby he must pay several times, in different ways, to different people, before services are rendered. He haggles also with a peep-show Girl through the Plexiglas wall that precludes their making physical contact, asking, "How can we get this barrier to come down?" (15). The repetition of this dynamic constitutes the conflict in the play, culminating finally in the episode with the Pimp. A middleman himself, the Pimp speaks frankly of the systemic financial entanglements in his business, identifying "the *police,* this man *here*" as other middlemen in their "trans*action*" (43, 44). When he turns on Edmond and attempts to rob him, thereby violating their contract, Edmond, by now sexually frustrated and infuriated by the barriers of duplicity and corruption, explodes in a frenzy of violence.

The scene is crucial in other ways, as well. Edmond admits later that, in the moment of his retaliation, "thirty years of prejudice came out of me" (49). The seeds of his prejudice are alluded to early, when Edmond implicitly agrees with the Man in the bar, who claims that blacks "have it *easy*" because "there are responsibilities they never have accepted" (10). As C. W. E.

Bigsby observes, Edmond sublimates his anger at an imposed "responsibility to understand or to act according to rational principles," and its attendant crush of moral imperatives, into racial hatred. Kicking the Pimp nearly to death while screaming "YOU MOTHERFUCKING NIGGER" satisfies his resentment of an imagined "superior freedom of the black race" as well as his "need to take violent action against a constraining fate."[8]

In a brilliant twist at play's end, this equation linking freedom from responsibility to criminality and race is ironically reasserted. Edmond's black cellmate corroborates Edmond's racist fears and preconceptions by forcing Edmond to fellate him. In so doing, however, he acts on precisely the same irrational impulses that drove Edmond into the night: he indulges both his sexual desires and his need to rebel violently against his "constraining fate," in this case the prison cell itself. That Edmond and his cellmate are fundamentally the same—or more precisely, as Robert Brustein puts it, that "Edmond becomes one with the hostile world he has invaded"—is signaled in the closing moment by their kiss goodnight.[9] This twist is predicted in the opening scene, in which the Fortune Teller tells Edmond, "The world seems to be crumbling around us. . . . And you are unsure what your place is. To what extent you are cause and to what an effect . . ."(2).

In this respect, *Edmond* recalls *Heart of Darkness*'s ironic treatment of the concepts of savagery and civilization. Edmond is a modernized Kurtz, at once loathing and greedily cultivating his primal instincts for survival and gratification.[10] He is, more importantly, Mamet's Everyman, and the play thus serves as a touchstone for the rest of Mamet's work. The primary through-line in the play is the systematic undressing, layer by layer, of man's core malignity. It elucidates not merely man's propensity for savagery, but also his predilection toward it, and concludes that behavior that modern jurisprudence and Judeo-Christian morality deem barbaric is bred not by socioeconomics but rather in the bone.

While Edmond demonstrates a growing awareness of his innate savagery along the way, by play's end he resists self-knowledge and responsibility, and struggles instead to construct some moral or cosmic order that would accommodate or even justify his actions. He dismisses the idea of God, for instance, and the moral imperatives pursuant thereto, for if God existed, He would not hold Edmond responsible for a morality that runs contrary to his nature; He would instead "let me walk *out* of here and be *free*" (73) to indulge those passions attendant to his humanity. A truly supreme being, he argues further, would "cause a new *day*. In a perfect land full of *life*. And *air*. Where people are *kind* to each other. . . . Where we grow up in *love*" (73–74).

Hence, except for the possibility that life is actually a "punishment," in effect a Hell, the notion of a God is philosophically inconvenient. Instead, Edmond embraces the possibility of "a destiny that shapes our ends" (77), and therefore removes from man a role in those ends. "You can't control," he tells his cellmate, "what you make of your life" (77). Fantastically and perhaps desperately, he and his cellmate speculate that they inhabit a world shared by aliens—dogs—whose thoughtless responses to their primal needs make them "superior." "Or maybe," his cellmate suggests, in a refrain that reverberates through Mamet's work, "*we're* the animals" (81).

Edmond's assault on the Pimp bears out his cellmate's suggestion. It represents an abdication of the codes of civilized morality—the "mess of intellectuality" (48)—that in his mind deaden and shelter humanity and prepare it only for victimization. It is "more comfortable," he tells Glenna, "to *accept* a law than question it and live your life" (47). He strikes back at the Pimp, he says, because "Something *spoke* to me, I got a *shock*" from the "warlike blood in *my* veins" (48–49) and is therefore now able to declare, "I am *alive*" (46). Invigorated by the shock not to his system, but *of* it, Edmond urges Glenna "to *live*" by acknowledging the violent hatred that "makes you whole" (50). In her refusal to do so is contained the play's central metaphor: role-playing.

Glenna identifies herself as an actress, but as Bigsby points out, "this turns out to be an elaborate piece of self-deception, the theatre becoming in her mind a kind of therapy, a route to self-realization."[11] Having never actually been in a play, the self she attempts to realize is as facadal as the characters whose lines she rehearses. "Then you are not an actress. . . ," Edmond tells her, "don't lie to yourself" (54). By the time he encounters her, Edmond has realized that almost everyone is, in one way or another, an actor. The Whore and peep-show Girl, the Pimp, the Fortune Teller, the Sharper—all are what the Bystander calls "shills, they're all part of an act" (18). Moreover, the masks they wear do not conceal or protect a fundamental benevolence or humanism; as Bigsby writes, such characters, in Mamet, "are their masks. They exist in and through their performances. Everyone, it seems, exploits everyone else, and when it appears otherwise . . . this proves illusory."[12]

Seeing through their masks has helped Edmond to recognize and remove his own. He now knows what he is. "I've *made* that discovery," he says, and getting Glenna to "Say it: I am a waitress" would be tantamount to extorting from her an unmasking of her self. "Be what you *are*," he pleads. "Say what you are. . . . Go *through* it. Go *through* with me" (54–55). Glenna, however, cannot capitulate; she takes pills to shield herself from the anxiety of introspection and clings to the belief that "I'm *good*" (57).

It is precisely her insistence on her own goodness that triggers Edmond's violent and fatal assault on her; with it, she refuses to validate his newly discovered darkness and in that sense be an accomplice to it. She also tacitly rejects his assessment of the world as "a piece of shit. . . . It is a shit house. . . . There is *NO LAW* . . . there is no *history* . . . there is just *now*" (51). Significantly, this assessment echoes Teach's description, in *American Buffalo,* of American survivalist-capitalism: "The Whole Entire World./ There Is No Law./There Is No Right and Wrong./The World Is Lies./There Is No Friendship."[13] For Teach, Edmond, and in fact all of Mamet's most negative characters, this *weltanschauung* becomes a rationale for breaking out of what Edmond calls the "fog" of imposed morality to indulge a self-interest untrammeled by conscience.[14] As such, it provides the strongest connective tissue between *Edmond* and *Glengarry Glen Ross.*

In a key speech in *Glengarry Glen Ross,* Richard Roma consoles a depressed restaurant patron—Lingk—by urging him to recast his concept of morality:

> When you *die* you're going to regret the things you don't do. You think you're *queer* . . . ? I'm going to tell you something: we're *all* queer. You think you're a *thief?* So *what?* You get befuddled by a middle-class morality . . . ? Get *shut* of it. Shut it out. You cheated on your wife . . . ? You *did* it, *live* with it. *(Pause.)* You fuck little girls, so *be* it. There's an absolute morality? May *be.* And *then* what? If you think there is, then *be* that thing. Bad people go to hell? I don't *think* so. If you think that, act that way. A hell exists on earth? Yes. I won't live in it. That's *me.* (27)

This speech is crucial because it works on two important levels. On the surface, Roma is playacting: in order to initiate a sale, he assumes the role of confessor, and as such absolves Lingk of whatever crime—the text suggests adultery—he is guilty of. Like Edmond, Roma advocates "*acting each day* without fear" (29) on whatever instincts or desires one may have. The beauty of Roma's system is that it uses Lingk's own transgressions against any absolute morality as *a priori* evidence of his abjuring it; it thereby neutralizes any values except expediency, justifies any action as emotionally authentic, and thus grants Lingk permission to be what he is. And as magically as Edmond's concept of "destiny," it indemnifies Lingk from the ramifications of his actions by classifying them under "THINGS THAT HAPPEN TO YOU" (29).

Beneath that, though, the speech crystallizes, with a breathtaking lack of hypocrisy, the ethic Roma uses to justify bilking Lingk and other buyers.

How is it, the other salesmen wonder, that Roma is able to close so many deals? By practicing exactly what he preaches. "I do those things," he says, "which seem correct to me *today*" (28–29). Though it sounds it, Roma's ethic is not entirely situational; that is, he does not operate amorally. The things he does are predicated entirely on what he is: a salesman. While he may have abjured the absoluteness of social or religious moralities, he nonetheless has identified and acts in accordance with that principle at the center of his reconstructed cosmos: profit.

Mamet fixates on characters like Edmond and Roma—they permeate his plays—for the same reason that the historical Caius Caligula fascinated Albert Camus. In *Caligula,* Camus portrayed his eponymous hero as an agent not of anarchy but of a precise and fixed, if ultimately corrosive, order. Having confronted, via his sister's death, the pointlessness of existence and thereby the irrelevance of morality, he creates Meaning by subscribing to his Intendant's insistence that "The Treasury's of prime importance."[15] Acting thereafter according to the maxim "If the Treasury has paramount importance, human life has none" (12), he proceeds to kill his subjects and plunder their fortunes for the sake of the budget, all the while maintaining—with astounding logic—that in doing so he is simply the creature of the state he serves.

Roma is, to Mamet's eye, such a creature. Roma has interpreted the American social landscape as a Darwinist jungle where the key to survival is dominance, the measure of dominance accumulation, and the means to accumulation, masculinity. In what is "not a world of men," he rhapsodizes over a survival-of-the-fittest style of capitalist "adventure" (72). While Lingk defines this adventure rather benignly, calling it "the power to negotiate" (62), to Mamet it is really a "frontier ethic [which] was always something for nothing,"[16] or the operative objective behind the American capitalist mythos: "How much money you can make."[17]

In the movie version of *Glengarry Glen Ross,* Roma's ethic is emphatically reinforced by the presence of a new character, Blake, a messenger from the pantheonic real estate moguls Mitch and Murray. In an early and extraordinarily brutal scene, he calls the salesmen "fucking faggots" and reminds them that selling real estate is a "man's game" that takes "brass balls." His method of inspiration is strictly a macho brand of demoralization that equates their identity with their earning power: "You can't close your leads? You can't close shit? *You are shit.*" When asked who he is to speak to them this way, he defines himself in terms they understand: "Fuck you, that's my name. You drove a Hyundai to get here tonight. I drove an $80,000 BMW, that's my name. And your name is you're *wanting.*" Their relationship, in other words, like all relationships in Mamet, is financial: "I made $920,000 last year. How much you make? You see, pal, that's who I am."[18]

Roma's (and Blake's) ethic is essentially what Moss calls a "mean streak" (45). In the same way, as Roma says, that thieves are "inured" to nervousness, he has so completely inured himself to conscience that he can, apparently out of pure reflex, cannibalize Levene's profits just moments after having defended and embraced Levene, and lie to Lingk in order to secure their transaction. Even Lingk's marriage is to Roma a loopholed "contract." Roma cryptically admits to having had some difficulty becoming what he is: "All train compartments," he says, summarizing with this metaphor the lifestyle of a salesman, "smell vaguely of shit." But after prolonged exposure to the fecal business atmosphere, he developed the moral organs necessary to breathe it: "It gets so you don't mind it. . . . You know how long it took me to get there? A long time" (27). Getting there, though, has secured him a dominant position on the sales board.

The hierarchy of salesmen, according to their standing on the sales board, forms a simple moral continuum. On one end—the top—Roma and Dave Moss scramble over one another not merely to dodge the relentless capitalist grinding wheel, but to direct it. In them, Mamet actualizes the cutthroat marketplace competitiveness that typifies his business plays. Sensing Roma's advantage in the Cadillac sweepstakes, Moss escalates the level of warfare and, after failing with Aaronow, convinces Levene to break into the office for the valuable new leads. The logic he employs, which we see in his negotiations with Aaronow, is as baffling and therefore as powerful as that which Roma uses to dodge Lingk's request for the return of his check. In subcontracting Levene, Moss in fact creates a paradigm for the corporate structure he sees looking up through the company's chain of command. Coveting the power and income of Mitch and Murray, who reap the profits of others' labor (and admiring the savvy of Jerry Graff, who went into business for himself), Moss casts himself in the role of executive and doles out the dirty work of breaking into the office to whoever is desperate enough to be his minion. Swindling a colleague proves no cause for consternation: he observes in Williamson, who knowingly doles out worthless leads to those salesmen whose livelihoods are in the most jeopardy, a model of corporate logic and efficiency, and so justifiably concludes that treachery is the surest path to success. For both Roma and Moss, accumulation is a simple matter of predation; their quarry, as the play progresses, is their clients, their colleagues, their office, and finally, in a brutal showdown near the end, each other. Sales competition devolves into direct confrontation in the form of verbal and near-physical violence.

On the other end of the continuum, and therefore at the bottom of the sales hierarchy, is Aaronow. He is, as Moss calls him, a "good man" (34), and functions as what Matthew Roudané terms "the one source of conscience" and "moral seriousness" in the play.[19] While naive to the point of being easily manipulated, he is at any rate the only character who seems to assume good faith in his business and personal relationships. As such, he is to Mamet the play's *raisonneur:*

> Aaronow has some degree of conscience, some awareness; he's troubled. Corruption troubles him. The question he's troubled by is whether his inability to succeed in the society in which he's placed is a defect—that is, is he manly or sharp enough?—or if it's, in effect, a positive attribute, which is to say that his conscience prohibits him.[20]

Yet Aaronow's presence is not enough to countervail the indictment the play makes of the American business wilderness. He is impotent to condemn or even identify corruption; he shrugs it off with "Oh, God, I hate this job," but settles, at play's end, into his desk chair, demonstrating his powerlessness to remove himself from it.

Between Roma and Moss on one end, and Aaronow on the other, is Levene. The central conflict in the play is the question of which pole—which ethic—he will gravitate toward, and as in *Edmond,* the central metaphor is role-playing. From his days as a real estate salesman, Mamet recalls his colleagues as being "primarily performers. They went into people's living rooms and performed their play about the investment properties."[21] For Levene, this description is particularly appropriate. Throughout the play, his identity is very fluid and chameleonic. In act 1, for instance, the various personae he adopts to negotiate with Williamson for the new leads demonstrate not only his desperation but also his dramatic range. In his attempts to strong-arm Williamson, then to beg, bribe, and finally threaten him, he assumes the guise first of proven salesman ("put a *closer* on the job" [1]); then of fellow man ("don't look at the *board,* look at *me.* Shelly Levene" [6]); of supplicant ("I'll give you ten percent" [7]); of family man ("John: my *daughter*" [9]) and finally of well-connected superior ("wasn't long I could pick up the phone, call *Murray* and I'd have your job" [9]). The language he and Williamson speak—real estate-ese—is prohibitively esoteric; it's the signature Mamet dynamic behind the language that drives the scene: one character has power, the other tries to extort it.

In act 2, that dynamic is reversed as Levene affects new roles. He blows through the door crowing about a sale, and immediately falls into a reenactment of his sales ploy. Significantly, that ploy is very much like the one Roma uses in act 1 to hook Lingk. "You have to believe in *yourself*"

(43), Levene says, recapitulating the pitch he made to the Nyborgs, replete with such Roma-isms as "see that opportunity . . . and *take* it" and "This is now" (47). While the transaction itself, as he describes it, had all the gaiety of a foreclosure, he nonetheless revels in reliving the "*old* days," a term that echoes Roma's fond reference to the "old stuff" of American-style salesmanship. Levene becomes, in essence, "Levene the Machine," and plays that role with bravado, crying, "Send me *out!* Send me *out!*" (48). In what amounts to his encore performance, Levene assumes the role of "D. Ray Morton," director of European sales for American Express, and in that persona pretends to hustle Roma away from the now-reticent Lingk. Roma, too, postures instantly and brilliantly; the ease with which both men fall into their *schtick* indicates that, in the business of acting, they are old hands.

Like Glenna, Levene insists on his own decency, telling Williamson, "I'm a good man" (5), and like her, he attempts to disassociate his image of himself from the things he must do to survive financially. Ultimately, the thing he thinks he must do is to burgle the office, and while this is the action that finally defines and condemns him, it is not the climactic event of the play; indeed, Mamet chose not to dramatize it at all. To Mamet, a climax is not such an action, but instead "something closer to the through-line of the protagonists," in this case a "condition."[22] As is the case with Edmond, it is Levene's changing *condition* that constitutes the arc he travels.

In *Strategies of Drama,* Oscar Brownstein corroborates Mamet's implied premise that a climactic event is not a single action, but rather a revision or reevaluation of the character. To Brownstein, the climax happens not on the stage, but rather in the audience or "the life of the spectator" in the form of a "perception shift." More than a "moment in the present," it is instead "one whole thing, an expanding sphere of discovered significance."[23] More specifically still, it is a revelation that should astonish us into a "revision of our understanding of [the central character], of his motives, and therefore of the significance of the play."[24]

In *Glengarry Glen Ross,* there is really no climax, per se. Rather, there is a point at which an audience realizes Levene has been gradually subsumed by the mask of "the Machine," and as such has become indistinguishable from the corrupt social elements he suspects conspire to destroy him. Stealing the leads amounts to essentially the same sort of rebellion Edmond mounted in killing the Pimp: Perceiving in the sales contest, and the threat of being fired, a constraining fate, Levene performs that act which he believes will free him. Instead, it traps him in a singular and defining role.

From behind the mask of "the Machine," Levene can bravely excoriate Williamson, and in effect convincingly appropriate power from him:

You have no idea of your job. A man's his job and you're *fucked* at yours. You hear what I'm saying to you . . .? What I'm saying to you: things can *change*. You *see*? This is where you fuck *up*, because this is something you don't *know*. You can't look down the *road*. . . . What are you, you're a *secretary*, John. Fuck *you*. That's my message to you. Fuck you and kiss my ass. You don't like it, I'll go talk to Jerry Graff. Period. Fuck you. Put me on the board. And I want three worthwhile leads today and I don't want any bullshit about them and I want 'em close together 'cause I'm going to hit them all today. That's all I have to say to you. (49–50)

Roma's adding, "He's right, Williamson" (50), brings closure both to the beat and to Levene's metamorphosis: in his sales tactics, his assault tactics, and particularly in the commitment he makes to secure his job—burglary—he is not merely allied to Roma; he becomes, to his horror and ours, another Roma. Succumbing to his own sales pitch, "'Why don't I get the opportunities . . .?'" (44) Levene does what seems right to him at the moment, seizes his opportunity, and steals on a higher and more pure level than Roma does when he "negotiates" with his clients. Upon being discovered as a thief, however, he attempts, in his negotiations with Williamson, to remask himself through his old devices of beggary and bribery, but finds in the end that he has become what he is by doing what he has done.

In his review of a recent London production of *Glengarry Glen Ross*, Sheridan Morley condemns "Mamet's resolute refusal to offer a moral or emotional frame" for his salesmen, who "exist only within their own terms of reference. We are never asked to judge or sympathize or understand, merely to observe varying degrees of desperation."[25] On this count, Morley is incorrect. Like Brecht, Mamet portrays extremes of behavior in order to encourage his audience to question his characters' choices. And while, like Brecht, he finds that these choices are conditioned at least in part by economic imperatives, beyond these are suppositions—a "moral frame"—about humanity's heart of darkness, suppositions that we are urged to refute, if we can.

To Mamet, the fundamental flaw in Adam Smith's "invisible hand" theory, which held that the common good would be automatically provided for if individual enterprise were given free reign, is that Smith did not fully account for human corruptibility, or for the idea that business actually nurtures latent corruption. This, at least, has been the theme of most of Mamet's plays since *American Buffalo*, which, as he says, directly equates crime with "the American ethic of business."[26] In his radio/stage/teleplay *The Water Engine*, Mamet makes his baldest indictment of American business by placing

Smith's theory in the mouth of unscrupulous lawyer Lawrence Oberman. "Who said," he asks, "that if every man just acted in his own best interests, this would be a paradise on Earth?"[27] Acting in his own best interests means, for Oberman, colluding in the blackmail of Charles Lang for the patent rights to his revolutionary water-powered engine. The nomenclature itself—the rich and powerful "superman" preying on and silencing the voice ("langue") of an industrious but disenfranchised laborer, ironically identifies the power nexus and with it the dichotomy between good and evil in the play. "You people," says Lang, referring to Oberman and the captains of American industry he represents, "are savages. You're animals" (39).

In Lang, Mamet offers one hero unsusceptible to the temptations of money: he rejects an early and substantial buy-out offer from Oberman, opting instead to protect his creation and with it his integrity. But Lang is an unusual character in Mamet; indeed, in none of his other plays is one character so clearly and irretrievably virtuous as Lang. But the statement the play makes is still bleak: the wages of virtue, for Lang and his sister, are death—at the hands of big business.

In Mamet, prostitution, pimping, swindling, thievery, murder—everything ordinarily associated with underworld vice—become metaphors for business, and business for life. Some of his characters, like Teach in *American Buffalo,* desperately disassociate themselves from the betrayals and violence they are actually agents of. Others, though, like Margaret in *House of Games,* discover in themselves a consanguinity with and even an attraction toward the depravity they despise. In a brief introspective moment, Edmond in fact admits that his descent into darkness was quite natural and even preordained. "I always knew," he says, in jail, "that I would end up here. . . . I think I'm going to like it here" (68). Levene, too, must ultimately recognize that his acceptance of the proposition that "a man's his job" (49) effectively eliminates his own sense of identity, and with it, morality. Given such observations, a deconstructionist reading of either *Edmond* or *Glengarry Glen Ross* would perhaps unearth an advocacy on Mamet's part for an absolute or at least civilizing morality, but such a reading would miss his bleak prognosis for humanity: life is a business, and business is savage because people are.

NOTES

1. Joseph Conrad, *Heart of Darkness* (Harmondsworth, Middlesex: Penguin, 1973), 98.

2. See C. W. E. Bigsby, *Modern American Drama* (Cambridge: Cambridge University Press, 1992), 225.

3. David Mamet, *Edmond* (New York: Grove Press, 1983), 65. Subsequent citations appear parenthetically in text.

4. Mamet, *Glengarry Glen Ross* (New York: Grove Press, 1982, 1983), 70.

Subsequent citations appear parenthetically in text.

5. See *Reflections on the Revolution in France* (Indianapolis: Bobbs-Merrill, Inc., 1955); and *The Correspondence of Edmund Burke*, ed. R.B. McDowell, et al. (Chicago: University of Chicago Press, 1958–1970).

6. George Kaiser, *From Morn to Midnight* (New York: Brentano's, 1922), 53. Subsequent citations appear parenthetically in text.

7. See C.W.E. Bigsby, *David Mamet* (London: Methuen, 1985), 107.

8. Ibid., 106.

9. Robert Brustein, "The Shape of the New," in *Reimagining American Theatre* (New York: Hill and Wang, 1991), 51.

10. The theme and in fact the basic situation of *Heart of Darkness* figure even more prominently in an earlier Mamet play, *Lone Canoe or The Explorer* (1979), in which a nineteenth-century explorer abandons his civilization to live with a remote tribe, which with himself he systematically corrupts.

11. Bigsby, *David Mamet*, 107–8.

12. Bigsby, *Modern American Drama*, 198.

13. Mamet, *American Buffalo* (New York: Grove Weidenfeld, 1976), 107.

14. Interestingly, if coincidentally, a "fog" is precisely what Marlowe sails through immediately before discovering Kurtz's camp in *Heart of Darkness*. In both Conrad and Mamet, then, a fog is a metaphor for the blurry distinction between order and chaos, the last marker one passes as he travels from one to the other.

15. Albert Camus, *Caligula and 3 Other Plays* (New York: Vintage, 1958), 11. Subsequent citations appear parenthetically in text.

16. Quoted in Bigsby, *David Mamet*, 111.

17. See *New York Times Magazine*, 28 March 1984, C19.

18. Quotations are from the film version of *Glengarry Glen Ross*, prod. Morris Ruskin and Nava Levin (Los Angeles: Zupnik Cinema Group, 1992).

19. Matthew Roudané, "Public Issues, Private Tensions: David Mamet's *Glengarry Glen Ross*," *South Carolina Review* 19, no. 1 (1986): 44.

20. Quoted in Matthew Roudané, "An Interview with David Mamet," *Studies in American Drama, 1945–Present* 1 (1986): 75.

21. See Henry Hewes, National Theatre's Education Department's *Background Notes for Teachers and Pupils for Glengarry Glen Ross* (1983), 7.

22. Quoted in David Savran, *In Their Own Words: Contemporary American Playwrights* (New York: Theatre Communications Group, 1988), 135.

23. Oscar Brownstein, *Strategies of Drama* (New York: Greenwood Press, 1991), 117–18.

24. Ibid., 115.

25. Sheridan Morley, "Onstage: London News," *Playbill*, 31 August 1994, 54.

26. Quoted in *New York Times*, 15 January 1978, 4D.

27. Mamet, *The Water Engine and Mr. Happiness* (New York: Grove Press, 1978), 43. Subsequent citations appear parenthetically in text.

10

DAVID MAMET, JEAN BAUDRILLARD
AND THE PERFORMANCE OF
AMERICA

Elizabeth Klaver

I went in search of astral *America.*[1]

—Jean Baudrillard

During the 1980s and the Reagan presidency, two versions of America saw performance and publication: David Mamet's *Glengarry Glen Ross* and Jean Baudrillard's *America*. At first glance, Mamet and Baudrillard seem more than an ocean apart, their visions of late-twentieth-century Western culture radically different. After all, Mamet has been called the most American of playwrights, while Baudrillard has been accused of writing an America no American would recognize. Mamet is seen as having a moral strategy, Baudrillard a fatal strategy. Mamet is seen as privileging the subject, Baudrillard the object. Nevertheless, by reading *Glengarry Glen Ross* against *America* we discover that both writers are constructing surprisingly comparable performances of America toward the end of the second millennium. We discover spectacles that are theatrical, visionary, and apocalyptic, as well as revelatory of a post-commodity culture in an astral landscape.

THE SEARCH

Mamet is really heir to a long line of American writers who have gone in search of America. Perhaps his nearest ancestor is Eugene O'Neill, whom Gregory Mosher, long-time director of Mamet's plays, speaks of sharing with Mamet the similar ability to look out at America and see things about the culture that no one else has observed.[2] Samuel Clemens as well offered a panoramic sweep of America, at least along the Mississippi River, and a portrayal of the American character(s). To Stephen Fender, the sort of national identity thus constructed includes not only the belief in a distinctive American singularity, but also the search to define it.[3] Certainly, a significant trait of some of America's most notable literary representations such as Huck Finn and Rip Van Winkle is their desire to "light out" in search of such definitions. While their fictional quests tropologically parallel the historical trek westward in search of land, they also parallel the effort of writers like Washington Irving and Benjamin Franklin to construct the nation's literary authority, its mythologies and personae.

Perhaps Franklin's project in his *Autobiography* stands as the paradigmatic search for America, for in seeking out and delineating an American definition Franklin installs himself as that definition. Franklin exhibits a certain self-consciousness in hoping that posterity will find his life "fit to be imitated."[4] As the original self-made man, Franklin makes of his own character, to apply a phrase spoken by Bobby Gould in *Speed-the-Plow*, *"that image people want to see."*[5] And yet it isn't only Americans who are interested in constructing America. At the same time Franklin was writing his *Autobiography*, the Frenchman Hector St. John de Crèvecoeur was writing his *Letters from an American Farmer*, including the essay entitled "What is an American." Like Franklin, Crèvecoeur sets out to define a nation whose inhabitants he sees as humanitarian but tied by definition specifically to the land. And, of course, fifty years later Alexis de Tocqueville will represent his Americans as "enterprising, fond of adventure and, above all, of novelty" in the book, *Democracy in America.*[6]

One can therefore recognize in Baudrillard's *America* a late-twentieth-century stage in the long-standing francophonic search for America, a search that is similar in its intent to that performed on the American side by Franklin, Clemens, and Mamet. And though Baudrillard's *America* is indeed shaped like a quest, it is one that circulates over the landscape rather than delving into it, and begins and ends in the desert of the Southwest. As he writes, "the crucial moment is that brutal instant which reveals that the journey has no end, that there is no longer any reason for it to come to an end" (10). Not in search of cultural or social America, Baudrillard begins his quest in the automobile, that most American of icons, to discover a vision of America in the excess of speed, in the obscenity of highway motels, in the hard surface of the Bonneville Salt Flats. And this vision explores the nation as astral, a land permeated by a sidereal vector that radiates out of the ecstatic form of the desert.

Baudrillard locates the desert as the pure expression of astral America because its emptiness reflects the desert of the sign, an emptiness that has affected every human institution (63). No longer a deep structure, culture has disappeared into "the lyrical nature of pure circulation" (27), and America, in the form of the desert, has become the perfect simulation. Baudrillard's America is without binary opposites. It is ecstatic, superlative, more than more. As fashion becomes the ecstasy of beauty, and pornography the ecstasy of sex,[7] the desert becomes the ecstasy of the land, the astral map of a geography that has disappeared. It is not surprising that Baudrillard would find the emptiness of Death Valley "the sublime natural phenomenon" and the theatricality of Las Vegas "the abject cultural phenomenon," reflecting each other across the desert expanse (67).

Mamet's plays constitute a remarkably similar sort of "lighting out," a voyage that ultimately mirrors Baudrillard's astral vision. For instance, like Baudrillard, Mamet is fascinated by Disneyland, which has been constructed as a miniature image of America and epitomizes the American enterprise system. Both writers have the view that Disneyland operates as an ideological institution, to Mamet exhibiting a totalitarian use of authority[8] and to Baudrillard filling the gap left by "real" America.[9] And just as Baudrillard travels across the phantasmagoria of the desert, Santa Barbara, New York, and Salt Lake City, Mamet travels across the film studios of Hollywood, the junkshops, bars, and real estate offices of Chicago, where he maps a superlative landscape *"bereft of Nature."* [10] Here, America has also become ecstatic.

This ecstatic form can be easily recognized in *Glengarry Glen Ross* as the disappearance of "real" estate for the appearance of "dream" estate signified by Glen Ross Farms and Glengarry Highlands. These empty signs of the land are skillfully manipulated by characters like Roma and Levene, those sleight of hand hustlers peopling Mamet's plays and whom Baudrillard reflects in his one "real" American in *America,* Ronald Reagan. In *Glengarry Glen Ross,* Mamet turns the selling of real estate into the ecstatic form of retail. Although he does not "drive" through America in quite the same way Baudrillard does, Mamet also features the automobile as excess, not as an excess of speed but as an excess of competition, the Cadillac as the ecstatic prize of American middle-class success. If Roma could win the Cadillac, perhaps Mamet's search for America would be over. The fast-talking con man of desert forms would merge with Cadillac Row. But the arrival is, of course, less achievable than projected, and the search continues to take place over the range of Mamet's vision.

The Performance

However, it is not merely a search for America that Mamet and Baudrillard conduct. In the course of their efforts, they produce spectacles that are staged, theatrical, and semiotic. Like their literary predecessors, Mamet and Baudrillard construct aesthetic visions of America, but ones that should never be confused with a sociological description. Certainly in Baudrillard's case, readers have had a tendency to mistake his *America* for a referential illustration of the United States and to reject it on the basis of inaccuracy. His work, like Mamet's, should rather be seen as distinctly performative, for it functions less as description and more as dramatic discourse in a network of "linguistic *interaction*."[11] Of course, Mamet's plays are less likely to be misconstrued in this way. They are indeed theatre pieces, performances in the literal sense of various opportunities and events the playwright imagines of America. We become the spectators of those projections he throws onto the stage and sometimes onto the movie and television screens. In fact, each of Mamet's plays, and prose pieces for that matter, acts as a Baudrillardian hologram of America.

To Baudrillard, the hologram applies perfectly to America "in the sense that information concerning the whole is contained in each of its elements" (29). One can glimpse America in every ray of light, in every Midwestern street, Burger King, cabin in Vermont, or real estate office. And certainly, *Glengarry Glen Ross* does act as an element of the whole. The sorts of hard sell, hustle, and theatricality that go on in the real estate office become a trope not only for cutthroat American business, but also for personal relations and the construction of the American character. In fact, Roma's sales pitch to Lingk during the restaurant scene in *Glengarry Glen Ross* provides an example of the way in which the hologram functions across Mamet's plays.

In the course of their "conversation," Roma recasts one of the most enduring definitions of America, one that extends at least back to Franklin— America as the land of opportunity. Roma makes a swerve by substituting for the dream of success the specter of loss that haunts the Willie Loman (or Shelly Levene) in every American's collective imagination. Extending such anxiety into the further reaches of "[s]tocks, bonds, objects of art, [and] real estate," Roma groups all such particulars under the rubric "opportunity." But to him, "opportunity" is an empty cipher waiting for a spin, a desert sign capable of circulating between making money and losing money, indulging oneself and learning. To Roma, "opportunity" is simply an event, most profoundly represented in this play as Levene's act of stealing the real estate leads.[12]

Interestingly though, opportunity-as-event also extends across Mamet's landscape from *American Buffalo* to *Oleanna,* ranging from the opportunity to steal the Buffalo-head nickel to the chance to advance one's political objective. In other words, the notion of opportunity-as-event in one play provides an element in which Mamet's oeuvre can be glimpsed, the opportunity-as-event performed in the other plays. And since *Glengarry Glen*

Ross itself is an opportunity or event where one can witness Mamet's vision, it can be recognized as holographic with respect to the other plays. In other words, each real estate or faculty office that is projected as a transitory beam of light across the blackness of a stage exhibits a range of those elements found in Mamet's vision of America.

Of course, in *America* Baudrillard also operates from a sense of the landscape as holographic. While his major image is the desert because of its paradigmatic emptiness, Baudrillard also recognizes each fragment of America as providing information about the whole. Each scene of Salt Lake City, New York City, or Santa Barbara reflects back America as a giant switching board of hyperbolic image, scenario, and disappearance. The New York Marathon, for instance, becomes "the mania for an empty victory" (20), while the Santa Barbara villas become a place for death in artificial serenity (30–31). For Baudrillard, each place, event, or opportunity acts like a stage dressed for some continuous performance. Yet America not only functions as a series of signs and formulas, it also reveals a fundamental lack or vacancy, the desert of the sign. Curiously though, this lack, which inhabits the matrix of every sign, is what empowers theatrical forms to generate themselves across time and space. The effect of disappearance in the sign can be explained as the opening of a gap that is always in the process of being filled by some other sign. In *America*, such a combination of elements—the sign, the image, the stage, disappearance—produces the astral phantasmagoria that radiates out of the desert and enables Baudrillard to envision America as a highly theatrical form.

In fact, Baudrillard sees theatre wherever he looks in America. The text revels in theatrical terms—backdrop, backcloth, scenario, scene, special effect, drama, spectacle, mask, performance. With its "impersonal roles" and "violent expressionism," New York alone is described as "act[ing] out its own catastrophe as a stage play" (22). (Several of Baudrillard's readers, such as Stephen Watt, have noted the connection between his writings and contemporary drama.)[13] But *America* as a literary construct can further be analyzed as acting out its own journey as a stage play as well, albeit one like *Speed-the-Plow* that circulates back to its point of departure. However, as Mike Gane points out, *America* has tended to elude critics, who have at times dismissed it as "ludicrous." They have not found a workable key for reading it.[14]

One has to grasp the notion that Baudrillard recognizes in the American landscape an instance of a fatal strategy, the catastrophic action of the object on the subject. This object theory allows him to remain on the surface of the journey, "a tourist" according to Gane.[15] As a sightseer in

America, Baudrillard acts the trope of a traveler who is distanced from his object of sight, protected by his own screens, voyeuristic and disengaged, but still more than capable of projecting the sweep of his own views. While Gane suggests that *America* eventually becomes discernible as dramatic event,[16] I would go a step further and posit that one key for reading the text is to look at it as the unfolding of performance. Baudrillard's search for an aesthetic construction of America, like Mamet's, emerges in a theatrical project.

Baudrillard sets the stage for *America* in the empty space of the desert. In projecting toward the "[v]anishing point," he takes us out on a journey not to discover a sociological reality, but to look upon a series of dramatic scenes, the episodic treatment of an ecstatic landscape. Here, he virtually conducts *America* as a *Lehrstück,* playing the Puritans, Tocqueville, and Reagan across a historical frame. However, his "learning" play, like *Glengarry Glen Ross,* makes a swerve in the already-constructed definitions of America. To Baudrillard, America has completed the Founding Fathers' vision of utopia, but it is a utopia that has utterly failed. Such a paradoxical assessment is undoubtedly aesthetic—"the tragedy of a utopian dream made reality" (30)—for Baudrillard envisions America as operating in a perpetual present of signs, an orgy of fashion where leadership is equated with "the advertising 'look'" (109). If society has to wear a mask, he asks, "Why not the mask of Reagan?" (118). America's power, based on the construct of a utopia, is delivered as a theatrical special effect, a postmodernist expressionism in which the emptiness of the desert lurks behind the projected face.

At the end of *America*, Baudrillard returns to the empty space of the desert, bringing the sunset down over the Pacific Ocean like a final curtain. Having opened and closed the performance in the eclipse of the sign, Baudrillard concludes with "Desert for ever," the immemorial "silence of the Badlands" (123), the pure expression of the astral. Interestingly, the text has not only constructed itself as the kind of performance associated with the theatre, but has also revealed performance of another sort in its vast network of signs, its screens of formulas and images, its dramatic discourse. *America* shows America becoming performative. This is the "real" Baudrillardian America.

POST-COMMODITY CULTURE

Baudrillard and Mamet are two writers who continually construct a vision of late-twentieth-century America as a landscape of signs, a post-commodity culture. Baudrillard associates the post-commodity culture with the current era of code and image, of DNA, computers and media, in which the "classical" configurations of Saussure and Marx have given way to the structural law of value. No longer in a world of articulating binaries (sign/referent, signifier/signified, product/value), the sign and value are now disengaged from representation and utility and circulate exclusively among themselves.[17] Binaries no longer cohere. Seduction replaces desire. Clearly, according to Baudrillard's theory, a humanism like Franklin's and Crèvecoeur's, which is based on the ability to fashion a bipartite set of values, has to vanish in these circumstances.[18]

Of course, Baudrillard's definition of the post-commodity culture is very similar to the sort of America Mamet stages in *Glengarry Glen Ross*. As critics have pointed out, Mamet's plays expose the vicious side of American capitalism. To Matthew C. Roudané, "fiscal capital replaces cultural and spiritual capital,"[19] and to Henry I. Schvey, *Glengarry Glen Ross* in particular displays "a society built on merciless exploitation."[20] Yet it is a form of capitalism radically different from that functioning at the beginning of the twentieth century when Saussure's and Marx's binaries could engage. As *Glengarry Glen Ross* demonstrates, at the end of the second millennium the referent or product is simply not in play.

What are the real estate salesmen actually selling? Is there any evidence in the play to suggest that they are selling real land? Do Glengarry Highlands and Glen Ross Farms exist even as good old American swampland? Or are these parcels simply the signs of an American dreamscape completely divorced from any referential anchorage? In fact, land appears in the play only in the context of real estate contracts, leads, and the swirl of talk and theatricality of the salesmen—the written and spoken languages of a semiotic and performative universe. In this exchange of buying and selling, only signs are available, and the value of the real estate becomes relative to the system rather than to a world of actual things. Witness Levene's desperate negotiations with Williamson not over the use value of the land, but over the exchange value of the clients. He bribes Williamson for the "opportunity" to sell, to spin desert signs in total relativity (23–27). In this play, the referent or product is about as necessary as an appendix and quietly atrophies. The seductive charm of Glen Ross Farms, Glengarry Highlands, and the Cadillac is what comes to pose as American desire. Indeed, according to Joe Mantegna, who played Roma in the U.S. premiere at the Goodman Theatre in Chicago, the sales maxim operating in *Glengarry Glen Ross* is "'sell the sizzle, not the steak.'"[21]

Mamet is clearly aware of the sort of America he is envisioning in *Glengarry Glen Ross*. Like Baudrillard, he recognizes the radical impact on society of certain technologies like the computer, which produce an economic world built around the shuffling of data. Data can generate an enterprise system unlimited in its ability to expand.[22] Because the post-commodity culture operates at the level of signs, Baudrillard's "era of simulation," infinite expansion indicates an explosion in the number of signs as well as in their circulation and, most important, their reversibility. Under the previous commodity law of value, when signs could articulate as binaries, desire could function as desire for something, and the system was capable of repressing reversibility. In this day and age when the structural law of value makes disarticulation and seduction the operative modes, signs are continually absorbing everything, even their own opposites. As Baudrillard writes, "Everywhere the same 'genesis of simulacra:' the interchangeability of the beautiful and the ugly in fashion; of the right and the left in politics; of the true and false in every media message."[23] To this list we might add the interchangeability or reversibility of buying and stealing, of legal and illegal acts, of American entrepreneurship and criminality.

In *Glengarry Glen Ross,* reversibility and seduction redefine the American trait of individualism, making Levene, who engages in both, the exemplary figure of the play. Contrary to Arthur Miller's examination in *Death of a Salesman* of a commodity culture still tense with binary contradictions, Mamet's play shows an erosion of differences. Rather than delineating a system that can beat down a good man, Mamet lets the edge of criminality lurk behind every aspect of the real estate venture from the bribery of Williamson by Levene to the seductive lure of Roma's language to the final break-in and robbery. Even though he gets caught, Levene is someone who can play in the game, who like Michael Milken can take reversibility right out to the infinite expanses of the system. And what does the post-commodity culture offer out there? Opportunity.

In an interview Leslie Kane conducted with Gregory Mosher in 1990, the following exchange took place:

> Mosher: What the guy wants to do is sell real estate.
> Kane: He doesn't want to save his neck?
> Mosher: In *Glengarry?* No, the guy's harder than that.[24]

And Mamet's play is harder than that as well, as hard as a shell game. As a holographic element of America, *Glengarry Glen Ross* slices through a landscape inhabited by Levenes, the con men who eventually emerge as Mamet's version of the American character. In a culture of superlatives, they become the ecstatic form of the entrepreneur; in a world of seduction, they become the archetypal postmodernist figure.

To be sure, America has been fatally attracted to the con artist for some time now, at least since Herman Melville's *The Confidence Man.* And the output of Hollywood over the last few years—*Butch Cassidy and the Sundance Kid, The Sting*—indicates a huge demand for a romantic, outlaw character. Mamet's own fascination with the underworld is clear from the number of screenplays he has written that feature versions of the petty criminal: *We're No Angels, House of Games.* Today, the con man seems to stand as the reigning manipulator of signs in a world that has lost the ground of referentiality.

The con man is appropriate to a post-commodity culture because he is the individual who operates best in the external realm of appearances; he is the ultimate spin-master of desert forms as they circulate on the surface. Nowhere is this ability to manipulate signs more clearly apparent than in the con man's bluff, a form of reversibility especially manifested in a game Mamet openly enjoys—poker.[25] Like the signs in a post-commodity culture, the cards in poker operate exclusively in relation to each other and are valued accordingly. Yet when a hand is being played, the players work with another set of signs written across their faces and gestures which diverts attention away from the cards. The brilliance of the game lies in the fact that, because one set of signs can be interchanged for the other, an inexperienced player will be seduced by the bluff's reversibility again and again. Of course, this is exactly what happens to Margaret in *House of Games,* an instance of America's love affair with the con man made literal.

In *Glengarry Glen Ross,* Roma's second encounter with Lingk operates like a poker game until the bluff is blown by Williamson. With Levene's help, Roma puts into motion one set of signs—Shelly as satisfied client—to divert attention away from another set of signs—Lingk's effort to renege on the sale. Roma's objective is to play out enough dazzling signs until Lingk misreads the "cards." All method acting, as Deborah R. Geis remarks,[26] it is Roma's attempt to reverse the signs that makes this display so spellbinding, a *coup de théâtre* by a man who is about to win with no hand. And even though the game eventually "crack[s]-out-of-turn" in this scene, the audience has still been seduced by "sights that few have seen."[27]

In such a world, seduction, reversibility, and opportunity not only take the place of referents and products, but also become something like ecstatic or metasigns, indicating the capacity of signs to turn into each other and turning into each other at the same time. In the process, they redefine Americans and America in particularly postmodernist fashion. The game player plays best in a house of games, a proposition that is implied by the sales-man in his real estate office in *Glengarry Glen Ross,* but which is ultimately hypostatized by Mamet and Baudrillard as the con man in Las Vegas. In-deed, at the end of *House of Games,* Mike is headed to Las Vegas, an astral mecca rising in all its neon intensity out of the emptiness of the desert where everything is valued according to the relativity of exchange. And Baudrillard in the last pages of *America* is headed to Las Vegas as well, to the "secret affinity" between that city of signs and the silence of the desert. To Baudrillard, gaming in Las Vegas tropologizes the lunatic fringe of exchange out at the edge of a system in its expansion, which draws America ever deeper into the heart of the desert and "leads men to seek the instantaneity of wealth" (128).

Conclusion

When Crèvecoeur posed the question "What is an American?" could he ever have envisioned a people so completely ensconced in a landscape of signs? It seems that Crèvecoeur's, Franklin's, and Clemens's construction of America rests on the capacity of the sign to anchor firmly to some real thing like a referent, a land, even a history. Their search was conducted in a "classical" age, when as Baudrillard puts it, there must have been some sort of "magi-cal obligation that kept the sign chained to the real."[28] According to Crèvecoeur, a free man is indeed a man invested with land, and a grouping of free men would be able to constitute a utopia called America, "the most perfect society now existing."[29] Ironically, at the end of the twentieth cen-tury, rather than a tie to the land, "freedom" has come to mean the eman-cipation of signs and their ability to circulate without touching land of any kind.[30] In Crèvecoeur's day, the land could be stolen; in Mamet's day, only the leads.

As the work of Baudrillard and Mamet suggests, America has become the failed utopia of Crèvecoeur's era, for it is constituted as the performance of a post-commodity culture in which its own face is now a mask. And surely a culture that wears itself as a mask must have an enormous effect on the way character is delineated. Baudrillard and Mamet's Americans, in oper-ating as the manipulators of signs, are clearly subject to reversibility them-selves, inevitably open to absorption into the matrix of signs. Certainly to Baudrillard's mind, Ronald Reagan appears as the quintessential postmodernist figure, the embodiment of a coded text manipulated across the screen of the American presidency. And Mamet in *Some Freaks* writes of political debate as a game in which the "talking head" is scored on how well he can deliver his prepared speech.[31] No one escapes manipulation, seduction, reversibility. Even con artists like Mike and Levene are susceptible to the hustle, the gaming, the edge of immorality and criminality that always threatens to reverse itself back onto their own performance.

Nevertheless, it must be acknowledged that the odd function of reversibility offers to Baudrillard a way of envisioning a strategy fatal to the post-commodity culture. Baudrillard sees a fatalism residing in the ecstatic form of the object rather than in the banal form of the subject. As a seismic abyss of inertia, the object is also superlative, more than the subject, more than the social. It is the challenge of the silent masses to the limits of an expanding system. Thus, Baudrillard looks to America as the repository of an apocalyptic performance, precisely because it is a landscape of signs. As the most saturated of systems, America is primed to implode around the desert at its heart. In this way, Baudrillard exhibits a curious twinge of nostalgia, for he seems to recognize America as responding to his quest for the return of a "cruel" culture, "the primitive society of the future" (7).[32]

Interestingly, Mamet also has a trace of nostalgia for an earlier version of America. Certainly in his latest prose work, *The Cabin,* with its obvious link to Thoreau, he makes wistful references to a heritage that is no longer available, to the writers who ghost the Chelsea Hotel in New York and to the bygone shipping community along the Hudson. Yet his nostalgia, rather than invoking Baudrillard's "cruel" society, informs the attempt to establish a moral strategy even though the universe may be amoral at its core.[33] While *Glengarry Glen Ross,* for example, depicts what America has become, Mamet's project also includes the critical exposure of a post-commodity culture gone far beyond the values of humanism. The epiphany of violence in the play, when Roma flings the worst of words at Williamson, is an element of the apocalyptic vision found throughout his work and indicates a system teetering on the edge. Despite privileging the agency of the subject over the passivity of the object, it is nevertheless apparent that Mamet makes even here a curious swerve back to Baudrillard. His con men would be the perfect advance forces of Baudrillard's fatal strategy.

Astral America. Mamet and Baudrillard's journey produces the shimmering refractions of a post-commodity culture that, according to Baudrillard, cannot be analyzed by a critical theory. Only the oblique ray of a poetic and theatrical conception can make an appropriate critique of a landscape of signs, images, and screens. And indeed, *Glengarry Glen Ross* and *America* meet on the sidereal vectors of such a visionary construction and commentary. Here, the performance of America emerges as Baudrillard's "empirical genius" as well as Mamet's prophetic lure: "Listen to what I'm going to tell you now:" (51).

NOTES

1. Jean Baudrillard, *America*, trans. Chris Turner (London and New York: Verso, 1988), 5. All further references will appear in the text.

2. Gregory Mosher, "Interview with Gregory Mosher," by Leslie Kane, in *David Mamet: A Casebook,* ed. Leslie Kane (New York and London: Garland, 1992), 236–37.

3. Stephen Fender, "Revolution, Succession and Natural Identity in American Literature," in *1992 Lectures and Memoirs: Proceedings of the British Academy* (Oxford: Oxford University Press, 1993), 286.

4. Benjamin Franklin, *Autobiography and Other Writings,* ed. Kenneth Silverman (New York: Penguin, 1986), 3.

5. David Mamet, *Speed-the-Plow* (New York: Grove, 1988), 56.

6. Alexis de Tocqueville, *Democracy in America,* Vol. 1, trans. Henry Reeve and Francis Bowen, ed. Phillips Bradley (New York: Knopf, 1945), 426.

7. Jean Baudrillard, "Fatal Strategies," in *Jean Baudrillard: Selected Writings,* ed. Mark Poster (Stanford: Stanford University Press, 1988), 186–89.

8. David Mamet, "A Party for Mickey Mouse," *Some Freaks* (New York: Viking, 1989), 80–82.

9. Jean Baudrillard, "Simulacra and Simulations," in *Jean Baudrillard: Selected Writings,* ed. Mark Poster (Stanford: Stanford University Press, 1988), 171–72.

10. Matthew C. Roudané, "Mamet's Mimetics," in *David Mamet: A Casebook,* ed. Leslie Kane (New York and London: Garland, 1992), 13.

11. Keir Elam, *The Semiotics of Theatre and Drama* (London and New York: Methuen, 1980), 159.

12. David Mamet, *Glengarry Glen Ross* (New York: Grove, 1984), 49–50. All further references will appear in the text.

13. Stephen Watt, "Baudrillard's America (and Ours?): Image, Virus, Catastrophe," in *Modernity and Mass Culture,* ed. James Naremore and Patrick Brantlinger (Bloomington and Indianapolis: Indiana University Press, 1991).

14. Mike Gane, *Baudrillard: Critical and Fatal Theory* (London and New York: Routledge, 1991), 178–82.

15. Ibid. 178.

16. Ibid. 188.

17. Jean Baudrillard, "Symbolic Exchange and Death," in *Jean Baudrillard: Selected Writings,* ed. Mark Poster (Stanford: Stanford University Press, 1988), 124–25.

18. Ibid. 128.

19. Roudané, 10.

20. Henry I. Schvey, "Power Plays: David Mamet's Theatre of Manipulation," in *David Mamet: A Casebook,* ed. Leslie Kane (New York and London: Garland, 1992), 102.

21. Joe Mantegna, "Interview with Joe Mantegna," by Leslie Kane, in *David Mamet: A Casebook,* ed. Leslie Kane (New York and London: Garland, 1992), 257.

22. Mamet, *Some Freaks,* 6.

23. Baudrillard, "Symbolic Exchange," 128.

24. Mosher, 239.

25. David Mamet, introduction to *House of Games* (New York: Grove, 1987), xvi.

26. Deborah R. Geis, "David Mamet and the Metadramatic Tradition: Seeing 'the Trick from the Back'," in *David Mamet: A Casebook,* ed. Leslie Kane (New York and London: Garland, 1992), 61.

27. Mamet, *House of Games,* 48, 67.

28. Baudrillard, "Symbolic Exchange," 126.

29. Hector St. John de Crèvecoeur, "What Is an American?" in *Letters from an American Farmer* (New York: Dutton, 1912), 41, 60.

30. Baudrillard, "Symbolic Exchange," 136.

31. Mamet, "A Speech for Michael Dukakis," *Some Freaks,* 110.

32. See Jean Baudrillard, "Fatal Strategies" and "The Masses: The Implosion of the Social in the Media," in *Jean Baudrillard: Selected Writings,* ed. Mark Poster (Stanford: Stanford University Press, 1988).

33. Roudané, 5.

11 VISIONS OF A PROMISED LAND

DAVID MAMET'S *GLENGARRY GLEN ROSS*

Tony J. Stafford

It is a critical given that David Mamet is a playwright with a social conscience. From his personal statements in interviews and his own prose writings to the avalanche of theater reviews and critical evaluations, his social concerns repeatedly draw the largest share of attention. The written assessments of *Glengarry Glen Ross,* for example, which opened on March 24, 1984 at the John Golden Theater, as well as his own statements, typify the comments surrounding most of his works. The play was greeted by various reviewers as an "indictment of American materialism and ethics," as a "corrosive . . . indictment of corruption," as depicting "American spiritual malaise," as a "howl of protest" against "our contemptible consumer society," and as a dramatization of the fact that "envy and greed are the engines that drive North American capitalism."[1] In a later scholarly opinion, Roudané writes that "avarice and greed form the nerve center of the play" and that the play shows that "public issues" and "business transactions" control "the individual's private world."[2] Even Mamet himself states that the play is about "how business corrupts" and about how "those in power in the business world . . . act unethically."[3] And assessments that acknowledge Mamet's interest in the individual do so in the context of social and commercial interaction: his interest in male relationships (Rich labels them "duels for domination, power, and survival")[4] the "individual's vocation,"[5] as Roudané calls it, as well as "the enervating influence selling exerts on the spirit of the individual"[6] which Harvey defines as the toll that the "rat's maze"[7] takes on human beings.

In this respect, Mamet appears to be no different from any other socially conscious American playwright, working in the tradition of Arthur Miller and Elmer Rice and dealing with such American matters as materialism, greed, competition, corruption, power, exploitation, and business ethics (as David Richards convincingly argues in his comparison of

Glengarry Glen Ross and *Death of a Salesman* in "The Lives of the Sales-men: From Miller and Mamet, Lessons for the Stage").[8] But Mamet is dif-ferent, and he transcends commonplace social criticism. Like any artist, so-cial or otherwise, he filters his social views through his own private experience of the world, and it is this individualization of his art that helps define him. Unlike Miller and Rice, Mamet in *Glengarry Glen Ross,* for ex-ample, draws upon his familiarity with Jewish traditions, the Old Testament, and Judeo-Christian history as a means of giving a moral and historical per-spective to the social issues of the play and an aesthetic for his images and language. In other words, Mamet is not just another angry, conscience-stricken social protester, but an artist who draws upon the historical pat-terns and connections within the Judeo-Christian tradition in such a way as to raise common ideas above the level of propaganda to a plane of a more abstract, philosophical treatment of the subject.

First, rather than being an ordinary examination of American greed and gain, *Glengarry Glen Ross* may be seen as a work with a more coher-ing and devastating central idea, and that is the theme of illusion. In this approach, the salesmen are seen as living in an illusory world, creating a phony reality, and using false appearances as a sales technique so that in the long run they deny their own reality, their client's reality, and the reality of the real world. Ultimately, in such a world, human values are destroyed and nothing means anything, for there is no truth and everything is what one merely says it is.

Since the primary illusion that the salesmen offer is based on land, the idea of land and illusion become joined in the play to create the motif of the "promised land," or more accurately, the perversion of the promised land, and the idea of the "promised land" is carried out in the title, the set-ting, the images, the structure, the action, and the characters.

The title itself has elicited contradicting opinions about it. Frank Rich says that "the only mellifluous words . . . are those of its title" and describes it as a musical title.[9] On the other hand, Brendan Gill says that it "suffers from the defect of being almost as instantly forgettable as it is chaste."[10] The title contains several hidden implications for the play and provides a clue as to the play's underlying intent. While the title is quite musical, due to its alliteration, repetition, and smooth flow, it stands in ironic contrast to the harshness and violence of the language of the play. Through its musical qual-ity, it conjures up illusions of beautiful places when in reality it ironically denotes worthless or nonexistent land.

Moreover, Glengarry Glen Ross, as a piece of real estate, is a mean-ingless entity, for it does not exist. The title is actually made up of the first half of the names of two different pieces of property, Glengarry Highlands and Glen Ross Farms. The combined names reveal yet another irony. Glengarry Highlands, connoting the lovely, green, heather-laden highlands of Scotland, is located in Florida, and a topographical map of that state reveals that there is hardly a hill in the entire state, let alone any height that would qualify as a "highland." While the audience never learns the actual geographical location of Glen Ross Farms, although it too is probably in Florida, irony still resides in the fact that a glen is a narrow, secluded, forested valley, which would defy cultivation as a "farm." Moreover, the most common geographical references of the name Ross are to the Ross Ice Shelf in Antarctica, in what is commonly known as Little America, and Ross county in northern Scotland, in what is known as Highland country. Since Florida has neither glens, mountains, ice shelves, nor highlands, either choice imbues the title with further irony, being a lie, and fosters the notion of land as an illusion.

The title opens up yet other possibilities. In suggesting geographical locations, it anticipates the recurring idea of geography, places, and land, for the play is replete with national and international place names. Finally, the title contains hidden in its juxtaposition of two real estate tracts the actual poles of the play. Glengarry Highlands is the project that the company is currently promoting with contests and prizes to the salesman who sells the most, and Richard Roma is the leader in this contest: he is also a decade or more younger than the older salesmen, who are in danger of losing their jobs. Glen Ross Farms represents a project of some years back, for Levene says "Sixty-*five*. When we were there, with Glen *Ross* Farms (3)."[11] The older salesmen brag that they sold a lot of this property long ago, for as Moss says to Aaronow, "*[D]idn't* we sell a bunch of that? . . ."(12). The central conflict of the play is in fact between the older salesmen, who represent the past and are faced with an uncertain future, and the younger salesman who is currently leading the company.

The mythological land motif is carried out in the setting and contains ironies as well. The off-stage setting is concrete and specific, in contrast to the phantasm of the on-stage setting. The temporal setting, including its values and cultural qualities, is late-twentieth-century America, and the geographical location, we can only assume, is Chicago. By contrast, the on-stage setting, consisting of a Chinese restaurant in act 1 and a plundered real estate office in act 2, is fraught with ironies and illusory properties.

The implications of the Chinese restaurant are rich and complex. In the first place, the China motif harmonizes with a geographical theme, consonant with the idea of land that pervades the play. Further, one can only assume that the decor of the "restaurant" visually establishes the image of China, especially given the fact that a number of reviewers of the New York production mention the look of the restaurant in writing about the "red banquette and black tables" and "banal oriental motif."[12] Another interesting feature of this set is its cheapness, featuring Formica tabletops and "shiny red vinyl"; it is also dark, "murky," and a place where one would not "touch an egg roll with a 10-foot chopstick."[13] Illusion and irony abound, for a Chinese restaurant, plunked down in the middle of Chicago, or any other American town for that matter, creates only the illusion of China but not the reality of China itself. China, which is ultimately only a piece of land, is a distant, rich, exotic, and ancient civilization; translated to Chicago, it is only a plastic phantom of the reality of China, a promise of the real thing, and an appropriate location for discussing bogus real estate.

The New York reviewers also note the quality of the real estate office in act 2, calling it "drab," "grubby," and a place that would "discourage the casual visitor, not to mention a staff member."[14] In ironic contrast to the sleazy quality of the real estate office is the beautiful, pastoral, scenic suggestion of the names of the land that is sold out of this office: Clear Meadows, Mountain View, and others. Even more to the point is the fact that the office has been robbed, pillaged, and vandalized and that it is no longer functioning as a real estate office. The "leads" with which the salesmen work have been stolen, some of the contracts of closed deals have been taken, and the telephones, typewriters, and cash are gone. It presents only the illusion, or "promise," of a real estate office, and much of the action of act 2 revolves around the frustration of the salesmen who cannot go out to sell on this day. It might also be suggested, parenthetically, that the disarray of the office parallels the moral condition of the job the salesmen perform.

Operating in conjunction with the setting are several clusters of images that reinforce the notion of illusory land. Geographical place names, for example, are repeated so constantly that they become like a sacred litany. Because the play deals with a shady real estate business, naturally the names of the properties recur from beginning to end; the salesmen invoke such names as Glengarry Highlands, Glen Ross Farms, Clear Meadows, Mountain View, Homestead, Rio Rancho, River Oaks, Brook Farms, River Glen, Black Creek, and Kenilworth. A close examination of each of these names would undoubtedly yield much irony, as for example, Rio (River) Rancho being located in the Arizona desert and Glengarry Highlands being placed in Florida swampland. But the place name reiteration extends far beyond real estate parcels and encompasses the United States as well as the rest of the world. There are references to Florida (51), Arizona (71), Des Plaines,

Illinois (8), Wisconsin (46), Pittsburgh (53), O'Hara (53), Platt (12), and Bermuda (9). In addition to the international suggestions of the bogus real estate tracts such as Scotland (highlands and glens), Mexico (Rio Rancho), and England (Kenilworth), there are also allusions to nationalities and international locations such as India (Patel, 12), Poland (Polacks, 11), France (53), Europe (52), Argentina (14), the Dutch (69), Ireland (Murray), Sweden (Nyborg), Italy (Roma), Russian (Aaronow), Spain (Seville), Switzerland (Como), and German (Graff and Getz). The total effect of this is a rather vague impression of global geography and pieces of land around the world, although there is no concrete experience within the play of journeying to foreign places.

In addition to proper name places, there are also invocations of land and places as a general concept: "the ground" (5), "earth" (27), "real estate" (29), "properties" (29), "piece of land" (29), "dirt" (39), "world" (45), "the plats [small pieces of land]" (51), "property" (51), "beautiful rolling land" (52), "quite a lot of land" (54), "acreage" (55), "downtown" (2, 3, 23, 57), and "world of men" (72). Moreover, there are a number of terms that connote travel that relates to the concept of traveling to distant lands: "on the street" (8, 66), "two hands and a map" (41), "takes out a small map" (29), "down the road" (50), "bus" (4), "train compartments" (27), "suitcase on the train" (47), "get you on the plane" (53), "courtesy class" (45), "get to O'Hare" (53), "harbor" (45), "waterfront" (51), and "hotel" (9, 10). Again, the idea of land and places is conjured up through repeated references, but it remains illusive and undefinable. Ironically, in spite of all this talk, within the action of the play, no one moves, no one goes anywhere, no land is actually seen, and the audience is left with vague allusions and even vaguer promises that remain unfulfilled.

The motif of illusion is carried out in the structure as well. Many critics have commented on the remarkable simplicity and workability of the structure. Act 1, located in the Chinese restaurant, is composed of three scenes, each of which pairs off two characters and lasts about ten minutes. Act 2, set in the real estate office, revolves around the question of which of the salesmen has committed the robbery. While the surface plot is quite simple (who robbed the office?), the subsurface is a progression of scenes in which one character or another is engaged in some form of illusion that is finally shattered by some contact with reality.

In act 1, scene 1, Levene, who has not been producing as of late, is trying to convince Williamson, the young boss, that he is in fact a good salesman and that all he needs are better leads in order to start selling again. As part of his argument, Levene talks about how productive he used to be, how he was the leader on the board, and how much money he has made for the company. Levene tries to convince Williamson of his past success: "Talk to Murray. Talk to Mitch. When we were on Peterson, who paid for his fucking car? . . . He came in, 'You bought that for me Shelly'" (3); or again, "Those guys lived on the business I brought in. They lived on it . . . You were here you'd of benefited from it too" (6); or, "Wasn't long I could pick up the phone, call Murray and I'd have your job. . . . 'Mur, this new kid burns my ass.' 'Shelly, he's out.' You're gone before I'm back from lunch. I bought him a trip to Bermuda once" (9). Williamson counters Levene's illusion with a brutal reality, pointing out that he, Levene, has not been on the board lately, that he has produced nothing, and implies that he, Williamson, has talked to Murray and Mitch about Levene's supposed successes and helps the audience to realize that Levene is not being honest about the past. Some readers and viewers have assumed that Levene has in fact been successful at some point in his career, but this assumption overlooks the fact that everything is an illusion in the world of this play.

In act 1, scene 2, Moss and Aaronow, both of whose future employment is in doubt, do as Levene does and blame the kind of clients they have for their own failure: Moss commiserates with Aaronow, "You miss a sale. Big deal. A deadbeat Polack" (11). Like Levene they also revel in past but dubious success: "Glen Ross Farms . . . didn't we sell a bunch of that?" (12). Moreover, their illusion consists in blaming the new managers: Moss says, "You know who's responsible? . . . It's Mitch and Murray. 'Cause it doesn't have to be this way" (15). They also suffer from the delusion that their competition, a man named Jerry Graff, is doing better, but in a flicker of honesty, Aaronow says, "I heard that they [the leads] were running cold" (16). It is this delusion that prompts Moss to steal the leads with Aaronow's help, sell them to Graff, and then go to work for him.

Act I, scene 3 is composed of a long harangue by Roma to a stranger named Lingk. The monologue by Roma consists of a kind of philosophizing about life in general. The speech dwells vaguely on the brevity of life, on the question of "what is our life," on the proper attitude toward wealth and investments, which, as Roma points out, are not for the purpose of making money but of finding out more about one's self. In this context, Roma takes out a map of Florida in order to ridicule the idea of investing in land there, only as a setup to begin his pitch. The phantasmal quality of the scene emerges from the irony that Roma has created the impression that he is not a salesman and that his speech is not a sales pitch, when in point of fact both are what they appear not to be. Roma's speech is a demonstration of what the salesmen call the "soft sale," and all these appearances are for the purpose of supporting the impression that the land he is talking about does not promise to be what it in fact is—worthless waste land.

While act 2 is one continuous action, it moves through a series of episodes based on the idea of illusion. One illusion that Mamet has created is the illusion that Aaronow is the one who robbed the office when it is in fact Levene. The act begins with Roma suffering under the delusion that he has closed a number of deals when in fact the contracts have been stolen and are no longer valid. When Levene enters, he boasts to everyone that he has just made a great sale; in his enthusiasm, he reenacts the scene in which he closed the deal, and the audience sees the illusion the salesmen create in that situation. Appropriately, Frank Rich comments that Levene treats the "ritual" of a closing "as if it were a grand religious rite."[15] Unfortunately, the reality is that the people he sold to are crazy and the check from them is no good: Williamson says to him, "They're nuts. . . . How can you delude yours[elf] . . . Forget [the check] . . . Frame it. It's worthless" (71). In another episode, Roma is confronted by James Lingk, whom he closed on the day before in the Chinese restaurant and who now has come to the office to break the contract. As a way of avoiding Lingk's determination, Roma, with the aid of Levene in Mamet's "play-within-a-play," creates the illusion that Levene is "D. Ray Morton, vice president of American Express in charge of European Sales," to whom he has sold many parcels of land and whom he must now get to the airport immediately in order to catch a plane. Roma creates one illusion after another to make the deal stick, including the illusion that he is Lingk's friend and wants what is best for him. Toward the end, Roma tries to create the illusion that Levene is his friend and wants to team up and work with him; after Levene leaves for his interrogation with Baylen, Roma seeks to exploit Levene by telling Williamson, "My stuff is *mine*, whatever he gets for himself, I'm taking half . . ." (74). The closing lines of the play counter all the illusions of the action as Aaronow says, "Oh, God, I hate this job" (75), and Roma ends it by saying, "I'll be at the restaurant" (75).

Finally, the overall polarity and conflict of the play are established by the opposition of two groups, just as Mamet divides them in his character list: On the one hand are the salesmen in their forties with Christian-sounding names: Williamson, the young manager of the office, and Roma, currently the most successful of the salesmen. Juxtaposed against these are the salesmen in their fifties, Aaronow, Levene, and Moss, whose jobs appear to be in jeopardy and whose names have Old Testament connotations. This division seems to resemble some latter-day reenactment of a Judeo-Christian struggle over and dispossession of the Jews from the Promised Land.

In the Judeo-Christian world, the idea of the Promised Land has become so embedded in Western consciousness that it has become a common metaphor for any concept presenting itself as some type of ideal that seems impossible to reach. The appropriateness of this well-known Judeo-Christian image to *Glengarry Glen Ross* seems to lodge in the desire of the salesmen to create in the minds of the customers the illusion of a land of mythic beauty. Moreover, there seems to be a historical inference as well: the older salesmen with the Old Testament–sounding names represent a more scrupulous ethical norm, while the younger, gentile types represent a new kind of religion that is destroying the old ways. In other words, the ancient religion is being displaced by a modern cult of materialism with its own set of commandments and sacraments.

Levene's name seems to suggests Levi, one of the twelve sons of Abraham and whose offspring became the Levites, the tribe of priests; Moss's name, with an *e* inserted, becomes Moses; and Aaronow's name without the last two letters becomes Aaron (and with the last two letters sounds like "Aaron" "now"—the Aaron of the present era). Moses and Aaron, it will be remembered, were charged by God with leading the Israelites to the Promised Land while the Levites were responsible for conducting the religious rituals. Appropriately, Roudané notes that Aaronow injects "moral seriousness" into the situation and that he is the one character with a "degree of conscience." These three represent the past, or, old way. When Levene has made his sale, he, in his enthusiasm, says, "The old ways. The old ways. . . . Like in the old days, Ricky" (47–48), and he admonishes Williamson with "you don't know history" (50). All three talk about the way things used to be, they talk about ethical and moral conduct, they object to the new regime and the way things are done in the present, they judge and condemn Mitch and Murray, and they decide, in Old Testament fashion, that revenge should be taken against the new bosses—as Moss says, "strike back" (18), "do something to them . . . pay them back . . . someone should hurt them. Murray and Mitch" (19).

A number of Old Testament images accrue around Aaronow, Moss, and Levene, these modern-day children of Israel: "judge" (2) [both the noun and the verb], "burning" (3) [Aaron was in charge of the burnt offerings], "the beginning" (71), "convert" (47), "my message" (50), "swear to God" (48), "a good trip" (46), "God's truth"(17), and Moss resents being treated like "children" (18), suggesting the idea of the children of Israel. Moss calls the new owners' approach "medieval" (15) [the era of the height of the power of the church at Rome] and uses terms that connote the Middle Ages as well as the Israelites' captivity in Egypt when he laments that they make themselves "thrall" (17) to Mitch and Murray and that the owners try to "enslave" (17,18) the salesmen.

Ricky Roma is now the leading salesman and is very much in command. His name, of course, suggests the Roman empire, which eventually dispossessed the Jews from their Promised Land; his name also suggests the city of Rome, which eventually became the chief site of the new religion. He is the representative of the new way of doing things, of the new religion in America, whose "fast-talking salesmanship wins him the top dog status every time."[17] Roudané fortuitously refers to Roma's attitude as a "business-as-sacrament stance."[18] Roma, more than any of the others, swears by the name of "Christ," is asked by Moss, "So you think you're the ruler of this place"(45), "What are you, Bishop Sheen" (46), and accused of thinking he is "sitting on top of the world" (45). Roma, like a good Roman, says, "Is this your farewell to the troops" (46), and uses Christian concepts such as "confess" (27), "morality" (27), "bad people go to hell" (27), "hell exists on earth" (27), "God protect me" (28), "thieves" (38), and the importance of "three days" (56); in suggesting the Judeo-Christian link, he tells Levene, "You taught me" (48).

Clearly, the Promised Land of the Israelites, while they were in Egypt, was not an illusion, although it was a collective memory of a past and a hope for the future. Although it represented an ideal land "flowing with milk and honey," it was simultaneously a real entity for which they struggled, fought, and died and toward which they marched and eventually possessed. On the other hand, the children of Israel eventually became once again dispossessed, primarily through the efforts of Rome and, later, the new Christian religion, and the Promised Land again became a nonreality, a memory of an ideal place, existing only in collective consciousness.

In a recent interview, Mamet quotes Robert Service, who "said it best" by noting that "there isn't a law of God or man that goes north of 10,000 bucks . . . money makes people cruel."[19] By inferring that even the "law of God" is subject to the tyranny of money, Mamet seems to suggest that ancient spiritual values and beliefs are susceptible of being destroyed and replaced by the new religion of money and commercialism. It is an extreme position, but having exposed the corrupting power of materialism on a human level (in other plays such as *American Buffalo*), Mamet goes a step beyond mere social criticism by enlisting the aid of his own religion to depict the omnipotent power of greed. The use of Judeo-Christian terminology and concepts may have the intended effect of institutionalizing this new religion of American materialism.

No one would go so far as to say that *Glengarry Glen Ross* is an allegory. On the other hand, the land and illusion motif help to develop the fraudulent real estate theme. The biblical names and allusions augment the idea of promised land. The division of the conflict into old versus new, age versus youth, previous values versus current values, and spiritual beliefs versus material beliefs gives a sense of historical perspective wherein the ancient traditions have been replaced with a modern day religion based on greed, deceit, and spiritual bankruptcy, with Roma(e) as its most successful, energetic representative.

NOTES

1. Clive Barnes, "Mamet's 'Glengarry': A Play to See and Cherish," *New York Post,* 26 March 1984, 36; Edwin Wilson, "Theatre: Lives of Salesmen," *Wall Street Journal,* 4 April 1984, 24. John Beaufort, "A Searing Look at the Sordid World of Salesmen," *Christian Science Monitor,* 10 April 1984, 25; Brendan Gill, *"Glengarry Glen Ross," New Yorker,* 2 April 1984, 114; John Bemrose, *"Glengarry Glen Ross," Maclean's,* 24 November 1986, 66.

2. Matthew C. Roudané, "Public Issues, Private Tensions: David Mamet's *Glengarry Glen Ross," South Carolina Review* 19, no. 1 (1986): 39, 35.

3. Matthew Roudané, "An Interview with David Mamet," *Studies in American Drama, 1945–Present,* 1, no. 1 (1986): 74.

4. Frank Rich, "Theater: A Mamet Play, 'Glengarry Glen Ross,'" *New York Times,* 26 March 1984, C17.

5. Roudané, "Public," 37.

6. Roudané, "Public," 40.

7. Stephen Harvey, *"Glengarry Glen Ross," Nation,* 31 March 1984, 396.

8. *The Washington Post,* 29 April 1984, H1.

9. Rich, C17.

10. Gill, 114.

11. David Mamet, *Glengarry Glen Ross* (London: Methuen, 1984). All citations are from this edition.

12. Howard Kissel, "'Glengarry Glen Ross,'" *Women's Wear Daily,* 27 March 1984, 24.

13. Douglas Watt, "A 'Dearth' of Honest Salesmen," *Daily News,* 26 March 1984, 16.

14. Watt, 26.

15. Rich, C17.

16. "Public," 44–45.

17. Leslie Bennetts, "The Hot-Shot Salesman of Mamet's 'Glengarry,'" *New York Times,* 18 May 1984, C4.

18. "Public," 42.

19. Geoffrey Norman and John Rezek, "Playboy Interview: David Mamet," *Playboy,* April 1995, 60.

12 THINGS (EX)CHANGE

THE VALUE OF MONEY IN DAVID MAMET'S
GLENGARRY GLEN ROSS

Linda Dorff

"Money is *tight*,"[1] Shelly Levene laments in the first scene of David Mamet's *Glengarry Glen Ross,* initiating a discourse about the shifting value of money and men in the real estate office and the world outside. As a medium of exchange, money signifies value in the dramatic economy of the play, in which a sale exchanges money for land, and talk negotiates the men's struggle for survival in the bureaucratic hierarchy. Although money is the holy grail the salesmen seek—the motivation behind their every word and action—it remains virtually invisible on stage. Levene's allusions to the past abundance and visibility of money foreground its absence in the present time of the play, when "real" money is scarce, having been replaced by a system of imaginary money that circulates through the office's capitalist bureaucracy in the form of checks and credit cards. "Real" money and imaginary money exemplify two types of theatrical signification that are at work in the play. Whereas imaginary money functions as a symbolic sign that refers to an object through abstract forms,[2] "real" money acts as an iconic sign, which usually resembles the object it signifies.[3] When cash is offered as a bribe at the beginning and end of the play, the iconic sign of money changes things, disrupting the office's imaginary universe and pointing to Levene's attempt, through crime, to subvert the capitalist system.

The shift in the value of money is reflected in semiotic transformations that money signs underwent as American frontier-style capitalism gave way to the existing shape of contemporary, bureaucratic capitalism. In all its forms, money is a sign, in that it "can be taken as *something standing for something else*,"[4] expressing value that is usually codified in terms of a gold standard. Gold is the ultimate iconic sign of money, resembling the glittering, precious ideal wealth it denotes,[5] making it a perfect target for Mamet, who has said that his plays are "iconoclastic," "in the sense of tearing down the icons of American business, and some of the myths about this country."[6]

Mamet has referred to the gold rush as being an integral part of the American past, identifying "a frontier ethic . . . the idea of go West and make your fortune, there's gold lying in the ground."[7] This image suggests that, like gold, money may have spontaneously generated from the ground, forging a visual, iconic link between money and land. The gold rush was a plot element in several nineteenth-century American melodramas,[8] which glorified the myth of the American West as a place of abundance where enormous fortunes could be made. The West was portrayed as a capitalist utopia, in which the ideal exchange was the frontier sale, wherein nothing (no money) is traded for something (gold). The epitome of the frontier exchange was something for free: gold was free and the gold rush soon turned into a rush for free land.

As capitalism became bureaucratic, gold money was displaced by a system of imaginary money signs, based on the concept of a promissory note, which was a symbolic sign that stood for a fixed amount of gold.[9] Paper money would appear to be a symbol, in that it does not resemble gold and denotes value through linguistic signs printed on each note. But, because of its infinite reproducibility, paper money has gradually lost its connection with gold, shifting into the position of an iconic signifier, which refers primarily to itself.[10] Paper money, therefore, has become an icon that looks like "real" money, or the thing it is supposed to signify. Brian Rotman observes that, as paper money comes to be the "creator, guarantor and sole evidence of wealth,"[11] it breaks with past notions about the value of money, replacing it with nothing but its own "scandalous capacity to create gold."[12] Yet, despite its potential for counterfeiting itself, "real" paper money remains scarce in *Glengarry Glen Ross*. "Real," iconic money, which is printed and regulated by a government, has been replaced by a symbolic system in which money signs can be written by any individual with a checkbook or credit line. In the new, corporate structure of symbolic money, exchanges are framed as competitions, illustrated by the sales contest, which substitutes symbolic rewards for money: The first prize is a Cadillac (symbolic wealth) and the second, a set of steak knives (symbolic food). The remaining salesmen—the losers—face a metaphoric death represented by being fired. The contest encodes sales as acts of competition that are recorded on a sales board, establishing a hierarchy that Moss explains as, "Somebody wins the Cadillac this month. P.S. Two guys get fucked" (36), portraying the contest as a desperate battle for survival that alters the value of money and life.

Money plays a shadowy, symbolic role in several Mamet plays and films, emerging as an unstable, shifting medium for exchanges and change. In *American Buffalo,* the buffalo nickel changes things. Although money is "hidden"[13] by coin collectors and its value is undetermined, Don and Teach plan to steal the nickel, much as the leads in *Glengarry Glen Ross* become the object of theft. Don has a book that shows list prices for rare coins, but "the values aren't *current*,"[14] and when Bob wants to sell a buffalo nickel he has bought, its value is indefinite:

> Don: What do you want for the coin?
> Bob: What it's worth only.
> Don: Okay, we'll look it up.
> Bob: But you still don't know.
> Don: But you got an idea, Bob. You got an idea you can *deviate* from.[15]

Don identifies value as an "idea" that can change, hinting that the coin's worth may be devalued. Although the coin is technically "real," iconic money worth five cents, the picture of the buffalo transforms it into a symbol for America's frontier past, in which gold and the buffalo were plentiful. Bob appreciates the pictorial representation of the buffalo, telling Teach that "I like 'em because of the art on it. . . . Because it looks like something."[16] The nickel's value as a symbol means little to Teach, who ignores Bob and turns to Don, asking, "Is this worth anything?"[17] Teach's philosophy of frontier capitalism, based upon "the freedom . . . Of the Individual . . . To Embark on Any Fucking Course that he sees fit,"[18] does not have room for aesthetics or history. But Teach's claim that he is all "business"[19] is shaken when Bob reveals that he bought the nickel for Don, opening up a possible space for a bond between the men that is not based on the value of money.[20]

In the film *Things Change,* the notion that a symbolic coin can change things is even more powerful. When Gino, a shoeshine man, is bribed to take the rap for a mob murder he did not commit, he does not understand what his "money's goin' to be worth in three years"[21] when he is released from prison. He is given an old Sicilian coin by a mob boss, who tells him: "'A big man knows the value of a small coin.' My friendship is a small coin, but it is all I have to offer you."[22] Like the buffalo nickel in *American Buffalo,* the Sicilian coin represents a symbolic connection to a historical past. Whereas in *American Buffalo,* the undetermined value of the buffalo nickel calls the myth of the American West into question, devaluing the past, in *Things Change,* the Sicilian coin reaffirms a link to history which is so powerful that iconic money becomes unnecessary. When Gino and Jerry spend a weekend in Lake Tahoe, they are told that "there is no bill. Your money is no good in this hotel."[23] Inside the casino, money is symbolic of a stronger bond between men that cancels the possibility of individual agency, replacing it with the medieval metaphysical concept of Fortuna, or a wheel of fortune that ultimately determines fate. When Gino bets on the "Wheel of Fortune," winning $35,000, and is compelled to "lose" it back to the casino, he ironically accepts that "things change . . ."[24] "Real," iconic money cannot buy Gino and Jerry freedom from a nearly feudal enslavement to the Mafia, but the coin gives Gino the symbolic power to appeal their fate, based upon the historical meaning of the bond between men represented by the coin. In contrast to *American Buffalo* and *Things Change, Glengarry Glen Ross* presents a far more cynical portrait of a medieval "world of men" (105), in which money only corrupts things.

The real estate office in *Glengarry Glen Ross* positions the play's critique of capitalism as an inquiry into exchanges that occur in the context of selling (supposedly) "real" land. The sale, or an exchange of one thing for another, becomes a paradigm for the dramatic action, which is developed through episodes of exchange that question the value of money. Talking is also a form of exchange in the play, foregrounded as dramatic storytelling in the sales narratives of Levene and Ricky Roma, in which the words *tell* and *sell* become linguistic correlatives. Nearly every time the word *"tell"* is used, it means *"sell,"* as illustrated when Ricky Roma moves in to close a sale, commanding his prospect to "listen to what I'm going to tell [sell] you" (51). The salesmen seek to hypnotize their audience through the medium of talk, which, even when they are without clients, seems to "ALWAYS BE CLOSING" (13) in on their prey. Although intent on the same goal—the sale—styles of talk differ, as do types of sales.

The play juxtaposes two basic models of the sale: The first type is located in the historical past of the play, when the salesmen were selling Glen Ross Farms. The Glen Ross model of the sale is the archetypal real estate sale, in which "real" money is exchanged for "real" land, or something of value is traded for something of value. But in the present time of the play, as the salesmen attempt to sell Florida swampland euphemistically named Glengarry Highlands, the model of the sale has changed and now approximates a contemporary version of plastic capitalism, in which credit cards or checks are exchanged for illusions fostered by the salesmen's storytelling. Credit cards are suggested to be plastic money and checks are symbols that are worthless until they are cashed, translating the writing on them into "real" money. When a check is written in Mamet's film *House of Games,* a gambler remarks that the "check had better be like gold,"[25] acknowledging that a check is a symbol (accepted on confidence) for the *idea* of money. The Glengarry model of the sale, staged in Roma's sales talk to Lingk at the end of act 1, exchanges Lingk's check, indirectly representing money, for land symbolized by a map. Roma, pointing to the map, says "look *here:* what is this? This is a piece of land" (51), equating a symbol for land with "real" land, suggesting that the land and its value are illusory, and marking the Glengarry sale as the exchange of something potentially valuable (the check) for something that is useless (the swamp).

Levene is strongly identified with the Glen Ross model of the sale—money for land—which flourished in the 1960s. He claims that money was clearly visible in the past: "You know what our sales contest used to be? *Money. A fortune.* Money lying on the ground" (20). This image echoes Mamet's allusion to the gold rush, in which gold, or "real," iconic money, was clearly visible, suggesting that the Glen Ross sale that Levene idealizes may resemble more closely the utopic frontier dream of free gold and land. Levene's nostalgia for the past is reflected in his melodramatic stories, which sentimentalize a past when money was clearly visible and salesmen were valued for their "talent" (77). Like miniature melodramas, his emotional sales pitches attempt to elicit a sympathetic response from his audience, whether the listeners are the Nyborgs or the other salesmen.[26] His narratives of the past, when he made his reputation as the "top man" (76) maintain that salesmen were independent agents who did not work from leads. As he mythologizes the golden Glen Ross days, Levene tells Williamson, the office manager, that his success was not based on luck, but that "it was *skill*" (18):

> . . . and you don't *remember.* 'Cause you weren't *around.* That's cold *calling.* Walk up to the door. I don't even know their *name.* I'm selling something they don't even *want.* You talk about soft sell . . . before we had a name for it . . . before we called it anything, we did it. (77)

Levene dramatizes himself as a pioneer in this narrative, suggesting that the Glen Ross salesmen invented the "soft sell," somehow mesmerizing unsuspecting people into buying land. Reciting a litany of dates and dollar amounts of money he made, he sounds like an old man reminiscing, outrageously claiming to have built the company: "Nineteen senny-*nine,* you know what I made? Senny-nine? Ninety-six thousand dollars. John? For Murray . . . For Mitch" (20).

Like "real" money in *Glengarry Glen Ross,* Mitch and Murray, the real owners of the company, also remain absent from the stage, their Godot-like presence represented through the figure of Williamson, the office manager. Mitch and Murray's absence suggests that the site of power is unseen—somewhere off stage—and that the businesslike front represented for the audience's gaze masquerades, as Philip C. Kolin has suggested, as a cover for a "shady operation."[27] Their absence is linked to a ubiquitous criminality that remains invisible, like money, hidden beneath the surface of ostensibly legitimate business transactions.

When Levene first tries to bribe Williamson to give him better leads, he pulls "real" money out of his pocket, transgressing the office's symbolic monetary system and marking Levene's action as a crime. Williamson initially agrees to the bribe, opening up the possibility, for a moment, that bureaucracy can be subverted. But when Levene does not have enough cash to pay him, he backs out, leaving the money untouched. Levene repeats, "You want to do business that way . . . ? You want to do business that way . . . ?" (26–27), suggesting that "business" should not be a transaction that follows bureaucratic rules. The appearance of bribe money reveals that Levene is not the resourceful, individualistic pioneer he would have everyone believe, for he has not been able to find much "real," legitimate money in the present-day imaginary landscape. His bribe acknowledges that things have changed and "this ain't sixty-five" (20), despite the claim of Mitch's and Murray's emissary, Blake, in the film version of *Glengarry,* who tells the salesmen that "real," iconic money is still as abundant as it was during the time of Glen Ross: "The money's out there. You pick it up. It's yours. You don't, I got no sympathy for you."[28] Changes in the form and value of money are reflected in the title *Glengarry Glen Ross,* which juxtaposes the lean Glengarry of the present with the past salad days of Glen Ross, pointing to the play's dialectic about the (past) valuation and (present) devaluation of money and people.

In the 1980s landscape of plastic capitalism where money is invisible, the salesmen's job has changed from the figure of a gold rush prospector, shifting to the role of a detective who seeks to solve the mystery of where money has been hidden. Instead of prospecting for clients, salesmen are given "leads" to steer them to prospects, a term that Mamet has noted may also be used "as a clue in a criminal case . . . [that] may lead to the suspect."[29] Williamson's "job is to marshal those leads" (18), doling them out to winners of the sales contest and robbing the salesmen of the type of individual initiative that Levene celebrates in his narratives of the past. In the film version the leads are shown to the salesmen as if they were a brick of gold, seeming to glitter, tied up with a gold ribbon and held under their noses to tantalize them. The salesmen suspect that clients have hidden their "real" money: Levene says, "They got their money in a *sock*" (21), and Roma echoes "money in the *mattress*" (62). "They hold on to their money" (28), Aaronow complains. When Levene closes his grand sale of eight units, he believes his clients have hidden "their money in *government* bonds" (72), or imaginary money. As a salesman of the old order, however, Levene is not as good at detection as others, for he fails to understand that his clients, the Nyborgs, have no money to hide. Levene tries to mythologize his "sit" with the Nyborgs as a Glen Ross sale, or an exchange of money for land. But he overlooks the fact that he is now selling swampland to people who cannot afford it, and his euphoric narrative of the sale reveals that he has become as self-deluded as his prospects. He tells them:

> This is now. This is the *thing* that you've been dreaming of, you're going to find that suitcase on the train, the guy comes to the door, the bag that's full of money. This is it, *Harriett* . . . (72).

Levene forgets that he is selling a melodramatic *dream,* seeming to fall into a trance along with Bruce and Harriett Nyborg. He describes the sale as if it were a religious experience, recalling Harry Hickey's evangelistic sales philosophy in Eugene O'Neill's *The Iceman Cometh.* Levene claims to have sold them according to "the *old* ways. The *old* ways . . . convert the motherfucker . . . *sell* him . . . *sell* him . . . *make him sign the check*" (72). He represents the signing of the check as a pledge that it can be translated into "real" money, describing the moment of signing as if it were a spiritual orgasm:

> It was *great.* It was fucking great. It was like they all wilted at once. No *gesture* . . . nothing. Like together. They, I swear to God, they both kind of *imperceptibly slumped.* And he reaches and takes the pen and signs, he passes it to her, she signs. It was so fucking solemn. (74)

He takes their hands, as a member of the clergy might, to bless the signing, after urging them to "believe in your*self*" (67). When he returns to the office, he appears to have sold himself on this belief, crowing to Roma, "I *did* it. I *did* it. Like in the *old* days, Ricky. Like I was taught . . . Like, like, like I *used* to do . . . I did it" (73). His need to believe in his own stories has blinded him to signs that Williamson claims he should have noticed:

> Williamson: . . . they're nuts . . . did you see how they were *living?*
> How can you delude yours . . .
> Levene: I've got the check . . .

Williamson: Forget it. Frame it. It's worthless.
(Pause.)
Levene: The check's no good? (103–4)

The check is a work of fiction authored by clients who have no money, exchanged for the illusion that Levene attempted to sell the Nyborgs.

Levene cannot stop selling even when he is alone with the other salesmen, witnessed by his frantic attempt to "tell" and "sell" Williamson on his value as a "closer" (15). After the Nyborg "sale," he badgers Williamson to call Mitch and Murray and "tell [sell] 'em my sale" (75), betraying his anxiety that his "sale" must be told/sold to his bosses, as well as to his clients. In the beginning of the play he claims that he has had a "bad *luck*" (16) and that, like reputations, "things get set . . . you get certain *mindset*" (15). Throughout the play he maintains a philosophy that "it's a streak and I'm going to turn it around" (22), repeatedly declaring that "things can change" (76), proclaiming his belief in the American Dream by his claim that he possesses the agency to change things. But when he returns to the office with the Nyborg's check—a sort of fool's gold— he reveals to everyone but himself that, despite his claims, things have not changed.

While Levene sells himself on his melodramas, the other older salesmen in the office are also at a loss in the plastic bureaucracy of Glengarry. George Aaronow, who cannot sell anything, complains about the presence of police in the office. Unlike the salesmen, who have become detectives in search of money, Baylen is a "real" detective who has been called in to search for the missing leads, or plastic money. After Baylen accuses him of stealing the leads, Aaronow complains, "No one should talk to a man that way. How are you *talking* to me like that . . . ?" (87) asserting that his position as a man in the office's "world of men" (105) has been devalued. As the architect of the robbery, Dave Moss is the most articulate critic of the play's devaluation of money and men, declaring that the new system is "*medieval* . . . it's wrong" (32). In contrast to Teach's individualistic, frontier philosophy of capitalism (stated above), Moss claims that the new bureaucratic system places the salesmen "in *thrall* to someone else. And we *enslave* ourselves. To *please*. To win some fucking *toaster*" (35), echoing Teach's claim that "fifty percent of some ["real," iconic] money is better than ninety percent of some broken *toaster*."[30] Moss remembers that in the days of "Glen Ross Farms . . . *didn't* we sell a bunch of that . . ." (30), and claims that "they fucked it up. . . . They killed the goose" (30). He explains the new sales mode of Glengarry as:

Guys come on: "Oh, the blah blah blah, *I* know what I'll do: I'll go in and rob everyone blind and go to Argentina cause nobody ever *thought* of this before." (32).

Although Moss recognizes that the seemingly empty "blah blah blah" of Glengarry sales patter is a front for robbery, he does not appreciate the irony of his revenge plot: by attempting to repay bureaucratic capitalism's hidden crimes with an overt act of robbery, he participates in a similar criminality.

Ricky Roma is the salesman who excels at exploiting the present-day Glengarry model of the sale, in which plastic, or symbolic, money is exchanged for swampland. As a master detective, Roma is the most skilled at locating "plastic" money and talking people out of it. In his early forties, he is younger than the other salesmen by at least ten years, and excels at the double-speak of postmodern Glengarry that the older salesmen cannot seem to master. The new sales philosophy articulated by Roma is vastly different from the theme of the *Glengarry* novels of Charles W. Gordon (Ralph Connor, pseudonym) to which Mamet's title may allude.[31] Gordon wrote about Scottish immigrants from the Glengarry Highlands who settled in Ontario, Canada, in works including *The Man from Glengarry* (1901), *Glengarry School Days* (1902) and *The Girl from Glengarry* (1933). The reference to Gordon's Glengarry is surely ironic, for the novels illustrated an idyllic morality that held that "not wealth, not enterprise, not energy can build a nation into greatness, but men, and only with the fear of God in their hearts and no other."[32] The ideology of Roma's imaginary Glengarry Highlands inverts Gordon's philosophy, replacing it with a credo based upon self-interest, which reverberates with the corporate-think of Reaganomics that prevailed in the mid 1980s when the play premiered:

> We say the *correct* way to deal with this is "There is a one-in-so-and-so chance this will happen . . . God *protect* me. I am powerless, let it not happen to me. . . . But no to *that*. I say. There's something else. What is it? If it happens, AS IT MAY for that is not within our powers, I will *deal* with it, just as I do *today* with what draws my concern today." I say *this* is how we must act. I do those things which seem correct to me *today*. I trust myself. And if security concerns me, I do that which *today* I think will make me secure (49).

Roma's sales pitch to Lingk reflects Mamet's observation that "the point is not to speak the desire [for money] but to speak that which is most likely going to bring about the desire."[33] By substituting the word *security* for *money,* Roma conceals an individualistic, capitalist philosophy that he shares with Teach, camouflaging it behind a linguistic gauze of simulated "opportunity" (49) to buy illusory "properties" (50). The value of "real," iconic money slips as Roma shows a brochure of Glengarry to Lingk, asking:

> What does it mean? What you *want* it to mean. *(Pause.)*
> Money? *(Pause.)* If that's what it signifies to you.
> Security? *(Pause.)* Comfort? *(Pause.)* All it is is THINGS THAT
> HAPPEN TO YOU (50).

Roma's words are captivating because they so easily transform the illusion of Glengarry Highlands into a play of signifiers, which can mean "what you want it to mean" (50). The Pinteresque pauses that follow each suggestion open a space of silence on stage, in which the question marks reverberate, inviting the audience to fill in the blanks with their own meaning(s). Unlike Levene, Roma does not fall under the spell of his own words. His sales pitch devalues money, reducing it to a series of "THINGS THAT HAPPEN TO YOU" (50), subtly hinting that, even in a chaotic universe, money can be an agent that makes things happen. The money Roma refers to, however, like his sales talk, is heavily camouflaged under a dense layer of symbolism. He first negates Lingk's (and the audience's) attempts to interpret the symbolic universe of Glengarry, setting them up for the sale by first withdrawing meaning, and then suggesting that he might be wrong: "I want to show you something. *(Pause.)* It might mean *nothing* to you . . . and it might not. I don't know. I don't know anymore" (50). Roma feigns confusion to disguise his commitment to Teach's frontier philosophy of individualism, for he is, after all, out for himself, playing each situation as it lays. Whereas Levene's melodramatic sales pitch to the Nyborgs solicits their sympathy through an almost religious ritual that imbues the act of signing a contract with an overload of meaning, Roma's storytelling to Lingk is an attempt to distract him from the sale, confusing him with a philosophic deconstruction of the meaning of life, property and money, which leaves each emptied of meaning. The most skilled con man in the office, Roma's protean duplicity leaves doubt about the veracity of everything he says, suggesting that the audience should, perhaps, distrust the dramatist's words as well. After Levene has been unmasked as the thief of the leads, Roma commiserates with him, seeming to critique the bureaucratic system that has actually benefited him, for as top man on the sales board, he is allowed to run wild. Yet, he says to Levene:

I swear . . . it's not a world of men . . . it's not a world of men, Machine . . . it's a world of clock watchers, bureaucrats, officeholders . . . what it is, it's a fucked-up world . . . there's no adventure *to* it. *(Pause.)* Dying breed. Yes it is. *(Pause.)* We are the members of a dying breed. That's . . . that's . . . that's why we have to stick together. Shel: I want to talk to you. I've wanted to talk to you for some time. For a long time, actually. I said, "The Machine, there's a man I would work with. There's a man. . . ." You know? (105)

Roma is practicing the sales maxim "ALWAYS BE CLOSING" (13) in this speech, in which his "we" is meant to gain Levene's trust, uniting them against the bureaucracy. When he says, "I want to talk to you" (105), the word *talk* is a cue that he is selling Levene something—perhaps nothing more than his confidence—and in this, he is like Levene, who cannot stop selling. When Lingk returns the next day to report that his wife is forcing him to cancel the sale, Roma quickly improvises a play-within-a-play, attempting to gain Lingk's confidence and prevent him from reneging on their deal. Roma concocts the story that Lingk's check has not been cashed, indicating that the money still remains in symbolic form, and nearly succeeds in convincing Lingk that "the deal's *dead*" (93). He instantly contrives a role and script for Levene:

You're a client. I just sold you five waterfront Glengarry Farms. I rub my head, throw me the cue "Kenilworth." (78)

Their "play" begins instantly as Lingk enters, and Roma and Levene toss the imaginary property names of "Black Creek" and "Kenilworth" back and forth. In Roma's play, not only is the property counterfeit, but Levene is represented as "Mr. Morton with American Express" (79), underscoring his plastic character. The con fails only when Williamson unwittingly bumbles into the scene, an uninvited and unscripted character, who cannot interpret the sales talk. Thinking he is playing along with Roma, he lies to Lingk, telling him that "your check was cashed yesterday afternoon" (95). As long as the check remains *un*cashed, money is imaginary, empowering Roma's symbolic sales rhetoric. But when Williamson suggests that the check has become *cash*, or translated from writing into "real" money, the sudden appearance of money reveals the criminal nature of the sale, disrupting Roma's "play" and unmasking him as a con artist.

Roma's metadramatic unmasking is quickly followed by Levene's exposure as a thief, ending the play with a doubled revelation that both the

Glengarry and Glen Ross models of the sale are fronts for robbery.[34] It is not difficult for the audience to accept that Roma's Glengarry world, with its plastic money and double-speak, is fraudulent, for its realistic surface too closely approximates the jaded look and feel of contemporary capitalism. It seems more improbable that Levene is the robber, whose attempts to hang onto the myth of a golden America render him pathetic, rather than subversive. Until the end of the play, the audience has been conned into believing that it was Aaronow who acted out Moss's plan to rob the office, much as the film *House of Games* deceives its audience. When he resorts to overt robbery, Levene abandons his futile attempts to make the Glen Ross sale work in a Glengarry world; a simple exchange of money for land has become impossible where there is no land of any value to sell and no visible money. When he finally resorts to robbery, Levene gives himself away with a "tell," like the bad poker player in *House of Games,* and Williamson detects the "lead" (clue) and accuses Levene of being the thief.

As Levene tries to bribe Williamson, money appears on stage for the second time, again from Levene's pockets. He displays twenty-five hundred dollars in cash, echoing his attempt to bribe Williamson for leads in the first scene of the play. The visual iconicity of money disrupts the symbolic network of the office, prompting Williamson to recognize Levene's bribes and robbery as subversions of his bureaucratic authority. Williamson refuses, saying, "No, I think I don't want your money. I think you fucked up my office" (102), recognizing "real" money as evidence that a crime has been committed. Levene, however, still argues that there is a difference between sales and robbery, maintaining that "I wasn't cut out to be a thief. I was cut out to be a salesman" (101–2), but the power has evaporated from his speech. Unlike Aaronow, who understands that he is going to lose the sales contest, Levene insists that "things can change" (76) and that his machine-like "skill . . . [and] talent" can prevail over theft, placing him "on the Cadillac board" (63). Even after his exposure as a criminal, like his nickname "the Machine," he continues to sell, claiming, "I turned this thing a . . . I can do *that,* I can do *anyth* . . ." (101). Now, however, his talk begins to wind down, fragmenting like the rattle of a broken machine that is unable to make any further (ex)changes.

Mamet's iconoclastic plays about business represent money signs as mediums of exchange *and* change, critiquing capitalism through its own language of money. Levene's model of the Glen Ross sale frames American frontier capitalism as a mythic "Machine" that can no longer transact the ideal exchange—plundering "real" gold from free land—because both "real" money and land have become scarce. Roma's postmodern Glengarry sale substitutes imaginary money for "real" money, breaking the historical link with gold (and the past), and devaluing money. In doing so, the Glengarry exchange foregrounds representation, erasing the myth with the medium. When Roma's play-within-a-play accidentally discloses that he is a con artist, it reflects Mamet's larger project in *Glengarry Glen Ross,* which, through the medium of money, masterfully reveals criminality hidden beneath the slick surface of plastic capitalism, and simultaneously points back to the frontier ethic, exposing both as fraud.

NOTES

1. David Mamet, *Glengarry Glen Ross* (New York: Grove Press, 1983), 20. All quotations from the play are from this edition; hereafter, page numbers will be included parenthetically in the text.

2. Keir Elam, *The Semiotics of Theatre and Drama* (New York: Routledge, 1980), 22. Elam states that "a *symbol* is a sign which refers to the object it denotes by virtue of a law, usually an association of general ideas" (22).

3. Elam, *The Semiotics of Theatre,* 21. According to Elam, "the governing principle in iconic signs is similitude" (21), following C.S. Peirce's definition of an iconic sign as one which "may represent its object mainly by its similarity," *Collected Papers* (Cambridge: Harvard University Press, 1931–1958), 2.276. Umberto Eco challenges the notion of similitude in reference to iconicity in his *A Theory of Semiotics,* Advances in Semiotics Series (Bloomington: Indiana University Press, 1976), arguing that: "The recognizability of the iconic sign depends on the selection of these features [recognition codes]. But the pertinent features must be *expressed.* Therefore, there must exist an *iconic code* which establishes the equivalence between a certain graphic device and a pertinent feature of the recognition code" (206).

Eco's objection to the definition of the icon as a sign recognized by similitude lies in the complexity by which the process of recognition of objects occurs. He notes that similarity extends beyond the visual dimension into a codified semantic system of cultural references, and that these must be taken into account as well. For example, a hundred dollar bill might look like "money," but it is also recognized through a screen of cultural data, which are not visual.

For a fascinating examination of the relation of iconicity to visibility, see J.L. Wing's "The Iconicity of Absence: Dario Fo and the Radical Invisible," *Theatre Journal* 45 (1993): 303–15.

4. Umberto Eco, *A Theory of Semiotics,* 16.

5. In *Signifying Nothing: The Semiotics of Zero* (Stanford: Stanford University Press, 1987), Brian Rotman notes that in the Middle Ages, gold was used in paintings "to signify the presence of God: gold as intrinsically beautiful, changeless, precious, immutable serves as the perfect icon of God who is beautiful, changeless and so on" (22).

6. Henry I. Schvey, "Celebrating the Capacity for Self-Knowledge," *New Theatre Quarterly* 4, no. 13 (February 1988): 92.

7. C.W.E. Bigsby, *Contemporary Writers—David Mamet* (London: Methuen, 1985), 111.

8. Jeffery D. Mason discusses the influence of the gold rush on the legend of the West in his study, *Melodrama and the Myth of America* (Bloomington: Indiana University Press, 1993). The gold rush began with James Marshall's discovery of a gold nugget at Sutter's Mill on 24 January 1848 (216n5), prompting a massive migration to California. Plots of several melodramas were based on the search for gold, including *My Partner* (1879) by Bartley Campbell, *Fast Folks* (1858), *Two Men of Sandy*

Bar (1876) by Bret Harte, and *Ah Sin* (1877) by Harte and Mark Twain (127). The gold rush theme carried over into the twentieth century, in plays such as David Belasco's *The Girl of the Golden West* (1905), Eugene O'Neill's *Desire Under the Elms* (1924), and Bertolt Brecht's *The Rise and Fall of the City of Mahagonny* (1930), as well as in Charlie Chaplin's silent film, *The Gold Rush* (1925).

9. Rotman, *Signifying Nothing,* 22.

10. In his *Theory of Semiotics,* Umberto Eco notes that "at a certain point, the iconic representation, however stylized it may be, appears more true than the real experience, and people begin to look at things through the glasses of iconic convention" (205).

11. Rotman, *Signifying Nothing,* 50.

12. Ibid., 53.

13. David Mamet, *American Buffalo* (New York: Grove Press, 1976), 46.

14. Ibid., 47.

15. Ibid., 61.

16. Ibid., 64.

17. Ibid., 64.

18. Ibid., 72–73.

19. Ibid., 83.

20. Robert Vorlicky's *Act Like a Man: Challenging Masculinities in American Drama* (Ann Arbor: University of Michigan Press, 1995), offers an insightful analysis of the way men talk to each other in *American Buffalo* and *Glengarry Glen Ross* (among several other plays). Vorlicky concludes that, in *American Buffalo,* "Mamet's play of talk ends neither in violence nor in business, but in sparse, personal dialogue" (227), opening up a space of self-awareness.

21. David Mamet and Shel Silverstein, *Things Change* (New York: Grove, 1988), 84.

22. Ibid., 9.

23. Ibid., 24.

24. Ibid., 39.

25. David Mamet, *House of Games* (New York: Grove Press, 1987), 23.

26. Some critics have labeled Levene's language as "mock-heroic," including Anne Dean (*David Mamet: Language as Dramatic Action,* 217) and Hersh Zeifman, "Phallus in Wonderland: Machismo and Business in David Mamet's *American Buffalo* and *Glengarry Glen Ross,*" *David Mamet: A Casebook,* ed. Leslie Kane (New York: Garland, 1992): 123–35. Although I recognize the mock-heroic impulse in Levene's rhetoric, I believe his speech also has a strong link to the tradition of American melodrama, for the subjects of his stories recall simplistically plotted melodramas about land and money, and the effect of his speech is calculated, as were melodramas, to inspire his audience to respond to him with a sentimental attitude of sympathy.

27. Philip C. Kolin, "Mitch and Murray in David Mamet's *Glengarry Glen Ross,*" *Notes on Contemporary Literature* 18, no. 2 (March 1988): 3.

28. David Mamet, screenwriter, *Glengarry Glen Ross,* directed by James Foley, with Al Pacino, Jack Lemmon, Ed Harris, and Alan Arkin, New Line, 1992. The character of Blake, who is sent by Mitch and Murray to deliver a sales talk in the film, does not exist in the play.

29. David Mamet, National Theatre Study Notes for *Glengarry Glen Ross,* 6.

30. Mamet, *American Buffalo,* 37.

31. Just as Mamet's *Glengarry Glen Ross* mirrors contemporary vernacular, so Charles W. Gordon's Glengarry novels reproduce patterns of Gaelic dialect. These moralistic stories are judged to be "generally rather dull novels" by Ian Pringle in his "Gaelic Substratum in the English of Glengarry County and Its Reflection in the Novels of Ralph Connor," *Canadian Journal of Linguistics* 26, no. 1 (Spring 1981): 139.

32. Ibid., 127–28.

33. David Savran, "Trading in the American Dream," *American Theatre* 4 (September 1987): 16.

34. For a discussion of Mamet's extensive use of metadramatic techniques, see Deborah Geis's "David Mamet and the Metadramatic Tradition: Seeing 'The Trick from the Back,'" in *David Mamet: A Casebook,* ed. Leslie Kane (New York: Garland, 1992): 49–68.

13

PERNICIOUS NOSTALGIA
IN *GLENGARRY GLEN ROSS*

Richard Brucher

Arthur Miller's *Death of a Salesman* (1949) and David Mamet's *Glengarry Glen Ross* (1983) have been soliciting comparisons since they ran concurrently on Broadway in 1984. For Robert Brustein, seeing the two plays back to back was "a compelling and enlightening experience— . . . a cultural broadcast of what is past and passing and to come." Although "Mamet follows Miller in making salesmen the metaphorical victims of a ruthless, venal, and corrupt system," their approaches "reflect significant differences in politics and practice, telling us more about the changing nature of American drama (and society) than a dozen theatre histories." By fashioning epiphanies out of dramatizing what the salesmen sell (real estate), Mamet clarifies a flaw in Miller's conception: the lack of detail about how Willy Loman actually makes his living. Miller's abstract realism is revealed to be a vestige of 1930s social realism, a theater of "pontifications and pronouncements." Miller tells us how to respond ("Attention must finally be paid to such a person"), whereas Mamet shows us, with concrete details and understatement, how "a totally honest realism can transcend itself."[1]

Subsequent criticism has tended to confirm Brustein's observations, particularly with regard to Mamet's use of selling as metaphor and the purity of his realism.[2] However, the cultural lesson, which transcends debate about realistic style, is complex, ironic, and perhaps delusive. Compared to the suppressed guilt and confused aspirations that drive Willy Loman, the sales contest that drives the salesmen in *Glengarry Glen Ross* has an "elegant simplicity."[3] The top seller wins a Cadillac, the runner-up wins steak knives, and the losers get fired. Mamet strips his characters of sentiment, history, and even coherent language, making *Death of a Salesman* seem, by contrast, "tendentious and sentimental."[4] The obscene, disjointed, and fragmented language used by Mamet's salesmen "*reflects* a frustration in all modern conventions and institutions," especially compared to Miller's "rational, generally coherent prose," which allegedly "implies an ultimate faith in current systems."[5] And yet it's Willy Loman's assaulted faith in democratic individualism that gets invoked at the end of *Glengarry Glen Ross*. Exhausted by his failure to defraud a customer, Ricky Roma laments the passing of the old ways: "I swear . . . it's not a world of men, Machine . . . it's a world of clock watchers, bureaucrats, office holders. . . . We are the members of a dying breed."[6] A number of critics, Brustein included, remark wistfully on this remnant of camaraderie, wishing to hear in it some hint of an alternative to the faceless venality of business. We also hear Willy Loman in Howard Wagner's office, pleading for his job and his life: in the old days, back when Dave Singleman was alive, "There was respect, and comradeship, and gratitude" in selling.[7] Behind both Roma and Loman we may also hear Emerson's observation in "Self-Reliance": "Society is a joint-stock company, in which the members agree, for the better securing of his bread to each shareholder, to surrender the liberty and culture of the eater."[8]

Roma's unexpected nostalgia hurtles us back to *Death of a Salesman*, the sentimental play *Glengarry Glen Ross* is supposed to replace, and to Emerson's essays, which are both a source for and an antidote to the individualism that deludes the salesmen who traffic in it. The appeal to the old ways, though, reaches beyond the characters and their situations. Mamet works assiduously in *Glengarry Glen Ross* to create an environment that refuses to credit Roma's gesture toward camaraderie. Consequently, if we put any stock in this flicker of fellow feeling, chances are we've been taken by Roma's appeal to our own need for community and tradition. Mamet has cleverly shifted nostalgia from characters to audience and critics. This deployment of nostalgia in *Glengarry Glen Ross* helps to illustrate Mamet's dramatic use of cultural history and to clarify his place in a tradition of social critics that includes Arthur Miller and Eugene O'Neill. Emerson creates subtext for all three dramatists.

By nostalgia I mean the traditional yearning for home, literally "homesickness," but also reminiscence about or longing for an idyllic or idealistic past, the more general connotation nostalgia has assumed in the twentieth century. In American drama, the expression of nostalgia often has political or ideological implications, as in evocations of Jeffersonian egalitarianism associated with pastoralism, Emersonian individualism associated with independent thinking and iconoclastic behavior, and the like.[9] By pernicious nostalgia I mean a deliberately insincere or malicious appeal to the usual signs and icons associated with nostalgic desire. Pernicious effects may accrue when the expression of nostalgia occurs in contexts that simply won't support it. In these circumstances the nostalgia is ironic, satiric, and critical, either of the character behaving nostalgically or of the object of nostalgia. Genuine nostalgia, as any melancholia, can be dangerous because it prevents the sufferer from engaging in present reality. Pernicious nostalgia is not suffered; it is deployed to conjure fake communal feelings intended to deceive people.

As American society changes—mostly for the worse in terms of its love of money and its capacity to take slogans for wisdom—our playwrights' responses to the spiritual malaise (and to earlier plays) have become increasingly caustic, ironic, and parodic. Although I'll be arguing that *Glengarry Glen Ross* rereads *Death of a Salesman* in often precise and parodic ways, it may be useful to pause first over O'Neill's *The Iceman Cometh,* the nostalgic salesman play against which, at least to some extent, Miller was writing in 1949. Miller, that is, extends and redirects O'Neill's dramatic use of nostalgia, and Mamet subverts the inherited line of nostalgia operating in Miller's play. It's important to note that the impulse to write *The Iceman Cometh,* O'Neill's late proletarian play, seems to have come from an angry impatience with stupid and deluded people who made a mess of the world. Mankind learned nothing from World War I, O'Neill wrote to his friend Lawrence Langner in 1939:

> The whole business from 1918 to now has been so criminally, hoggishly stupid. That is what sticks in one's gorge, that man can never learn but be always the same old God damned greedy, murderous, suicidal ass! I foresee a world in which any lover of liberty will continue to live with reluctance and be relieved to die.[10]

In *The Iceman Cometh* the implied death wish gets expressed in Larry Slade's waiting for death in the grandstand and in the general impulse shared by all the habitués of Harry Hope's saloon to retreat to pipe dreams about the good old days. According to John Raleigh, "Nostalgia is the only kind of sentimentality that is honest."[11] That may be true in *The Iceman Cometh* because neither O'Neill nor his characters mock the past, except as pipe dream that can never quite be realized. Affectionately dismissing Cora's aspirations to marriage and a farm in New Jersey as "de same old crap,"[12] Margie, another tart, summarizes both Cora's pipe dream and O'Neill's comic-satiric use of agrarian myth in *The Iceman Cometh.* Tradition and pipe dream, past and future, merge as comforting delusion. Deadbeats fantasizing in 1912 about the good old days, the corrupt 1890s, engage post-Depression audiences in conflicts between reality depicted on stage and reality outside the theater. Our sense of history impinges anachronistically on the characters' nostalgia to emphasize failed economic and political promises, as well as personal irresponsibility.

The various personal nostalgias have their analog in a kind of national nostalgia, which is both embodied in and travestied by Hickey's story of spiritual rebirth, commercial success, domestic violence, and profound delusion. Hickey seems not to have deluded himself at all about why he became a salesman: it was for the good time, the freedom to roam, joke, womanize, and make a buck with a gift of gab. He secularized and commercialized his preacher father's ability to sell salvation to hicks. As Hickey explains early in his act 4 confession,

> Listening to my old man whooping up hell fire and scaring those Hoosier suckers into shelling out their dough only handed me a laugh, although I had to hand it to him, the way he sold them nothing for something. I guess I take after him, and that's what made me a good salesman. (232)

His story both affirms the American dream—a bright young man can make a success of himself with nothing more than personality and the ability to size up people—and blasts it. He deluded himself that he could marry and lead a middle-class, middle-American life with Evelyn, his pious, doting wife. The dream wife stifles the man with guilt, and he murders her.

> I remember I stood by the bed and suddenly I had to laugh. I couldn't help it, and I knew Evelyn would forgive me. I remember I heard myself speaking to her, as if it was something I'd always wanted to say: "Well, you know what you can do with your pipe dream now, you damned bitch!" (241)

The combination of Christian evangelicalism and sales patter in Hickey's speech travesties the American dream both as romantic quest and commercial enterprise. His hateful "truth" reveals his salvation to be nihilism, worse than fraud. Hickey, as false prophet and purveyor of fake security, certainly anticipates the likes of Ricky Roma.[13]

In the mid 1930s, Arthur Miller thought O'Neill was "archaic," "the playwright of the mystical rich, of high society and the Theatre Guild and escapist 'culture.'" By the late forties, Miller changed his mind. Even the weak original production of The Iceman Cometh in 1946 realized "O'Neill's radical hostility to bourgeois civilization, far greater than anything Odets had expressed. Odets's characters were alienated because . . . they couldn't get into the system, O'Neill's because they so desperately needed to get out of it, to junk it with all its boastful self-congratulation. . . ."[14] I think it's Hickey's story that Miller wanted to turn on its head, to tell from home in Brooklyn rather than from a bar in lower Manhattan or a hotel room in Boston. I don't mean to suggest that Hickey is a direct source of Willy Loman; Miller's uncle Manny Newman, a wonderful grotesque, appears to be Willy's primary model.[15] I think, though, that Miller meant to both domesticate and nationalize Hickey's story. That is, Willy's moments of recall make palpable the troubling consequences of misapplied myth by making even more explicit than Hickey's story does the incompatibility of commercial and domestic cultures.[16] We see and hear Willy's love for his boys and his faith in American social mythology; but the language Willy uses to "sell" his boys reveals how much his labor has alienated him from his family. "I'll show you all the towns," Willy promises his sons in his notion of a civics lesson:

> America is full of beautiful towns and fine, upstanding people. And they know me, boys, they know me up and down New England. The finest people. And when I bring you fellas up, there'll be open sesame for all of us, 'cause one things, boys: I have friends. I can park my car in any street in New England, and the cops protect it like their own. This summer, eh? (31)

Miller, like O'Neill and Mamet, is deeply interested in myth as a source of social dislocation. Like O'Neill, Miller uses nostalgia because that kind of sentiment captures poignant discrepancies between troubling reality and lost but yearned-for idealism. Willy's sales talk unintentionally commodifies genuine family love in painful and precise ways.

As an aging salesman who desperately needs some success and who must humiliate himself before his younger boss, Shelly Levene obviously recalls Willy Loman. Mamet promotes the comparison by giving Levene lines that echo Willy's. For example, act 1, scene 1, of *Glengarry Glen Ross,* in which Levene tries to save his job by negotiating leads with his office manager, John Williamson, clearly recalls the scene in *Death of a Salesman* in which Willy pleads for his job with Howard Wagner. Willy claims 1928 was his "big year" (82); Levene claims 1979: "Nineteen senny-*nine,* you know what I made? Senny-*nine?* Ninety-six thousand dollars" (20). And like Willy, Levene claims not to want any favors: "Do I want charity? Do I want *pity?* I want *sits*" (22). The echoes set off stylistic and ideological differences. As Brustein notes, Willy, facing termination, moans about intrinsic human worth, while Levene, unable to make good on his bribe, heaps invective on his boss's head.[17] "You can't eat the orange and throw the peel away—a man is not a piece of fruit!" (82), Willy pleads to Howard. "You fucking asshole" (25), Levene accuses Williamson. It's as if Levene's obscenity rebukes Willy for groveling as well as Williamson for being a bureaucrat.

Levene insists that he's "the *man* to sell" (19), but to judge Levene's virility (relative to Willy's) by his vituperation is to endorse the value system that defeats and deludes both salesmen, as Mamet surely knows.[18] Mamet's indictment of business sensibility takes a more subtle and ironic tack. Willy's preoccupation with his sons is echoed in Levene's references to his daughter. However, Biff and Happy make real appearances, both in the present and in the past; and they are crucial to the play's examination of masculine American mythology. Biff's aborted football career reflects and mocks Willy's best chance to achieve vicariously the glamorous success he associates with his brother and father, and Happy's squalid career as buyer mocks his father's infidelity. By giving Levene a daughter, Mamet offers the possibility of redirecting this gender-generation problem. Instead, Levene's daughter remains ineffable. Even when she is invoked as a boast (she's better educated than Biff Loman), she testifies to her father's preoccupation with work: "And I put a kid through *school*. She . . . and . . . Cold *calling,* fella" (77). We don't know anything about Levene's relationship with his daughter; we don't know for sure that she exists. She comes up, never as a name, just as "my *daughter*" (26, 104) when Levene reaches a certain level of desperation in a sales pitch. Levene invokes her twice with Williamson, both times when all other ploys have failed. To an extratextual question that has long nagged me—Would having a daughter save Willy Loman?—Mamet provides a witty and derisive answer: No, he'd sell her.

Flashbacks test the assumptions on which nostalgia is based in *Death of a Salesman,* but Miller's most resonant social criticism issues from misappropriated tropes that are designed to evoke a rich cultural past as well as a deluded personal present. I have in mind Willy's long speech to Howard Wagner in which, on the verge of being fired, he links commerce with the American frontier, apotheosizes Dave Singleman, and reveals his own terrible isolation. Meeting Dave Singleman in the Parker House changed Willy's mind about seeking his father in Alaska and settling in the North.

> And he was eighty-four years old, and he'd drummed merchandise in thirty-one states. And old Dave, he'd go up to his room, y'understand, put on his green velvet slippers—I'll never forget—and pick up his phone and call the buyers, and without ever leaving his room, at the age of eighty-four, he made his living. And when I saw that, I realized that selling was the greatest career a man could want. (81)

In light of *Glengarry Glen Ross,* the Dave Singleman story seems to be sheer fantasy. Of course it was mostly fantasy in 1949, and perhaps even in the first decade of the twentieth century when Willy would have met Singleman in the Parker House in Boston. Willy's version of selling completely sanitizes Hickey's story, and it omits any sense of the face-to-face work that must have gone into making the contacts that Singleman, in his old age, could then call on. By mistaking Singleman's phone work for personal work, Willy reveals how oblivious he is to the professional and cultural transformations Singleman represents.[19] Willy tells the Singleman story because it affirms his career choice even as it laments the passing of the old ways. Nothing we see in *Death of a Salesman* confirms the accuracy of the story or its equivalence to the adventuresome careers of Willy's father and brother (which also are simplified and glorified into myth). The Emersonian echo early in the speech—"We've got quite a little streak of self-reliance in our family" (81)— sounds like an advertising or political slogan. Far from being self-reliant and of independent thought, Willy is a conforming consumer, a salesman who believes his own pitches and the advertisements he reads in the paper. And yet the speech, Willy's longest, has passion, conviction, and sincerity (as well as Whitmanesque sweep, balance, and rhythm). Willy's Emersonian reflections mock him (as does the voice of Howard's son in the background, naming on the wire recorder the capitals of the states), but they also endow selling with epic qualities and give Willy a sense of ennobling work.

American Buffalo (1976), Mamet's first play about business ethics, boisterously parodies the kinds of national sentiments that Willy Loman thrives on. Teach, for example, defines free enterprise as "The freedom . . . Of the *Individual* . . . To Embark on Any Fucking Course that he sees fit. . . . In order to secure his honest chance to make a profit."[20] Teach's definition legitimizes robbery and deadly force ("*honest* chance" [emphasis added] is the embedded cliché), and it transforms sex into swindle. *Glengarry Glen Ross* has little of this kind of declamation, although there are ironic remnants of it. Dave Moss rails against businessmen who seem to operate according to Teach's principles: "Oh, the blah blah blah, *I* know what I'll do: I'll go in and rob everyone blind and go to Argentina cause nobody ever *thought* of this before" (32). Overt satire of business practices is part of the play's methodology; but *Glengarry Glen Ross,* like *The Iceman Cometh* and *Death of a Salesman* before it, develops its wittiest, most penetrating criticism by unexpectedly invoking and then breaking cultural icons. For example, the railroad figures romantically in Willy Loman's vision of selling as a respectable, even epic enterprise, as indeed the railroad actually did figure in the expansion of interstate commerce. Dave Singleman "died the death of a salesman, in his green velvet slippers in the smoker of the New York, New Haven and Hartford, going into Boston" (81). With the first words he speaks in *Glengarry Glen Ross,* in act 1, scene 3, Ricky Roma says, "all train compartments smell vaguely of shit. It gets so you don't mind it" (47).

Ricky Roma, the most successful salesman, deploys Emerson in ways Willy Loman, in his innocence, would never dream of. This is most evident in Roma's pitch to James Lingk, a virtual monologue that touches on train compartments, middle-class morality, food, sex, chance, opportunity, fear, fate, investment, and finally Florida real estate ("Florida. *Bullshit.*" [47–51]). Despite its convolutions and non sequiturs, Roma's speech is closer to what Mamet has said it is—"inspirational . . . classic Stoic philosophy"—than to the "cleverly worded nonsense" that some reviewers took it for.[21] Most reviewers and critics have favored Roma's speech, although characterizations of it vary widely. It has been called "one of the finest Dionysion swirls in twentieth-century American drama" as well as "an improbable amalgam of sentimentality and down-market existentialism" that "none the less touches on areas of genuine anxiety."[22] The spiel is intended to coax and disorient Lingk, to never give him an easy place to intervene or redirect the conversation. It is also redolent of Emerson and the vocabulary of independence and promise, with echoes of the major essays, wittily adulterated by popular inspirational materials. "Eh? What I'm saying, what is our life? *(Pause.)* It's looking forward or it's looking back. And that's our life" (48). The sentiment could come from Emerson's "Experience," which opens with a question it then proceeds to answer: "Where do we find ourselves? In a series of which we do not know the extremes, and believe that it has none."[23] Roma's answering call to confidence and action seems to turn "Self-Reliance" against Lingk. "I trust myself" (49), Roma boasts, clearly enjoining Lingk to trust him as a means for trusting himself. Willy Loman sought in Emerson and popular American jingoism an affirmation; not requiring one, Roma proceeds to raze Emerson's premises and sell off parcels of a subdivided Nature.

Far from eschewing the deployment of nostalgia as a device for writing social criticism, Mamet internalizes and understates the nostalgia, and in some cases ritualizes it. For example, Dave Moss reminisces fondly over lunch with his colleague George Aaronow, seemingly in opposition to the sales contest that will no doubt cost Aaronow his job. In answer to Aaronow's remark that the competition is "not right to the *customers,*" Moss says: "I know it's not. I'll tell you . . . what did I learn as a kid on Western? Don't sell a guy one car. Sell him *five* cars over fifteen years" (31). But even as Moss uses the reminiscence to expose greedy and fraudulent management practices, he's luring Aaronow into complicity in a burglary. Later, Levene,

reliving his morning sale to the Nyborgs, hits on a toast as a vaguely ethnic, domestic ritual:

> They, I swear to God, they both kind of *imperceptibly slumped.* And
> he reaches and takes the pen and signs, he passes it for her, she signs.
> It was so fucking solemn. . . . I'm beaming at them. I'm nodding like
> this. I point back in the living room, back to the sideboard. *(Pause.)*
> *I didn't fucking know there was a sideboard there!!* He goes back,
> he brings us a drink. Little shot glasses. A pattern in 'em. And we
> toast. In silence. (74)

One reviewer noted a reminiscence of Willy Loman in this speech, Levene's
pride in the details of his performance being analogous to Willy's self-ag-
grandizing stories.[24] But as Anne Dean points out, there's "a sublime nasti-
ness" in the way the sale gets wrapped in quasi-religious terms, a "noxious
sentimentality" in Levene's details.[25] The Nyborgs are expendable, however,
because they have no domestic standards. The crumb cake Levene takes as
sacrament was "[f]rom the store." "Fuck *her*" (72) is Roma's judgment. Nostalgia may be understated and seemingly incidental, but it is also almost always hostile, specious, or parodic.

For someone who purports not to care about food, Roma keeps
bringing up the subject. Is it possible that he is sincere in rebuking Harriett
Nyborg for buying her crumb cake? In his pitch to Lingk in the Chinese
restaurant in act 1, he claims that "a great meal fades in reflection. . . .
'Cause it's only food. This shit we eat, it keeps us going. But it's only food"
(48). Yet when Lingk returns in act 2, to break the sales contract and get
his money back, Roma again invokes food, this time championing Jinny
Lingk's cooking. "But I'm saying you haven't had *a meal* until you've
tasted . . ." (79), Roma explains to Levene, who is pretending to be an out-
of-town client, D. Ray Morton of American Express. Again, the circumstances won't credit the sentimentality. In what comes off as a brilliant bit
of comic-desperate improvisation, Roma parleys praise for Mrs. Lingk's
cooking into a new "service feature" (79) American Express is develop-
ing in Europe:

> Roma: "Home Cooking" . . . what did you call it, you said it . . . it
>   was a tag phrase that you had . . .
> Levene: Uh . . .
> Roma: Home . . .
> Levene: Home cooking . . . (80)

What begins as a tactic to divert Lingk, intended to keep Lingk's relationship with Roma personal and sentimental, quickly gets merchandised, and then gets lost in the chaos that erupts in the already trashed office. Aaronow bursts from the inner-office, outraged by Officer Baylen's interrogation; and Williamson, harried by the burglary and anxious about Mitch and Murray, loses his temper with Aaronow. Meanwhile, Levene works his cues as Roma, with increasing effort, tries to stall Lingk. The ploy almost works, until Baylen starts demanding to see Levene, and Williamson, either to calm Lingk or to entrap the burglar, decides to intervene in Roma's scam. This is the action that explodes "Home Cooking" and that exhausts Roma, prompting him to call Williamson a "child" (97) and to lament the passing of the old ways. "Home Cooking" is a momentary stay against ethics. Nostalgia is just as pernicious for Roma as it is for Levene and Moss. Society is a joint-stock company still, and Williamson is the hated "company man" (96). But if "[a] man's his job" (75), as Levene insists, the salesmen are no less alienated from human nature than Williamson. Their gestures toward camaraderie are audience traps.

Although Mamet doesn't say so, this self-conscious use of cultural past may be part of his conception of vitality in the theatre. It is true that the theatre is always dying, he says, "and, rather than being decried, it should be understood." An expression of our national dream life, theatre "responds to that which is best, most troubled, most visionary in our society. As the society changes, the theater changes." Theatre people, Mamet argues, work out of "necessity": "What we act out, design, write, springs not from meaningless individual fancy, but from the soul of the times. . . ." So, "It is not theater which is dying, but men and women—society. And as it dies a new group of explorers, artists, arises whose reports are disregarded, then enshrined, then disregarded."[26] The ambivalence of "disregarded, then enshrined, then disregarded" calls attention to consumer whimsy rather than to any planned obsolescence in art or competition among artists, complicating Brustein's idea of what's past and passing and to come. One aspect of the problem may be outmoded dramatic style and didacticism. Another part of the problem is an audience's capacity to distance itself from the action. We delude ourselves into thinking that plays are somehow about aspects of our society but not about us personally. Travesty and other forms of ironic inversion are useful techniques for entrapping complacent audiences.

Mamet has said that he accepts the human need for a well-made dramatic form;[27] but, as William Desmastes has argued, the well-madeness is an artifice rather than a reflection of social or moral order, "a convenience that works to console or set at ease the audience." Still, Demastes may miss a major irony when he suggests that "the mystery-plot second act" of *Glengarry Glen Ross* is "anti-climactic," a structure there only to appease "those looking for . . . closure."[28] The play distills a history of capitalism into ninety minutes of sleazy real estate dealing and an office robbery. Act 1's three scenes, three conversations in a Chinese restaurant, redefine reality as vitriolic desperation, personal betrayal, and surrealistic seduction. These three scenes, depicting personal power plays, feed into act 2, a deeper, more ironic examination of the institution of selling. Act 2, set in a trashed real estate office, creates a vortex that sucks salesmen, the office manager, a client, and a cop into a comic-savage indictment of work ethics. Admittedly, the resolution doesn't resolve anything, even though a crime has been planned, carried out, and solved. Instead, act 2 both repeats and undoes the business of act 1, now in hyped-up continuous action. Aaronow has kept his word not to squeal on Moss but has again been humiliated, this time by "*gestapo* tactics" (89). Roma, even with Levene's improvisational help, has failed to defraud James Lingk (mainly because of Lingk's apologetic refusal to leave). Levene, despite boasting that he's got his balls back, has another sale kick out, a professional affront almost worse than betraying himself as the burglar. As in act 1, scene 1, Levene again fails to consummate a deal with Williamson. The play opens in a Chinese restaurant with Levene trying to cut in on Roma's sales; it ends with Roma, after insisting that Williamson give him half of Levene's commissions, heading to the Chinese restaurant. As Christopher Bigsby has observed, the circularity of structure "reflects the production-consumption cycle of capitalism" and, even more alarmingly, a "profound and disturbing hermeticism." The characters rail against "a system whose principles they have long since internalized," and so they can't escape.[29]

Mamet's *American Buffalo* ruthlessly excludes its audience. We're inhabitants of the hostile environment outside Don's junk shop; we're the "Fuckin' *fruits*" (*American Buffalo*, 32), as Teach puts it, who inhibit these guys' livings and who consequently justify their robbing us. The salesmen in *Glengarry Glen Ross* are more like us, almost mainstream, in their struggles to make livings in an abusive economic system. Mamet counts on our need to connect with a character, to identify with at least one character whose behavior might provide some ethical foundation, some vague possibility of redemption or salvation. Again Mamet refuses to supply such a character. Lingk reflects this need explicitly, and we're as vulnerable to Roma's sales pitch as he is (by virtue of having no superior knowledge of Roma's motives), but Lingk proves to be a gull who will have to seek solace in the attorney general's office. Aaronow speaks the most reasonable words in the entire play—"Oh, God, I hate this job" (108)—but he's a loser, and anyway Roma steps on his line on his way out. Roma appeals because he's successful. That doesn't mean we all have a chance to win. As Willy Loman's life and career demonstrate, that appeal is a sucker's game. Roma's success—as Joe Mantegna's brilliant performance in 1984 demonstrated—means that we are apt to buy his bill of goods. The only likable characters in the play never appear on stage. I mean "Harriett and blah blah Nyborg," the two loonies who "just like talking to salesmen" (104) and who, by remaining silent and absolutely still for twenty-two minutes before signing a contract for eight units of Mountain View, fool Levene into thinking he has made a career-saving sale. Anne Dean, among others, accurately calls Roma's pitch a betrayal of Lingk and of the audience.[30] *Glengarry Glen Ross* proceeds by betrayal. One of the things that's "totally honest" about the realism of *Glengarry Glen Ross* is that you can never really believe any of the characters. The actors are always in character; and the characters are always selling, acting: to their clients, to one another, to the audience. The well-made structure of *Glengarry Glen Ross* is not so much an "artifice" or a "consolation;" it is, more complexly, a con. So may be its radical departure from *Death of a Salesman.*

Mamet has said that his "job is to create a closed moral universe" and to leave evaluation of the characters' behavior to the audience.[31] That's fair enough. He means the evaluation to be difficult rather than easy and for the audience to squirm on the hook. As Mamet has said in "Decay: Some Thoughts for Actors," "We need not fall victim to the liberal fallacy of assuming that because we can perceive a problem we are, de facto, not part of the problem." In the same piece—originally a lecture given at Harvard in 1986—Mamet offers some precepts, both practical and mystical, that may suggest a way to transcend this liberal fallacy. Theatre workers are "born" to it, "thrown up by destiny to attempt to bring *order* to the stage. . . ."[32] In an earlier piece, Mamet, in mock-Puritan fashion, said theatre workers "are elected to supply the dreams of the body politic."[33] In "Decay," with deadpan evangelicalism, he invokes a fate that is closer to grace or calling than to Greek destiny.

> Our civilization is convulsed and dying, and it has not yet gotten the message. It is sinking, but it has not sunk into complete barbarity, and I often think that nuclear war exists for no other reason than to spare us that indignity.
>
> We might have wished these things not to be the case, but they *are* the case; and, for you young people, to quote Marcus Aurelius

again: you receive a bad augury before a battle, *so what?* It's *still* your job to fight.[34]

Mamet's sense of destiny turns out to be astonishingly Emersonian, a combination of the rueful sage writing in "Experience" (1844)—"It is very unhappy, but too late to be helped, the discovery we have made, that we exist"[35]—and the more exhilarated huckster writing in "Self-Reliance" (1841)—"Do that which is assigned you, and you cannot hope too much or dare too much."[36]

Emersonian thoughts resonate in Mamet's theatre essays, just as they do in his plays and in those of Miller and O'Neill. As a purveyor of possibility and unbridled individualism, Emerson is a major creator of the cultural baggage that Theodore Hickey, Willy Loman, Shelly Levene, and Richard Roma trade in. As a stoical antimaterialist and skeptic about the ability of language to reveal reality, he is a progenitor of O'Neill, Miller, and Mamet. I think that each of these writers deliberately travesties Emerson, and probably one another, to find an original and promising American thought. Viewed this way, Mamet doesn't "improve" Miller or O'Neill—as if their dramatic styles or politics got the cultural problems wrong—so much as he seeks to engage his audience with its own time, (re)see persistent communal problems, and play with audience myopia. Unlike Miller (and perhaps O'Neill), Mamet refuses to reveal his position, either in his plays or his theatre essays. Richard Roma mimics Emerson with disconcerting persuasiveness; and Mamet, especially when he seems most sincere in his theatre essays, sounds like Roma.

In my analysis, admittedly, nostalgia for icons of idyllic American life—home cooking, trains, dignified work, and the like—has been displaced by nostalgia for models of redemptive behavior and social improvement. That is a risky venture. To persist too longingly in hearing Emerson in Mamet, as if Emerson is the true and only fix, is also to grow perniciously nostalgic. In this Mamet has his way, too. If we take seriously the Emersonian premises, then we must take to heart Mamet's reminder that recognizing the problem doesn't give us any special dispensation. Perceiving the salesmen as creative or even heroic victims of a corrupt system doesn't exonerate them or us. Individuals must reform themselves before society can be reformed. If they or we prove incorrigible—and that's one implication of the O'Neill-Miller-Mamet connection—then we might recall Teach's singularly un-Emersonian premise in *American Buffalo:* "The only way to teach these people is to kill them" (11). Emersonian premises in Mamet's essays antagonize [Emersonian and other nostalgic remnants] in Mamet's plays, leaving readers and viewers on our own. Arguably, this is where we should be. Mamet refuses to tell us whom or what to trust. If we try to take our cue from any one character or perspective—as from Roma because he talks so persuasively and wins—we're apt to be suckered.

NOTES

1. Robert Brustein, "Show and Tell," in *Who Needs Theatre: Dramatic Opinions* (New York: Atlantic Monthly Press, 1987), 67–68.

2. For example, Stanley Kauffmann, in his review of the film version of *Glengarry Glen Ross*, remarks that in his play "Mamet achieved the work about the fake-smiling drudges of the business world that, some thirty-five years earlier, Arthur Miller had been groping for." See "Deaths of Salesmen," *The New Republic* (26 October 1992), 31. Also see Richard Corliss, "Pitchmen Caught in the Act," *Time* 123:15 (9 April 1984), 105; Anne Dean, *David Mamet: Language as Dramatic Action* (Rutherford and Madison, NJ: Fairleigh Dickinson University Press, 1990), 200, 217–19; and William W. Demastes, *Beyond Naturalism: A New Realism in American Theatre* (New York: Greenwood Press, 1988), 70–71, 86–92.

3. I borrow C.W.E. Bigsby's characterization. See his *David Mamet* (London: Methuen, 1985), 113. "The elegant simplicity of this arrangement serves to expose the operation of a system in which success, defined in purely financial terms, is rewarded, and failure summarily punished."

4. Dennis Carroll, *David Mamet* (New York: St Martin's, 1987), 49–50.

5. Demastes, *Beyond Naturalism,* 92. At least in terms of refusing to offer tidy social analysis and resolution, Mamet concurs. Actions and events that "can be dealt with rationally," he has said, "probably don't belong in my theatre." He concedes that "There are other people who feel differently and work that way brilliantly. One of them is Arthur Miller." Quoted in Demastes, 70.

6. David Mamet, *Glengarry Glen Ross* (New York: Grove Press, 1984), 105. All quotations are from this edition.

7. Arthur Miller, *Death of a Salesman* (1949; Rpt. New York: Penguin Books, 1976), 81. All quotations are from this edition.

8. Ralph Waldo Emerson, "Self-Reliance," in *Ralph Waldo Emerson,* ed. Richard Poirier (Oxford: Oxford University Press, 1990), 133.

9. Timothy B. Spears argues that the traveling salesman entered the national literature and popular imagination as a nostalgic figure. The traveling salesman spent his time on the road, separated from home; and, as a commercial figure in the rural (nineteenth-century) landscape, he mediated between pastoralism and modern industrialization. See *100 Years on the Road: The Traveling Salesman in American Culture* (New Haven: Yale University Press, 1995), 9–15. I came upon Spears' fascinating book too late in my revisions to make full use of it. It seems to confirm some of the cultural implications about which this essay speculates.

10. Quoted in Travis Bogard, *Contour in Time: The Plays of Eugene O'Neill* (New York: Oxford University Press, 1972), 418.

11. John Raleigh, *The Plays of Eugene O'Neill* (Carbondale: Southern Illinois University Press, 1965), 66–67.

12. Eugene O'Neill, *The Iceman Cometh* (1940; Rpt. New York: Vintage Books, 1967), 99. All quotations are from this edition.

13. Bigsby compares Roma to Hickey in *David Mamet,* 113 and 119; Raleigh discusses Hickey as nihilist in *The Plays of Eugene O'Neill,* 166–68.

14. Arthur Miller, *Timebends: A Life* (New York: Grove Press, 1987), 228.

15. Miller, *Timebends,* 122–31.

16. See Spears, *100 Years on the Road,* 232–33.

17. Brustein, 69–70.

18. See Granger Babcock, "'What's the Secret?': Willy Loman as Desiring Machine," *American Drama* 2, no. 1 (Fall 1992): 62. Babcock argues that "In constructing Willy, Miller exposes the liberal subject as a fiction, as part of a structure of value that is an effect of the economy. To dismiss Willy as 'pathetic' because he does not have the strength of character to understand his situation or because he has made the wrong choices is to recode the play according to the protocols of the apparatus (i.e., a man is either a success or he is a failure)." In *Glengarry Glen Ross*, George Aaronow makes the consequences of this value system painfully clear. Aaronow is the gentlest, most decent of Mamet's salesmen; but because his name is not on "the board" he must conclude, "I'm no fucking good" (56–57).

19. On the aptness of Miller's cultural typing, see Spears, *100 Years on the Road*, 223–24.

20. David Mamet, *American Buffalo* (New York: Grove Press, 1976), 72–73. Quotations are from this edition.

21. Dean, *David Mamet: Language as Dramatic Action*, 204. Mamet's remark is quoted in Dean, 204. Dean argues, wrongly I think, that Roma's long speech is simply "vacuous and pretentious" and that "the only type of listener who would be impressed by such verbiage would be someone like Lingk, a gullible, easily swayed individual, apparently with few opinions of his own" (204).

22. Kauffmann, "Deaths of Salesmen," 31; and Bigsby, *David Mamet*, 118.

23. Emerson, "Experience," in Poirier, 216.

24. Gerald Weales, "Rewarding Salesmen: New from Mamet; Old from Miller," *Commonweal* (4 May 1984): 278.

25. Dean, 209–10.

26. David Mamet, *Writing in Restaurants* (New York: Viking, 1986), 19–20.

27. See Matthew C. Roudané, "An Interview with David Mamet," *Studies in American Drama, 1945–Present* 1 (1986): 77. "I'm sure *trying* to do the well-made play. . . . Everybody wants to hear a story with a beginning, middle, and end."

28. Demastes, 69, 87.

29. Bigsby, 125, 119.

30. Dean, 207. Also see Bigsby, 117–19.

31. Quoted in Dean, 192.

32. Mamet, *Writing in Restaurants*, 114–15.

33. Mamet, *Writing in Restaurants*, 19.

34. Mamet, *Writing in Restaurants*, 116.

35. Emerson, "Experience," in Poirier, 230.

36. Emerson, "Self-Reliance," in Poirier, 148.

14

A Japanese
Glengarry Glen Ross

Robert T. Rolf

David Mamet's *Glengarry Glen Ross* was performed in Japan by members
of the Bungakuza (or "Literary Theatre") at the Parco Theatre in Tokyo,
4–21 February, 1988, under the direction of Emori Tōru (b. 1944), who also
translated the work.[1] As is often the case for productions by large theatre
troupes in Japan, it subsequently traveled to various other cities—Yokohama,
Iwata, Kyoto, Osaka, Nagoya, Kobe—from May 12 through 29.

Emori is an accomplished actor, who has played the full range of roles
available to the modern Japanese actor—from Shakespeare and Molière to
twentieth-century works by both Japanese and non-Japanese playwrights.
He is also, incidentally, somewhat of a celebrity in Japan, appearing regularly on all manner of television programs from serious dramas to quiz
shows. His voice is possibly even better known than his face, as his narra-
tions of various TV documentaries are broadcast almost daily. However,
Emori has also increasingly pursued a directing career. It is his work as a
director and translator that interests us here; he was not a member of the
Glengarry Glen Ross cast.

Emori and Bungakuza again tackled *Glengarry Glen Ross* in 1990,
putting it on at the Haiyūza Theatre in Tokyo, 8–21 February. The production was then taken to many cities in Western Japan, 6 March to 7 April.
The cast was the same as in 1988 with the exception of the actor playing
Williamson; that role was given a different interpretation than in the earlier
version. This study discusses both the 1988 and 1990 productions, with
emphasis decidedly on the latter, as well as such related matters as the advertising approach employed in Japan for the film version of *Glengarry Glen
Ross* (dir. James Foley, 1992).

There are inherent problems, inevitable obstacles, in the transference
of the product of one culture to another. There are difficulties imbedded in
language, thinking, and the intricate intermesh between the two. One should

be wary of overemphasizing cultural differences; the essence of the work should generally remain intact. Still, it sometimes seems that Japanese and American artists, and audiences, can look at the same work and see rather different things. It is hoped that an examination of Emori's directorial approach to *Glengarry Glen Ross,* the details of the Japanese productions, and—important with a play that depends greatly upon language for its success—Emori's translation, will help illuminate in some small way the complexity of the undertaking. First, however, a historical and cultural context must be provided for this production and the style of Japanese theatre it represents.

BUNGAKUZA AND THE HISTORICAL CONTEXT OF NONTRADITIONAL THEATRE

The impetus for a new Japanese theatre differing from that in the traditional forms came from the example of Western theatre. That the Japanese would turn their attention in that direction is not surprising. During the long Edo period (1603–1867), when Japan was under the tight, relentless control of the Tokugawa family shogunate, the country was almost entirely closed to the outside world. The door to Japan opened a crack in the aftermath of the visits of Admiral Matthew C. Perry's intimidating American fleet in 1853–1854. The downfall of the Tokugawas and the restoration of nominal imperial rule that ushered in the Meiji period (1868–1912) led to the opening of the nation to large-scale commercial and cultural contact with other nations after nearly three centuries of isolation.

This new state of affairs produced an enthusiasm for modernization that probably has few historical parallels. In a way, modernization meant Westernization, inasmuch as the technology and expertise required for Japan's hurried version of the industrial revolution came primarily from the West. European and North American technicians and teachers were employed on a vast scale in Meiji Japan. In one way or another Westernization touched most areas of Japanese society. The Japanese response to the phenomenon of Westernization provides a central dilemma—one that often resembles a conundrum—in understanding twentieth-century Japan. There is sometimes even the sense that the Japanese are somehow uncomfortable with the new cultural identity created in the process. This is true of both artistic expression and the broader societal phenomena it reflects. And there is the persistent but sometimes apparently unanswerable question of how deep Japan's Westernization goes.

By the turn of the century the thirst for Western knowledge had reached the arts, including literature and theatre. In both poetry and fiction the influence of Western models was enormous. Likewise, in theatre, there began a slow process of searching for an art that could engage problems of a changing society in the manner of Ibsen's *The Doll's House* or *Enemy of the People*, or depict modern ennui and alienation with the artistic impact of Chekhov's *The Cherry Orchard* or *Three Sisters.* Ibsen, for example, loomed large as a model for the type of rational, thoroughly modern approach to art that many Japanese writers were groping toward in the first decade or so of this century. The Ibsen Society *(Ibsen-kai)* was a monthly study group in 1907–1908 that read and discussed the works of the great Norwegian playwright. It included several writers who became associated with literary Naturalism *(shizenshugi bungaku),* which was perhaps Japan's first major modern literary movement, as well as Osanai Kaoru (1881–1928), who would play a major role in the development of a modern Japanese theatre.[2]

What finally resulted was a "new theatre," or *shingeki,* which saw its first period of intense activity in the mid-1920s, especially beginning in 1924 amidst the rebuilding of Tokyo after the mass destruction of the Great Kanto Earthquake on 1 September 1923. Osanai Kaoru led the formation of the Tsukiji Little Theatre *(Tsukiji Shōgekijō),* which became the most prominent venue for a modern theatre. It focused on translated Western works, but Japanese writers were also caught up in the general enthusiasm for theatre. One former participant in the Ibsen Society, Masamune Hakuchō (1879–1962), a novelist and essayist associated with Naturalism, wrote more than twenty-five plays during the period between 1924 and 1927.

In what specific ways did the new theatre differ from the traditional? The most obvious difference is that it was wedded to realism, which is not surprising given that Ibsen and Chekhov were prominent among its gods. Whereas *nō* and *kabuki* are highly stylized, *shingeki* is even today characterized by realism.

Secondly, the advent of the new theatre opened the Japanese stage to women. One interesting Meiji response to the desire to modernize Japanese theatre had been *shimpa,* or "new school" [of *kabuki*], which introduced female actors while at the same time retaining the tradition of male actors who specialize in female roles *(onnagata).* The realistic approach of *shingeki* required that all female roles be played by women. The first *shingeki* actress to achieve considerable fame was Matsui Sumako (1886–1919), whose successful roles included Nora in *The Doll's House.* She also impressed audiences with her Ophelia. The irony of her success in a Western classic reveals part of the dilemma of the modern Japanese theatre artist even today, for she (like her male colleagues) was completely cut off from the major venues for the Japanese classics.

Another significant difference between traditional and modern Japanese drama is language. By the time of the Ibsen Society, Japanese fiction had begun to "free" itself from the traditional literary language that differed greatly from the spoken idiom. Modern Japanese drama also has developed mostly within the context of the colloquial idiom.

At the risk of some oversimplification, one can say that by the 1930s the new Japanese theatre was being pulled in two different directions. On the one hand, a very sociopolitical approach sought to express its ideological viewpoint through drama. An excellent example is available in English translation: Kubo Sakae's *Land of Volcanic Ash* (*Kazanbaichi,* 1938), a vast seven-act drama of the struggle of a humanistic man of science, an agronomist, against the grasping proclivities of "the company," which seeks to use its enormous capital to gain control of an agricultural region and force its will on the farmer inhabitants. This is not the sort of material with which traditional Japanese drama typically deals.[3]

The other approach is an ostensibly apolitical one, which seeks to invest drama with psychological or lyrical complexity. It was perhaps best exemplified by the work of Kishida Kunio (1890–1954), who was instrumental in the founding in 1937 of the Bungakuza, or Literary Theatre (whose artists would perform Mamet's *Glengarry Glen Ross* a half-century later). Despite the serious question of Kishida's enthusiastic support for the war effort, his better works remain compelling explorations of family relationships that ring true in a way that the works of perhaps few of his Japanese contemporaries do.[4]

Bungakuza was launched with a statement of purpose that included the following ideas:

> Avoiding makeshifts, pedantry, or subservience to politics, we would like to offer to the intelligent general public through the medium of the stage a glimpse of a genuine "entertainment for the soul." We wish to avoid both the vague "theatrical" atmosphere that has been part of the drama in Japan until now, as well as the various crude aspects of the radical elements in the New Theatre movement. We wish to create a theatre with an intimate connection with the emotional realities of contemporary life.[5]

It is clear that the Literary Theatre wished to steer clear of both the theatrical spectacle of *kabuki* and the political ideology of the theatre of the Left. They were "serious" about life and theatre, but sought to avoid ideological confrontation and controversy. Their stance seems to represent an amalgam of aestheticism and humanism. A word in the above Bungakuza statement that needs emphasizing is "intelligent," for one of the major contributions of *shingeki* (whether the new theatre of the Left or the Right) has been the addition of an intellectual dimension to Japanese theatre.

The early Bungakuza offerings were mostly of works by such contemporary Japanese artists as Kishida, Kubota Mantarō, Tanaka Chikao, Mafune Yutaka, and Morimoto Kaoru. Productions of foreign works were mostly of French plays, but Bungakuza's first staging of an American work was of Morimoto's translation of Wilder's *Our Town* in July 1941, then again in September and November of the same year, on the eve of Japan's spectacular sudden attack on Pearl Harbor.

Bungakuza's apolitical stance and cooperative attitude toward the war effort allowed them to remain active throughout the war. Inevitably perhaps, their wartime work occasionally included such jingoistic offerings as *Onward One Hundred Million Fireballs! (Susume Ichioku Hi no Tama,* July 1943). The troupe's statement of purpose in 1946 describes how they had managed to continue their work despite the various restrictions placed upon them "during this period leading up to the worst of all possible events, defeat in the war."[6]

Bungakuza's first major postwar production of an American work was once more of *Our Town,* in June 1948 and again in May 1949. (Clifford Odets's *Golden Boy* had received a studio performance in February 1946.) Other American works done by Bungakuza in those early postwar years include William Saroyan's *My Heart's in the Highlands* (September 1949), and Thornton Wilder's *The Happy Journey* (October 1950; January 1951). Wilder's *The Long Christmas Dinner* was then performed together with *The Long Goodbye* by Tennessee Williams in March 1951. Nevertheless, although the troupe has put on its share of productions of American works over the years, it has never been noted especially for its American connection.

Bungakuza has a central position in the history of twentieth-century nontraditional Japanese theatre. It remains the oldest and arguably most prestigious *shingeki* troupe, one whose productions range from revivals of its earlier Japanese works to small theatre premieres of plays by Betsuyaku Minoru, one of the more important Japanese playwrights active today. Betsuyaku is one of the many artists who appeared as part of the reaction against *shingeki* in the 1960s, the artistic phenomenon known variously as the Little Theatre Movement *(shōgekijō undō)* and "underground" *(angura)* theatre, the phase of nontraditional Japanese theatre that has received the most attention from non-Japanese scholars in recent years. Japan's "underground" theatre was an attempt to free nontraditional theatre from the prevailing realism, and to reconnect it somehow with a more autochthonous sensibility than that of the heavily Western-oriented *shingeki*. Although a response to domestic Japanese artistic and sociopolitical circumstances, it was also to a great extent in step with alternative forms of theatre in America and Europe, the international avant-garde. It was greatly influenced by the style and values of the youth culture of the 1960s. Although its ideological stance is largely absent in Japanese theatre today, its stylistic legacy is considerable. And it produced many directors and playwrights who achieved international recognition, such as the late Terayama Shūji, Suzuki Tadashi, Ninagawa Yukio, Ōta Shōgo, Shimizu Kunio, and Betsuyaku.[7]

Of course, the presence of the traditional theatre forms such as *nō, bunraku,* and especially *kabuki* is formidable. *Shingeki* and the alternative theatre approaches that sprang up in opposition to it in the 1960s have never come close to acquiring the official recognition and cultural cachet of the older forms. Still, it can hardly be denied that what I refer to as nontraditional Japanese theatre is the representative theatre of twentieth-century Japan.

A JAPANESE *GLENGARRY GLEN ROSS:* THE DIRECTORIAL CONCEPT

Emori Tōru came to David Mamet's *Glengarry Glen Ross* by way of his *American Buffalo*. Finding the latter a very good read, he was led to the former, the language of which so impressed him with its "power" that he determined to stage a Japanese version.[8] Not surprisingly for an artist who has spent his career with Bungakuza, director/translator Emori Tōru approaches theatre with a strong faith in realism. Emori claims that in both his 1988 and 1990 productions of *Glengarry Glen Ross* his directorial concept—his primary artistic objective—was to create "real" dialogue. He feels he came closer to realizing this goal in the 1990 version, but in both productions he was after this reality of language. Few things are as difficult to pin down as notions of "reality" or "real" language, but as Emori describes it, he refers to a kind of believability of both diction and dramatic situation. One cannot base one's understanding of a theatre production too unreservedly upon the statements of its participants, but they seem highly instructive in trying to gauge the conception of *Glengarry Glen Ross* held by Emori and his actors as well. Of his notion of "'real' dialogue," Emori says:

> By "real" dialogue I mean that I was after a "real" psychology. For example, you go by yourself into a coffee shop or restaurant, or a bar, and you overhear a couple of other customers talking at the next table. You can hear what they say clearly, but at first you don't know

what they're talking about. Still, as you listen, you gradually do. And then you want to hear more and more. That's the kind of reality I was after.

Of course, as will be seen in the discussion of the translation, one problem is that the distinctive nature of the English original—Mamet's (English's?) heavy reliance on scatological expressions—forces the translator into some nearly impossible situations and difficult choices, because Japanese does not rely heavily upon scatological language. And there is the further question of the reality—the authenticity—of the language of the Mamet original. He creates a compelling, complex work structured on language, but *Glengarry Glen Ross* remains a creation, part scatological poetry, part intellectual exercise with a well-defined sociopolitical objective. Mamet's language in *Glengarry Glen Ross* has an air of authenticity but, curiously, also a feel of language existing for the sake of its sound as much as for its meaning. Its power, which attracted Emori, helps create emotional intensity, but seems a far cry from the natural and powerful language of another American play known for its intensity and psychological complexity—O'Neill's *Long Day's Journey into Night*. Still, it was the preservation or re-creation of the power and psychological reality of Mamet's language that Emori saw as his main directorial task in staging *Glengarry Glen Ross* in Japan.

In addition to the believability that Emori perceives in Mamet's language, he also finds a thematic universality in *Glengarry Glen Ross*. For Emori, the play is a universal drama of the daily struggle of the common man. In this respect, as we shall see, his understanding of the work differs somewhat from that of some American critics and perhaps Mamet himself. Such works as *American Buffalo* and *Glengarry Glen Ross* are commonly described as attacks on a pernicious American brand of capitalism.[9] In discussing these two works, Hersh Zeifman speaks of "the apparently oxymoronic term 'American business ethics.'"[10] Henry I. Schvey quotes Mamet on *American Buffalo*: "The play 'is about the American ethic of business, . . . about how we excuse all sorts of great and small betrayals and ethical compromises called business.'" Emori would seem closer to Schvey himself, who quickly adds that "only a small part of the play's success comes as a result of its explicit attack on American values."[11] Schvey characterizes *Glengarry Glen Ross* as "a small masterpiece which reveals with extraordinary perspicacity the treachery of the materialistic world we live in,"[12] and which contains an "excoriating attack on American business values."[13] If *Glengarry Glen Ross* is relevant in Japan, however, it is because of what its Japanese performance implies about Japanese, or all, business.

Mamet's *Glengarry Glen Ross* (1983) is a rather early response to an era of massive savings and loan scandals, the rise of the Yuppie and apparent fall of the trade unionist, and a steady decline in the nation's manufacturing base that even today continues to exacerbate the widening gap between the wealthy and the majority of Americans. The painful emotional and moral complexity of hostile corporate takeovers would be the subject of Jerry Sterner's thought-provoking play, *Other People's Money* (1987). The Japanese performances of *Glengarry Glen Ross,* on the other hand, were during the Bubble Economy era, a time of an almost giddy national confidence and overreaching when, at the end of the 1980s, Japan and its economy seemed nearly invincible. Americans, among many others, could be seen scurrying about seeking ways to "learn from Japan," or at the very least get in on the Japanese overseas investment phenomenon. Emori produced his *Glengarry Glen Ross* during an extraordinary time when the Japanese national mood was compounded of euphoric exuberance, a sometimes almost overbearing self-satisfaction, and a strong sense of disbelief and even anxiety at Japan's new global economic preeminence. It was also a time when Japanese engaged in much public discussion of the costs of success: The English loanword *stress,* already in the Japanese vocabulary, was now on everyone's lips, and the Japanese neologism for a newly recognized pathology, *karōshi* (death from overwork), became known to the world. Indeed, of course, there soon would be a price to pay. By 1993, Japanese stock prices would plummet, losing about half their value; Japan's extraordinarily inflated real estate values would fall dramatically; and wave after wave of enormous scandals would break, involving many of the nation's most prestigious brokerage firms, banking institutions, and manufacturing companies. Finally, perhaps the greatest shock of all would occur—the fall of the Liberal Democratic Party, which had had uninterrupted political control for about four decades.[14]

As for how clearly Japanese audiences of *Glengarry Glen Ross* might have actually perceived this relevance, Emori (probably relying on the audience reaction questionnaires routinely used by Japanese theatre troupes, and not totally indulging in wishful thinking) says:

> I think the reaction of both men and women was sympathetic. Probably because they face the same difficulties in their lives. The productions were at the beginning and during the middle of the so-called Bubble [Economy]. So even male company employees, who are not normally interested in theatre, seemed to find the play interesting. Many of the women in the audience—of course the working women,

but even housewives and young women too—felt that they gained a new realization of the hardships their husbands or fathers are exposed to outside. At any rate, in *Glengarry Glen Ross,* Mamet depicts, in his distinctive idiom, with a blend of humor and poignancy, problems of people living in modern society that are universal and apply equally to both the East and West.

So, for Emori, *Glengarry Glen Ross* is not about a peculiarly American phenomenon. Likewise, it is not merely about capitalism or materialism in his view. As will be seen below, Emori understands modern life's corrosive effect on community, and the concomitant isolation and mistrust that the competitive nature of life in a capitalist society brings. But, like most contemporary Japanese theatre artists of all ages, he does not seem to suggest that a change in economic systems would bring about an end to life's essential suffering and uncertainty, and might even find it naive to believe that theatre could lead the way to such a change anyway. In this regard, Emori would be in step with most Japanese theatre artists today, who are reluctant to draw moral conclusions, to make ideological pronouncements, to use theatre as a tool for sociopolitical statements. Unlike the theatre of the 1960s and early 1970s, Japanese theatre of the past fifteen years or so has become increasingly apolitical and relativistic.[15] Rather than merely a "treacherous materialistic world," it is a difficult existence that Emori seems to find in Mamet's play. Emori, the Japanese artist, while fully cognizant of the toll exacted by the competitive rat race, is capable of a wider view. He knows that the world is treacherous, but seems to ask by implication how it could be anything but materialistic.

When asked specifically about the "significance" of *Glengarry Glen Ross* though, and what he thinks Mamet is trying to say and accomplish through this work, Emori was rather explicit:

This is the most difficult question. First of all, more than anything, I felt that it was a work that depicted people living right in the midst of modern civilization and culture. It depicts men who must earn money to stay alive.

Once Neanderthal and Cro-Magnon men had to go out on grueling hunts to support their families, their clansmen. Today the hunt has assumed a different form—men's jobs. Now it involves difficulties and complexities unimaginable to the Stone Age hunter. One is no longer certain when the game is before one's eyes. The hunt is no longer a cooperative effort. So, it stands to reason that the dejection and pain when a hunt comes up empty surpass that of the Stone Age.

There's no need to ask whether the way one lives is right or wrong. The point is daily survival—the urgency of earning a daily living, above all. Philosophy doesn't fill empty stomachs—that's the reality.

The accompanying jealousy, contempt, and hate in the play are all believable. I can't say exactly what Mamet wanted to say or hoped to accomplish. As for myself, it's an extremely fascinating work that portrays truly lifelike men that we can believe really do exist.

As is perhaps becoming obvious from Emori's statements, *Glengarry Glen Ross* strikes him as an impressive depiction of life's difficulty, especially the trials of the working *man*. He appreciates the fact that the work is a man's play, and even seems to expect it to win some overdue understanding of— even sympathy for—the difficult existence of the traditional male family provider. Although, like most educated Japanese today, Emori must certainly be aware of the existence of such views of society, he gives no indication that he wants to approach *Glengarry Glen Ross* as an indictment of the business world, or any other, as a phallocentric institution. The Japanese actors, in fact, seem to relish the play's maleness, the rare opportunity to perform in a work with no actresses. The thoughts of the cast of the 1988 production are contained in the program. Kawabe Kyūzō (Moss) laments the dearth of all-male plays, which he finds characterized by their vehemence, sublimity, and "dryness" (that is, cerebral, as opposed to emotional, quality). Takahara Toshio (Aaronow), although not wanting to make too much of it, finds an unusually straightforward and efficient communication at the all-male rehearsals.[16]

The actors seem to show genuine enthusiasm for the play and the production, although of course their conceptions of *Glengarry Glen Ross* might have been influenced by that of director Emori. Kitamura Kazuo (Levene) finds *Glengarry Glen Ross* a difficult play in that it is entirely concerned with work, and has no ostensible hero. The lives of the middle-aged actors he sees as essentially the same as those of the play's middle-aged realtors struggling to survive; this overlapping of his own life with that of his character makes the role more difficult to act. On the other hand, Kawabe finds little need for the customary preparation for the role of the realtor Moss, for he is middle-aged like himself: he has only to bare himself honestly on the stage.[17] A curious twist to the 1988 production was that actor Oide Shun played Williamson as a homosexual, a choice apparently dictated by Emori's taking too literally Roma's virulent attack on Williamson in act 2. In the 1990 production Emori abandoned that interpretation and employed a different actor for Williamson. One gets the impression that to some extent the 1990 production was intended to make up for the omissions of the earlier effort, rather than to reproduce a past triumph.

The film version of *Glengarry Glen Ross* received a modest run in Japanese theatres in late 1993. Mamet's enigmatic title was replaced with a grander one, *Matenrō o yumemite* (literally, "dreaming of skyscrapers"), meant to suggest the romance and drama of the big city, as well as perhaps to connect with the common Japanese notion of *otoko no roman* (a man's *roman*), a phrase that alludes to the possibility of drama and adventure in a man's life, as if in a novel. In his screenplay, unlike the play, Mamet creates a somewhat sympathetic realtor, the pathetic Levene, constantly phoning to check on the condition of his daughter (whose photo we see always on his desk). The notion of the businessman in a three-piece suit being a kind of contemporary warrior was drawn upon for the film's main advertising slogan: *"Otokotachi wa sūtsu to puraido de busō suru"*—that is, "The men arm themselves with a suit and their pride." The film's program (these popular, handsome items are nearly always printed for films in Japan) continues this marketing approach somewhat, although it does also show an understanding of Mamet's intended meanings. For one thing, a paragraph toward the back of the program is devoted to Mamet's excoriating comments on the American "system." The program's balance between text and photographs, however, is tilted heavily toward the latter. For example, the first two pages are dominated by an approximately 12-inch by 13-inch black-and-white still of a scowling Al Pacino, seated behind his realtor's desk, coat off, tie loosened, fists clenched—in short, ready for battle. The caption running down the right margin of page two reads, "1993. The men arm themselves with a suit and their pride."[18]

Glengarry Glen Ross: The Bungakuza Production

When a straight play such as *Glengarry Glen Ross* is done with a realistic approach, rather than a directorial concept that undermines or somehow calls into question the literal meaning of the dramatic text, much of the burden of the performance's success falls on the acting. As we have seen, Emori sought believability; the rather ordinary sets and lighting for the Japanese *Glengarry Glen Ross* merely augmented that. The 1988 and 1990 productions were similar, but it seems simpler (and kinder) to discuss the Bungakuza *Glengarry Glen Ross* with the latter in mind.

The three scenes of act 1 introduce in successive pairs the six main characters, five realtors and a customer. Each pairing creates an unequal relationship, as Williamson asserts his power over Levene in scene 1, Moss over Aaronow in scene 2, and Roma over Lingk in scene 3. In the opening scene of the Japanese *Glengarry Glen Ross,* Williamson appears neat, even dapper, cutting a classier appearance than the other realtors. He is well-mannered and patient with Levene at first, then calmly, coldly drives his hard bargain. Levene, by contrast, is somewhat sloppy in appearance, a man who often speaks in whining tones although he does employ a rather strong tone when he loudly and emphatically makes his point about what a crack salesman he really is. The sales leads in Emori's production are written down in notebooks. Frustrated, Levene slams the notebook with the bad leads several times in his opening scene with Williamson.

Scene 2 reveals a Japanese Moss who is slick, sleazy, and self-important—in short, an extremely distasteful character, as he should be. Still, he is capable of whining, which might be considered a likely, "believable" way for a Japanese adult to plead his case, but also has the effect of hinting at underlying self-doubt. Moss boldly, excitedly expounds the importance of getting one's own leads, of taking the initiative in life. He is extremely bitter about not being his own boss, about not being the one to think of starting a business first. Aaronow is quiet and unassuming, a perfect foil for Moss. In this scene at least, realtor though he be, Aaronow seems to qualify as a victim of Mamet's "system," but he does not necessarily elicit our sympathy. We are just as likely to be repelled by his weakness. It must be that very weakness in his character (a lack of mental toughness as much as moral turpitude) that leads Moss to try to rope him into his criminal plot so mercilessly in the first place. That he might strike us more as wimpish loser than victim could constitute one of Mamet's more telling indictments of the extent to which capitalism distorts American values. Then again, it could merely be the nature of unequal relationships: the dupe is foolish, even a figure of fun. The manipulator, the user of the weak, may be repulsive but tends to fascinate us with his power and maliciousness. The Japanese interpretation of Aaronow, by Takahara Toshio, seems almost a caricature (an unconscious parody) of a weak man. In the second act, the Japanese Aaronow will be whining loudly and desperately, sometimes almost wailing.

In act 1, scene 3, Roma employs much physical movement; he is mostly on his feet as he entraps Lingk. His delivery is, of course, quiet. Lingk is bemused by Roma's line in the restaurant; he is not played as a born mark at this point. We will know little of his thoughts until his desperate reappearance in the second act, when we might find ourselves fascinated with the "professionalism" of Roma and Levene's deft improvisation, rather than moved by Lingk's plight. For, in fact, the scene seems to be a humorous example of a black comedy. Perhaps this shows Mamet's lack of sympathy for his characters and their predicament, or then again that it might be human nature to laugh at a dupe, however unfortunate. Whatever the interpretation, the clever play within a play is perhaps *Glengarry*'s most purely enjoyable scene. At the close of both act 1 and the play itself, Emori reinforces the irony of the consequences of greed, as well as the symbiosis involved in predatory relationships, through his choice of music. Putting aside how well Japanese audiences could be expected to understand them, the cynical English lyrics are highly appropriate: "Sweet dreams are made of this; who am I to disagree? I traveled the world and the seven seas; everybody is looking for something. Some of them want to use you; some of them want to be used by you. Some of them want to abuse you; some of them want to be abused."[19]

In busy act 2, Roma is berserk upon his entrance, as he tries to learn the fate of his contract with James Lingk. Still, he almost always seems to act from a position of strength and confidence, no doubt simply because his name is highest "on the board." Although he sometimes shows a tender side, the Japanese Roma (Kobayashi Katsuya) can also chase Baylen, the detective, back into the office simply by screaming, "You got it . . . ?" Aaronow remains consistent and one-dimensional. He whines loudly and uncontrollably, moving from the realm of the wimp into that of the infant. "I'm no fucking good" (57), he says and collapses, near tears. Even the line "They stole the phones" (58) he whines with palpable pain in his voice. Moss, too, is simple, the personification of angry insecurity. As for Williamson, he can shout at Levene on occasion, but also be devastated by the tongue-lashing from Roma and Levene, after which he slumps down on a chair and hangs his head.

Levene and Lingk present the most problematic (and perhaps interesting) interpretations. Levene is a crucial character—believer in the salesman's creed, has-been, criminal. The parabolic trajectory of his career and his almost mystic embrace of the salesman's life—the sale—mark him as an heir to Willy Loman. The Japanese Levene attempts to cover a broad range of emotions. He delivers his Bruce and Harriett speech with exaggerated feeling, almost as if reciting lyric poetry, but is violent as he berates Williamson, who knows neither *"history"* nor *"the shot."* When his guilt has been detected and he is about to be taken into the back room by Baylen, Levene gives a long, loud, anguished cry. Such a raw expression of emotion is not called for in Mamet's stage directions, and most likely at odds with American notions of "realism," but not surprising within the context of Japanese *shingeki*.

Lingk is similarly demonstrative in act 2. His expression of his fear of his wife is seized upon as an occasion for emoting. "I can't talk to you, you met my wife . . ." (92), he says to Roma and dissolves into tears. He goes on sobbing until Baylen reappears to summon Roma. When told that his check has been cashed, Lingk begins a primeval moan, which he continues as he staggers about the office, even knocking Roma down at the line, "Don't follow me" (95), before finally exiting. Some of the decisions of Emori and his actors seem due to the conventions of *shingeki* "realism." Recently playwright/director Hirata Orisa and his troupe Seinendan (Youth Group) have begun to draw critical attention and approval for their subdued, (almost unnaturally) "natural" acting methods, which shows that there is a receptivity for underplaying in Japan, where notions of theatre are understandably heavily influenced by *kabuki*. A Seinendan performance is ninety minutes of quiet talk. However, such restraint remains somewhat of an anomaly, even among artists who seek "believability" in their performances. The frequently booming voices of the Japanese actors of *Glengarry Glen Ross* created a performance that, while fascinating in its own way, at times curiously seemed to dissipate, rather than heighten, tension. And, although the whining of many of the actors—Levene, Aaronow, Lingk—might be plausible for people in this desperate situation, it combined with the shouting to reduce the level of menace in the characters and the situation. There was less of a sense of malice—whether of characters, deeds, or "systems"—in the Japanese version of *Glengarry Glen Ross*. Although there is inevitability in both, the feeling was more of a group of lost, pathetic men in the same sad predicament, as if writhing in some Buddhist hell, than of a collection of "sleazeballs," as it were, forced by a system to do wrong.

Glengarry Glen Ross: THE JAPANESE TRANSLATION

The strongest insults in Japanese might be those to another's intelligence (or also perhaps integrity). Scatological language exists, but is not as prevalent as in English. Above all, there is no Japanese equivalent of English's versatile "F" word. This vulgar but common linguistic phenomenon poses problems for Japanese translators. There is probably no Japanese translation that possesses the vulgarity, syntactic versatility, and semantic resonance of the original.[20] *Glengarry Glen Ross* is virtually held together by the "F" word.[21] The play has a strong plot (with twists), but also seems to derive much of its structural coherence from verbal repetition, above all the obscenity "fuck," which appears in various forms more than 150 times, almost as if one were dealing with free verse. Other obscenities that further flesh out the dirty world of Mamet's real estate office are rectal/genital references (ass/

cock/cunt), at least thirty-five occurrences, and what might be termed excremental obscenities (shit/bullshit), forty occurrences or more. Also deserving mention is the verb "to close," which is used more than thirty times, at least twenty in act 2. There is nothing patently obscene about "closing," but in Mamet's hands it acquires a sinister ring. Mamet seizes upon this—"Always Be Closing"—in his screenplay for the film *Glengarry Glen Ross,* which might show its importance to his mind.

The obscenity "fuck" that dominates *Glengarry Glen Ross* has no equivalent in the language of the translation, which creates a considerable dilemma for the translator. It is like the difficulty of rendering into English a Japanese play that depends on a specific dialect for its effect, for example, many of Okabe Kōdai's works in Nagasaki dialect. Ignore the dialect and one could be changing the play. How does Emori deal with this translation problem? Levene, Moss, and Roma are the play's masters of filth; when they appear together in act 2 the obscenities fly. In a page of text culminating in Moss's exit, some form or other of "to fuck" appears seventeen times, "shit" three, and "farts" once. The "closing" motif is sounded before, during, and after this scene—"closed," "closes," and "Always Be Closing." A look here reveals some of the translation strategies Emori employs: one way to deal with the "F" word is to find a suitably vulgar Japanese expression; another way is to employ (c)rude speech to approximate the effect of the English original; another, simply ignore it.

Examples of the first two approaches are seen when Moss exits with a flourish: "Fuck you. Fuck the lot of you. Fuck you *all*" (71). The Japanese translation is: "*Kusokurae da, omae nanza. Omae dake janai. Doitsumo koitsumo da.*" Translated somewhat literally back into English: "You eat shit. Not just you. The whole lot of you." *Kusokurae* (eat shit) is an example of the substitution translation strategy, but English cannot express the bluntness and impoliteness of some of the other words, for example *omae* (you). The use of such personal pronouns is complex in Japanese, as they can reflect the relative status of speaker and listener. Depending on the situation, the second person pronoun *omae* can express superiority, rudeness, informality, and familiarity. Emori's is a reasonable translation. The job gets done, but at the inevitable cost of the effect of the staccato "Fuck. . . . Fuck. . . . Fuck. . . ." in Mamet's original.

Examples of "fuck" being ignored abound. Roma asks Moss rhetorically, "Who said 'Fuck the Machine?'" (70). The Japanese translation "*Jibun wa dō nandai?*" (literally, "What about you?") continues the idea of harboring an insult. It ignores both "fuck" and Levene's interesting rhyming epithet "the Machine." Japanese has five vowels and one final consonant;

such rhymes are too common to be interesting. The epithet is untranslated throughout.

Profanity, in the traditional sense of irreverent expressions, is common in English, but not Japanese. Having lost much of its power to offend in English, it has little place in *Glengarry Glen Ross*. With expressions ranging from "crissake" to "goddam," there are fifteen or so instances of profanity. Still, when Lingk realizes his worst fears in act 2 and says "Oh, Christ. . . . Oh, Christ" (95), it seems a more expressive word choice than having him exclaim, for example, "Oh, shit," which could convey more or less the same meaning. Lingk is a mark, a victim; he exists to be victimized. His is a necessary presence in a story of predators; he even begs Roma's forgiveness. Lingk is a victim—if not Everyman, then Everyconsumer—whose whining, wimpish manner serves as a foil to, indeed makes possible, the predatory masculinity of the archetypal Businessman-as-Ogre upon which the play depends. We have seen that the Japanese Lingk staggers and moans here. The resonant "Oh, Christ" is rendered as *"Ā, nante koto da"* (something like "Oh, what a thing" [to happen]), which expresses extreme disappointment and bewilderment, though without all the possibilities of the original.

The scatological language of *Glengarry Glen Ross* is perhaps impossible to recapture as such in Japanese. Much of the power of the dialogue that Emori so admires is inevitably lost. Still, he succeeds in creating a script that is sufficiently vulgar, angry, and rude. The conventions of Japanese *shingeki* produce acting approaches that sometimes seem at odds with American notions of "realism," but the core of the play is communicated. The frustration and insecurity of the characters come through. Whether in English or Japanese, the question becomes: What makes them so? American critics and Mamet himself often point to socioeconomic causes, whereas Emori, while apparently able to accept that interpretive approach, seems to add to it a strong overlay of resignation.

NOTES

1. Japanese names are rendered in the Japanese order, surname first.

2. For a discussion of Osanai Kaoru and the Tsukiji Little Theatre, see Brian Powell, "Japan's First Modern Theatre—The Tsukiji Shōgekijō and Its Company, 1924–1926," *Monumenta Nipponica*, 30, no. 1, (1975): 69–85.

3. See *Land of Volcanic Ash: A Play in Two Parts by Kubo Sakae*, trans. David G. Goodman. (Ithaca, N.Y.: Cornell University East Asia Papers, 1986).

4. For translations of Kishida's works, see *Five Plays by Kishida Kunio*, ed. David G. Goodman. (Ithaca, N.Y.: Cornell University East Asia Papers, 1989). For a study of Kishida's career and its relation to the development of *shingeki*, see *Toward a Modern Japanese Theatre: Kishida Kunio*, ed. J. Thomas Rimer (Princeton: Princeton University Press, 1974).

5. Rimer, *Toward a Modern Japanese Theatre*, 118–19. Also quoted in Goodman, *Five Plays by Kishida Kunio*, 13.

6. *Bungakuza-shi* (A history of the Bungakuza), ed. Tatsuoka Shin (Tokyo: Bungakuza, 1977), 26. Information on Bungakuza productions also is taken from here.

7. Works on 1960s Japanese theatre include Robert T. Rolf and John K. Gillespie, eds., *Alternative Japanese Drama: Ten Plays* (Honolulu: University of Hawaii Press, 1992), and David G. Goodman, *Japanese Drama and Culture in the 1960s: The Return of the Gods* (Armonk, N.Y.: M.E. Sharpe, 1988).

8. Correspondence with Emori Tōru, December 15, 1994. All subsequent references to, and quotations of Emori's thoughts on *Glengarry Glen Ross* are from this source.

9. For many examples, see the annotated bibliography in *David Mamet: A Casebook*, ed. Leslie Kane (New York: Garland, 1992).

10. Hersh Zeifman, "Phallus in Wonderland: Machismo and Business in David Mamet's *American Buffalo* and *Glengarry Glen Ross*," in *David Mamet: A Casebook*, 124.

11. Henry I. Schvey, "Power Plays: David Mamet's Theatre of Manipulation," in *David Mamet: A Casebook*, 96.

12. Schvey, 103.

13. Schvey, 106.

14. For analyses of the Bubble Economy and its aftermath, see Christopher Wood's books, *The Bubble Economy: The Japanese Economic Collapse* (Tokyo: Tuttle, 1993), and *The End of Japan Inc.: And How the New Japan Will Look* (New York: Simon & Schuster, 1994).

15. See Robert T. Rolf, "Japanese Theatre from the 1980s: The Ludic Conspiracy," *Modern Drama 35*, no. 1 (1992): 127–36.

16. Program for 1988 Japanese production of *Glengarry Glen Ross*, February 1988, 10.

17. Ibid., 11–12.

18. Program for Japanese showings of the film *Glengarry Glen Ross*, September 1993.

19. The song used in this production was "Sweet Dreams," recorded by Annie Lenox and the Eurythmics.

20. See the chapter "Comparative Profanity" in *Japanese and the Japanese*, Herbert Passin (Tokyo: Kinseido, 1980), 75–92.

21. For a discussion of Mamet's use of obscenities, see Ruby Cohn, "How Are Things Made Round," in *David Mamet: A Casebook*, 117–19.

15 A Conversation

SAM MENDES AND LESLIE KANE

Leslie Kane

Having left Cambridge University in 1987, Sam Mendes began his theatrical career under the aegis of John Gale at the Chichester Festival Theatre, where in successive seasons he ran the Chichester Festival Theatre Tent, the venue at which he directed productions of *Translations* by Brian Friel and *Heartlands* by Tim Firth, as well as the newly built Minerva Studio, where he directed an acclaimed production of Gorky's *Summerfolk* and Shakespeare's *Love's Labour Lost*.

In that same year, he directed *London Assurance* with Paul Eddington, which transferred to the Theatre Royal, Haymarket, and for Michael Codron, *The Cherry Orchard* at the Aldwych with Judi Dench, which won him the Critics' Circle Award for Most Promising Newcomer.

In 1991 Sam Mendes went to the RSC (Royal Shakespeare Company) where he has worked consistently, directing highly successful productions of *Troilus and Cressida*, Ben Jonson's *The Alchemist, Richard III* with Simon Russell Beale, and most recently *The Tempest* with Alec McCowen.

His work in London has included productions of Jean Paul Sartre's *Kean*, starring Derek Jacobi at The Old Vic, Sean O'Casey's *The Plough and the Stars* at The Young Vic, and productions at the Royal National Theatre of *The Sea* by Edward Bond (Lyttleton), *The Rise and Fall of Little Voice* by Jim Cartwright (Cottsloe) with Alison Steadman and Jane Horrocks that transferred to the Aldwych and won the Olivier and Evening Standard awards for Best Comedy, and *The Birthday Party* by Harold Pinter (Lyttleton) with Dora Bryan and Bob Peck. He most recently directed *Oliver!* with Jonathan Pryce at the London Palladium, Tennessee Williams's *Glass Menagerie* and Stephen Sondheim's *Company* at the Donmar during the 1995–1996 theatrical season.

Sam Mendes was appointed artistic director of the Donmar Warehouse in 1992, where he directed the British premiere of Steven Sondheim's and John Weidman's *Assassins,* which won the Critics' Circle Award 1993, *Translations* by Brian Friel, and a hugely successful production of Kander and Ebb's *Cabaret.* His production of David Mamet's *Glengarry Glen Ross* garnered rave reviews. During his tenure as artistic director, the Donmar Warehouse has been nominated for nineteen Olivier awards—winning four— and has also won two Evening Standard awards, three Critics' Circle awards, and The Times Critics Award in 1993.

On television he has co-directed his own production of *Cabaret* for Carlton Television, which won the Gold Carrera Award at the United States International Film Festival in Chicago.

Sam Mendes is a soft-spoken, charming, and congenial man with a marvelous, easy wit. Despite the fact that he was engrossed in rehearsals for another production immediately following the run of *Glengarry Glen Ross* at the Donmar Warehouse, he graciously agreed to meet with me on very short notice. This conversation was conducted at the Donmar on 22 July 1994, on an unusually brilliant morning in London immediately following my attendance at Mendes's production of *Glengarry Glen Ross* on the previous evening.

Kane: In your professional career as a director, you have directed a wide variety of classical and modern dramatists. What has attracted you to the work of David Mamet and to *Glengarry Glen Ross* in particular?

Mendes: Well, it's this particular play. I find I have a fascination with words and my criteria for going into rehearsal with a play is wanting to see how it works. There's a tremendous verbal complexity with this work which fascinates me, and I wanted to explore that. Interestingly enough, I'd just worked on *The Birthday Party,* which I directed at the National Theatre, and *Glengarry* seemed to me to be a natural extension of the work that I was doing on that, and a natural conclusion to it, because it brought it forward thirty years—that sort of verbal precision. As a play, I felt it has a genuine universality. Like all great plays it resonates far beyond itself, far beyond the shores of its own country, far beyond the specifics of its world and the specifics of its characters. There are many layers to it. I mean—you know all this—it's not just a critique of capitalism. It's not just a story of one particular man who can no longer stand the pressure and snaps, or makes an error of judgment. It's about the layers beyond that: the Mitch and Murray who never appear, who control that world, and the people beyond that. There's one character, as you know, Lemkin, who's mentioned just once.

Roma says, "I'm going to Lemkin." That actually does remind me of *The Birthday Party*, in many ways. At the very end of *The Birthday Party*, Petey says, "Where are you taking him?" And Goldberg says, "I'm taking him to Monty." Even sounds like Mitch and Murray a little bit. (Laughter). And, it's that sort of distancing device, that sense of desperation, that sense of them being unaware of performing for the people that we never see. Somebody downtown takes the cream.

I could be more specific, but the play also fascinates me, just purely personally, because I very much enjoy doing ensemble pieces. I always find it very stimulating. I don't enjoy a hierarchical rehearsal process, and I find it very difficult and work very hard when I'm doing Shakespeare to make the company feel like a unit, even when people, as is inevitable in Shakespeare, have nothing to say. I very much enjoy doing ensemble work, and what fascinates me about *Glengarry* is that here is an "ensemble" of characters, who would *gladly* stab each other in the back, given a second chance, and yet, somehow you're having to design a rehearsal atmosphere in which there is a huge amount of bonding and mutual dependence between the actors. In fact, within the context of an office, which is at one point almost like a theatre—a play within a play—there is a certain amount of mutual dependence and improvisatory cunning, you know, in which they become willing partners in crime. So, that also fascinated me. Also, I think that David Mamet stands between two areas which I'm very fond of, and very fascinated by: One is the tradition of the "American play," if you like—forgive me for generalizing on this—which is a discussion, if you like, of the "American Dream" and of the notion of all those clichés. In other words, it does come from a tradition which involves Miller and goes way back.

Kane: To O'Neill?

Mendes: Yeah, O'Neill. Hickey is a storyteller and a salesman. And, in *American Buffalo* I think Mamet quite deliberately toys with history. And, with *Glengarry* he can't be unaware of *Death of a Salesman*.

Kane: Isn't Mamet toying with history, to use your phrase, in *Glengarry Glen Ross* when Levene tells Williamson that he doesn't know his history, as if one can't survive without knowing history?

Mendes: (Laughter). He does indeed. Well, there you are. There's your answer, I think. But, it's the other aspect of Mamet that I think I keyed into first: that he's also European. He uses language in a far more Beckettian or Pinteresque way. Beckett is equally valid as a parallel. And, so he stands between the two. I think that's probably the reason why he is so popular in this country.

Kane: Currently two successful Mamet productions, your *Glengarry Glen Ross* and Gregory Mosher's *The Cryptogram* are running concurrently in London, constituting a mini-Mamet festival. To what do you attribute Mamet's critical reception in Great Britain?

Mendes: Well, I don't think you can ever quite quantify what somebody's appeal is in bold terms, you know. I think you're asking something that is partly spiritual: Why do audiences in this country come to see these plays? Partly, there is a linguistic, rhythmical fascination, whatever it is, whether it's the fascination of the alien, as it were, or the fascination with a nationality. But at the moment, as has happened for the last five or ten years, there is a shared fascination in Britain with America and all things American, and I do think we're becoming far more American as a race. I think that High Street fashions are now not just American, but black American fashions. Ten, fifteen years ago, it was all absolutely rooted in England. The whole punk culture was English, the whole New Wave Movement was English. So, youth culture has changed, as well.

With that there has been a whole renewed interest in American drama, and a continued interest in *Glengarry*. I think there's somehow a density to it, a rhythm which sets it aside from most contemporary English playwrights, as well. Of course, you have to hold him up as a stylist, as well. Who would you say are the big commercially successful playwrights in this country in the last ten years? Well, there aren't any real stylists apart from (Tom) Stoppard. They're all storytellers. There's Alan Ayckbourn, Simon Gray, there's (Michael) Frayn, a theatrical stylist, a wonderful man, a wonderful playwright, but there are no linguistic stylists. There are no wordsmiths. There are no people who spin characters out of nothing. It's very narrative-based now. I think Pinter is still treated with great suspicion in this country because he doesn't deal in story.

Kane: The beauty of Pinter's work is, I think, that he weaves a number of stories into each play, but gives the impression that they aren't stories at all by providing alternative versions of them.

Mendes: Yes.

Kane: It appears in *Glengarry* that the hierarchical business system tends to corrupt, or as the playwright has said, quoting theorist Thorstein Veblen, "Sharp practice inevitably shades over into fraud." In your view how does Mamet dramatize this inevitability and the fear of men whose lives and livelihood are equated? In your stunning production, this shading from sharp practice to fraud, it seems to me, is brilliantly underscored by the use of a revolve and blazing red wall that focuses our attention on the characters engaged in a series of deals. How does it shade over?

Mendes: Well, I mean, that is the glory of the play. It's done with immense subtlety. I always see the first act, that blood-red wall, and clinical, rather dead-pan audience involvement that the revolve asks for, very filmic, very . . . almost like a specimen on a revolving desk.

Kane: And it reflects off Williamson's face.

Mendes: Absolutely, absolutely. And, until he understands what's happening, a lot of what George (Aaronow) is doing is also quite deadpan. But for me the first act is the crime and the second act the post-mortem. In actual fact, the crime happens in the first act, you know. The robbery happens in spirit in the first act; the second act is merely the shit, the mess, the mistake, which is what Shelly (Levene) makes. He's an idiot. He has a big mouth. He says one thing too many.

Kane: Whereas it's (Dave) Moss who says, "I have a big mouth."

Mendes: Yeah. Yet, Moss is intelligent enough to admit it! (Laughter). Shelly never really admits it. He's too proud.

Kane: But isn't that Mamet's point, though, that the one who is clever is smart enough to admit it?

Mendes: Oh, absolutely. I think that Shelly is partly blind. He's blind in the context of the play because he doesn't know himself well enough to be honest. There's also a red herring for a second: this pause when Moss leaves the office in the second act. Roma says, "Come on, snap out of it. You're sitting in the kitchen eating her crumb cake," and Shelly says, "Oh yeah. I'm eating her crumb cake," and they go back into it, you know, but he's been caught up. That's when Shelly should walk out and go down the road with Moss and say, "Hey, now what happened last night? What happened in the room? What's going on here?" Because if you actually look beneath the surface of the play, there's an incredible, complex web of communication that's gone on off-stage. Moss and Levene must have had a meeting. They must have struck a deal.

Kane: When Moss realized that Aaronow was never going to be able to go through with it?

Mendes: Of course, yeah, when George said, "Look, I'm going to have a nervous breakdown if I do this," and Moss says, "Okay, well fuck you," then he must have gone off to catch Shelly. And one really does imagine that they've met, that it's rainy, it's midnight, and they're both two desperate men. But Levene comes in having made the sale to the Nyborgs, and Dave is already in the room, you know—he's already in interrogation—so he can't have known what's going on, but then Dave has rung up Ricky, telling him, "We've had a robbery." The cop says to Ricky, "How do you know we've had a robbery?" He said, "Moss told me," so Moss must have rung him earlier in the morning. We spent a lot of time working out exactly what happened. But getting back to your earlier point, part of the first act can be seen as a discussion of the point in the first act where "sale" becomes "bribe." Where you're no longer merely asking someone to buy something, you're *giving* them something to buy it.

Kane: Doesn't Levene do this with the Nyborgs when he gives them encouragement and confidence so that he can make the sale?

Mendes: Absolutely. All that is "sale as crime" in a sense. And, in the first act, you know, from the moment the lights go up, Levene is selling. He's selling an idea.

Kane: But so is Williamson, and he ups the ante.

Mendes: Yes, although he doesn't like entering into it, and he regrets it the moment he does it. And then he jumps at any opportunity he gets to withdraw. He does, of course, withdraw. He's lucky that Levene doesn't have the money for the bribe, anyway. In fact, he may *suspect* that he has no money at all, but he doesn't *know* that. The point, obviously, where it shades into fraud, as you say, is when Levene pushes his final button. He says, "Look, put me out with Roma. We'll double-team 'em," and John says, "Dream on." "Okay, okay," says Shelly, "Look, I'll give you ten percent." So he has a sort of game-plan. It's confused, it's driven by panic—panic and fear and desperation. But, he knows inevitably he's going to have to try bribery in the end when muscle-flexing, bullying, and all the other, as it were, actions on his list have failed. That's the specific point. But, as to where it shades over into fraud in the *second* scene of act 1—who knows? I mean, that's the glory of it. You don't know. You, the audience, are George in that scene. I have a *notion* about the moment it happens. There's a long pause and George says, "Well, how much would we get for it?" What Dave Moss says is, "What somebody should do notionally is rob the office in an ideal world. We're not saying anything is going to happen . . ." and George says, "How much can we get for it?" And, the moment that he says that, Dave knows he's more than just "talking." What George should say is: "There's no way. We're not even going to talk about it. It's a crime." When he says the wrong thing, he's lost it. That's the actual, specific point. From then on, the glory of it is watching it grow in momentum and scale.

Kane: It seems to me that in your production of *Glengarry* George is much more befuddled than in other productions that I have seen, just as many of the other characters appear more desperate. Yet, I had the strong impression that, like Carol in *Oleanna,* George is not nearly as naive as he appears.

Mendes: No. I think he is somebody who acts the role that he has been given by others. We had an improvisation one evening and the actor playing Moss said, "George couldn't sell matches to Prometheus" (laughter), which I thought was very good. But there is a sense in which everybody is assigned a role. Shelly is called "The Machine." In actual fact he isn't "The Machine" anymore. They give him that because they know he needs it. He's a man who needs it. He's a man who needs that feeding constantly to survive. Moss is the loud mouth, Williamson is the cold fish, George is the klutz. The only person who hasn't got a role is Ricky because he's not controllable . . . because he's too good. You don't give the best salesman a nickname because nicknames are controlling devices to make people feel superior to each other. Everybody adopts a role within the context of the office. In any office there's a hierarchy. There has to be.

Indeed, here the hierarchy is on the wall; it's written on the bloody wall. You can't deny there's a hierarchy, so everybody has to fit in with whatever the order is on the board. But then suddenly the hierarchy will change. Someone will make a big sale and go up. Then, the relationships are changed, then somebody who's been friendly with you the previous week is your enemy and rival. Like Dave has been friendly with Shelly when Shelly's not made a sale . . . and Shelly makes a sale; "Fuck you," Dave says. It means

Moss has gone down. There's an extraordinary shifting ground of egos, a huge amount of desperation just within the context of the room. But, coming back to your point, I think you're right about George. George is cannier than he lets on. I mean, he knows what's happening.

Kane: As you said, if he didn't, he would have backed out in a minute and said, "I'm not interested."

Mendes: Exactly.

Kane: Mamet has characterized *Glengarry Glen Ross* as a "kind of . . . bastard play . . . a gang comedy in the tradition of *The Front Page* or *Man in White*. Assuming that a gang comedy reveals the "specific . . . unifying natures" of a group of people engaged in a single enterprise whose confrontation is between individuals and their environment, these individuals split into protagonist and antagonist in competition with each other. What accounts for your particular perspective on this play? That is, the fact that you have staged what reviewers have characterized as a "ferociously effective" production in which the salesmen appear far more vicious or cunning than in previous productions, a reading, I think, that also delimits the comedy apparent in other productions. Certainly, those with Joe Mantegna.

Mendes: Yeah. Well, it's not in any way intentional. I must stress I don't go into a play thinking I'm gonna do a desperate production of this. I'm gonna bring out this, that, the other. What we find as a group in the play, what chemical reactions happen in rehearsal are very difficult to actually predict, you know. But, I think what I was very clear about was I wanted to believe in their predicament. That's all. I have to believe. The fact is: they're losers. They are all losers. Otherwise, they wouldn't be working in this office in the first place. Ricky says, and he means it, "What am I gonna do this month?" And, he means it, because if he loses those fucking leads, he's bust, for the time being. They're not what they say they are. They all think they're Mr. Slick. If any of them had been really cool, they'd be Mitch and Murray or they'd be Jerry Graff setting up on their own, but they're not. Ricky, okay, has a sort of middle-ground. He operates on sort of a middle ground.

Kane: But you don't believe he has two months put away to protect him.

Mendes: No. He has those lines: "What am I going to do?" I believe that. You could easily play that as a "kvetch."

Kane: I think that's especially apparent in Pacino's portrayal.

Mendes: Yeah. Brilliant. I think that Pacino was superb, and I think also what the film did was establish a definite place. I mean that it was about a shop and the way the train was rattling past and all that sort of stuff. I loved that. I know we could get many more laughs in Dave's and George's scene. But, I also know the scene works when that stuff about the Indians is sublimated to the super-objective of that scene which is the *deal*. It is not about two guys being really funny and, you know, making racist jokes. It's actually about a man who has finished a meal. He knows he has to do the deal tonight. He knows he has only one opportunity. He knows he has to be very careful how he says it, and he's flanneling until the point he can find a way of getting into the conversation. And, it's a very, very slow spiral downwards. If you look at it the way Mamet's written that speech about the Indians, there are pauses all over it, and it's because Moss isn't feeling relaxed. He's a very clever man, a very clever wordsmith. So, the actor should play that gradual progression to-wards the moment he first broaches the subject of the deal, *not* look for laughs (although the scene remains very funny). Again, Ron (Cook) playing the role of Ricky could get many more laughs. He knows he could get more laughs, and he could do it if he wanted to, but I think what fascinates him and me about it is what the rhythm does and the rhythmical complexities of that speech that give Lingk the impression that he's hearing great truths. And in actual fact, it's air. There's nothing there at all. And he finds some other way of doing it, another way of persuading Lingk beyond meaning, which is fascinating.

Kane: Would you characterize *Glengarry Glen Ross* as a play about who has the power and who's got the most power? Lingk, like the *Glengarry* sales-men to a certain degree, obviously lacks power, a point that he underscores in his crucial line, "I don't have the *power.*" What do you view as Lingk's role in the play?

Mendes: Well, he's us. Isn't he? The audience. I wanted the audience to feel that somebody just walked in, you know, off the street, and that he's found himself in a play by David Mamet, and he doesn't have the lines. He doesn't have any of the means of expression. He's just, "Shit," you know, "Where am I and why are all these people watching?" (Laughter). Well, I think there's a bit of that. There's no question for me that I think he's us. He's the *link*. And, he's the heart of the play.

Kane: If Lingk is "the link" to us, do you think that link is to his powerlessness? His blindness? And, how in your view does that link differ from, say, Aaronow's link to us?

Mendes: For me, those are the two hearts of the play, if that isn't a contradiction in terms? I think Lingk is one heart. When you see the destruction wrought on him by Roma in the second act and the sheer disinterest in his plight when he leaves, I think it is very moving, very moving, and clearly intended to be, and the fact that he asks for forgiveness is absolutely awful. And George is touching because he doesn't betray Dave. That's why he is really touching. Because, he's clearly fighting like hell in that room with the cop, and he comes out dripping with sweat, but the fact is that he does know—at least he thinks he knows who has robbed the office. And, there's that wonderful moment when he comes out and asks for some coffee and Dave says, "How ya doin?" (Laughter). "Fine." And, they can't let on anything because Ricky and Shelly are watching, they just have eye contact.

Kane: Mamet's aesthetic imagination appears to be engaged by the idea of honor among thieves consistent with your previous point that the play depicts a family. However, what he always portrays, it seems to me, is betrayal on every level.

Mendes: Yes, absolutely. The betrayal within the family. There's no question about that. But you see, here the relationships aren't real, anyway.

Kane: None of them?

Mendes: Because I think that the relationship is between their *acted* roles within the complexity of the office, who they *feel* themselves to be. They are not actually being themselves. Though you could argue that in a family, as well, people aren't actually themselves within the family. They're merely a son, daughter, elder. "Hey, hey, that's the Machine," Ricky says. "The Machine, there's somebody I could work with. It's not a world of men, Machine." All this stuff. I mean, it's a very ironic line. (Laughter). It's a wonderful line: "It's not a world of men, Machine." You can't get more ironic than that.

Kane: Isn't that Ricky's point when he tells Williamson that he can't work with men, you know, that he's a "fucking child." The question, it seems to me, is: Will all the men in this room please stand up? We're not quite sure who they are when we see how Aaronow and Levene fall apart. Speaking of men and families, Levene is the only one who we know is a family man. Presumably Williamson is also because he says that he stayed home with his children on the night of the break-in.

Mendes: He didn't say that.

Kane: Have I confused this line with the screenplay?

Mendes: He may say that in the movie. I think he does say that in the movie. He doesn't say that in the play, but I think it's right. I think Williamson indeed does have a family. I mean, it's the conclusion we came to very early on, because he's the only person who actually seems not to confuse his work identity and his real identity. When they're going at him, he just sort of cuts off, sort of shuts down. He's probably a very emotional man, actually, but he learns how to deal with it. The fact is that he must have a family. He must have another life, because of the way in which he performs within the context of the office. So, I think they do set up this sort of surrogate family within the office, and I think it is therefore a betrayal within the family.

Kane: In the portrayal of the American family, in the plays of O'Neill and Miller, in particular, to which you referred earlier, we find betrayal in the family. How then are we to account for the loyalty to family implicit in Levene's allusive and poignant references to his daughter? This is in the play, isn't it?

Mendes: Yes. (Laughter). That is in the play.

Kane: Shelly's references to his daughter are intensified in the film, but certainly in the play his allusions to his daughter both in the first scene and the final moments of the play call attention to her, as if she were an ill or dependent daughter, arousing our compassion, if not curiosity. "John: my daughter," he says to Williamson. In other words, why does Shelly have a daughter? Isn't he pathetic enough without Mamet giving him a dependent daughter?

Mendes: No. I think he has something none of the salesmen have because *there* is a man who has clearly coped with . . . I think Mamet, it may be the sentimentalist in him, in a sense, but he does want to portray an element to Levene which is a good man. There's an element to Shelly which is the emotional core of the play, whereas Ricky is its balls, you know. But there's no question for me that Levene is the central part and the central thread through it. It's *the* part. In a sense its journey is the journey of the play. Ricky doesn't have a journey. Ricky, at the end, is returning to the restaurant where you first saw him. And, he'll be doing exactly the same thing as when you first saw him . . . selling. But with Levene, I think the most eloquent line, almost, in the play, is the two-word split line, about his daughter. Shelly says, "I put a kid through school," and then he says, "She's . . . and . . . cold *calling* fella, door to door." He says these two words, and he's about to say something about his daughter, and he can't say it. Why he can't say it, I don't know. I don't know if he's too emotional, or he doesn't want to bring it up, or it's too difficult and he can't express it. I tend to favor the latter. And, then he goes back to shouting at Williamson, but he's got . . . suddenly there's a huge whirl of emotion that is barely suppressed then is added to this next speech to Williamson which is: "*Fuck* you and kiss my ass." And that's very quiet, very deliberate. "That's my message to you. Put me on the board." He feels he's done it. He feels he's survived. He's made it. He's made the eighty-two grand sale and the twelve grand commission. He can pay for his daughter's whatever.

Kane: Whatever?

Mendes: Whatever. I mean whatever it is; it doesn't matter. It really doesn't matter. It's very interesting. One of my friends who said he hadn't seen the film said, "The whole bit about Levene paying for his daughter's operation." I said, "Well, how do you know it was an operation?" He said, "Didn't they say operation?" I said, "No, no, just daughter." But then somebody else said, "It's like she's had to be sent away. He's clearly split up from his wife or the wife has died and so maybe she's at a school and he has to pay, I don't know, whatever. College, it could be."

Kane: College could easily cost eighty-two thousand dollars. (Laughter).

Mendes: Absolutely. College is more expensive than the operation. So all those things. The sense of protection of a woman in a man's world, also. It is quite sentimental. I think it's very, very, very cleverly handled in the play. I think it is not cleverly handled in the film. I think its seriously overwritten and overplayed. I mean, Jack Lemmon flashing his false teeth. It's too much, you know. You think, "Oh, come on now; don't be so corny." It's cheesy for me because the glory of this play is *absolute* lack of sentiment. It just drops in two tiny pieces of information, and they spread right through the play. And, they're absolutely perfectly timed and the most crucial points. You know, one of my serious arguments with the film is that it's all paraphrased. They do not speak the text that is written in the play. Certainly whatever Jack Lemmon says as Levene bears very little resemblance to what is written in the play.

Kane: Earlier you said that you see the first act of the play as the crime. In the author's program notes, David Mamet draws an analogy between a lead in a criminal case and a lead to a sale. I presume that your conception for the production preceded the playwright's remarks included in the program. Did you have discussions with Mamet prior to your staging of *Glengarry?*

Mendes: No, no, I didn't because of Rebecca Pigeon (Mamet's wife) having babies and things, and he's been filming *Oleanna,* so I didn't talk to him. He's not even seen *The Cryptogram;* he's not been over at all. For me, I wanted something more epic. It sounds terribly pretentious, but *Glengarry* has an element of classical tragedy in it, of tragic flaw in a character, of an inevitability. In the very beginning you think something's gonna happen, and there's gotta be something that gives you the sense, beyond the words, the sense that there is something going on above and beyond what is being said. That here is a particular night, or a particular year, which has a resonance beyond itself. It's the best way I can put it, really. And the blood-red wall and . . . and the threat. I mean, when Harold (Pinter) came to see the production early on, he said, "What's fascinating about the revolve is that it's so threatening. We don't know why there's something so frightening about those first scenes, because what is being said is in many ways very petty." I'm delighted by that because there is a danger throughout that fuels the character.

Kane: Pinter's comment is fascinating given that the use of the revolve in his play *Betrayal* facilitates a series of flashbacks and imbues the past with a clarity, whereas, it seems to me, the revolve in your production heightens the tension of the present moment, enhances anticipation about the future, and intensifies our awareness of Shelly's irrevocable personal and professional decision, the point to which he can never return.

Mendes: I think there is that absolutely. I think there is an inevitability to the play.

Kane: For all of them? I think for Aaronow, who hates his job, it will not be the same. Even for Roma, who will be back, as you said, to make another deal, there is a new reality. He knows when he says to Williamson, at least it seems to me, "I GET HIS ACTION," that Levene is guilty, especially when Levene hangs back in the office and says, "I think I better stay." Doesn't this confirm Roma's theories and conclude his criminal investigation?

Mendes: Yeah, he *knows* Shelly did it by the end. But he found out it's not George very early on.

Kane: Mamet has observed that Aaronow is troubled by the corruption that surrounds him, and that he comes closest to being a kind of *raisonneur* in exhibiting a degree of conscience. Is that what you mean by his being us? Because it would seem to me that *some* of us in the audience might have, like him, bought into the deal. How would you characterize his dilemma?

Mendes: He's us in that first act. He's not in the second when he's clearly very, very uncomfortable and unhappy and driven to a certain amount of despair by what is going on around him. I don't think he's . . . No, I think he probably, in the end, is as guilty as any of them, because he doesn't say anything.

Kane: So that is his dilemma? That he knows but doesn't say?

Mendes: Yes, well, he thinks he knows, and actually he doesn't know.

Kane: Although Mamet's plays can be read for their cynicism, and there's certainly enough of that in this play, would you agree that there's a simultaneous rhythm of self-motivation and self-knowledge?

Mendes: I don't know about his other plays. Yes, *Glengarry,* is full of cynicism, but David loves these guys. No question about it. All of them. I mean he worked in an office, and I guarantee, I feel from doing this play that there's a great, deep well of emotion about these people, because he both pities them and criticizes them. And yet also, it's a hymn to their absurd genius, their self-delusions and their comic inventions.

Kane: Because they invent themselves everyday?

Mendes: Yeah, they're storytellers. They spin stories out of nothing. I mean, the Roma-Levene-Lingk sequence is absolute genius. You can tell David loves that, absolutely loves that, and he also loves the story that Levene spins about the Nyborgs . . . "twenty-two minutes by the kitchen clock." Shelly's creating his own myth there; he wants that to be repeated. "Guess what 'The Machine' did: twenty-two minutes by the kitchen clock." He was there . . . his pen was in his hand . . . he needs that self-propagation. So there's no question in my mind that the reason it works is that there is a huge affection in the portrait at the same time as being an absolute calculation—not calculation—a total honesty of his viewing of the motives, of what drives them.

What's the difference between selling a house that, maybe, somebody wants and a piece of land somebody doesn't want? The answer is in actuality you have to be much cleverer at selling something people don't want. I mean there's that wonderful line Shelly has: "We're going up to the door and I don't even know their names. I'm selling them something they don't even *want*," he says. (Laughter). I mean, that's the ultimate compliment! Roma starts by putting it down, as if he was a buyer: "What is this? This is a piece of land . . . Florida *Bullshit* . . . and, that's what I said." And, then there's this amazing creation out of nothing.

Kane: The teacher-student dynamic is a central one in Mamet's work, notable in such disparate plays as *American Buffalo, The Shawl,* and *A Life in the Theatre.* And, I think there's a lesson implicit when Shelly steps over the line and brings tragedy upon himself. Would you agree that Mamet has chosen the pedagogical relationship to explore the myths we perpetuate about ourselves?

Mendes: I don't know. I mean, I can only speak for this play, really. I don't really know enough about the other plays, but you know, I'm not sure about it in this play. I think it is parodied, because Ricky says to Shelly, "Like you taught me."

Kane: Yes. Well, what exactly has Ricky learned from Shelly?

Mendes: How *not* to be, perhaps. But Ricky learns from everybody because he listens. He's the only person in the office who listens. He listens, he hears, he takes it in. He doesn't say, "I've heard you." He just listens and that's why he's on top of the board because he takes what he needs from Levene's story, nothing more, maybe a couple of tiny details, but it's been filed. It's been logged. But for me, Ricky says "like you taught me" because Shelly needs it.

Kane: He compliments him, but not because it's true?

Mendes: Yeah, absolutely. But, I think it's designed to make Shelly feel better, and if it does, "Well, if I did then I'm glad it did." And then Shelly goes on with his story.

Kane: Is that what you meant earlier by David Mamet caring about these men? I mean, even Ricky, who at moments is utterly despicable—who we all know we've been set up by and will be again—is decent to men who more than one reviewer has referred to as "jackals in jackets."

Mendes: That's what I said about the love, the affection . . . that it is not bleak. In one sense he is fair. He abides by the rules of the game, that is the rules that are his, not anybody else's. What he considers to be stepping over the mark he makes perfectly clear. For instance, Roma's question to Lingk: "Why did she do that, Jim? Who did she call?" I mean, *that* steps over the mark. "She called the consumer, whatever it is, the consumer office?" And there's that moment, that flash of: "Are you serious? I'm selling you a bit of land. You want to put me out of business?" from Ricky. So, there are rules that are established, and I think within that he's fair. But it never becomes sentimental. For instance, Roma says to George, "Hey, fuck that shit, you're a good man, George, you've hit a bad streak," and is comforting him, but in the same sentence, "Look at this, fifteen units, Mountain View, and the fucking things got stole." It's an unbroken line. He says, "Yeah, yeah, don't worry George, you're a good man . . ." but he's really interested in what's gone from his drawers. So, it's only marginally there. It's only there because he wants to keep everybody in order, and "okay," "don't worry," and "you're a good man," but I think it's never allowed to get beyond that. I don't think Roma has many redeeming features, actually, but as you say, there's something about him that's attractive.

Kane: I remember Joe Mantegna telling me that when he first read the role of Ricky Roma he thought, "Oh God, look at this guy. This guy's really despicable." But then he looked at Roma and thought, "all these attributes that perhaps to somebody else were sleazy or despicable, to me were all attributes. He has confidence and I have confidence—I went to one of the schools, you know, where they tell you that you can sell yourself, and that's what I'm doing. I'm selling myself. I'm a good man." I could barely control my laughter as he told me this story, but having seen his brilliant performance, I could easily visualize how Ricky Roma was transformed from contemptible to skillful, even admirable.

Mendes: Mantegna was very, very charming, indeed. I mean, he played that first scene in a much more charming and much more daredevil way, and it was wonderful. The glory of it is that there are many ways to do it.

Kane: Yes, that's one of the aspects of your production that is so marvelous. I have seen Joe Mantegna in a number of Mamet roles, and one of the things that we spoke about when I interviewed him on the set of *Homicide* is that Mamet's work is characterized by key words or phrases that the actor must repeat with differing inflection. In *Glengarry,* the words *leads* and Mitch and Murray, for example, gain a kind of totemic power. As the director, how do you intensify each repetition of say, "the board. . . . Put me on the board"?

Mendes: I don't think you really attempt to make each repetition different. I think that what you do is say, you know, each part of a speech serves a different purpose, a different objective within the context of the scene, so I think they are by necessity different. *Sometimes* they are the same. I actually rather like, "Will you go to lunch?" "Just go to lunch." "Will you go to lunch?" all being the same. What more can you say: "Just go to lunch." That's all it is. Sometimes they're the same and sometimes not. The power of it is rhythmical and cumulative. I don't think it's because you give it a different inflection or consciously throw a different color at it—or you're lighter with it at the beginning—I think actually the play reads the word differently. When it's been ten minutes or longer of stage time behind those words, they gradually come to mean something far greater than the sum of their parts. I very consciously chose to use a very monochromatic set in the second half of *Glengarry* that is sort of washed out, bleached as if the salesmen were under a search light, a spot light, a beam, just that raking light and heat and the sense of sweat, and the fans. And, the leads are bright colors. They're red, pink, and yellow cards. They're the only bit of color that really comes on stage. That's quite deliberate.

Kane: Was your mounting of the revival of *Glengarry Glen Ross* deliberately planned to coincide with the premiere of Mamet's newest play, *The Cryptogram?*

Mendes: No. *Cryptogram* originally was going to open a month before us, and then there were difficulties casting it. In the end, you know, we both fed off each other's coverage, but we've had a good deal more coverage than *Cryptogram*, rather than the other way around! Obviously, because it was his new play, the press tended to come out on one side or the other. There was a bit of, "It's not quite as good as *Glengarry Glen Ross*," unfortunately.

Kane: Do you think there is a correspondence between the two plays, both of which dramatize betrayal in the family?

Mendes: I think there has to be. I do think there's a correspondence between the plays of any single author! There has to be because they're writtten from the same mind. And, I do think it's a story about betrayal, and that there are themes that reappear, but *Glengarry* and *Cryptogram* are water and gin. It's a very different part of David—a mystical, spiritual side—that's written *Cryptogram*. It's very, very private, isn't it? It's very distant, and I think very touching, but I think it's not got the comic twinkle of his realistic plays. But, very obviously, they bear some relation. I'd say if there were going to be a Mamet play revived while *Cryptogram* was on, this would probably be the least competitive.

Kane: In his review of *Glengarry Glen Ross* Benedict Nightingale posited that 1994 should be called "The Year of Mamet." Actually he said, "The Year of *the* Mamet," as in "The Year of the Dog." Given a critically acclaimed production of *Oleanna*, a fine production of *The Cryptogram*, and your gripping production of *Glengarry Glen Ross*, Nightingale observed that all that was missing was a production of *American Buffalo*. I looked at your schedule, and it looks as if you're quite booked up for the rest of the year. Do you know if a production is planned?

Mendes: There's been talk of it elsewhere, actually. Yes, I would love to do one, and for me, it's on a par with *Glengarry*. I think people will give it a rest for a year or so because there's been so much coverage. And, I think, you have to have a particular actor in mind. I mean, you have to have someone who can play Teach. It's not one of those plays that you can do without that. I mean, it's really true. It's about like doing *The Caretaker*. I've said to Harold (Pinter) that you could quite easily crosscast *The Caretaker* and *American Buffalo*. It would be very interesting to see how *that* works.

BIBLIOGRAPHY OF
GLENGARRY GLEN ROSS,
1983-1995

Janice A. Sauer

PRIMARY TEXTS

Barnes, Clive, ed. *Best American Plays: 1983-1992.* Ninth Series. John Gassner Best Play Series. New York: Crown, 1993.

Cohen, Robert, ed. *Twelve Plays for Theatre.* Mountain View, Calif.: Mayfield Pub., 1994.

Glengarry Glen Ross. [videotape of the New York production] TOFT [Theatre on Film and Tape] Collection, Billy Rose Theatre Collection. New York Public Library at Lincoln Center.

Guernsey, Otis L., Jr., ed. *Best Plays of 1983-1984.* New York: Dodd, Mead, 1984, 201-16.

Mamet, David. *Glengarry Glen Ross: A Play.* New York: S. French, 1983.

———. *Glengarry Glen Ross.* New York: Grove, 1984; London: Methuen, 1984.

———. *Glengarry Glen Ross.* Screenplay. Dir. James Foley. Prod. Jerry Tokogsky. Videocassette and videodisk. Live Home Video, 1993.

INTERVIEWS WITH DAVID MAMET

Allen, Jennifer. "David Mamet's Hard Sell." *New York,* 9 April 1984, 38–41.

Booth, John E. *The Critic, Power, and the Performing Arts.* New York: Columbia University Press, 1991.

Cantwell, Mary. "David Mamet: Bulldog of the Middle Class." *Vogue,* July 1984, 216ff.

Case, Brian. "The Hot Property Man." *Times Magazine* (London), 18 September 1983, 72–73.

Christy, Desmond. "A Man for the Forgotten Frontier." *Guardian,* 16 September 1983, 15.

DeVries, Hilary. "In David Mamet's Hands a Pen Becomes a Whip." *Christian Science Monitor,* 21 March 1984, 21–22.

Harriott, Esther. "Interview with David Mamet." In *American Voices: Five Contemporary Playwrights in Essays and Interviews,* 76–97. Jefferson, N.C.: McFarland, 1988.

Lahr, John. "Winners and Losers." *New Society,* 29 September 1983, 476–77.

Nuwer, Hank. "A Life in the Theatre: David Mamet." *Rendezvous: Journal of Arts and Letters* 2, no. 1 (1985): 1–7.

———. "Two Gentlemen of Chicago: David Mamet and Stuart Gordon." *South Carolina Review,* 17 (Spring 1985): 9–20.

"Playboy Interview: David Mamet." *Playboy,* April 1995, 51ff.

Roudané, Matthew C. "An Interview With David Mamet." *Studies in American Drama, 1945—Present* 1, no. 1 (1986): 73–81.

Savran, David. "Trading in the American Dream." *American Theatre* 4, no. 6 (September 1987): 13–18.

———. "David Mamet." In *Their Own Words: Contemporary American Playwrights*, 132–44. New York: Theatre Communications Group, 1988.

Schvey, Henry I. "Celebrating the Capacity for Self-Knowledge." *New Theatre Quarterly* 4, no. 13 (1988): 89–96.

Taylor, Clarke. "Mamet Is 'Thrilled' by His Pulitzer." *Los Angeles Times*, 19 April 1984, F7.

SCHOLARLY STUDIES

Adler, Thomas P. *Mirror on the Stage: The Pulitzer Plays as an Approach to American Drama*, 105–7. West Lafayette, Ind.: Purdue University Press, 1987.

Almansi, Guido. "David Mamet, A Virtuoso of Invective." In *Critical Angles: European View of Contemporary American Literature*, 191–207, ed. Marc Chénetier. Carbondale: Southern Illinois University Press, 1986.

Berkowitz, Gerald M. "David Mamet." In *American Drama of the Twentieth Century*, 190–94. London: Longman, 1992.

Bigsby, C.W.E. "David Mamet: All True Stories." In *Modern American Drama, 1945–1990*, 195–230. Cambridge: Cambridge University Press, 1992.

———. *David Mamet*. Contemporary Writers Series. London: Methuen, 1985.

———. "David Mamet." In *A Critical Introduction to Twentieth-Century American Drama: Beyond Broadway*. Vol. 3, 251–90. New York: Cambridge University Press, 1985.

Blumberg, Marcia. "Eloquent Stammering in the Fog: O'Neill's Heritage in Mamet." In *Perspectives on O'Neill: New Essays*, ed. Shyamal Bagchee, 97–111. Victoria: University of Victoria, 1988.

Brewer, Gay. "Another Furious Season: Glengarry Glen Ross, Hoffa, Ad Infinitum." In *David Mamet and Film: Illusion/Disillusion in a Wounded Land*, 163–70. Jefferson, N.C.: McFarland, 1993.

Bruster, Douglas. "David Mamet and Ben Jonson: City Comedy Past and Present." *Modern Drama* 33, no. 3 (1990): 333–46.

Carroll, Dennis. *David Mamet*. Modern Dramatists Series. New York: St. Martin's, 1987.

———. "The Recent Mamet Films: 'Business' versus Communion." In *David Mamet: A Casebook*, ed. Leslie Kane, 175–90. New York: Garland, 1992.

Christiansen, Richard. "David Mamet." In *Contemporary Dramatists*, 4th ed., ed. D.L. Kirkpatrick, 338–40. Chicago: St. James, 1988.

Cohn, Ruby. "Eloquent Energies: Mamet, Shepard." In *New American Dramatists 1960–1990*, 2nd ed., 160–84. London: Macmillan, 1991.

———. "How Are Things Made Round." In *David Mamet: A Casebook*, ed. Leslie Kane, 109–22. New York: Garland, 1992.

———. "Phrasal energies: Harold Pinter and David Mamet." In *Anglo-American Interplay in Recent Drama*, 58–94. Cambridge: Cambridge University Press, 1995.

Cullick, Jonathan S. "'Always Be Closing': Competition and the Discourse of Closure in David Mamet's *Glengarry Glen Ross*." *Journal of Dramatic Theory and Criticism* 8, no. 2 (1994): 23–36.

Davis, J. Madison, and John Coleman. "David Mamet: A Classified Bibliography." *Studies in American Drama, 1945–Present* 1 (1986): 83–101.

Dean, Anne. "Glengarry Glen Ross." In *David Mamet: Language as Dramatic Action*, 189–221. Rutherford, N.J.: Fairleigh Dickinson University Press, 1990.

Demastes, William W. "David Mamet's Dis-Integrating Drama." In *Beyond Naturalism: A New Realism in American Theatre*, 67–94. Westport: Greenwood, 1988.

Forbes, Daniel. "Dirty Dealing." *American Theatre* 4, no. 2 (1988): 13–18.

Freedman, Samuel G. "The Gritty Eloquence of David Mamet." *New York Times Magazine,* 21 April 1985, 32ff.

Geis, Deborah R. "David Mamet and the Metadramatic Tradition: Seeing 'The Trick from the Back.'" In *David Mamet: A Casebook,* ed. Leslie Kane, 49–68. New York: Garland, 1992.

———. "The Theater as House of Games: David Mamet's (Con)Artistry and the Monologic Voice." In *Postmodern Theatric[k]s: Monologue in Contemporary American Drama,* 89–116. Ann Arbor: University of Michigan Press, 1993.

"Glengarry Glen Ross." In *Contemporary Literary Criticism: Yearbook 1984,* ed. Sharon K. Hall, 217–24. Detroit: Gale Research Company, 1985.

Harriott, Esther. "Comedies of Bad Manners." In *American Voices: Five Contemporary Playwrights in Essays and Interviews,* 61–76. Jefferson, N.C.: McFarland, 1988.

Hasenberg, Peter. "'Always be Closing': Struktur und Thema von David Mamets *Glengarry Glen Ross.*" *Anglistik und Englischunterricht* 35 (1988): 177–91.

Herman, William. "Theatrical Diversity from Chicago." In *Understanding Contemporary American Drama,* 125–60. Columbia: University of South Carolina Press, 1987.

Hubert-Leibler, Pascale. "Dominance and Anguish: The Teacher-Student Relationship in the Plays of David Mamet." *Modern Drama* 31, no. 4 (1988): 557–70.

Hudgins, Christopher C. "Comedy and Humor in the Plays of David Mamet." In *David Mamet: A Casebook,* ed. Leslie Kane, 191–230. New York: Garland, 1992.

Jacobs, Dorothy H. "Working Worlds in David Mamet's Dramas." In *Midwestern Miscellany, Being Essays on Chicago Writers,* ed. David D. Anderson, 47–57. East Lansing: Michigan State University Press, 1986.

Joki, Ilkka. *Mamet, Bakhtin, and the Dramatic: The Demotic as a Variable of Addressivity.* Abo: Abo Akademis Forlag, 1993.

———. "David Mamet's Drama: The Dialogicality of Grotesque Realism." *Critical Studies* 3/4, no. 2 (1993): 80–98.

Jones, Nesta, and Steven Dykes. *File on Mamet.* London: Methuen Drama, 1991.

Kane, Leslie. "Time Passages." *Pinter Review* (1990): 30–49.

———. "Interview with Gregory Mosher." In *David Mamet: A Casebook,* ed. Leslie Kane, 229–47. New York: Garland, 1992.

———. "Interview with Joe Mantegna." In *David Mamet: A Casebook,* ed. Leslie Kane, 248–69. New York: Garland, 1992.

Kim, Yun Cheol. "Degradation of the American Success Ethic: *Death of a Salesman, That Championship Season,* and *Glengarry Glen Ross.*" *Journal of English Language and Literature* [Korea] 37, no. 1 (1991): 233–48.

Kolin, Philip C. "Mitch and Murray in David Mamet's *Glengarry Glen Ross.*" *Notes on Contemporary Literature* 18, no. 2 (1988): 3–5.

Lawley, Paul. "Glengarry Glen Ross." In *International Directory of Theatre: Plays,* ed. Mark Hawkins-Dady, 294–95. Chicago: St. James Press, 1992.

Lundin, Edward. "Mamet and Mystery." In *Publications of the Mississippi Philological Association,* ed. K. A. Berney, 106–14. Jackson, Miss: Mississippi Philological Association, 1988.

McDonough, Carla J. "Every Fear Hides a Wish: Unstable Masculinity in Mamet's Drama." *Theatre Journal* 44, no. 2 (1992): 195–205.

McNaughton, Howard. "David (Alan) Mamet." In *Contemporary American Dramatists,* ed. K. A. Berney, 373–77. Detroit: St. James Press, 1994.

Malkin, Jeanette. "David Mamet, *American Buffalo* and *Glengarry Glen Ross.*" In *Verbal Violence in Contemporary Drama from Handke to Shepard,* 145–61. Cambridge: Cambridge University Press, 1992.

Peereboom, J. J. "Mamet from Afar." In *New Essays on American Drama,* eds. Gilbert Debusscher and Henry I. Schvey, 189–99. Amsterdam: Rodopi Editions, 1989.

Radavich, David. "Mamet among Men: David Mamet's Homosocial Order." *American Drama* 1 (1991): 46–60.

Roudané, Matthew C. "Public Issues, Private Tensions: David Mamet's *Glengarry Glen Ross.*" *South Carolina Review* 19, no. 1 (1986): 35–47.

Schvey, Henry I. "The Plays of David Mamet: Games of Manipulation and Power." *New Theatre Quarterly* 4 (February 1988): 77–86.

———. "Power Plays: David Mamet's Theatre of Manipulation." In *David Mamet: A Casebook,* ed. Leslie Kane, 87–108. New York: Garland, 1992.

Showalter, Elaine. "Glengarry Glen Ross." *Times Literary Supplement,* 6 November 1992, 16–17.

Vorlicky, Robert. "The American Masculine Ethos, Male Mythologies, and Absent Women." In *Act Like a Man: Challenging Masculinities in American Drama,* 25–56. Ann Arbor: University of Michigan Press, 1995.

Weales, Gerald. "American Theater Watch: 1983–1984." *Georgia Review* 38 (1984): 594–96.

Wolter, Jürgen C. "David Mamet in German Speaking Countries: A Classified Bibliography." *Studies in American Drama, 1945–Present* 5 (1990): 67–87.

Worster, David. "How to Do Things with Salesmen: David Mamet's Speech-Act Play." *Modern Drama* 37, no. 3 (1994): 375–90.

Zeifman, Hersh. "Phallus in Wonderland: Machismo and Business in David Mamet's *American Buffalo* and *Glengarry Glen Ross.*" In *David Mamet: A Casebook,* ed. Leslie Kane, 123–35. New York: Garland, 1992.

Zinman, Toby Silverman. "Jewish Aporia: The Rhythm of Talking in Mamet." *Theatre Journal* 44 (May 1992): 207–15.

DISSERTATIONS

Beckwith, Jeanne Joan. *Deviancy and the Stage in the Plays of David Mamet and Peter Barnes.* Diss. University of Georgia, 1994.

Blondell, John. *Myth and Anti-Myth in the Plays of David Mamet.* Diss. University of California, Santa Barbara, 1990.

Chi, Wei-jan. *The Role of Language in the Plays of Mamet, Wilson, and Rabe.* Diss. University of Iowa, 1991.

Dawson, Barbara Gail. *Sacred and Profane Dynamics in Contemporary American Drama: An Analytical Approach Based on Concepts of the Sacred and the Profane Applied to the Pulitzer Prize Plays of the 1980s.* Diss. University of Missouri, 1993.

Demastes, William Willis. *American New Realism in the Theatre of the 80s (Fuller, Henley, Norman, Rabe, Mamet, Shepard).* Diss. University of Wisconsin, 1986.

Erickson, Steven Craig. *The Drama of Dispossession in Selected Plays of Six Major American Playwrights.* Diss. University of Texas at Dallas, 1991.

Myers, Mary Kay Zettl. *Closure in the Twentieth-Century American Problem Play.* Diss. University of Delaware, 1992.

Ryan, Steven Daniel. *David Mamet: Dramatic Craftsman.* Diss. Fordham, 1988.

LONDON PREMIERE

Dir. Bill Bryden. Cottesloe Theatre at the National Theatre, London, 21 September 1983.

Asquith, R. "Glengarry Glen Ross." *City Limits,* 30 September–6 October 1983, 54. Rpt. *London Theatre Record,* 10–23 September 1983, 822.

Barber, John. "Glengarry Glen Ross." *Daily Telegraph,* 23 September, 1983, 15. Rpt. *London Theatre Record,* 10–23 September 1983, 822.

Billington, Michael. "Glengarry Glen Ross." *Guardian,* 22 September 1983, 15. Rpt. *London Theatre Record,* 10–23 September 1983, 822.

———. "Theater in London: Mamet Turns to the World of Salesmen." *New York Times,* 9 October 1983, B6ff.

Brook, Stephen. "On the Line." *New Statesman,* 30 September 1983, 34ff. Rpt. *London Theatre Record,* 10–23 September 1983, 824.

Coveney, Michael. "Glengarry Glen Ross." *Financial Times,* 22 September 1983, 15. Rpt. *London Theatre Record,* 10–23 September 1983, 824–25.

Cushman, Robert. "All American Boys." *Observer,* 25 September 1983, 33.

Fenton, James. "Okay, as a Favour, I'll Tell You What I'll Do." *Sunday Times,* 25 September 1983, 39.

Gordon, Giles. "Transatlantic." *Spectator,* 1 October 1983, 27. Rpt. *London Theatre Record,* 10–23, September 1983, 823.

Hayman, Ronald. "Following the Lead: David Mamet, *Glengarry Glen Ross,* Cottesloe Theater." *Times Literary Supplement,* 30 September 1983, 1042.

Hirschorn, Clive. "Glengarry Glen Ross." *Sunday Express.* Rpt. *London Theatre Record,* 10–23 September 1983, 824.

Lahr, John. "Winners and Losers." *New Society,* 29 September 1983, 476–77.

Mackenzie, Suzie. "Glengarry Glen Ross." *Time Out.* Rpt. *London Theatre Record,* 10–23 September 1983, 823–24.

"New Mamet Play Clicks in London; Due in Chi in Jan." *Variety,* 5 October 1983, 132.

Say, Rosemary. "Dog Days." *Sunday Telegraph,* 25 September 1983, 16. Rpt. *London Theatre Record,* 10–23 September 1983, 825.

Shulman, Milton. "Glengarry Glen Ross." *Standard,* 22 September 1983, 26. Rpt. *London Theatre Record,* 10–23 September 1983, 824.

Wardle, Irving. "Con-Men Sold on American Dream." *The Times,* 22 September 1983, 14.

CHICAGO PREMIERE

Dir. Gregory Mosher. Goodman Theatre, 6 February 1984. [27 January 1984, preview].

Christiansen, Richard. "'Glengarry' Refines Map of Explored Terrain." *Chicago Tribune,* 7 February 1984, sec. 5, 2.

Syse, Glenna. "'Glengarry Glen Ross' Rings Up Another for Mamet." *Chicago Sun Times,* 7 February 1984, 44.

NEW YORK PRODUCTION

Dir. Gregory Mosher. John Golden Theatre, 25 March 1984.

Allen, Jennifer. "David Mamet's Hard Sell." *New York,* 9 April 1984: 38–41.

Baker, Russell. "Playing for Keeps." *New York Times,* 26 May 1984, sec. 1, 23.

Barnes, Clive. "Language, Death—and Life." *New York Post,* 26 May 1984, 11.

———. "Mamet's 'Glengarry': A Play to See and Cherish." *New York Post,* 26 March 1984, 15. Rpt. *New York Theatre Critics' Reviews,* 5–11 March 1984, 336–37.

Beaufort, John. "A Searing Look at the Sordid World of Salesmen." *Christian Science Monitor,* 10 April 1984, 25. Rpt. *New York Theatre Critics' Reviews,* 5–11 March 1984, 339.

Bennetts, Leslie. "New Face: Joe Mantegna, The Hot Shot Salesman of Mamet's 'Glengarry.'" *New York Times,* 18 May 1984, C4.

Blacker, David. "'Glengarry Glen Ross' It's Selling on Broadway." *Broadway Bill of Fare,* 28 June 1984, 14.

Brustein, Robert. "Show and Tell." *New Republic,* 7 May 1984, 27–29.

Canby, Vincent. "Mamet's Real Estate Sharks and Their Prey." *New York Times,* 30 September 1992, C15.

Christiansen, Richard. " 'Glengarry' Gets Rave, Coolly Favorable New York Reviews." *Chicago Tribune,* 27 March 1984, sec. 5, 1, 3.

Cook, James. "Life of a Salesman." *Forbes,* 21 May 1984, 56.

Corliss, Richard. "Pitchmen Caught in the Act." *Time,* 9 April 1984, 105. Rpt. *New York Theatre Critics' Reviews,* 5–11 March 1984, 338.

Cunningham, Dennis. WCBS-TV2, 25 March 1984. *New York Theatre Critics' Reviews,* 5–11 March 1984, 338.

Edwards, Christopher. "Glengarry Glen Ross." *Drama* 151 (1984): 23–24.

Freedman, Samuel J. "The Cast that Put Mamet on the Board." *New York Times,* 18 April 1984, C21.

———. "'Glengarry' Is Helped by Pulitzer." *New York Times,* 24 April 1984. sec. 3, 15.

———. "Pulitzer Increases Play's Business." *Atlanta Constitution,* 26 April 1984, C15.

Gill, Brendan. "The Theater: The Lower Depths." *New Yorker,* 2 April 1984, 114.

"'Glengarry Glen Ross' What a Pulitzer Means." *Daily News* [New York], 18 April 1984, 37.

Gluck, Victor. "Theatre: The Time of the Salesmen." *Wisdom's Child,* 16 April 1984, 7.

Gussow, Mel. "Real Estate World a Model for Mamet." *New York Times,* 28 March 1984, C19.

Harvey, Stephen. "Glengarry Glen Ross." *The Nation,* 28 April 1984, 522–23.

Hayman, Edward. "Mamet's Pulitzer Winner Dissects a Sellers' World." *Detroit News,* 20 April 1984, D4.

Helbing, Terry. "Desperate Salesmen." *New York Native,* 23 April 1984, 42.

"His Words Get under the Skin." *Los Angeles Times,* 17 June 1984, C40.

Holmberg, Arthur. "Stage View: Playwrights Who Take a Dim View of Business." *New York Times,* 2 December 1984, sec. 2, 3.

Hughes, Catherine. "Salesmen." *America,* 28 April 1984, 320.

Humm [R. Hummler]. "Glengarry Glen Ross." *Variety,* 28 March 1984, 104.

Jenner, C. Lee. "Glengarry Glen Ross." *Stages,* May 1984, 6–7.

Kauffmann, Stanley. "American Past and Present." *Saturday Review,* November/December 1984, 58–59.

Kelly, Kevin. "'Glengarry' Is Mamet Magic." *Boston Globe,* 2 March 1984, 49ff.

———. "Pulitzers for Writing Spring No Surprises." *Boston Globe,* 18 April 1984, 70.

Kissel, Howard. "Glengarry Glen Ross." *Women's Wear Daily,* 27 March 1984, 20. *New York Theatre Critics' Reviews,* 5–11 March 1984, 335–36.

———. "Miller and Mamet." *Playbill,* June 1984, 6.

———. "Tinkering with Mamet: Part of the Job." *Women's Wear Daily,* 18 April 1984, 18.

Kroll, Jack. "Mamet's Jackals in Jackets." *Newsweek,* 9 April 1984, 109. Rpt. *New York Theatre Critics' Reviews,* 5–11 March 1984, 337–38.

Lawson, Carol. "Mamet's New Play about Real Estate to Open in March." *New York Times,* 24 February 1984, C2.

Levett, Karl. "Mamet 'Glengarry Glen Ross.'" *Drama,* 153 (1984): 42–43.

Merschmeier, Michael. "Willy Loman Lebt Weiter: New York Szenen im Frühjahr." *Theater Heute,* (June 1984): 16–21.

Munk, Erika. "Glengarry Glen Ross." *Village Voice,* 17 April 1984, 105.

Nightingale, Benedict. "Is Mamet the Bard of Modern Immorality?" *New York Times,* 1 April 1984, B5ff.

Novick, Julius. "Men's Business." *Village Voice,* 3 April 1984, 89.

Rich, Frank. "Theater: A Mamet Play, 'Glengarry Glen Ross.'" *New York Times,* 26 March 1984, C17ff. Rpt. *New York Theatre Critics Reviews,* 5–11 March 1984, 334.

———. "Theatre's Gender Gap Is a Chasm." *New York Times,* 30 April 1984, sec. 2, 1.

Richards, David. "Lives of the Salesmen: From Miller and Mamet Lessons for the Stage." *Washington Post,* 29 May 1984, H1.

Sauvage, Leo. "Corrupted Salesmen." *New Leader,* 16 April 1984, 20–21.

Schecter, J. "Glengarry Glen Ross." *In These Times*, 9 May 1984, 14.
Siegel, Joel. "Glengarry Glen Ross." WABC-TV7, New York, 25 March 1984. Rpt. *New York Theatre Critics' Reviews*, 5–11 March 1984, 339.
Simon, John. "Salesmen Go, Salesmen Come." *New York*, 9 April 1984, 72–74.
Stitt, Milan. "The Union Jacking of Broadway." *Horizon*, July/August 1984, 16ff.
Syna, Sy. "Mamet's 'Glengarry Glen Ross' Gripping Play of Hustlers, Suckers." *New York Tribune*, 26 March 1984, 5B.
Templeton, Jane. "Broadway Revives the Myth of the Salesman." *Sales & Marketing Management*, 13 August 1984, 55.
Watt, Douglas. " A 'Dearth' of Honest Salesmen." *New York Daily News*, 26 March 1984. Rpt. *New York Theatre Critics' Reviews*, 5–11 March 1984, 337.
Weales, Gerald. "Rewarding Salesmen: New from Mamet, Old from Miller." *Commonweal*, 4 May 1984, 278–79.
Wilson, Edwin. "Theater: Lives of Salesmen." *Wall Street Journal*, 4 April 1984. Rpt. *New York Theatre Critics' Reviews*, 5–11 March 1984, 337.

London Revival Production

Dir. Sam Mendes. Donmar Warehouse, 22 June 1994.

Billington, Michael. "Glengarry, Glen Ross." *Guardian*, 24 June 1994, sec. 2, 13. Rpt. *Theatre Record*, 18 June–1 July 1994, 792.
Core, Susan, and George Core. "Glengarry Glen Ross." *Sewanee Review* 10, no. 4 (1994): 694ff.
Coveney, Michael. "Glengarry Glen Ross." *Observer*, 26 June 1994. Rpt. *Theatre Record*, 18 June–1 July 1994, 793.
de Jongh, Nicholas. "Powerful Tragedy in a Combat Zone Nightmare." *Evening Standard*, 23 June 1994. Rpt. *Theatre Record*, 18 June–1 July 1994, 794.
Doughty, Louise. "Glengarry Glen Ross." *Mail on Sunday*, 26 June 1994. Rpt. *Theatre Record*, 18 June–1 July 1994, 792.
Edwards, Jane. "Glengarry Glen Ross." *Time Out*, 29 June 1994. Rpt. *Theatre Record*, 18 June–1 July 1994, 791.
Gross, John. "Tragedies of Good and Bad Manners." *Sunday Telegraph*, 26 June 1994. Rpt. *Theatre Record*, 18 June–1 July 1994, 788.
Hagerty, Bill. "Slice of Life at a Bargain Price." *Today*, 23 June 1994. Rpt. *Theatre Record*, 18 June–1 July 1994, 794.
Hirschorn, Clive. "Glengarry Glen Ross." *Sunday Express*, 26 June 1994. Rpt. *Theatre Record*, 18 June–1 July 1994, 791.
Hoyle, Martin. "The American Dream Distorted." *Financial Times*, 24 June 1994. Rpt. *Theatre Record*, 18 June–1 July 1994, 792.
Morley, Sheridan. "Theatre: Copacabana, Home, Glengarry Glen Ross." *Spectator*, 2 July 1994, 42. Rpt. *Theatre Record*, 18 June–1 July 1994, 792.
Nathan, David. "Glengarry Glen Ross." *Jewish Chronicle*, 1 July 1994. Rpt. *Theatre Record*, 18 June–1 July 1994, 792–93.
Nightingale, Benedict. "The Sharks Still Have Bite." *The Times*, 24 June 1994. Rpt. *Theatre Record*, 18 June–1 July 1994, 793.
Paton, Maureen. "Theatre." *Daily Express*, 2 July 1994. Rpt. *Theatre Record*, 18 June–1 July 1994, 791.
Smith, Neil. "Glengarry Glen Ross." *What's On*, 29 June 1994. Rpt. *Theatre Record*, 18 June–1 July 1994, 793.
Spenser, Charles. "The Arts: Dog-Eat-Dog in Mamet's Savage Sales Pitch." *Daily Telegraph*, 24 June 1994, 19. Rpt. *Theatre Record*, 18 June–1 July 1994, 794–95.
Taylor, John Russell. "Glengarry Glen Ross." *Plays & Players*, December 1983, 27–29.
Taylor, Paul. "Brute Strength." *The Independent*, 24 June 1994, 19. Rpt. *Theatre Record*, 18 June–1 July 1994, 793–94.

——. "Home Truths." *The Independent,* 20 June 1994, 23.

Wardle, Irving. "A Crazy Way to Make a Living." *The Independent on Sunday,* 26 June 1994, 14. Rpt. *Theatre Record,* 18 June–1 July 1994, 788–89.

OTHER PERFORMANCES

Dir. Daniel Freudenberger. Habimah National Theatre, Tel Aviv, 7 August 1984.
Dir. Bobby Heaney. Alexander Theatre, Johannesburg, 11 April 1985.
Dir. Louis Lentin. Abbey Theatre, at the Peacock, Dublin, 8 May 1985.
Dir. Marcel Marechal. Theatre National de Marseilles, 19 November 1985.
Dir. Gregory Mosher. Curran Theater, San Francisco, 27 October 1985.
Dir. Tony Giodano. Syracuse Stage, Syracuse, N.Y., 12 November 1985.
Dir. Gregory Mosher. Henry Ford Theater, Los Angeles, 26 November 1985.
Dir. Luca Barbareschi. Teatro Stabile, Genoa, 16 January 1986.
Dir. Douglas C. Wager. Arena Stage, Washington, D.C., 5 February 1986.
Dir. Gregory Mosher. Wilbur Theater, Boston, 11 February 1986.
Dir. Bill Bryden. Mermaid Theatre, London, 24 February 1986.
Dir. Gregory Mosher. Blackstone Theater, Chicago, 5 March 1986.
Dir. Michael Arndt. Mixed Blood Theatre, Minneapolis, 27 March 1986.
Dir. Neil Armfield. Sidney Opera Playhouse, 10 April 1986.
Dir. John Dillon. Todd Wehr Theater, Milwaukee, 11 April 1986.
Dir. Jean-Pierre Malo. Theatre de Vidy, Lausanne, 2 December 1986.
Dir. Tony Giodano. Trinity Repertory, Providence, Rhode Island, 17 February 1987.
Dir. Emori Tōru. Haiyūza Theatre, Tokyo, 4 February 1988.
Dir. Antti Einari Halonen. Teatterikor Keakoulu, Helsinki, 9 February 1989.
Dir. Gordon Edelstein. Plays & Players Theater. Philadelphia, 31 March 1989.
Dir. Emori Tōru. Haiyūza Theatre, Tokyo, 8 February 1990.
Dir. Sam Mendes. Donmar Warehouse, London, 22 June 1994.

OTHER REVIEWS

Barber, John. "Glengarry Glen Ross." [Mermaid Theatre, London] *Daily Telegraph,* 26 February 1986. Rpt. *London Theatre Record,* 12–25 February 1986, 178–79.

Bemrose, John. "Glengarry Glen Ross." [Bathurst Street Theatre, Toronto] *Maclean's,* 24 November 1986, 66.

Brown, Joe. "It's Business—and Personal." Review of Arena Stage Production. *Washington Post,* 6 February 1987, sec. Weekend, N9.

Conlogue, Ray. "Citadel Almost Matches Mamet's Excitement." *Globe & Mail* [Toronto], 30 January 1985, M7.

de Jongh, Nicholas. "Glengarry Glen Ross." [Mermaid Theatre, London] *Guardian,* 22 February 1986. Rpt. *London Theatre Record,* 12–25 February 1986, 177.

Denby, David. "Stranger in a Strange Land: A Moviegoer at the Theater." *Atlantic,* January 1985, 48–50.

Dodds, Richard. "'Glengarry' Skillfully Comes to Life." *Times-Picayune* [New Orleans], 7 November 1989, D8.

——. "Mamet's 'Glengarry' to Launch Theater Company." *Times-Picayune* [New Orleans], 14 September 1989, E14.

Edwards, Christopher. "Glengarry Glen Ross." [Mermaid Theatre, London] *Spectator,* 14 March 1986. Rpt. *London Theatre Record,* 12–25 February 1986, 179–80.

Farson, Sibyl. "In Bitter Comedy, Hard Look at Life." [Boston production] *Telegram* [Worcester, Mass.], 16 February 1986.

Goodman, Walter. "Critic's Notebook: Once Again, Salesmen Are Nobody's Heroes." *New York Times,* 2 April 1987, late city ed., C22.

Grant, Steve. "Glengarry Glen Ross." [Mermaid Theatre, London] *Time Out,* 27 Feb. 1986. Rpt. *London Theatre Record,* 12–25 February 1986, 177.

Hoyle, Martin. "Glengarry Glen Ross." [Mermaid Theatre, London] *Financial Times,* 25 February 1986. Rpt. *London Theatre Record,* 12–25 February 1986, 179.

Jacobs, Gerald. "Glengarry Glen Ross." [Mermaid Theatre, London] *Jewish Chronicle,* 28 February 1986. Rpt. *London Theatre Record,* 12–25 February 1986, 177.

King, Francis. "Glengarry Glen Ross." [Mermaid Theatre, London] *Sunday Telegraph,* 2 March 1986. Rpt. *London Theatre Record,* 12–25 February 1986, 177.

Lambert, Mikel. "'Glengarry Glen Ross' Proves a Winning Challenge." [Port City Playhouse] *Washington Post,* 22 June 1989, 17.

McColloh, T.H. "Glengarry Glen Ross." *Drama-Logue,* 5 December 1985, 6. [rev. of Los Angeles production].

Morley, Sheridan. "Glengarry Glen Ross." *Punch,* 12 March 1986. Rpt. *London Theatre Record,* 12–25 February 1986, 178.

Nicholls, Liz. "Shysters—Taut and Funny." *Edmonton Journal,* 19 January 1985, C3.

Richards, David. "'Glengarry,' to the Good." [Arena Stage] *Washington Post,* 6 February 1987, final ed., C1.

Shulman, Milton. "Glengarry Glen Ross." [Mermaid Theatre, London] *London Standard,* 25 Feb. 1986. Rpt. *London Theatre Record,* 12–25 February 1986, 178.

Smith, Sid. "'Glengarry' Comes Back to Sparkle at Blackstone." *Chicago Tribune,* 6 March 1986, 9.

Sullivan, Dan. "'Glengarry' Takes Care of Business." *Los Angeles Times,* 29 November 1985, 5, no. 1.

Temkine, R. "Mamet 'Glengarry Glen Ross.'" *Europe: Revue Litteraire Mensuelle,* 66, no. 715 (1988): 224.

Tinker, Jack. "Glengarry Glen Ross." [Mermaid Theatre, London] *Daily Mail* 25 February 1986. Rpt. *London Theatre Record,* 12–25 February 1986, 179.

Touret, M. "Francis Perrin in a New Adaptation of David Mamet's 'Glengarry Glen Ross.'" *Avant Scene Theatre,* 838 (1988): 59.

Weiner, Bernard. "Mamet's Seedy Salesman." [Marin Theatre Co.] *San Francisco Chronicle,* 16 January 1990, E3.

Weiss, Hedy. "Falk & Mantegna Peddle a Good Line." [Chicago, Blackstone production] *Chicago Sun-Times,* 7 March 1986, 39.

Wong, Herman. "Stereotype or Truth?: Business Insiders Review Harsh 'Glengarry Glen Ross.'" *Los Angeles Times,* 22 November 1987, Orange County ed., 57C.

FILM AND VIDEO REVIEWS

Adams, Michael. "Glengarry Glen Ross." *Magill's Cinema Annual 1993,* ed. Frank N. Magill, 140–43. Englewood Cliffs, N.J.: Salem Press, 1993.

Allen, K. Linn. "'Glengarry' Hits Home." *Chicago Tribune,* 16 October 1992, sec. 5, 1.

Arnold, Gary. "'Glengarry' Salesmen Seal Amusing Deal for Film Fans." *Washington Times,* 2 October 1992, E1.

Baron, David. "'Glengarry Glen Ross': Biting Exposé of Big-City Life." *Times-Picayune* [New Orleans], 2 October 1992, LAG, 25.

Beck, Marilyn. "Segal Snares a Big Role in 'Glengarry Glen Ross.'" *New York Daily News,* 15 September 1986, sec. Extra, 11.

Blanchard, Jayne M. "'Glengarry' Hits the Screen with the Joys of Male Angst." *Washington Times,* 27 September 1992, D1.

———. "Movies & Video—Glengarry Glen Ross." *Washingtonian,* October 1992, 31.

Bourget, J. L. "Glengarry Glen Ross." *Positif,* November 1992, 49.

Brown, Georgia. "Men of Doom—Glengarry Glen Ross." *Village Voice,* 6 October 1992, 60.

Butler, Charles. "What Is the Secret?" *Sales & Marketing Management,* May 1995, 6.

Calhoun, John. "Dead End." *TCI,* Nov. 1992, 9.

Canby, Vincent. "Mamet's Real Estate Sharks and Their Prey." *New York Times,* 30 September 1992, C15.

Carr, Jay. "'Glengarry': 80s Requiem Potent in 90s." *Boston Globe*, 2 October 1992, 45.

——. "Potent Adaptation of 'Glengarry Glen Ross.'" *Boston Globe*, 16 September 1992, 72.

Christiansen, Richard. "Flawless Transfers." [review of laser disc] *Chicago Tribune*, 24 May 1994, sec. 5, 3.

Clark, Mike. "'Glengarry': A Prime Piece of Filmmaking." *USA Today*, 30 September 1992, D1.

Combs, P. "Glengarry Glen Ross." *Sight and Sound*, 2 (November 1992): 43.

Corliss, Richard. "Sweating Out Loud." *Time*, 12 October 1992, 84.

Crisp, Quentin. "Glengarry Glen Ross." *Christopher Street*, 7 December 1992, 10–12.

Daly, Steve, and Lisa Karlin. "Language Barrier." *Entertainment Weekly*, 9 October 1992, 41.

Denby, David. "A Few Bad Men." *New York*, 12 October 1992, 64–65.

Ebert, Roger. "'Glengarry' Resonates with Despair, Pathos." *Chicago Sun-Times*, 2 October 1992, 45.

Fagan, Gregory P. "Laser Fare." *Playboy*, June 1994, 28.

Faust, M. "Glengarry Glen Ross." *Video*, June 1993, 72–73.

Foley, James. "James Foley's Guilty Pleasures." *Film Comment*, September/October 1992, 76ff.

Galloway, Paul. "Blank Verse Versus (Blank) Verse." *Chicago Tribune*, 12 October 1992, sec. 5, 1.

Gleiberman, Owen. "Pros and Cons." *Entertainment Weekly*, 9 October 1992, 40.

Goodman, Walter. "In Mamet's World, You Are How You Speak." *New York Times*, 4 October 1992, H24.

Grant, Edmond. "Glengarry Glen Ross." *Films in Review*, March/April 1993, 125–26.

Howe, Desson. "'Glengarry': Cold Property." *Washington Post*, 2 October 1992, sec. WW, 42.

Hulbert, Dan. "Mamet's Script Draws All-Stars to 'Glengarry.'" *Atlanta Journal Constitution*, 27 September 1992, N1.

Johnson, Brian D. "Closing for the Kill." *Maclean's*, 5 October 1992, 63.

——. "Reel Men Never Win." *Maclean's*, 9 November 1992, 106.

Kauffmann, Stanley. "Deaths of Salesmen." *New Republic*, 26 October 1992, 30.

Kempley, Rita. "Glengarry Glen Ross." *Washington Post*, 20 May 1993, D7.

——. "Mamet's Moral Swamp." *Washington Post*, 2 October 1992, C1.

Kehr, Dave. "Hard Sell." *Chicago Tribune*, 2 October 1992, sec. 7, A19.

Kermode, Mark. "Video—Glengarry Glen Ross." *Sight & Sound*, June 1993, 66.

Krohn, Bill. "Glengarry Glen Ross." *Cahiers du Cinema*, January 1993, 56–57.

Kroll, Jack. "Heels, Heroes and Hustlers." *Newsweek*, 5 October 1992, 73–74.

LaSalle, Mick. "'Glengarry' Is a Tough Sell." *San Francisco Chronicle*, 2 October 1992, C1.

Letts, Vanessa. "Cinema." *Spectator*, 7 November 1992, 64.

Leydon, Joe. "'Glengarry Glen Ross' Reveals Working Man's Desperation." *Houston Post*, 2 October 1992, E1.

Linklater, John. "Subtle Tyrant of the Finer Lines." *Herald*, 28 June 1994, 20.

Lurie, Rod. "Yak-Yak-Yak—Glengarry Glen Ross." *Los Angeles*, September 1992, 114–17.

McCabe, Bruce. "The Darker Side of Capitalism." *Boston Globe*, 23 August 1992, Television 2.

McCarthy, Todd. "Glengarry Glen Ross." *Variety*, 31 August 1992, 59ff.

Mallet, Gina. "Pacino's Charm Wins the Rat Race." *Chatelaine*, November 1992, 10.

Mitchell, Sean. "A Slice of Lemmon." *Premiere*, November 1992, 106.

Movshovitz, Howie. "'Glengarry Glen Ross' Can't Sell Overworked Inventory." *Denver Post*, 2 October 1992, sec. Week, 6.

Murray, Steve. "Shark Attack." *Atlanta Constitution,* 2 October 1992, D1.
Novak, Ralph. "Picks & Pans—Glengarry Glen Ross." *People Weekly,* 5 October 1992, 23.
Pollack, Joe. "Desperate Straits Make a Powerful Story." *St. Louis Post-Dispatch,* 2 October 1992, G3.
Powers, John. "SWF Seeks Same." *Harper's Bazaar,* September 1992, 128.
Rea, Steven. "All-Star Cast of Real-Estate Scammers at Work in Glengarry." *Philadelphia Enquirer,* 2 October 1992, WK, D3.
Rottenberger-Murtha, Kerry. "Now Showing: A Retrospective of Sales in the Movies." *Sales & Marketing Management,* October 1993, 142–44.
Ryan, James. "Playing Mamet's Music." *Boston Globe,* 27 September 1992, B33.
Simon, John. "Worst Guys Finish First." *National Review,* 2 November 1992, 62.
Sheehy, Catherine. "Editors' Choice: Mamet Dammit." *American Theatre* (October 1992): 53.
Sragow, Michael. "Glengarry Glen Ross." *New Yorker,* 5 October 1992, 164.
Stark, Susan. "Survival-of-the-Slickest." *Detroit News,* 2 October 1992, D3.
Sterritt, David. "Cutthroat Americana." *Christian Science Monitor,* 29 September 1992, 11.
Travers, Peter. "Glengarry Glen Ross." *Rolling Stone,* 1 October 1992, 74.
Turan, Kenneth. "Gang that Couldn't Sell Straight." *Los Angeles Times,* 30 September 1992, F1.
Weinraub, Bernard. "The 'Glengarry' Math: Add Money and Stars, Then Subtract Ego." *New York Times,* 12 October 1992, C11.
Westbrook, Bruce. "Glengarry Glen Ross." *Houston Chronicle,* 21 May 1993, D3.
Wheeler, Drew. "Marquee Values." *Billboard,* 17 April 1993, 62.
Williamson, Bruce. "Movies—Glengarry Glen Ross." *Playboy,* October 1992, 22.
———. "Now Playing . . . Glengarry Glen Ross." *New Woman,* October 1992, 24.

MISCELLANY

Benson, Alan, dir. and prod. *David Mamet.* Profile of a Writer Series. Videocassette, Home Vision, 1985.
Brown, Joe. "It's Business—and Personal." *Washington Post,* 6 February 1987, N9.
Cammuso, Frank and Hart Seeley. "Glengarry Glen Plaid." [humor] *New Yorker,* 9 May 1994, 108.
Christiansen, Richard. "Chicago Playwright Wins Pulitzer Prize." *Chicago Tribune,* 17 April 1984, A1.
———. "Mamet's 'Glengarry' Wins London Award for Best Play." *Chicago Tribune,* 24 January 1984, sec. 5, 3.
Dowd, Maureen. "Novel 'Ironweed' and Mamet Play Are Awarded 1984 Pulitzer Prize." *New York Times,* 17 April 1984, sec. 1, 1.
Lamont, Rosette C. "When the Political Message Is Submerged." *New York Times,* 24 March 1985, sec. 2, 3.
"Mamet New Fave on Worldwide Front; 'Glengarry,' 'Plow' Lead the Pack." *Variety,* 7 December 1988, 93.
"Shows Abroad." *Variety,* 19 October 1988, 502.

CONTRIBUTORS

RICHARD BRUCHER is associate professor of English at the University of Maine, Orono, where he teaches courses in drama. As well as writing and presenting critical essays on Mamet, Miller, O'Neill, Hellman, and Shakespeare, he has acted locally in Mamet's *Reunion, Dark Pony,* and *Glengarry Glen Ross.*

ANNE DEAN holds a Ph.D. in theatre studies from Royal Holloway & Bedford New College, University of London. Currently she holds the position as head of the Postgraduate Education Department at the Royal College of Psychiatrists in London. Her publications include two books on contemporary American drama: *David Mamet: Language as Dramatic Action,* a revised version of her doctoral dissertation, and *Discovery and Invention,* a critical study of Lanford Wilson's urban plays. A poem, "Vacation America" has recently appeared in *The American Literary Review.*

LINDA DORFF is a visiting instructor of modern drama at Oberlin College. Professor Dorff holds a Ph.D. in English from New York University, having recently defended her doctoral dissertation on the late plays of Tennessee Williams. Her most recent publication is "The Double-sided Kandinsky and the Politics of Art in John Guare's *Six Degrees of Separation,*" in *John Guare: A Casebook.*

DEBORAH R. GEIS is associate professor of English at Queens College, CUNY. Her publications include *Postmodern Theatric(k)s* (University of Michigan Press, 1993), and articles on Shange, Fornes, Rabe, Mamet, and others. She is co-editor (with Steven F. Kruger) of a forthcoming anthology on Tony Kushner's *Angels in America.* Professor Geis serves as book review editor for *The David Mamet Review.*

CHRISTOPHER C. HUDGINS, recently completing nine year's tenure as the chair of the University of Nevada, Las Vegas English Department, is the author of numerous articles on David Mamet, Harold Pinter, and Stanley Kubrick. He is currently writing an essay about Harold Pinter's script for *Lolita* and continues work on his long-term project, a book on Pinter's filmscripts. Professor Hudgins serves as vice president of the Harold Pinter Society, vice president and treasurer of the David Mamet Society, and production editor of *The David Mamet Review*.

DOROTHY H. JACOBS is an associate professor in the Department of English of the University of Rhode Island. She has sustained scholarly interest in Mamet's drama, and was one of the first scholars to note the prominence of "working worlds" in his work. Currently, she is working on a history of the Trinity Repertory Company.

LESLIE KANE is professor of English at Westfield State College. She is the author of *The Language of Silence: On the Unspoken and the Unspeakable in Modern Drama,* and the editor of *David Mamet: A Casebook* and *Israel Horovitz: A Collection of Critical Essays.* Her essays, interviews, and reviews on Pinter, Mamet, Norman, Shepard, Miller, Horovitz, and Pirandello have appeared in *The Pinter Review, American Drama, American Theatre, Theatre Journal,* and *The Yearbook of English Studies.* President of the David Mamet Society, editor of *The David Mamet Review,* and a Fulbright scholar, Kane is currently working on *Weasels and Wisemen,* a study of Jewish tropes in the work of David Mamet.

ELIZABETH KLAVER is an assistant professor of English at Southern Illinois University at Carbondale. She has published on television and contemporary drama, Beckett, Ionesco, and the plays of William Carlos Williams. She is currently working on a book on theatre and the media culture.

STEVEN PRICE is a lecturer in English at the University of Wales, Bangor, and received his Ph.D. from the University of London for his work on David Mamet. He has published essays on Mamet and Beckett, writes on modern American drama for *The Year's Work in English Studies,* and is co-author of a forthcoming book on Oscar Wilde's *Salome* (Cambridge University Press).

ROBERT T. ROLF received his Ph.D. in Japanese literature at the University of Hawaii. During his academic career, he has held the positions of assistant professor of Japanese and Chinese at Duke University, Japanese literature and language at the University of Florida, Gainesville, and Washington University, as well as foreign lecturer of American literature, language, and culture at Fukuoka University and Yokohama University, Japan. Currently he holds the position of professor of American Literature, School of Literature, Komazawa University, Tokyo. His scholarship includes studies of various aspects of Japanese and American drama and fiction, as well as English translations of plays of several contemporary Japanese playwrights.

DAVID K. SAUER is professor of English at Spring Hill College, where he also directs theatrical productions. Inspired to work on American drama by Howard Stein in an NEH Seminar (1992) and performance by Lois Potter in a Folger Shakespeare Library NEH Institute (1993–1994), Sauer has pursued both in an NEH Independent Study Grant (1995). He has published recently on Etherege, Guare, and Mamet, and in the *Shaw and Shakespeare Quarterly*. He is bibliographer for *The David Mamet Review*.

JANICE A. SAUER is assistant librarian in the position of instructional services librarian at the University of South Alabama. She has also taught for the School of Library and Information Studies of the University of Alabama. She has recently published in the journal *College and Undergraduate Studies,* as well as *Information for a New Age* (1995). She is bibliographer for *The David Mamet Review.*

TONY J. STAFFORD is professor of English at the University of Texas at El Paso. He has presented papers and published on Shakespeare, the English Renaissance drama, Shaw, and contemporary dramatists such as McCullers, Rabe, Albee, Barry, Gray, Mamet, and August Wilson. He is also a playwright who has been produced from Los Angeles to Washington, D.C. and many cities in between. He is currently finishing his first novel.

JON TUTTLE is an assistant professor of English at Francis Marion University and the author of articles on Arthur Miller, Harold Pinter, Samuel Beckett, and Truman Capote. His plays, among them *Hammerstone* and *Terminal Café,* have been performed in New York, Los Angeles, Atlanta, and elsewhere around the country.

ROBERT H. VORLICKY is associate professor of English and Theater at Marymount College, where he also serves as chair of Fine and Performing Arts. A former Fulbright scholar in Zagreb, Croatia, and recipient of a National Endowment for the Humanities Fellowship, Vorlicky is the author of

Act Like a Man: Challenging Masculinities in American Drama (University of Michigan Press, 1995), the first comprehensive study of published American male-cast plays.

DAVID WORSTER is a Ph.D. candidate at the University of North Carolina at Chapel Hill. His other publications include "*Macbeth,* 1.3.89–95: Editorial Glosses and Theatrical Alternatives" in *English Language Notes* and "The Linguistic Hierarchy in *Emma*" in *Language and Style*. His area of dissertation research is Early Modern Drama.